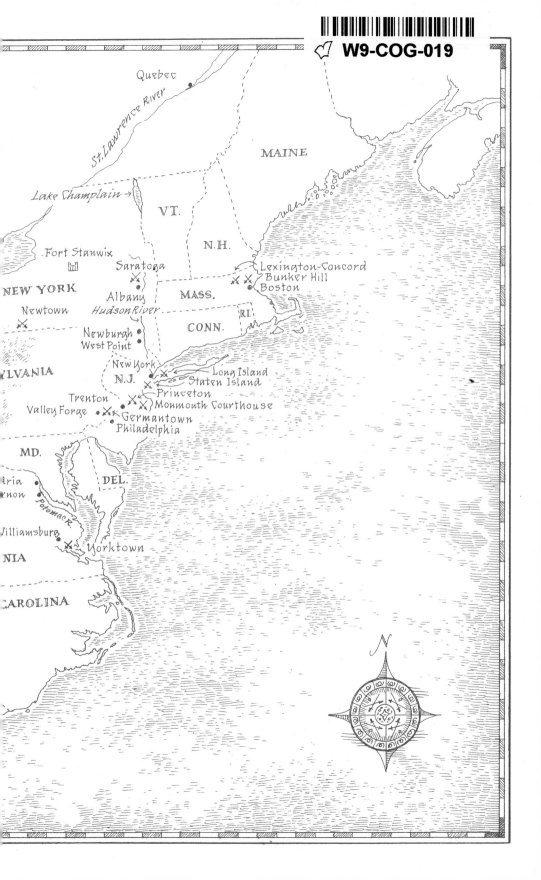

Quebec

St. Lawrence River

MAINE

Lake Champlain →

VT.

N.H.

Fort Stanwix

Saratoga

NEW YORK

Newtown

Albany
Hudson River

MASS.

RI

Lexington-Concord
Bunker Hill
Boston

CONN.

Newburgh
West Point

New York

N.J.

Long Island
Staten Island

Trenton

Princeton

Valley Forge

Monmouth Courthouse

Germantown
Philadelphia

MD.

...ria
...non

DEL.

Potomac R.

...illiamsburg

...NIA

Yorktown

...CAROLINA

N

Our First Civil War

ALSO BY H. W. BRANDS

The Reckless Decade

T.R.

The First American

The Age of Gold

Lone Star Nation

Andrew Jackson

Traitor to His Class

American Colossus

The Murder of Jim Fisk for the Love of Josie Mansfield

The Heartbreak of Aaron Burr

The Man Who Saved the Union

Reagan

The General vs. the President

Heirs of the Founders

Dreams of El Dorado

The Zealot and the Emancipator

Our First Civil War

Patriots and Loyalists in the American Revolution

H. W. BRANDS

DOUBLEDAY · New York

All rights reserved. Published in the United States by Doubleday,
a division of Penguin Random House LLC, New York, and distributed
in Canada by Penguin Random House Canada Limited, Toronto.

www.doubleday.com

DOUBLEDAY and the portrayal of an anchor with a dolphin
are registered trademarks of Penguin Random House LLC.

Front-of-jacket images: Battle of Bunker Hill, Battle of Lexington
and American Revolutionary War (details) © Paul Popper/Popperfoto/
Getty Images; Union Jack © Heritage Images/Getty Images;
crown © Transcendental Graphics/Getty Images;
floral elements © Komar Art / Shutterstock

Jacket design by Michael J. Windsor
Endpaper map by John Burgoyne
Text design by Cassandra J. Pappas

Library of Congress Cataloging-in-Publication Data
Names: Brands, H. W., author.
Title: Our first civil war : patriots and loyalists in the
American Revolution / H. W. Brands.
Other titles: Patriots and loyalists in the American Revolution
Description: First edition. | New York : Doubleday, [2021] | Includes index.
Identifiers: LCCN 2020043860 (print) | LCCN 2020043861 (ebook) |
ISBN 9780385546515 (hardcover) | ISBN 9780385546522 (ebook)
Subjects: LCSH: United States—History—Revolution, 1775–1783—
Causes. | Revolutionaries—United States—History—18th century. |
American loyalists. | United States—History—Revolution, 1775–1783—
Social aspects. | United States—Politics and government—to 1775. |
United States—History, Military.
Classification: LCC E210 .B736 2021 (print) |
LCC E210 (ebook) | DDC 973.3/11—dc23
LC record available at https://lccn.loc.gov/2020043860
LC ebook record available at https://lccn.loc.gov/2020043861

MANUFACTURED IN THE UNITED STATES OF AMERICA
1 3 5 7 9 10 8 6 4 2
First Edition

Contents

Prologue

THE FIGHTING HAD BEEN vicious in the Carolinas since the start of the war. And it was the more vicious for pitting not American against Briton, nor even American against Hessian, but American against American. John Adams would say that the American Revolution was in the "minds and hearts" of the American people before it produced the armed struggle between the United States and Britain; what Adams neglected to mention was the degree to which those minds and hearts were at odds, one American against another. In every colony, and then every state, were thousands of men and women who wanted nothing to do with independence. They valued the freedom and security they had enjoyed under British rule, and they resented the rebel Patriots for bringing on the war. These Loyalists cast their lot with their mother country; the result was the shattering of trust among neighbors, the rending of families, and murderous conflict like that convulsing the Carolina backcountry.

There, in the Waxhaws region on the border of North and South Carolina in the summer of 1780, a column of Loyalists led by a British lieutenant colonel named Banastre Tarleton gave chase to a Patriot force commanded by Abraham Buford. Tarleton and the Loyalists soon caught Buford and the Patriots, and Tarleton demanded the surrender of Buford's force. He claimed more men than he possessed, hoping to frighten the untested recruits who formed a large part of the Patriot contingent. The ruse failed; Buford rejected the demand, and fighting commenced.

It went badly for the Patriots. Tarleton's cavalry ripped through the lines of Buford's infantry, and Buford quickly reconsidered his defiance. He sent a truce flag to Tarleton, but the message to cease fire didn't reach all of Buford's own men, and firing from their side persisted. Tarleton's horse was killed, and Tarleton was pinned beneath it. His Loyalist troops, watching him fall, thought he had been killed and blamed the Patriots for faking a truce. They responded with what Tarleton called "a vindictive asperity not easily restrained."

The Patriots called it a massacre. Robert Brownfield, a surgeon's aide with Buford, afterward wrote that the Patriots, seeing the Loyalists resuming the fight, attempted to put themselves in a defensive position. "But before this was fully effected," Brownfield said, "Tarleton with his cruel myrmidons was in the midst of them, when commenced a scene of indiscriminate carnage never surpassed by the ruthless atrocities of the most barbarous savages. The demand for quarters, seldom refused to a vanquished foe, was at once found to be in vain. Not a man was spared. And it was the concurrent testimony of all the survivors that for fifteen minutes after every man was prostrate, they went over the ground plunging their bayonets into every one that exhibited any signs of life. And in some instances, where several had fallen one over the other, these monsters were seen to throw off on the point of the bayonet the uppermost, to come at those beneath."

The savagery of the Loyalists was summarized by their treatment of one Patriot, a man named Stokes, who barely lived to tell Brownfield the tale. "He received twenty-three wounds, and as he never for a moment lost his recollection, he often repeated to me the manner and order in which they were inflicted," Brownfield said. "Early in the sanguinary conflict he was attacked by a dragoon, who aimed many deadly blows at his head, all of which by the dextrous use of the small sword he easily parried; when another on the right, by one stroke, cut off his right hand through the metacarpal bones. He was then assailed by both, and instinctively attempted to defend his head with his left arm until the forefinger was cut off, and the arm hacked in eight or ten places from the wrist to the shoulder. His head was then laid open almost the whole length of the crown to the eye brows. After he fell he received several cuts on the face and shoulders. A soldier passing on in the work of death, asked if he expected quarters. Stokes answered I have not, nor do I mean to ask quarters, finish me as soon as possible; he then transfixed him twice with his bayonet."

The Battle of Waxhaws left the Patriots reeling, but also seething. Their anger spilled over the mountains into what would become Tennessee, where a Patriot regiment mustered to avenge the Loyalist atrocities. These "over-mountain men" had their chance at Kings Mountain in October 1780. "Their numbers enabled them to surround us," wrote Anthony Allaire, a member of one Loyalist company. "Our poor little detachment, which consisted of only seventy men when we marched to the field of action, were all killed and wounded but twenty." Other Loyalist companies were similarly mauled, with nearly three hundred Loyalists dying on the battlefield, many after surrendering.

Isaac Shelby, a commander of the Patriots, acknowledged the slaughter of the Loyalists. "They were ordered to throw down their arms, which they did, and surrendered themselves prisoners at discretion," Shelby recounted. "It was some time before a complete cessation of the firing, on our part, could be effected. Our men, who had been scattered in the battle, were continually coming up, and continued to fire, without comprehending in the heat of the moment, what had happened; and some, who had heard that at Buford's defeat the British had refused quarters to many who asked it, were willing to follow that bad example. Owing to these causes, the ignorance of some, and the disposition of others to retaliate, it required some time, and some exertion on the part of the officers, to put an entire stop to the firing."

WHAT CAUSES A MAN to forsake his country and take arms against it? What prompts others, hardly distinguishable in station or success, to defend that country against the rebels?

George Washington and Benjamin Franklin were the unlikeliest of rebels, from all outward appearance. Washington in the 1770s stood at the apex of Virginia society, possessing everything material a man of his place and time could desire. Franklin was more successful still, having risen from humble origins to world fame, a feat he could have accomplished in no other sphere than the British empire. John Adams might have seemed a more obvious candidate for rebellion, being of cantankerous temperament generally. Even so, Adams revered the law, and rebellion begins with an overthrow of existing laws. Yet all three men became rebels against the regime that had fostered their success.

William Franklin might have been expected to join his father, Benjamin, in rebellion, the young often being more disposed to overthrow existing standards than the old. But William Franklin remained loyal to the British crown. Thomas Hutchinson grew up near Benjamin Franklin in Boston and worked closely with him in the Albany

Congress during the French and Indian War. Yet though Hutchinson often criticized British policy toward the colonies, he refused to break with London. Joseph Galloway led the Pennsylvania provincial assembly in its challenge to the privileges of the colony's founding family. But when that challenge evolved into a revolt against Parliament and the Crown, Galloway stepped back.

The American Revolution turned accepted notions of allegiance on their heads. Even before the Declaration of Independence proclaimed the severing of American ties to Britain, individuals like William Franklin, Thomas Hutchinson and Joseph Galloway heard themselves denounced as traitors—for *not* having betrayed the country they had grown up in and long served. The Declaration gave the denunciations bite, and the Loyalists became subject to arrest, imprisonment, violence and death.

Benedict Arnold embodied the confusing demands of allegiance. As a young man, Arnold had enlisted on Britain's behalf in the French and Indian War. Fifteen years later he fought *against* Britain, as the most energetic and valued of George Washington's lieutenants. Then he switched sides again, turning coat from the Patriot cause to the Loyalist and accepting a commission in the British army. Arnold's case was unusual for its visibility; his name would become synonymous in American minds with treachery. But he was hardly alone in reconsidering choices made under the duress of a complicated and often dispiriting war.

Joseph Brant brought a different perspective to the questions of allegiance and loyalty. Brant was a war chief of the Mohawks, one of the Six Nations of the Iroquois Confederacy. For more than a century the Iroquois and the other native peoples of North America had maneuvered among the competing groups of interlopers from Europe; in the long struggle between the British and the French, the Iroquois had tilted toward the British. But the American Revolution split the British, and Brant and the Iroquois had to choose between Patriots and Loyalists. Brant and most of the Iroquois chose the British; others of the confederacy sided with the Patriots. Thus the civil war among the British Americans became a civil war among the Native Americans.

As fraught as the choice of allegiance was for the free inhabitants of the American colonies, it was more parlous still for the enslaved. Slavery existed in all thirteen colonies at the outbreak of the American Revolution, and slave-owners were found among both Patriots and Loyalists. The slave-owners typically demanded that their bondsmen follow their lead. But British officials offered freedom to slaves of Patriot masters if the slaves would cross to the British and Loyalist side. The offer was tempting yet dangerous, for the slaves knew they could expect no mercy if they fell back into Patriot hands. Some took the chance; others sat tight. A modest number even fought on the Patriot side, helping secure the liberties of those who enslaved them. Such were the paradoxes of this disorienting era.

After the revolution, it served the unifying purposes of the victors to portray the conflict as one of Americans against Britons. The Patriots were cast as heroes and founding fathers; the Loyalists were relegated to bit parts better forgotten. But amid the struggle, the bitter fight among the Americans—for minds and hearts, for political allegiance and material support, for control of the destiny of the homeland both sides laid claim to—was crucial in determining the outcome of the contest between nations. Before America could win its revolution against Britain, the Patriots had to win their civil war against the Loyalists.

Part I

Seeds of Doubt

· 1 ·

IN THE SPRING OF 1754 a regiment of Virginia militia set off from Alexandria for the Ohio River, under the command of a twenty-two-year-old lieutenant colonel named George Washington. The Washington family name was well known on the Potomac River, but chiefly for its connection to a more distinguished name: Fairfax. Thomas Fairfax was the sixth and current Lord Fairfax of Cameron, in England; besides the title he had inherited five million acres in western Virginia, from which he hoped to derive an income to support his lordly manner of living. His cousin William Fairfax headed the family's American wing, with a plantation, Belvoir, on the Potomac that anchored Virginia's Tidewater aristocracy.

George Washington was no aristocrat, but he had come to know the Fairfaxes through proximity and marriage. The Fairfaxes lived a few miles from Mount Vernon, the Washington family home, and George Washington grew up playing with the Fairfax boys. Washington's elder half-brother Lawrence married into the Fairfax clan, making Washington an in-law. After Augustine Washington, the father of Lawrence and George, died, when George was eleven, William Fairfax took a paternal interest in the lad. George Fairfax, eight years older than Washington, stood in as an elder brother.

At the age of sixteen, Washington made a journey with George Fairfax across the mountains into western Virginia. The purpose of the journey was to scout the Fairfax holdings, in particular a parcel George Fairfax had his eye on. Although the death of his father had kept Washington from receiving much formal education, brother Lawrence saw that he got practical training in surveying and the mathematical and topographic arts that underlay it, and when George Fairfax sought a companion for his scouting journey, Washington was a natural to invite along.

The expedition lasted several weeks and required all the resourcefulness and stamina the two young men could summon. They endured the snow and rain of late winter and early spring, high water in the numerous streams athwart their path, short rations and miserable camping conditions, rugged and unmapped terrain, and threatening if not downright hostile Indians and white frontiersmen. Washington loved every minute, and George Fairfax marked him as someone who could find his way around the wilderness. He shared the opinion with his family and friends.

Among the latter was Robert Dinwiddie, the acting governor of Virginia. Dinwiddie was an appointee of the British crown, and his chief assignment in the early 1750s was securing the Ohio Valley for Britain. During the previous century, while the British were establishing footholds on North America's eastern seaboard, French explorers and soldiers had probed the heartland of the continent. They traveled by water, from the north along the St. Lawrence River, from the south via the Mississippi. In the grandiose manner of the age, French explorers claimed for the French crown all the lands drained by the two great rivers. The English, for their part, were no more restrained: Virginia's charter gave its proprietors title to a swath of land from the Atlantic to the Pacific. The inevitable result, once reality caught up with the claims, was a clash between Britain and France for control of the parts of North America where their claims overlapped.

Indians and occasional western travelers brought tales of increasing French activity in the Ohio Valley. At this point the Virginians had little active presence that far west; their settlements, aside from a few trading posts, were confined to the lands that sloped toward the Atlantic. But the Virginians were looking to the future.

For an influential few of them, the future included the Ohio Valley in a special way. The Ohio Company of Virginia had been created in the 1740s by investors engaged in what was becoming a signature enterprise of the American economy: land speculation. The Ohio Company pulled strings in London to receive a royal grant of 500,000 acres in the Ohio Valley. The investors, who included George Washington's elder brothers Lawrence and Augustine Washington, and Robert Dinwiddie, were eager to lay hold of the lands, that they might begin the process of selling parcels to actual settlers and thereby grow rich.

The French expansion into the Ohio country put their plans in jeopardy. Not only did the French reject the right of the British crown to grant lands in Ohio to the Ohio Company or anyone else, but a French presence in Ohio would render the region insecure for Anglo-American settlers. The French themselves would be hostile; more threateningly, they would turn the Indians of the region hostile. The various tribes there understood the competition between the two European empires, and they played one against the other, to their own benefit. Part of the benefit consisted of trade goods that made the lives of the Indians easier—firearms, steel knives and the like; another part entailed military support in the rivalries of the tribes against one another. The sum of the interplay of empires and tribes was a welter of intrigues and conflicts on the frontier: British against French, British against France's Indian allies, Britain's Indian allies against the French and the French Indians, Indians against Indians. There was even competition between Virginians and residents of other British colonies, notably Pennsylvania and New York, who had their own claims to the Ohio country.

In 1753 Governor Dinwiddie summoned Washington to Williamsburg, the Virginia capital, and handed him a letter, to be conveyed to the commandant of French forces in Ohio. The drafting of the letter was beyond Washington's purview, but its gist was evident from the public attitude of Dinwiddie and the British government toward the French in Ohio—namely, that they had no right to be there and must depart at once.

There was more to Washington's assignment. While seeking out the French commandant, he was to conduct a reconnaissance of Ohio, identifying and describing French forts and trading posts, and locating likely spots for British positions. With another war looming, Washington was to scout the western theater with an eye toward bolstering Britain's prospects there.

Finally, Washington was to cultivate the Indian tribes of the region, and especially their leaders. He was to gauge the attitudes of the Indians he encountered, and with modest presents and larger promises persuade them to side with Britain in the event of war with France.

The journey to the Ohio proved an even sterner test of Washington's mettle than his trip with George Fairfax. This time he rode into the teeth of winter, carrying an unwelcome message across contested ground to a military officer of his country's historic foe. He had to recruit guides, translators and baggage handlers; he had to find friends among the Indians of the region and dodge Indian enemies. He had to gather intelligence about the French and the Indians, which they would be reluctant to reveal to the envoy of their enemy.

He succeeded even better than before. He delivered Dinwiddie's letter and brought back the reply from the French commandant. Its essence wasn't unexpected: that the British were the ones who had no business in Ohio, and *they* must abandon any claims to the region.

Yet Dinwiddie was mightily impressed with the young man's work, and the more so on reading the journal Washington had kept of the trip. The governor all but snatched the journal from Washington's hand and rushed it into print. When it was reproduced in newspapers around the other American colonies, the name George Washington acquired a sudden currency. People asked about this resourceful, intrepid fellow—diplomat, spy, Indian agent—and many marveled to learn that he was barely twenty-two years old. If the future of Britain in North America lay in hands like his, most thought, it was a bright future indeed.

WASHINGTON HAD LITTLE TIME to relish his new distinction before Dinwiddie put him back to work. The intelligence Washington brought home regarding French initiatives in the Ohio country was alarming; the French threat was greater than Dinwiddie or other British officials had realized. French forts in Ohio endangered Britain's American frontier, and they bid fair to block the efforts of the Ohio Company to make Dinwiddie, the Washington brothers (now including George) and its other investors rich. The French must be rooted out of Ohio.

To this end, Dinwiddie in March 1754 named Washington a lieutenant colonel and ordered him to lead a regiment of Virginia militia to Ohio to counter the French presence by building forts of Virginia's own, in preparation for driving the French from the region. Dinwiddie understood that Virginia's volunteers by themselves couldn't oust the French, but they could make a stand, perhaps bloody the French, and engage the interests of the British empire as a whole.

How much of this thinking Dinwiddie shared with Washington is unclear. Quite possibly he recognized in Washington one who didn't need to have things spelled out. In any event, Washington understood his orders as being to march his regiment to the Ohio, there "to build forts, and to defend the possessions of His Majesty against the attempts and hostilities of the French," as he subsequently put it.

They set off from Alexandria in early April. As a military column they traveled more slowly than Washington had five months earlier, and they were still far from the Ohio when a messenger brought word that a thousand French troops had arrived at the Forks of the Ohio—the junction of the Monongahela and Allegheny Rivers, which there form the Ohio—and taken possession of that strategic site.

Washington wondered if he was already too late. Additional reports told of the sixty bateaus—flat-bottomed rivercraft—and three hundred canoes of the French expedition, and the eighteen cannons they had carried to the Forks.

The French invasion alarmed many of the Indians of the Ohio country. Even tribes allied with the French grew worried at this large increase in French troops, which could only bode ill for Indian control of the region. Washington encountered Indians who had fled before the French and now urged the British to beat them back. The Indians didn't love the British, nor did they want the British to drive the French entirely out of Ohio. Instead they sought a restoration of the previous balance.

A runner from Tanacharison, a Seneca chief the British called the Half King, brought a message. It took the form of a speech, which Washington was supposed to imagine the Half King giving to Governor Dinwiddie. The chief promised the aid of his people in a campaign against the French. "We are now ready to fall upon them, waiting only for your succor," he said. "Have good courage, and come as soon as possible; you will find us as ready to encounter with them as you are yourselves." The runner had instructions to deliver the chief's message to the governor of Pennsylvania as well; the Half King hoped to ally with the two British colonies against the French. But whatever action was taken must be taken soon. "If you do not come to our assistance now, we are entirely undone, and imagine we shall never meet together again. I speak it with a heart full of grief."

Washington weighed his options. Against the French force of a thousand, he commanded but 150 men. More might be coming, but they weren't available yet. It would be suicide to challenge the French directly, and the destruction of his regiment would render the French position all but impregnable.

On the other hand, he couldn't ignore the plea of the Half King, which gained credence from similar calls by other Indian leaders. To leave friendly Indians exposed might result in their destruction and likely would cause other Indians to yield to the inevitable and ally with the French.

Washington split the difference. He ordered his men to push forward, building a road as they went. The road would speed the arrival of any reinforcements that might be dispatched. Washington would approach the Forks but stop well short of the French post under construction there. His presence would signal that Britain wasn't surrendering its claim to Ohio, but it needn't provoke the French to a pitched battle, which Washington's smaller force would certainly lose.

He held a council of war, at which he let representatives of the various tribes air their views. A speech of his own told the Half King, through the runner, that Washington had heard his plea and was coming. "This young man will inform you where he found a small part of our army making towards you, clearing the roads for a great number of our warriors, who are ready to follow us with our great guns, our ammunition and provisions," Washington said. "We know the character of the treacherous French, and our conduct shall plainly shew you how much we have it at heart." He sent along the currency of alliance on the frontier. "I present you with these bunches of wampum, to assure you of the sincerity of my speech, and that you may remember how much I am your friend and brother."

Washington's column advanced steadily. By the middle of May he was issuing orders to be on the lookout for French troops. His men should not initiate a battle without further orders; if they made contact with the French they should withdraw. Yet they might capture stragglers. "If they should find any Frenchman apart from the rest, seize him and bring him to us," Washington directed. Such a prisoner would be interrogated about French dispositions and plans.

New reports from the Ohio elaborated on the earlier ones. Two Indians had just been at the Forks. "They relate that the French forces are all employed in building their fort, that it is already breast-high, and the thickness of twelve feet, and filled up with earth and stone, etc.," Washington noted. "They have cut down and burnt up all the

trees which were about it, and sown grain instead." More French soldiers were en route to the Forks. "They expect a greater number in a
few days, which may amount to 1600. Then, they say, they can defy
the English."

Some fifty miles from the Forks, Washington found a promising
spot for his own fort. A large meadow spared him the labor of clearing
the ground, and it allowed sightlines for observing any advance by the
enemy. He put his men to work.

A report of French troops in the vicinity prompted Washington to
investigate. "Detached a party to go along the roads, and other small
parties to the woods, to see if they could make any discovery," Washington wrote on May 25. "I gave the horsemen orders to examine the
country well, and endeavor to get some news of the French, of their
forces, and of their motions, etc." The search was futile. "At night all
these parties returned without having discovered anything, though
they had been a great way towards the place from whence it was said
the party was coming."

Washington was determined to avoid an ambush. To be caught
unawares would be personally mortifying, not to mention militarily
disastrous. He continued the patrols, chasing down every rumor and
hint of French forces nearby. On the night of May 27 he got word
from the Half King, who was on his way to join him, that a French
contingent was lurking in the vicinity. Washington decided at once to
meet the Half King on the way. "That very moment I sent out forty
men, and ordered my ammunition to be put in a place of safety, under
a strong guard to defend it, fearing it to be a stratagem of the French
to attack our camp, and with the rest of my men set out in a heavy rain,
and in a night as dark as pitch, along a patch scarce broad enough for
one man," he wrote. "We were sometimes fifteen or twenty minutes
out of the path, before we could come to it again, and so dark, that
we would often strike one against another." They kept at it all night.
"About sunrise, we arrived at the Indian camp, where, after having
held a council with the Half King, it was concluded we should fall on
them"—the French—"together."

Washington and the Half King dispatched scouts, who discovered
the precise location of the French column. "We formed ourselves for
an engagement, marching one after the other, in the Indian manner,"
Washington recounted. "We were advanced pretty near to them, as we

thought, when they discovered us, whereupon I ordered my company to fire."

The engagement was brief but intense. Washington and a subordinate officer led their companies into the thickest of the fight. "My company and his received the whole fire of the French during the greatest part of the action, which only lasted a quarter of an hour before the enemy was routed," Washington recalled. He added, "We killed Mr. de Jumonville, the commander of that party, as also nine others. We wounded one and made twenty-one prisoners." The Half King's men claimed prizes. "The Indians scalped the dead, and took away the most part of their arms."

Washington had never been in battle before this, and he found the experience thrilling. In a letter to his younger brother John, he relived the experience. "Three days ago we had an engagement with the French, that is, between a party of theirs and ours," he said. "Most of our men were out upon other detachments, so that I had scarcely 40 men under my command, and about ten or a dozen Indians. Nevertheless we obtained a most signal victory. The battle lasted about 10 or 15 minutes, sharp firing on both sides, when the French gave ground and run, but to no great purpose. There were 12 killed, among which was Monsieur De Jumonville, the commander. . . . We had but one man killed, two or three wounded and a great many more within an inch of being shot."

WASHINGTON'S SURPRISE ATTACK on Jumonville's column infuriated the French, who deemed the attack an unwarranted ambush, and the killing of Jumonville a criminal assassination. They moved at once to avenge the killing and repulse its perpetrators.

Washington readied Fort Necessity, as he called his work in progress, for the counterattack. He set his men to digging trenches and completing the construction of the fort. He had learned that reinforcements were on the road from Virginia; he sent a message urging them to make all haste.

Not everyone heeded the orders of the young lieutenant colonel. A company of British regulars sent from South Carolina had joined Washington's force; they declared ditch-digging beneath them and said that, anyway, they took orders only from officers of the British army, not from provincials.

Washington was nowhere near ready when the French attack came, on July 3. "Our sentinel gave notice, about eleven o'clock, of their approach, by firing his piece, which he did at the enemy, and as we learned afterwards killed three of their men, on which they began to fire upon us, at about 600 yards distance, but without any effect," he wrote afterward. He ordered his men to hold their fire until the French got closer. "They"—the French—"then advanced in a very irregular manner to another point of woods, about 60 yards off, and from thence made a second discharge; upon which, finding they had no intention of attacking us in the open field, we retired into our trenches, and still reserved our fire, as we expected from their great superiority of numbers that they would endeavour to force our trenches."

But the French still refused to engage frontally. Washington evaluated his position. Rain was falling and his men were unsheltered, making their powder liable to wetting. He surmised that more French troops would arrive before any reinforcements to his side. Hostile Indians, too, had joined the French, and seemed eager to have at the British. Concluding that time was not on his side, Washington gave the order to fire.

The French returned the fire, with an intensity reflecting their greater numbers. Washington's men acquitted themselves well but were overmatched. "We continued this unequal fight, with an enemy sheltered behind the trees, ourselves without shelter, in trenches full of water, in a settled rain, and the enemy galling us on all sides incessantly from the woods, till 8 o'clock at night, when the French called to parley," he wrote.

The French commander, Louis de Villiers, who happened to be the brother of the slain Jumonville, demanded that Washington surrender Fort Necessity and retire from the area. He said his demand was reasonable and in the best interests of Washington and his men, who could not hope to hold out against the much larger French force. "I told him that, as we were not at war, we were very willing to save them from the cruelties to which they exposed themselves, on account of the Indians," Villiers recalled afterward. "But if they were stubborn, we would take away from them all hopes of escaping; that we consented to be favourable to them at present, as we were come only to revenge my brother's assassination, and to oblige them to quit the lands of the King our master."

Washington couldn't deny the logic of Villiers's argument. Yet neither could he read Villiers's French, and so when he signed the articles of capitulation, he unwittingly conceded responsibility for "l'assasinat du Sr de Jumonville." Later, he hotly denied understanding what he had signed. He blamed a bad translation. And he most vehemently rejected the allegation that Jumonville's death was anything other than a legitimate casualty of war.

What he could not deny was that the expedition to the Forks of the Ohio had been a failure. He had been ordered to drive the French from the region; instead the French had driven *him* from the region. The resources devoted to the expedition were a dead loss. The French killed most of the horses of Washington's command during the battle, and the Indians contrived to steal much of their baggage afterward. Britain's fortunes in America's west had suffered a body blow.

All the same, Washington took from the expedition a feeling he would never forget. In the letter to his younger brother describing his first firefight, he added an emotional note. He told of the heavy casualties around him, declared himself fortunate to have escaped unhurt, and then remarked, "I heard bullets whistle and, believe me, there was something charming in the sound."

"FRIDAY LAST AN EXPRESS ARRIVED here from Major Washington," reported the *Pennsylvania Gazette* in Philadelphia a short while later. The owner and publisher of the paper was Benjamin Franklin, who, with everyone else in Pennsylvania, watched the events in the Ohio country with keen interest. Pennsylvania's claims to Ohio overlapped those of Virginia, and Pennsylvanians, including Franklin, were no less active than the Virginians in pursuing possibilities for land speculation there. Moreover, the danger of attack from Indians allied with the French was greater in the Pennsylvania backcountry than in the Virginia hinterland, due to the nearer proximity of Pennsylvania to the French base in Canada.

Franklin had been closely involved with frontier defense, as he had been involved in all manner of civic affairs in his adopted province for years. His residence in Philadelphia reflected sibling rivalry, professional ambition and dumb luck. He was born in Boston in the first decade of the eighteenth century, the fifteenth child of his father and the eighth of his mother. His father, Josiah, secured a roof over their many heads, and his mother, Abiah, put food on the table, but the family's resources didn't stretch much farther than that. Ben received but two years of formal schooling; at ten he was drafted for work in Josiah's chandlery, making candles from the rendered fat of slaughtered animals. A revolting smell suffused the process, and young Ben duly revolted, threatening to run away to sea if his father tried to make him stay in the shop. Escape by sea was a real possibility for a Boston boy; one of Josiah's older sons had done just that, and been lost when his ship foundered. Josiah couldn't bear the thought of losing another, and he yielded to Ben's threat. He apprenticed Ben to Ben's older brother James, a printer.

The decision was inspired and ill-fated. Printing played to Ben's manual dexterity and especially his way with words; he had been an early reader and was a precocious writer. Too precocious, in fact, for when James, insisting on the prerogatives of the master and elder brother, declined to accept Ben's offer to write for the newspaper James published, Ben fashioned an alter ego and submitted essays under that name. The letters of "Silence Dogood" proved popular with James's readers, and James eagerly but unknowingly solicited more. Ben drew quiet satisfaction from Silence's success, yet ultimately couldn't resist twitting James with her true identity. Fisticuffs ensued, with the brothers brawling on the shop floor. They appealed to their father. Josiah ruled in favor of James. Ben decided to break his indenture contract and flee Boston.

He covertly boarded a ship for New York. The captain tolerated the stowaway, who had saved enough money to pay for the passage. Franklin, confident of his skills, expected to find work in New York. But the descendants of the Dutch burghers who had founded the city were too busy buying and selling to read much, and no jobs in the printing trade appeared.

One of the printers who rejected Franklin's application said there might be a job in Philadelphia. So to Philadelphia Franklin headed, crossing New Jersey on foot and hitching a ride down the Delaware River. He reached the Pennsylvania capital city tired, dirty and almost without resources. Three copper pennies and the clothes on his back were the sum of his worldly possessions. When the pennies bought breakfast, his cash balance hit zero.

Yet Franklin thrived in the tolerant atmosphere of William Penn's city. He built a printing business, publishing the *Pennsylvania Gazette*, which he made into the most influential newspaper in North America, and *Poor Richard's Almanack*, a witty, sometimes racy version of the glorified calendars found in nearly every home. He applied his versatile intelligence to the improvement of civic life in Philadelphia, organizing a fire department, founding a philosophical society, sponsoring a lending library, and spearheading establishment of a hospital and a college. He invented an improved wood-burning stove that kept people warmer and forests fuller; his lightning rod preserved buildings from destruction and their inhabitants from electrocution. When he elevated his gaze from the affairs of Philadelphia to those of Pennsylvania, he proposed the creation of a militia to protect against the French and their Indian allies. And he became an envoy from the Pennsylvania assembly to the friendly tribes of the frontier.

In dealing with frontier issues, Franklin encountered a problem that had vexed colonial relations for decades. Just as the Indians played the British against the French, they played the Pennsylvanians against the Virginians and New Yorkers. They were able to do this because the different colonies refused to cooperate with one another. Sometimes the refusal took assertive form, as when Washington led Virginia militia into territory claimed by Pennsylvania. Sometimes the lack of cooperation appeared negatively, when one colony—typically Quaker-influenced Pennsylvania—refused to do its share for frontier defense.

Franklin proposed a simple solution: a confederation among the colonies, charged with coordinating their actions. As early as 1751 he made this suggestion amid a contretemps among the colonies regarding Indian policy. Citing the Iroquois Confederacy as a model, he observed, "It would be a very strange thing if six nations of ignorant savages should be capable of forming a scheme for such an union, and be able to execute it in such a manner as that it has subsisted ages and appears indissoluble; and yet that a like union should be impracticable for ten or a dozen English colonies, to whom it is more necessary, and must be more advantageous; and who cannot be supposed to want an equal understanding of their interests."

Franklin's suggestion fell on stony ground. The very rivalries that made cooperation necessary also made it impossible. He set his proposal aside. But when Washington's report from the frontier revealed that armed hostilities with the French had begun, he brought it out again. He observed that it was bold of the French to invade Ohio, given that the British in the area greatly outnumbered the French. Yet though bold, it wasn't without basis. "The confidence of the French in this undertaking seems well-grounded on the present disunited state of the British colonies and the extreme difficulty of bringing so many different governments and assemblies to agree in any speedy and effectual measures for our common defense and security, while our enemies have the very great advantage of being under one direction, with one council, and one purse," Franklin wrote in the *Pennsylvania Gazette*. The French realized they could get away with murder, figuratively and literally. "They presume that they may with impunity violate the most solemn treaties subsisting between the two crowns, kill, seize and imprison our traders, and confiscate their effects at pleasure (as they have done for several years past), murder and scalp our farmers, with their wives and children, and take an easy possession of such parts of the British territory as they find most convenient for them, which if they are permitted to do, must end in the destruction of the British interest, trade and plantations in America."

Accompanying Franklin's editorial was an illustration, a drawing of a snake severed into eight pieces. The pieces were labeled for the colonies, with the five New England colonies counting as one, and Delaware, having no frontier, omitted. Beneath the drawing was a caption: "Join, or Die."

Franklin's image would come to be considered the first political cartoon in American history; like many of its genre, it was no joke. In the 1750s the future of the British colonies in America couldn't be taken for granted. The French threatened them; the Indians threatened them. More crucially, British policy threatened them, Franklin judged. During much of the time since the first colonies were founded, London had let the colonies more or less govern themselves. Occasionally the Crown regathered the threads of power, but the effects of the retrenchment rarely lasted long. Each colony came to think of itself almost as a sovereign state, with little responsibility to the British government or people, and less to the other colonies.

The British government reciprocated. The colonies were styled "plantations," and like plantations they were valued for what they produced—in this case, raw materials and profits for the home country. London weighed the interests and desires of the American colonists almost not at all.

Franklin's second try at an American confederation, following Washington's report of the loss of Fort Necessity, received a warmer reception. Franklin presented his plan to a meeting at Albany, New York, of representatives from seven of the colonies, gathered to consider colonial defense. The Albany Congress, as it called itself, was intrigued enough to ask Franklin to flesh out the plan, which to this point existed only in outline. He did so, and debate ensued. "We had a great deal of disputation about it, almost every article being contested by one or another," Franklin afterward told a friend. The heat of the discussion reflected the engagement of the delegates rather than their opposition, and in the end the congress heartily endorsed Franklin's plan and referred it to the colonies for approval.

A FRANKLIN ALLY at Albany was a delegate from Massachusetts named Thomas Hutchinson. Born in Boston, like Franklin, and of comparable age, Hutchinson had roamed the same streets as young Ben, and perhaps crossed paths with him, although not so either recalled. Yet where Franklin left Boston as a teenager, Hutchinson stuck around. Hutchinson liked things as they were, and in their place. He shunned controversy. "My temper does not incline to enthusiasm," he said. He was conservative to the core, adopting as his motto "What is, is best." Hutchinson's forebears being merchants, he followed their lead, with a punctiliousness of his own. "All the time he was at college," he afterward wrote of himself, "he carried on a little trade by sending ventures in his father's vessels, and kept a little paper journal and ledger and entered in it every dinner, supper, breakfast, and every article of expense, even of a shilling; which practice soon became pleasant, and he found it of great use all his life, as so exact a knowledge of his cash kept him from involvement of which he would have been in danger. And having been a very few instances negligent in this respect for a short time only, he saw the consequence of this neglect in a very strong light, and became more observant ever after."

Hutchinson entered politics while still in his twenties. He served as a selectman in Boston, and then as a member of the Massachusetts provincial assembly. Before long he became speaker of the assembly. His obvious talent didn't guarantee him popularity, though, and he lost his assembly seat to a challenger. Almost at once he received appointment to the governor's council, which restored some of his influence even as it cost him further popularity. The assembly was the people's body, the council the governor's. And because the governor was a royal appointee, the council members were often seen as the king's men.

Hutchinson encountered—or re-encountered—Benjamin Franklin at Albany, where they worked together to strengthen the British colonies against France and France's Indian allies. Hutchinson headed a committee of the Albany congress charged with drafting a justification for the confederation Franklin proposed. The Hutchinson report lamented the "divided, disunited state" of the British colonies, and observed, "There never has been any joint exertion of their force or counsels to repel or defeat the measures of the French." The colonies must learn to coordinate their efforts, and the most effective means to this end would be "a union of His Majesty's several governments on the continent, so that their counsels, treasure, and strength may be employed in due proportion against their common enemy."

THE COLONIAL GOVERNORS WERE less enthusiastic about an American confederation than the Albany delegates were. Franklin proposed to give the people of the colonies a large role in the selection of delegates to the confederation government; the governors were loath to allow the people such authority. Massachusetts governor William Shirley said the British government should have the power of selection.

Franklin replied that this would fatally weaken the confederation. The critical issue was the funding of frontier defense, which would require new taxes, a sensitive subject for Englishmen since the time of Magna Carta, and no less sensitive for the English in America. "It is supposed an undoubted right of Englishmen not to be taxed but by their own consent given through their representatives," Franklin wrote to Shirley. So far the British government had honored this right with respect to the Americans.

The governor answered Franklin's objection by declaring that the British government should grant the Americans representation in Parliament.

Franklin doubted that Parliament would agree. But supposing it might, he raised the stakes. He broadened his idea of a confederation among the American colonies into a union of the American colonies with Britain itself. "Such an union would be very acceptable to the colonies," Franklin predicted, "provided they had a reasonable number of representatives allowed them, and that all the old acts of Parliament restraining the trade or cramping the manufactures of the colonies be at the same time repealed, and the British subjects on this side the water put, in those respects, on the same footing with those in Great Britain." American representation in Parliament would strengthen British policy for the American frontier, and it would improve imperial governance generally. "It is not that I imagine so many representatives will be allowed the colonies as to have any great weight by their numbers, but I think there might be sufficient to occasion those laws to be better and more impartially considered, and perhaps to overcome the private interest of a petty corporation, or of any particular set of artificers or traders in England, who heretofore seem, in some instances, to have been more regarded than all the colonies, or than was consistent with the general interest or best national good."

The more Franklin thought about it, the better he liked the idea of a transatlantic union, with America eventually assuming a role equal to Britain's. Here he was thinking beyond taxes and trade. "I should hope too, that by such an union, the people of Great Britain and the people of the colonies would learn to consider themselves not as belonging to different communities with different interests, but to one community with one interest, which I imagine would contribute to strengthen the whole, and greatly lessen the danger of future separations."

A union would benefit all parts of the empire, Franklin said. Size mattered in world affairs. "It is, I suppose, agreed to be the general interest of any state that its people be numerous and rich: men enough to fight in its defense, and enough to pay sufficient taxes to defray the charge, for these circumstances tend to the security of the state, and its protection from foreign power." A union would amalgamate multiple interests, to the benefit of all. "It seems not of so much importance whether the fighting be done by John or Thomas, or the tax paid by William or Charles," Franklin wrote. "The iron manufacture employs and enriches British subjects, but is it of any importance to the state whether the manufacturers live at Birmingham or Sheffield, or both, since they are still within its bounds, and their wealth and persons at its command?" The same reasoning might extend to the American colonies, making Boston interchangeable with Manchester, and New York with Newcastle.

The concept was simple but profound. "The strength and wealth of the parts is the strength and wealth of the whole," Franklin asserted. The questions that followed from the concept answered themselves. "What imports it to the general state whether a merchant, a smith, or a hatter grow rich in *Old* or *New* England? And if, through increase of people, two smiths are wanted for one employed before, why may not the *new* smith be allowed to live and thrive in the *new Country*, as well as the *old* one in the *Old*? In fine, why should the countenance of a state be *partially* afforded to its people, unless it be most in favour of those who have most merit? And if there be any difference, those who have most contributed to enlarge Britain's empire and commerce, increase her strength, her wealth, and the numbers of her people, at the risque of their own lives and private fortunes in new and strange countries, methinks ought rather to expect some preference."

Franklin was willing to waive preference. But he thought equality in the empire was America's right.

WHEN FRANKLIN SPOKE of the increase in American numbers, he relied on data he had been gathering for some time. He was a keen observer of all manner of things: lightning, patterns of wind and rain, the Gulf Stream, lead poisoning in printers, the growth of the population of the British colonies in America. This last, demographic question prompted Franklin to write an essay titled "Observations concerning the Increase of Mankind, Peopling of Countries, etc." The essay consisted of a series of assertions, based on what Franklin had seen, what he had read, and what he could conjecture about human procreation and the influences upon it. "People increase in proportion to the number of marriages, and that is greater in proportion to the ease and convenience of supporting a family," he said. "When families can be easily supported, more persons marry, and earlier in life." Supporting a family, in a largely agricultural age, required access to land. In Europe land was scarce, in America plenty and therefore cheap. "A labouring man that understands husbandry can in a short time save money enough to purchase a piece of new land sufficient for a plantation, whereon he may subsist a family," Franklin said of the situation in America. "Such are not afraid to marry, for if they even look far enough forward to consider how their children when grown up are to be provided for, they see that more land is to be had at rates equally easy, all circumstances considered."

The arithmetic was straightforward, and to America's enduring advantage over Europe. "If it is reckoned there that there is but one marriage per annum among 100 persons, perhaps we may here reckon two," Franklin said. "And if in Europe they have but 4 births to a marriage (many of their marriages being late) we may here reckon 8, of which if one half grow up and our marriages are made, reckoning one with another at 20 years of age, our people must at least be doubled every 20 years."

And yet America was not about to fill up. "So vast is the territory of North America that it will require many ages to settle it fully," Franklin said. "And till it is fully settled, labour will never be cheap here, where no man continues long a labourer for others, but gets a plantation of his own. No man continues long a journeyman to a trade, but goes among those new settlers, and sets up for himself." The evidence of this appeared in American wage rates, which remained high. Franklin cited his own province and spoke from his own experience. "Labour is no cheaper now in Pennsylvania than it was 30 years ago, though so many thousand labouring people have been imported."

This had implications for policy. "The danger therefore of these colonies interfering with their Mother Country in trades that depend on labour, manufactures, etc., is too remote to require the attention of Great Britain," Franklin said. Britain should not restrain American manufactures. "A wise and good mother will not do it. To distress, is to weaken, and weakening the children, weakens the whole family."

The government and people of Britain, far from feeling threatened by the growth of the American colonies, should encourage that growth, which in any event was certain to continue. "There are supposed to be now upwards of one million English souls in North America (though 'tis thought scarce 80,000 have been brought over sea) and yet perhaps there is not one the fewer in Britain, but rather many more, on account of the employment the colonies afford to manufacturers at home," Franklin wrote. "This million doubling, suppose but once in 25 years, will in another century be more than the people of England, and the greatest number of Englishmen will be on this side the water. What an accession of power to the British empire by sea as well as land! What increase of trade and navigation! What numbers of ships and seamen!"

GEORGE WASHINGTON'S DEFEAT at Fort Necessity prompted the British government to take the French threat on the American frontier more seriously, with the result that what London had previously left to provincials like Washington and the Virginia militia, it now assigned to British regulars. Heading the force the government sent to America was Edward Braddock, a type specimen of a certain sort of British general. Braddock was the son of Edward Braddock, a major general in the Coldstream Guards, a regiment with roots in the New Model Army of Oliver Cromwell. The father found a spot for his fifteen-year-old in the Coldstream Guards, as an ensign, and from there the younger man successively purchased promotions—a standard practice—to lieutenant colonel by the 1740s. The War of the Austrian Succession—called King George's War in America—found him not on the battlefield but in the wood-paneled bunkers of the army staff. By this time Braddock had reached middle age, which brought a kind of career crisis. He transferred from the Coldstreams to another regiment, and was sent, now a full colonel, to Gibraltar, Britain's booty from an earlier conflict with Spain.

Horace Walpole, London's most famous gossip, besides being the son of a prime minister, observed Braddock's rise with fascination. "He once had a duel with Colonel Gumley, Lady Bath's brother, who had been his great friend," Walpole wrote to an acquaintance. "As they were going to engage, Gumley, who had good humour and wit (Braddock had the latter) said, 'Braddock, you are a poor dog! Here take my purse; if you kill me you will be forced to run away, and then you will not have a shilling to support you.' Braddock refused the purse, insisted on the duel, was disarmed, and would not even ask his life. However, with all his brutality, he has lately been Governor of Gibraltar, where he made himself adored, and where scarce any Governor was endured before."

Braddock's performance at Gibraltar won him promotion to major general. And it put him in line for a posting to America. His temperament appeared admirably suited for the frontier. "Braddock is a very Iroquois in disposition," Walpole wrote to the same acquaintance. "He had a sister, who having gamed away all her little fortune at Bath, hanged herself with a truly English deliberation, leaving only a note upon the table with those lines 'To die is landing on some silent shore,' etc. When Braddock was told of it, he only said, 'Poor Fanny! I always thought she would play till she would be forced *to tuck herself up!*'"

Yet there was another side to Braddock. "A more ridiculous story of him, and which is recorded in heroics by Fielding in his 'Covent-Garden Tragedy,' was an amorous discussion he had formerly with a Mrs. Upton, who kept him," Walpole continued. "He had gone the greatest lengths with her pin-money, and was still craving. One day that he was very pressing, she pulled out her purse and showed him that she had but twelve or fourteen shillings left; he twitched it from her, 'Let me see that.' Tied up at the other end he found five guineas; he took them, tossed the empty purse in her face, saying, 'Did you mean to cheat me?' and never went near her more." Walpole concluded: "Now you are acquainted with General Braddock."

The suspicious side of Braddock surfaced early in his dealings with the Americans. He gathered the governors of the colonies with the greatest stake in the frontier, to coordinate military planning and arrange appropriations. Talks went well on the former front and poorly on the latter. Braddock, with the rest of the British government, expected the colonies to contribute to their own defense. But the colonial assemblies, two in particular, were slow in voting funds. Braddock reacted as he had to the hidden guineas. "I cannot sufficiently express my indignation against the provinces of Pennsylvania and Maryland, whose interest being alike concerned in the event of this expedition, and much more so than any other on this continent, refuse to contribute anything towards the project," Braddock informed his London superiors. He planted a seed that would bear portentous fruit a decade hence. "I cannot but take the liberty to represent to you the necessity of laying a tax upon all His Majesty's dominions in America," he said. If the colonies wouldn't voluntarily pay for their own defense, they must be compelled to do so.

Braddock knew he needed the colonial support because his British backing was insufficient. George Anne Bellamy, an intimate friend, recalled their last moments together in London. "General Braddock, to whom I had been known from my infancy, and who was particularly fond of me, the evening before his departure for America supped with me," she wrote. "Before we parted, the General told me he should never see me more, for he was going, with a handful of men, to conquer whole nations, and to do this they must cut their way through unknown woods. He produced a map of the country, saying, at the same time, 'Dear Pop, we are sent like sacrifices to the altar.'"

Braddock exaggerated, for Pop's benefit and his own, but his lament wasn't without basis. His handful of men was actually two regiments. Yet they weren't staffed at capacity. And his mission indeed was to conquer whole nations. He was to capture Fort Duquesne, as the French called their post at the Forks of the Ohio, and proceed to roll the French back to Montreal and Quebec. In the bargain he would punish the Indian nations allied to the French, winning them to Britain's side or destroying their ability to wage war.

From the perspective of Britain's armchair strategists in London, Braddock's charge wasn't outlandish. The population of the British colonies in America was far greater than that of the French colonies, and the disparity in wealth and resources commensurate. By sheer weight alone, French Canada must fall into British hands. Beyond this, the British government had implicit confidence in the fighting ability of British soldiers and the battlefield tactics of British officers. With an experienced commander like Braddock, the campaign against the French had every likelihood of success.

BENJAMIN FRANKLIN MET Braddock on the march, and he brought with him his son. William Franklin's relationship with his father hadn't always been of a sort that suggested partnership. The problems started with William's illegitimate birth. Franklin and a young woman of Philadelphia, Deborah Read, had arranged to be married, but Franklin's printing work took him to London, to acquire equipment, and he was so charmed by the imperial capital that he overstayed his business. His letters to Debbie grew less frequent, and his liaisons with other women more so. Finally he stopped writing entirely. Debbie found another suitor and married him. But he proved more faithless than Franklin, and abandoned her, leaving her legally wed yet practically a widow. Eventually Franklin returned to Philadelphia, and he and Debbie resumed their relationship. Once more they engaged to be married, albeit as common-law spouses, because of the legal limbo Debbie inhabited. But before the happy day arrived, Franklin informed Debbie he was going to be a father, with another woman. The child of this affair was William, whom Franklin took into his and Debbie's home from birth.

Debbie wasn't thrilled at the idea of raising another woman's child, especially one who embodied her husband's infidelity. Her resentment gave rise to shouting matches, duly noted by the neighbors, between her and William as the boy grew older. The atmosphere in the household improved after Debbie and Franklin had a child, Francis, together. But the respite ended abruptly and tragically when Francis died of smallpox at the age of four. A second child, Sarah, again allayed the friction between stepmother and stepson, yet the Franklin home remained tense.

William attempted escape at the age of fifteen. Philadelphia's harbor boasted fewer vessels than Boston's, but like the latter in Ben's youth, it beckoned to a lad eager to make his own way in the world. And amid King George's War, it offered work even to a novice willing to take his chances on a privateer—a vessel licensed to prey on the commerce of the enemy, with the officers and crew splitting the booty. With no word to his father, William packed a duffel of clothes and personal items and found a berth on a privateer about to sail.

Ben hadn't lived in Philadelphia twenty years for nothing; his network of friends and associates alerted him to William's imminent departure. Ben marched down to the dock, boarded the vessel, grabbed William by the scruff and hauled him home.

Yet he knew the solution was temporary. William would simply do a better job running off next time. Ben had lost a brother at sea, and didn't want to lose a son the same way. So he let William know that if a taste of war was what he wanted, he might enlist in a regiment being mustered for an invasion of Canada. William seized the offer, bought a uniform, and marched off toward Albany in the service of king and empire.

Ben hoped his son's enthusiasm would diminish on exposure to camp and campaign. Instead it only grew. "Billy is so fond of military life that he will by no means hear of leaving," Franklin remarked. Political differences and bureaucratic bungling prevented the invasion from even reaching the Canadian border; the troops spent a painfully cold winter outside Albany. But William remained in the service, winning promotion to captain. A career in the army appeared possible, even likely. "My son (who will wait upon you with this)," Franklin wrote to an Albany friend, to whom William was carrying a letter on his way back from furlough, "is returning to the army, his military inclinations (which I hoped would have been cooled with the last winter) continuing as warm as ever."

The war ended before William could be tested in battle. The regiment was disbanded and his military career suspended. "As peace cuts off his prospect of advancement in that way, he will apply himself to other business," Ben wrote to a friend.

Some of that other business was with Ben. William assisted in Ben's experiments, including the kite experiment that made the elder Franklin world-famous. As William approached manhood, Franklin saw a good deal of himself in his son. "A tall proper youth, and much of a beau," he described William to his own mother. Too much of a beau, it turned out, and too much like the father: William eventually sired a son out of wedlock.

In other respects, William was quite different from Franklin. He wasn't obviously ambitious, and he fancied he would inherit a living from his father. Franklin brought him up short. "I have assured him that I intend to spend what little I have, myself, if it please God I live long enough," Franklin told his mother.

To encourage self-sufficiency, Franklin promoted William's career. After Franklin was elected to the Pennsylvania assembly, he got William a job as clerk to the legislative body. Following Franklin's appointment as postmaster for the American colonies, he made William postmaster of Philadelphia. Father and son speculated in Ohio lands together. And when Franklin traveled from Philadelphia to meet

General Braddock on the march toward the Forks of the Ohio, William rode with him.

BRADDOCK HAD LAUNCHED the campaign from Alexandria, and he proceeded with the van of his army to western Maryland, where Franklin, sent out by the Pennsylvania assembly, and William intercepted him. The assembly's leaders understood that Braddock was livid at them, and they instructed Franklin to say he was acting in his capacity as postmaster general of the colonies, not as their agent. He should offer that he wished to ensure smooth communications between the general and the governors and assemblies of the several colonies. If opportunity arose, he might mollify Braddock by explaining that the assembly in fact was willing to do more than it had let on.

"We found the general at Fredericktown, waiting impatiently for the return of those he had sent through the back parts of Maryland and Virginia to collect wagons," Franklin recalled later. Braddock was seeking 150 wagons to transport the baggage and provisions of his troops. "I stayed with him several days, dined with him daily, and had full opportunity of removing all his prejudices, by the information of what the Assembly had before his arrival actually done, and were still willing to do, to facilitate his operations."

As Franklin was preparing to head back to Philadelphia, the results of Braddock's wagon-raising campaign started trickling in. A mere twenty-five wagons, many almost unusable, were offered. "The general and all the officers were surprised, declared the expedition was then at an end, being impossible, and exclaimed against the ministers for ignorantly landing them in a country destitute of the means of conveying their stores, baggage, etc., not less than one hundred and fifty wagons being necessary," Franklin recounted.

He tactfully spoke up. "I happened to say I thought it was a pity they had not been landed rather in Pennsylvania"—instead of Virginia—"as in that country almost every farmer had his wagon."

Braddock locked on to Franklin's words. "Then you, sir, who are a man of interest there, can probably procure them for us," he said. "And I beg you will undertake it."

Franklin knew the Pennsylvanians would have to be paid. "I asked what terms were to be offered the owners of the wagons," he recalled.

Braddock told Franklin to write down what he thought the farmers would accept. Franklin did so, and Braddock approved.

Franklin composed a call for wagons, which he arranged to run in a newspaper at Lancaster. The call piqued the interest of farmers in the vicinity, yet many were skeptical, unsure that they were going to be paid. They didn't know General Braddock, and they didn't trust his promise of payment. They doubted they could sue a British general and collect. Franklin, on the other hand, they *did* know. And Franklin was subject to the laws and courts of Pennsylvania. If Franklin would post bond for their payment, they said, Braddock could have his wagons.

Franklin agreed. Within two weeks, the wagons appeared.

Braddock judged Franklin a remarkable fellow. He thought even better of him after Franklin persuaded the Pennsylvania assembly to send provisions Braddock particularly needed. Braddock then requested that Franklin procure other provisions. Franklin did so, paying for them with a thousand pounds of his own money, on promise of reimbursement from the British treasury.

Franklin developed a mixed view of Braddock. "This general was, I think, a brave man, and might probably have made a figure as a good officer in some European war," he said afterward. "But he had too much self-confidence, too high an opinion of the validity of regular troops, and too mean a one of both Americans and Indians." Braddock had boasted of the victories he would swiftly win. "After taking Fort Duquesne," he said, "I am to proceed to Niagara; and, having taken that, to Frontenac, if the season will allow time; and I suppose it will, for Duquesne can hardly detain me above three or four days; and then I see nothing that can obstruct my march to Niagara."

Franklin thought Braddock unduly optimistic. He tried to point this out. "To be sure, sir, if you arrive well before Duquesne, with these fine troops, so well provided with artillery, that place, not yet completely fortified, and as we hear with no very strong garrison, can probably make but a short resistance. The only danger I apprehend of obstruction to your march is from ambuscades of Indians, who, by constant practice, are dexterous in laying and executing them; and the slender line, near four miles long, which your army must make, may expose it to be attacked by surprise in its flanks, and to be cut like a thread into several pieces, which, from their distance, cannot come up in time to support each other."

Braddock would have none of it. "He smiled at my ignorance," Franklin recalled, "and replied, 'These savages may, indeed, be a formidable enemy to your raw American militia, but upon the king's regular and disciplined troops, sir, it is impossible they should make any impression."

Franklin fell silent. "I was conscious of an impropriety in my disputing with a military man in matters of his profession, and said no more."

To GEORGE WASHINGTON, Edward Braddock seemed the answer to a young soldier's dreams, or at least his ambitions.

On arrival in Virginia, Braddock had inquired about soldiers who knew the backcountry; informed of Washington's two expeditions to the Ohio, he invited the young man along. Washington was delighted to accept. A reorganization of the Virginia militia had left him with the unappealing prospect of accepting a demotion if he remained on duty. He thought he deserved better, and resigned. But his appetite for action hadn't diminished, and he hoped to take part in a campaign that ended in victory rather than defeat. Braddock's presence signaled British seriousness about driving the French from the Ohio. If Washington impressed Braddock, others in the British chain of command might notice.

"I wish earnestly to attain some knowledge on the military profession," he wrote to Braddock's adjutant, in response to the invitation. "And believing a more favorable opportunity cannot offer than to serve under a gentleman of General Braddock's ability and experience, it does, as you may reasonably suppose, not a little contribute to influence my choice." For Braddock's benefit Washington drew a map of the Ohio country, "which though imperfect and roughly drawn, for want of proper instruments, may give you a better knowledge of the parts designated than you have hitherto had an opportunity of acquiring."

Meanwhile Washington asserted to friends that his participation was motivated solely by concern for the welfare of his country. "I can very truly say I have no views either of profiting by it or rising in the service, as I go a volunteer without pay, and am certain it is not in General Braddock's power to give a commission that I would accept." Washington protested—perhaps too much—that joining the campaign would actually *cost* him. "So far from being serviceable, I am thoroughly convinced it will prove very detrimental to my private affairs." The busy season of plowing and planting was upon Mount Vernon, and by leaving the work to others, Washington risked its being poorly done. "But however prejudicial this may be," he said, "it shall not keep me from going."

Washington blended easily into Braddock's "family," as the general's personal staff was called. "I have met with much complaisance in this family, especially from the General, who I hope to please without ceremonious attentions or difficulty," Washington wrote to his brother John. To his mother he said, "I am very happy in the General's family, being treated with a complaisant freedom which is quite agreeable to me and have no reason to doubt the satisfaction I hoped for in making the campaign."

He would have been happier still if the campaign had unfolded more rapidly. "We proceeded by slow marches to this place," Washington informed brother Augustine from Fort Cumberland, on the Maryland side of the Potomac at Wills Creek. "I fear we shall remain some time, for want of horses and carriages to convey our baggage etc. over the mountains, but more especially for want of forage, as it cannot be imagined that so many horses as we require will be subsisted without a great deal." As things happened, Benjamin Franklin solved the transport problem, but the lack of forage remained a hindrance.

Scanty intelligence regarding the enemy posed another problem. "We hear nothing in particular from the Ohio except that the French are in hourly expectation of being joined by a large body of Indians," Washington told Augustine.

Yet Braddock didn't seem worried. At his conference with the governors he had been promised attacks on other parts of Canada. These would keep the French from concentrating on the Ohio, the general judged.

Washington was willing to defer to Braddock on this. "I fancy they will find themselves so warmly attacked in other places that it will not be convenient for them to spare many," he wrote.

Washington remained hopeful as the summer approached. "We are to halt here till forage can be brought from Philadelphia, which I suppose will introduce the month of June," he explained to a friend. "And then we are to proceed upon our tremendous undertaking of transporting the heavy artillery over the mountains, which I believe will compose the greatest difficulty of the campaign." The French were almost an afterthought. "As to any apprehensions of the enemy, I think they are more to be provided against than regarded, as I fancy the French will be obliged to draw their force from the Ohio to repel the attacks in the north." In another letter Washington was even more categorical. "As to any danger from the enemy, I look upon it as trifling," he said.

The delay served the self-interest Washington had taken pains to deny. "The general has appointed me one of his aides de camp, in which character I shall serve this campaign agreeably enough," he recorded. "I am thereby freed from all commands but his, and give his orders to all, which must be implicitly obeyed. I have now a good opportunity, and shall not neglect it, of forming an acquaintance which may be serviceable hereafter if I shall find it worthwhile pushing my fortune in the military line."

Braddock consulted Washington more frequently as they approached the Forks. He asked for details about the terrain, points of access, and routes for men and materiel. He flattered Washington by inquiring how *he* would engage the French.

"I urged it in the warmest terms I was able to push forward, even if we did it with a small but chosen band, with such artillery and light stores as were absolutely necessary, leaving the heavy artillery, baggage etc. with the rear division of the army to follow by slow and easy marches, which they might do safely while we were advanced in front," Washington recounted to John. "As one reason to support this opinion, I urged that if we could credit our intelligence, the French were weak at the Forks at present, but hourly expected reinforcements, which to my certain knowledge could not arrive with provisions or any supplies during the continuance of the drought which we were experiencing, as the Buffalo River (River Le Boeuf), down which was their only communication to Venango, must be as dry as we now found the great crossing of the Youghiogheny, which may be passed dry shod."

Braddock was impressed. "This advice prevailed," Washington boasted to John. "And it was determined that the general, with 1200 chosen men and officers from all the different corps, under the following field officers"—Washington listed several, including Lieutenant Colonel Thomas Gage—"with such a certain number of wagons as the train would absolutely require, should march as soon as things could be got in readiness for them."

The preparations were made, and the march began. "We set out with less than 30 carriages (including those that transported the ammunition for the howitzers, 12-pounders, 6-pounders etc.) and all of them strongly horsed, which was a prospect that conveyed infinite delight to my mind," Washington wrote.

Events soon diminished his delight. Braddock could not bring even this flying column to move swiftly. "Instead of pushing on with vigour, without regarding a little rough road, they were halting to level every mole hill and to erect bridges over every brook, by which means we were 4 days getting 12 miles," Washington grumbled.

His disappointment at the column's slowness was compounded just then by illness. Braddock's army had been accompanied by the bane of every army in those times: infectious disease caused or aggravated by the close, unsanitary quarters in which the men ate, slept and performed the other functions of daily life. Washington had been spared, not least by eating and tenting with Braddock's staff, but finally he too fell ill. "I was seized by violent fever and pains in my head," he told John. The worst of it lasted a week. "My illness was too violent to suffer me to ride; therefore I was indebted to a covered wagon for some part of my transportation. But even in this I could not continue far, for the jolting was so great that I was left upon the road with a guard and necessities, to wait the arrival of Colonel Dunbar's detachment, which was two days' march behind us." Washington tried to refuse this special treatment, but Braddock insisted. "The general giving me his word of honour that I should be brought up before he reached the French fort, this promise, and the doctor's threats that if I persevered in my attempts to get on, in the condition I was, my life would be endangered, determined me to halt for the above detachment."

Washington's condition gradually improved, but he fretted that he might miss the big event, notwithstanding Braddock's promise. "I have now been six days with Colonel Dunbar's corps, who are in a miserable condition for want of horses," he wrote on June 28. Each passing day caused him to fret the more. Word from the van told of encounters between the British and the enemy. "They have had frequent alarms and several men have been scalped," Washington recorded. He hoped the tales were exaggerated, or that the attacks didn't amount to much. "This is done with no other design than to retard the march and harass the men," he said of the French strategy.

His spirits lifted shortly. "We are advanced almost as far as the Great Meadows," he wrote on July 2. "I shall set out tomorrow morning for my own corps." The battle wouldn't begin without him. "My fears and doubts on that head are now removed."

Everything was falling into place for Braddock, and for Washington, who soon caught up with him. Braddock's spies said the French garrison at Fort Duquesne was still undermanned; the fort could be captured with little difficulty. Yet Braddock took no chances. He avoided narrow places where his column could be ambushed, sometimes marching many miles to secure a safer path forward. He sent scouts ahead of his troops and posted guards behind them. He left nothing to chance. After all the frustrations of the campaign in terms of funding, provisioning and lack of local support, his first major objective was within reach.

The portents remained good as they neared the Forks. "We continued our march from Fort Cumberland to Frazer's (which is within 7 Miles of Duquesne) without meeting any extraordinary event, having only a straggler or two picked up by the French Indians," Washington wrote. His early impatience had vanished. He now felt only confidence in Braddock and respect for the British style of campaigning.

AND THEN DISASTER STRUCK. "Our numbers consisted of about 1300 well-armed men, chiefly regulars," Washington wrote afterward of Braddock's column as it moved closer to Fort Duquesne. The general remained cautious and vigilant; his scouts continued to probe the forests beside the road on which his soldiers advanced.

But somehow they missed the Indians and French Canadians who lay concealed there. And when the Indians and French opened fire, the British troops were thrown into "such an inconceivable panic that nothing but confusion and disobedience of orders prevailed amongst them," Washington reported to Governor Dinwiddie. Until this moment Washington had accorded the British regulars the respect and even deference militia men and officers typically displayed toward professionals in the art of war. But he now discovered that the regulars' experience and training hadn't prepared them for the kind of fighting practiced on the American frontier. Most had never fought in the forest; under sudden fire from an enemy hidden by trees, they didn't know whether to go forward or back, and so they simply milled around. Eventually they heard an order to fall back, but in obeying, they collided with troops from the rear who had been ordered to rush forward. The collision increased the confusion, with the result that even as the British troops were raked by the fire of the French and Indians, many were killed or wounded by fire from their comrades.

The officers did what they could to stem the panic. "The officers in general behaved with incomparable bravery," Washington reported. Yet their gallantry, combined with their visibility on horseback, rendered them easy targets for enemy fire. "They greatly suffered, there being near 60 killed and wounded, a large proportion out of the number we had," Washington said.

The Virginia militia made Washington proud. "The Virginian companies behaved like men, and died like soldiers, for I believe out of 3 companies that were on the ground that day, scarce 30 were left alive," he wrote. "Captain Peyrouny and all his officers down to a corporal were killed; Captain Polson shared almost as hard a fate, for only one of his escaped."

It was the British troops who failed miserably. "The dastardly behaviour of the regular troops exposed all those who were inclined to do their duty to almost certain death; and at length, in despite of every effort to the contrary, they broke and ran as sheep before hounds, leaving the artillery, ammunition, provision, baggage and in short everything a prey to the enemy. And when we endeavoured to rally them in hopes of regaining the ground and what we had left upon it, it was with as little success as if we had attempted to have stopped the wild bears of the mountains, or rivulets with our feet, for they would break by in spite of every effort that could be made to prevent it."

Washington could easily have been killed in the effort. "I had four bullets through my coat, and two horses shot under," he told John. This summary didn't do justice to the effort Washington expended and the risks he took. He galloped ceaselessly along the line of the troops, carrying orders from Braddock to the front and rear and back again. He shouted to the soldiers to obey, appealing to their pride; when pride failed, he cajoled and threatened. He was a tall man, and on horseback he looked towering. Some who saw him, in the thickest part of the fight, reported that he had been killed; no one, they assumed, could have survived such a tempest of lead. Yet the bullets all missed him. Among the Indians spread word he had a protective form of magic. Washington himself credited a higher power. "By the all-powerful dispensations of Providence, I have been protected beyond all human probability and expectation," he said.

Washington never forgot that day, or the night that followed. "The shocking scenes which presented themselves in this night's march are not to be described," he recalled decades later. "The dead, the dying, the groans, lamentations and cries along the road of the wounded for help . . . were enough to pierce a heart of adamant. The gloom and horror of which was not a little increased by the impervious darkness occasioned by the close shade of thick woods which in places rendered it impossible for the two guides which attended to know when they were in, or out of the track but by groping on the ground with their hands."

Among the dying was Braddock himself. The general had tried, futilely, to rally his men, and in the process had made himself a tempting target for the sharpshooters of the enemy. Or it might have been a stray bullet from one of his own men that pierced his shoulder and chest. In either case the wound seemed mortal, and in seventy-two hours it turned out to be.

Braddock never learned the full extent of the disaster on the Monongahela. Nearly a thousand officers and men on the British side were killed or wounded, against a tenth as many on the French side. It was one of the costliest days in the history of British arms until then. Braddock went to his death wondering what had befallen him. Robert Orme, a friend of Washington on Braddock's staff, stayed with the general from the moment of his wounding until his death. Orme afterward told Benjamin Franklin that Braddock had said almost nothing the whole time. But on the general's last night, Orme heard him mutter, "Who would have thought it?" And the next day: "We shall better know how to deal with them another time." Then he lapsed into silence and expired.

George Washington helped bury Braddock. The remains were interred beneath the road over which the army traveled on its retreat from the scene of its humiliation. The boots of the men, the hooves of the horses, and the wheels of the wagons and gun carriages obliterated all sign of the interment—"to guard against a savage triumph, if the place should be discovered," Washington explained.

———

THE EPIPHANY GEORGE WASHINGTON experienced amid the chaos of Braddock's defeat—that British power wasn't what he had thought—was recapitulated throughout the American colonies as news of the debacle spread. The bright red line of defense Americans had counted on to secure their frontier against attack by Indians in league with the French had been shown, as the redcoats panicked and ran, to be no line at all. Many colonists had hoped to acquire land in Ohio and improve their fortunes; the rout at the Forks blew those hopes to bits. For the time being, the colonists would be lucky to hold the territory they already occupied.

To most of the colonists, as to Washington, the British army had been the standard for martial effectiveness. The part-time militias of Virginia, Pennsylvania and the other states had seemed inferior imitations of the career officers and tested rank-and-file of His Majesty's service. But then, in an hour in the American backcountry, the image of British indomitability vanished. Washington's Virginians outperformed Braddock's British regulars on the basic measures of aptitude and courage; Washington himself, at twenty-three, had proven more than a match for soldiers twice his age and with many times his experience. Benjamin Franklin observed, "This whole transaction gave us Americans the first suspicion that our exalted ideas of the prowess of British regulars had not been well founded."

Part II

When the Winds Blow

A S SHOCKING AS the slaughter on the Monongahela was, more dismaying to the residents of Pennsylvania and Virginia was the decision of Braddock's battlefield heir, Thomas Dunbar, to abandon the entire campaign and flee east. Cannons and other equipment, hauled to the west at great effort and cost, were destroyed or simply left to the French and the Indians. Dunbar's retreat didn't halt until he reached Philadelphia, which in high summer he proclaimed to be his winter quarters.

His decision left the frontier defenseless. The French and their Indian allies were as emboldened as the Anglo-Americans were dispirited. Jean-Daniel Dumas, the French commander at Fort Duquesne, unleashed a wave of terror against the settlers of western Pennsylvania, Maryland and Virginia. "I have succeeded in setting against the English all the tribes of this region who had been their most faithful allies," Dumas wrote to his superiors. "I have succeeded in making almost all of them attack the English, and if any of them resisted I have always managed to destroy them, so that I have put the Iroquois in fear of the Delawares and Shawnees unless they follow their example."

Dumas detailed his strategy of sending out war parties of Indians, each headed by a Frenchman, to terrorize the western zones of British settlement. "It is by means such as I have mentioned that I have succeeded in ruining the three adjacent provinces, Pennsylvania, Maryland, and Virginia, driving off the inhabitants and totally destroying the settlements over a tract of country thirty leagues wide, reckoning from the line of Fort Cumberland." The system leveraged the small number of Frenchmen most effectively. "Thus far we have lost only two officers and a few soldiers, but the Indian villages are full of prisoners of every age and sex." As bad as Braddock's defeat had been for the English, this campaign was much worse. "The enemy has lost far more since the battle than on the day of the defeat," Dumas boasted.

The terror spread up and down the frontier, with each week bringing new atrocities. "The inhabitants of the Great Cove were all murdered or taken captive, and their houses and barns all in flames," a western Pennsylvanian wrote to Robert Morris, the Pennsylvania governor. "We, to be sure, are in as bad circumstances as ever any poor Christians were ever in, for the cries of widowers, widows, fatherless and motherless children, with many others of their relations, are enough to pierce the most hardest of hearts. Likewise, it's a very sorrowful spectacle to those yet escaped with their lives with not a mouthful to eat, or bed to lie on, or clothes to cover their nakedness or keep them warm, but all they had consumed into ashes." The tales of the survivors were harrowing in the extreme. "It is really very shocking—it must be—for the husband to see the wife of his bosom, her head cut off, and children's blood drank like water by these bloody and cruel savages."

The alarm and dread extended far beyond the scene of the violence. "We are now in a grievous condition: the barbarous, inhuman, ungrateful natives weekly murdering our back country inhabitants; and those few Indians that profess some friendship to us are mostly watching for an opportunity to ruin us," wrote John Bartram, a friend of Franklin, in Philadelphia. A particularly appalling aspect of the violence was its treachery. "By what we can understand by the reports of our back inhabitants, most of the Indians which are so cruel are such as were almost daily familiars at their house: ate, drank, cursed and swore together—were even intimate playmates; and now, without any provocation, destroy all before them with fire, ball and tomahawk."

The raiding parties employed a murderously efficient style, Bartram reported. "If they attack a house that is pretty well manned, they creep behind some fence or hedge or tree, and shoot red-hot iron slugs, or punk, into the roof, and fire the house over their heads; and if they run out they are sure to be shot at, and most or all of them killed. If they come to a house where most of the family are women and children, they break into it, kill them all, plunder the house, and burn it with the dead in it; or if any escape out, they pursue and kill them. If the cattle are in the stable, they fire it, and burn the cattle; if they are out, they are shot, and the barn burnt." The raiding parties were implacable. "They are like the Angel of Death," Bartram said. He didn't know what would become of his province. "O Pennsylvania! Thou that was the most flourishing and peaceable province in North America art now scourged by the most barbarous creatures in the universe. All ages, sexes and stations have no mercy extended to them."

PENNSYLVANIANS FELT PECULIARLY aggrieved under the assault. The Quaker values that had inspired the founding of their colony had caused them to treat the Indians with comparative respect. Indeed, relations between the Pennsylvanians and the Indians had been good, measured by the aggressive standards of the provinces to the north and south of Pennsylvania. They had to be, for the Quakers who long dominated Pennsylvania politics typically refused to take up arms in the colony's defense, and they objected even to paying taxes earmarked for defense. The proprietors of the province—the English descendants of William Penn—retained a veto over provincial legislation through the governors they appointed, and they steadfastly rejected defense bills.

Benjamin Franklin endeavored to change their minds. Franklin had tangled with the Quakers and the Penns on the subject of defense for years. Frustrated by their recurrent vetoes of provincial defense bills, he had proposed the establishment of an extra-governmental militia, to be called the "Association." Members would be volunteers; they would bring their own weapons, furnish their own provisions, elect their own officers, and draw up their own regulations. In a draft charter for the Association, Franklin explained that he didn't suggest this circumvention of government lightly. "Where a government takes proper measures to protect the people under its care, such a proceeding might have been thought both unnecessary and unjustifiable. But here it is quite the reverse, for in our state (and perhaps if you search the world through, you will find it in ours only) the government, that part of it at least that holds the purse, has always, from religious considerations, refused to use the common means for the defence of the country against an enemy."

Franklin's fellow Pennsylvanians thought the Association a brilliant idea. Within days a thousand men had enlisted in Philadelphia; before long ten thousand from across the province had taken the pledge. The enlistees began drilling, to acquire military discipline to complement the skill with weapons they had learned at their fathers' knees. Women's auxiliaries pitched in to sew uniforms and flags.

Of small arms the Association had plenty; to acquire artillery, which had to be purchased, Franklin proposed another scheme: a lottery. The Association would sell twenty thousand pounds sterling worth of tickets, and pay out seventeen thousand in prizes. The balance of three thousand would go for cannons. Again, Franklin's plan proved wildly successful. The tickets sold out almost at once, and the Association purchased eighteen cannons.

Franklin had long enjoyed a reputation as a leading citizen of Philadelphia, but his measures on behalf of Pennsylvania defense made him a hero of the province. The Association's volunteers voted to make him their colonel. He expressed thanks for the honor, but declined the office as beyond his expertise. Others were better suited, he said.

THOMAS PENN JUDGED Franklin not a hero but an incipient traitor. Penn was a son of William Penn, and the current head of the proprietary group. "This Association is founded on a contempt to government, and cannot end in anything but anarchy and confusion," he declared. Penn saw something in the Association that Franklin declined to admit, though he certainly recognized it. The Association showed the people they could act independently of government. If this were allowed, Penn said, "why should they not act against it?"

Why not, indeed? With the Association, Franklin started Pennsylvania down the path all the colonies would take in 1776. His justification for the independent militia—that the government of Pennsylvania was failing to serve the interest of Pennsylvanians, and therefore that the Pennsylvanians must take matters into their own hands—was the same justification Thomas Jefferson would write into the Declaration of Independence almost three decades later.

Thomas Penn called Franklin's actions "little less than treason." Penn added of Franklin, "He is a dangerous man and I should be very glad he inhabited any other country, as I believe him of a very uneasy spirit." Yet Penn understood the political realities of the moment. "As he is a sort of tribune of the people, he must be treated with regard."

THE ASSOCIATION NEVER HAD to take the field; the conflict that had prompted it—King George's War—ended before the need arose. Franklin's idea lingered, however, and several years later, in the aftermath of the Braddock fiasco, it was revived.

The terror on the frontier prompted even many Quakers to support a land tax earmarked for defense. Yet the proprietors insisted that Governor Morris reject it if it included their lands on the list of taxable properties. It did, and he did, and the defense bill failed.

A bitter standoff developed between Franklin and the assembly, on one side, and Morris and the proprietors, on the other. The killing and burning on the frontier eventually caused the proprietors to offer a compromise: without yielding to the proposed tax and the precedent it would establish, they offered a free grant of five thousand pounds. It was a shrewd maneuver, for with women and children being butchered, Franklin and the assembly couldn't reject anything that might save others from such a ghastly fate. The assembly accepted the gift and passed a defense bill that left the proprietors' property untaxed.

The defense law named Franklin as one of the commissioners to oversee spending of the appropriated funds. He supervised the raising and training of troops, many of them former Association members. When a new attack a mere fifty miles from Philadelphia sent residents of the area fleeing toward the city, Franklin headed an expedition to construct a chain of blockhouses in which people could take refuge at the approach of French and Indian raiders. The structures were simple, built of pine logs planted vertically in trenches three feet deep, with rough planks affixed a few feet below the top of the walls, on the inside, from which the defenders could fire at attackers. Franklin marveled at the facility of the axmen; out of scientific curiosity he timed two of them as they felled a tree he measured at fourteen inches in diameter. In six minutes they had it down. The first fort was finished in a week, despite breaks for heavy rain.

The speed of construction owed much to the fear of renewed attack. Upon its completion Franklin led a reconnaissance of the surrounding area and discovered that he and his men had been observed. They found fire pits dug into the ground on a hilltop above the fort. Inside the pits were ashes of fires that had warmed the feet and legs of Indians as they sat and watched the construction. The pits and the method of building the fires kept the flames from view, and the rain and clouds disguised the smoke. "It appeared that their number was not great," Franklin remarked of the Indian observers, "and it seems they saw we were too many to be attacked by them with prospect of advantage."

The governor summoned Franklin back to Philadelphia, where the assembly was gathering again. Morris hoped Franklin would help sustain the cooperative spirit the collective danger had evoked. He wasn't pleased when the officers of the new regiment elected Franklin colonel, and this time Franklin accepted. The regiment was in fine fettle. "We paraded about twelve hundred well-looking men, with a company of artillery, who had been furnished with six brass field-pieces, which they had become so expert in the use of as to fire twelve times in a minute," Franklin recalled. The men insisted on marching Franklin to his house, where he kept scientific instruments, some made of glass. The salutes the men fired in his honor resulted in the shattering of several pieces.

Morris decided to test Franklin's popularity. He proposed that Franklin lead a new expedition against Fort Duquesne, now that the British had abandoned the cause. He offered to make Franklin a general.

Franklin saw through Morris's maneuver. "I had not so good an opinion of my military abilities as he professed to have, and I believe his professions must have exceeded his real sentiments," he said. Franklin reckoned that Morris wanted to parlay his—Franklin's—popularity into further appropriations from the assembly, without taxes on the proprietors' lands. Franklin foiled the scheme by declining, and Morris dropped it.

Nor did Franklin's colonelcy last. After his efforts helped stabilize the situation on the part of the frontier closest to Philadelphia, and the moment of greatest alarm passed, the proprietors' resentment of Franklin and his independent ideas took hold again. Franklin's commission was rescinded, at Thomas Penn's request, by a parliamentary override of the provincial law authorizing it.

FRANKLIN TOOK THE FIGHT against the Penns to England. In 1757 the Pennsylvania assembly named him its representative to the British government. The impasse between the assembly and the proprietors over defense and taxation persisted, and the assembly decided to dispatch its most persuasive member—Franklin—to talk sense into the Penns or, failing that, to find allies in Parliament to offset them.

Franklin was an apt choice, for beyond being persuasive, he was the most celebrated American in the world. His scientific experiments, especially in electricity, had won him renown in every country involved in the scientific revolution of that era. He had struck up correspondence with leading figures in England, Scotland and continental Europe. As a result, men who had never met him awaited his arrival in England most eagerly. Peter Collinson, a famous English botanist and a member of the Royal Society, offered to house Franklin until he found suitable quarters to let. William Strahan, the publisher of Samuel Johnson, Adam Smith and other literary stars, thought the world of Franklin. "I never saw a man who was, in every respect, so perfectly agreeable to me," Strahan wrote. "Some are amiable in one view, some in another, he in all."

Yet if Franklin had friends in England, so did Thomas Penn. Lord Granville was the president of the Privy Council, the group of closest advisers to King George II; he was also Penn's brother-in-law. Granville greeted Franklin with skepticism. "You Americans have wrong ideas of the nature of your constitution," he told Franklin at their first interview, according to Franklin's recollection immediately after. "You contend that the king's instructions to his governors are not laws, and think yourselves at liberty to disregard them at your own discretion. But those instructions are not like the pocket instructions given to a minister going abroad, for regulating his conduct in some trifling point of ceremony. They are first drawn up by judges learned in the laws; they are then considered, debated and perhaps amended in council, after which they are signed by the king. They are then so far as relates to you, the *law of the land*, for the king is the legislator of the colonies."

Franklin demurred. "I told his lordship this was new doctrine to me," he recorded. "I had always understood from our charters that our laws were to be made by our assemblies, to be presented indeed to the king for his royal assent, but that being once given, the king could not repeal or alter them. And as the assemblies could not make permanent laws without his assent, so neither could he make a law for them without theirs."

Granville would have none of it. "He assured me I was totally mistaken," Franklin wrote.

"I did not think so, however," he went on. "And his lordship's conversation having a little alarmed me as to what might be the sentiments of the court concerning us, I wrote it down as soon as I returned to my lodgings."

Franklin's alarm was apt, and prescient. For the first time he had encountered directly the question that would break up the empire two decades hence: Who legislated for the colonies? Franklin in 1757 couldn't know that the fate of the empire and of America would turn on this question. He hoped it wouldn't. He hoped Granville's view wasn't shared by everyone of influence in London, or, if it was, that it might be modified.

HE DISCOVERED THAT the modifying wouldn't come easily. Robert Morris, by this time the former governor of Pennsylvania, had warned Thomas Penn against Franklin. "Mr. Franklin will be in England soon, exhibiting his complaints against the proprietors, as is thought and expected by many that sent him," Morris wrote. "But I imagine his own schemes are very different from those of his employers. He is a sensible, artful man, very knowing in American affairs, and was his heart as sound as his head, few men would be fitter for public trust. But that is far from being the case. He has nothing in view but to serve himself, and however he may give another turn to what he says and does, yet you may be assured that is at the bottom, and in the end will shew itself."

Penn, aided by his brother and fellow proprietor Richard Penn, orchestrated a campaign against Franklin in the London press and in the salons of the city. Editorials and rumors cast doubt on Franklin's intentions and integrity.

Franklin fired back with an open letter to the editor of *The Citizen*, subsequently reprinted in other papers and magazines. Franklin had long employed aliases in making political arguments; in this case the alias was William Franklin, who had accompanied Franklin to London and now purported to defend his father against the Penns' attacks. Franklin-as-William argued that the proprietors' interpretation of their prerogatives flew in the face of centuries of English constitutional theory and practice. It threatened to deprive the Pennsylvanians of "the privileges long enjoyed by the people, and which they think they have a right to not only as Pennsylvanians but as Englishmen."

This would be the ground on which the American Revolution was made: that the Americans were defending their rights as Englishmen. For now it furnished the basis for Franklin's campaign against the proprietors.

And it failed. The Penns' allies proved more powerful than Franklin's. The proprietors' position held firm.

EVENTS IN NORTH AMERICA soon took the edge off the fight between Franklin and the Pennsylvanians, on the one side, and the Penns and the British government, on the other. The British eventually recovered from the shock of Braddock's defeat and mounted another expedition against the French on the Ohio. George Washington joined the staff of British general John Forbes and soon began offering local advice on the conduct of the campaign. The Cherokees and other potentially friendly Indians must be cultivated, Washington said. "On the assistance of these people does the security of our march very much depend." It would be a tricky business. "The Indians are mercenary; every service of theirs must be purchased; and they are easily offended, being thoroughly sensible of their own importance." Some Indians who had usually been helpful were flagging in their support. "The Catawbas have not this year brought in one prisoner or scalp," Washington said. "There hath been no prisoner taken by any of our friendly Indians this season." Things were moving in the wrong direction on the Indian front. "It gave me no small uneasiness when I was informed of the resolution which some of the Cherokees had made to wander towards the Indian settlements in Maryland and Pennsylvania, clearly foreseeing the bad consequences such a peregrination would produce." The Cherokees seemed to be soliciting French offers to switch sides. "Such is the nature of Indians that nothing will prevent their going where they have any reason to expect presents, and their cravings are insatiable."

Even when the Indians seemed to be doing good work, they couldn't be trusted, Washington said. One Cherokee warrior had gone out on a reconnaissance. He found no enemies, but refused to admit his failure. "On his return hither, he brought two white men's scalps which he brought from his own nation"—whose members had acquired them in a previous raid—"and wanted to pass them for the enemy's taken in his unsuccessful scout," Washington wrote. Thankfully, his tribesmen refused to go along. "In this villainy he was detected by the other warriors, who were highly offended at so base a deceit, and threatened to kill him for it."

Under different circumstances Washington might have recommended that General Forbes simply send the Indians packing, but he realized the British side couldn't manage without them. "These scalping parties of Indians we send out will more effectually harass the enemy (by keeping them under continual alarms) than any parties of white people can do," Washington explained. "Small parties of ours are not equal to the undertaking, and large ones must be discovered by their scalping parties early enough to give the enemy time to repel them by a superior force." Yet though the Indians were essential, they still weren't reliable. "The malbehaviour of our Indians gives me great concern. If they were hearty in our interest their services would be infinitely valuable, as I cannot conceive the best white men to be equal to them in the woods. But I fear they are too sensible of their high importance to us to render us any very acceptable service."

Indians aside, the new campaign confronted familiar issues, including how to transport soldiers and weapons across the mountains to the Ohio. General Forbes, blaming Braddock's defeat on his slowness in moving his army from Virginia, pondered cutting a new road through Pennsylvania. In this he was supported by key members of his staff, led by Colonel Henry Bouquet.

He was opposed, most vehemently, by Washington. "If Colonel Bouquet succeeds in this point with the general," Washington declared, "all is lost—all is lost, by Heavens!—our enterprise ruined, and we stopped at the Laurel Hill"—a notoriously steep stretch—"for this winter." Making a new road would squander the effort that had gone into the Braddock route; it would also imperil Virginia and the colonies to Virginia's south. "The southern Indians turn against us, and these colonies become desolate by such an accession to the enemy's strength. These are the consequences of a miscarriage, and a miscarriage the consequence of the attempt."

Washington won this argument, and the Forbes expedition proceeded by Braddock's road. Washington's hopes for success, finally, against the French began to revive. But they were soon threatened by the same kind of political wrangling that had dogged the earlier campaigns. The provincial assemblies refused to appropriate needed moneys, with each blaming the others for stingy shortsightedness.

Washington gnashed his teeth; frustration, mounting almost to despair, supplanted his budding optimism. "That appearance of glory once in view, that hope, that laudable ambition of serving our country, and meriting its applause, is now no more. 'Tis dwindled into ease, sloth and fatal inactivity," he lamented to John Robinson, the speaker of the Virginia house of burgesses. Washington concluded that his years of striving and suffering had been one large exercise in futility. "Nothing now but a miracle can bring this campaign to a happy issue."

But then came the miracle. The French evacuated Fort Duquesne without a shot being fired. "The enemy, after letting us get within a day's march of the place, burned the fort and ran away (by the light of it) at night, going down the Ohio by water," Washington reported.

He was stunned at first, along with Forbes and the rest of the Anglo-American army. But he and they gradually realized that the troubles that had hindered their military operations in the wilderness afflicted the French too, and must have prompted their sudden withdrawal. "We cannot attribute it to more probable causes than the weakness of the enemy, want of provisions, and the defection of their Indians," Washington said.

Even so, there was an element of luck in the turn of events. Forbes had already decided to winter in a camp southeast of the Forks, and to make the final push in the spring. "A council of war had determined that it was not advisable to advance this season," Washington wrote. But a scouting party seized some prisoners, who revealed the French decision to abandon the Forks. "We have thus happily succeeded," he said, in grateful summary.

THE TAKING OF FORT DUQUESNE was merely one part of a broad British offensive in Canada and the Ohio Valley. A British naval squadron attacked a French fortress at Louisbourg in Nova Scotia and captured it. A British army ascended the St. Lawrence toward Quebec, the heart of French Canada. The city seemed nearly impregnable, protected from the sea by the rapids of the St. Lawrence and from infantry assault by the escarpment on which the city sat. Yet British boats found a way past the rapids, to the discomfiture of the officers and men of the French garrison at Quebec. And British troops scaled the bluffs behind the city, to the defenders' greater dismay. British commander James Wolfe was killed in the final battle on the Plains of Abraham, as was his French counterpart, the Marquis de Montcalm, but the British prevailed, and Quebec was taken.

A modest part of the British campaign that season had major implications for what would come after. The Mohawk Valley of the colony of New York was the home of the tribe that had long played the leading role in the Iroquois confederation. The Mohawks, like the other tribes, had had to choose between the British and the French as allies and sponsors. They leaned toward the British, in part because of the adept personal diplomacy of William Johnson, the Indian agent for the British crown in the region, who settled among the Mohawks and married into the tribe. His wife—the British called her his consort— was a young woman named Konwatsi'tsiaienni, known among the British as Molly Brant, the daughter of a Mohawk chief. Johnson took pains to cultivate the Mohawks, and the eight children he had with Molly Brant helped secure his status as a de facto chief.

William Johnson persuaded the Mohawks that in the war against the French, the interests of the tribe paralleled the interests of Britain. He enlisted a thousand Mohawk and other Iroquois warriors in an assault on a French fort near Niagara Falls, along the portage between Lake Ontario and Lake Erie. The attack was a rousing success, and Johnson won acclaim as a hero to both the British and the Iroquois.

In Johnson's army was a young man of sixteen, a brother of Molly Brant. His Mohawk name was Thayendanegea; among the British he was called Joseph Brant. He was brave and able; for his service in the Niagara campaign and after, he received a silver medal from the British.

Partly because he was Molly Brant's brother, but also because he showed unusual promise, Joseph Brant was enrolled, at William Johnson's expense, in a Connecticut school for Indians that within a decade would move to New Hampshire and be renamed Dartmouth College. Brant's smattering of English became fluency, and he acquired the essentials of an English education, including familiarity with the classics and mathematics. The headmaster of the school was as impressed as William Johnson had been; he characterized Brant as being "of a sprightly genius, a manly and gentle deportment, and of a modest, courteous and benevolent temper." The schoolmaster recommended, and Johnson agreed, that upon completion of his studies in Connecticut, Joseph Brant should enroll at King's College in New York.

THE CAPTURE OF QUEBEC, after the reduction of Fort Duquesne and Louisbourg, elicited celebration throughout the Anglo-American colonies. The expulsion of the French from Canada would terminate their evil influence with the Indians; the frontier would be more secure than it had been in years. As it related to Franklin's mission, the good news from Canada diminished the need for defense funding in Pennsylvania and consequently for a swift resolution of the impasse between the Pennsylvania assembly and the Penns.

But before long reports began circulating that Canada might be returned to the French. Guadeloupe, a French sugar island in the Caribbean, had likewise fallen to British forces, and conventional wisdom held that France couldn't be deprived of both without making a peace settlement impossible. Either Canada or Guadeloupe would be restored to French control. The question was, which?

Franklin labored mightily to ensure that it was Guadeloupe. He commenced sarcastically, publishing a list of facetious arguments why Canada should be the territory restored to France. "Because an uninterrupted trade with the Indians throughout a vast country, where the communication by water is so easy, would increase our commerce,

already too great, and occasion a large additional demand for our manufactures, *already too dear*," he wrote. "Lest through a greater plenty
of beaver, broad-brimmed hats become cheaper to that unmannerly
sect, the Quakers . . . That we may *soon* have a new war, and another
opportunity of spending two or three millions a year in America; there
being great danger of our growing too rich, our European expences
not being sufficient to drain our immense treasures. . . . That we may
have occasion constantly to employ, in time of war, a fleet and army in
those parts; for otherwise we might be too strong at home. . . . That
the French may, by means of their Indians, carry on, (as they have
done for these 100 years past even in times of peace between the two
crowns) a constant scalping war against our colonies, and thereby stint
their growth; for, otherwise, the children might in time be as tall as
their mother." Franklin concluded, "Should we not restore Canada, it
would look as if our statesmen had *courage* as well as our soldiers; but
what have statesmen to do with *courage*?"

Franklin complemented his satiric barbs with serious broadsides.
He printed a pamphlet arguing that Britain's imperial interests required
keeping Canada. Advocates of the opposite course—keeping Guadeloupe and restoring Canada to France—contended that the problem of
border security in America could be solved by placing forts in the passes
in the mountains of the frontier. Franklin dismissed such reasoning as
revealing utter ignorance of the American west. "If the Indians when
at war marched like the Europeans, with great armies, heavy cannon,
baggage and carriages, the passes through which alone such armies
could penetrate our country or receive their supplies, being secured, all
might be sufficiently secure," he said. "But the case is widely different.
They go to war, as they call it, in small parties, from fifty men down
to five. Their hunting life has made them acquainted with the whole
country, and scarce any part of it is impracticable to such a party. They
can travel through the woods even by night, and know how to conceal
their tracks. They pass easily between your forts undiscovered, and
privately approach the settlements of your frontier inhabitants. They
need no convoys of provisions to follow them; for whether they are
shifting from place to place in the woods, or lying in wait for an opportunity to strike a blow, every thicket and every stream furnishes so
small a number with sufficient subsistence. When they have surprized
separately, and murdered and scalped a dozen families, they are gone

with inconceivable expedition through unknown ways, and 'tis very rare that pursuers have any chance of coming up with them." Forts could never safeguard the frontier populations. "The inhabitants of Hackney"—a London borough—"might as well rely upon the Tower of London to secure them against highwaymen and housebreakers."

Advocates of keeping Guadeloupe cited the lucrative trade of the island. Franklin pointed out that the trade to the Anglo-American colonies was already greater, and would become very much greater with the growth of the population of those colonies—as long as they weren't hemmed in by a hostile French presence on their border. Some in the Guadeloupe camp warned of an overly strong Anglo-America, united against Britain. Franklin waved aside the worry. "There are so many causes that must operate to prevent it, that I will venture to say, an union amongst them for such a purpose is not merely improbable, it is impossible."

Unless Britain did something really foolish. "When I say such an union is impossible, I mean without the most grievous tyranny and oppression," Franklin explained. "People who have property in a country which they may lose, and privileges which they may endanger, are generally disposed to be quiet, and even to bear much, rather than hazard all. While the government is mild and just, while important civil and religious rights are secure, such subjects will be dutiful and obedient. The waves do not rise, but when the winds blow."

FRANKLIN DIDN'T WANT it to come to that. And he didn't think it would. For all his concerns over certain aspects of British policy, he thought the British empire a jewel of modern civilization. And he delighted in his time in Britain. With William, he visited Northamptonshire, the home of their forebears. He met a cousin, and learned of an uncle who possessed the same inquisitive spirit as his own. He was intrigued to learn that this uncle had died four years to the day before he was born. William remarked that it almost seemed there had been a transmigration of souls, uncle to nephew, across the years and over the ocean.

They traveled to Scotland, where Edinburgh awarded him the freedom of the city, and the University of St. Andrews conferred an honorary doctorate. He made new friends among the great and good, who seconded his English friends in urging him to stay in Britain permanently. William Strahan wrote to Deborah Franklin, begging her to come to London, where her husband was so loved and admired. Debbie resisted, claiming fear of the sea and its crossing. More likely it was her fear of the deeper waters of British life and politics that put her off. She was a Philadelphia girl, and pleased to be one; a Philadelphia girl she intended to remain.

Franklin himself sought to change her mind. His sojourn finally at an end, he prepared to sail for America. But he told Strahan he expected to return. They had spoken of vibrating strings, among many other topics of mutual scientific interest; Franklin now drew an analogy to himself crossing the Atlantic. "I shall probably make but this one vibration and settle here forever," he said. "Nothing will prevent it, if I can, as I hope I can, prevail with Mrs. Franklin to accompany me."

To Franklin, England was feeling like home. And he increasingly envisioned America and Britain as two equal parts of a new, improved British empire. "I have long been of opinion that the foundations of the future grandeur and stability of the British Empire lie in America," he wrote to Lord Kames, a Scottish friend and admirer. "And though, like other foundations, they are low and little seen, they are nevertheless broad and strong enough to support the greatest political structure human wisdom ever yet erected." This was another reason, the most important, why Britain must retain Canada. "If we keep it, all the country from the St. Lawrence to the Mississippi will in another century be filled with British people. Britain itself will become vastly more populous by the immense increase of its commerce; the Atlantic Sea will be covered with your trading ships; and your naval power thence continually increasing, will extend your influence round the whole globe, and awe the world!"

Should he live so long, no one would celebrate Britain's global glory more than Franklin, who told Kames he spoke "not merely as I am a colonist, but as I am a Briton."

Part III

So Widely Different

FRANKLIN GOT HIS WISH regarding Canada. In early 1763 nego-
tiators in Paris concluded the most recent installment of the age-
old struggle between Britain and France; the treaty confirming the
close specified that Britain would keep Canada, and France get back
Guadeloupe. The decision brought joy and satisfaction to Benjamin
and William Franklin, to George Washington and Thomas Hutchinson, and to nearly all the Anglo-Americans. Some, like Washington,
had risked their lives to secure the western frontier against French and
Indian attack; the acquisition of Canada capped their efforts with success. Others, notably Franklin, had risked their fortunes in the same
endeavor. The Franklins, like Washington and the other partners in
the Ohio Company, looked to the Ohio country as a field for speculation and profits. Benjamin Franklin, hoping the British would perceive
the wisdom in a transatlantic union of equals, saw the land beyond the
mountains as part of the enlightened British empire of his dreams.

The hopes and dreams for the West had a short life. In the autumn
of 1763 the British government issued a proclamation forbidding settlement beyond the mountains, which was declared an Indian reserve.
The proclamation suspended land grants in Ohio, including that of
the Ohio Company, jeopardizing investments already made and profits anticipated. The modest number of settlers who had been living
across the mountains before the war, and been driven east by the violence, were told they couldn't return.

The proclamation was puzzling and infuriating, in equal parts.
Puzzling, because why had the British government expended such
effort conquering Canada, merely to hand it over to the Indians, many
of whom had fought on the side of the enemy? Infuriating, because the
Americans had contributed crucially to the conquest, and now were

being denied the spoils of victory. They were treated as pawns on a chessboard controlled by powerful interests in London.

The puzzling part of the decision to fence off Ohio was clarified before long, but in a way that made the decision more infuriating. In 1764 Parliament approved the Sugar Act, which cleverly aimed to increase the revenues London derived from the American colonies through taxes on imports of molasses, the raw material for rum. The cleverness lay, first, in the observation that the Americans had never seriously protested Parliament's authority to regulate the commerce of the colonies, via "navigation acts." Various such measures had been in force for decades, with little complaint from the colonies. It was a Frenchman, Jean-Baptiste Colbert, who said that the art of taxation was to pluck as many feathers from the goose as possible with the least amount of hissing, but the British ministries in London understood the principle and acted on it. Yet the greater cleverness lay in the fact that the larger revenues would result from a *reduction* in the tax rates. At that time, as before and after, taxes prompted efforts to evade them. In the case of molasses, high taxes encouraged smuggling, which became a cottage industry along the American coast. But smuggling wasn't cheap, and by lowering the rates, the government undercut the smugglers and made honest men of the molasses importers. Sterner anti-smuggling efforts accompanied the new rates, doubling the damage done to the smuggling industry. The final dollop of cleverness lay in recognition, on both sides of the Atlantic, that the aggrieved smugglers couldn't complain without convicting themselves of previous illegality.

The Sugar Act revealed the deeper meaning of the Proclamation of 1763. The British government had gone uncomfortably into debt funding the war against France. Bondholders—the wealthy and hence powerful people who had loaned money to the government—demanded repayment, lest they withhold future loans and work to replace the current government with one more amenable to their demands. The government scrambled to rebalance its books, by cutting expenditures and increasing revenues. The proclamation promised to do the first, by reducing the need for a British military presence in America. With the French gone, the only source of friction would be between the Indians and the colonists. The proclamation erected a legal fence between the two groups. The British government wasn't so naïve as to think the proclamation alone would keep all settlers out of Ohio. Squatters had taken up land there before the war; they would continue to do so. But the proclamation *would* foil organized speculators like George Washington and the Franklins, whose interest lay not in relocating to Ohio themselves but in selling land to actual settlers. Selling land required obtaining title to the land, which the proclamation prevented.

Even as the Proclamation of 1763 reduced expenditures, the Sugar Act would increase revenues. Governments always hesitate to raise taxes, preferring not to anger the goose. But when they find new taxes necessary, they typically seek to levy them on parties unable to retaliate. The Americans, electing no representatives to Parliament, couldn't retaliate in the manner that meant most in British politics. The unacceptable alternative was to raise taxes on Britons, who *could* retaliate, by voting the tax-raisers out of office.

BEFORE THE AMERICANS HAD much chance to protest the Sugar Act, they were slapped with something even more provocative. The British government's accountants reckoned that the reduction in expenditures resulting from the Proclamation, combined with the addition to revenues from the Sugar Act, would still leave the hole in the budget dangerously large. A bigger fix was required. George Grenville, who doubled as prime minister and chancellor of the exchequer, laid before Parliament a bill to authorize a tax on the paper used in documents, newspapers, playing cards and other items employed in daily life in America. Called a stamp tax, for the stamps affixed to the paper, the measure would be felt by the Americans in a way they'd felt no taxes before.

Benjamin Franklin did what he could to head off the stamp law. He joined agents from other American colonies to express their collective concern to Grenville. One of the agents, Jared Ingersoll of Connecticut, summarized the gist of the meeting a short time afterward. "Mr. Grenville gave us a full hearing," Ingersoll wrote. "Told us he took no pleasure in giving the Americans so much uneasiness as he found he did. That it was the duty of his office to manage the revenue. That he really was made to believe that considering the whole of the circumstances of the mother country and the colonies, the latter could and ought to pay something, and that he knew of no better way than that now pursuing to lay such tax, but that if we could tell of a better he would adopt it."

Franklin and the others objected that if there must be a tax, the colonial assemblies should be allowed to lay it themselves. "It would at least seem to be their own act, and prevent that uneasiness and jealousy which otherwise we found would take place," Ingersoll recorded of the conversation. "They could raise the money best by their own officers."

Grenville listened, then noted some problems with the agents' proposal. "Mr. Grenville asked us if we could agree upon the several proportions each colony should raise," Ingersoll wrote. The agents conceded they could not. Grenville said he himself didn't have the information to make a fair apportionment. And even if he did, it would soon become outdated. "The colonies by their constant increase will be constantly varying in their proportion of numbers," he said. A fair scheme this year would be unfair before long. Grenville said his stamp plan would accommodate such change.

Grenville assured the agents he would relate their objections to the full House of Commons, which would do what it thought best for the empire as a whole. He cautioned the Americans against carrying their opposition too far. "He said he wished we would preserve a coolness and moderation in America," Ingersoll wrote. "That he had no need to tell us that resentments indecently and unbecomingly expressed on one side the water would naturally produce resentments on t'other side, and that we could not hope to get any good by a controversy with the mother country."

FRANKLIN STILL HOPED to stave off the stamp tax. Taking Grenville at his word about listening to other ideas, Franklin proposed an alternative scheme. A shortage of money had vexed the colonies for decades, as a result of the mercantilist policies of the British government, which drew specie—gold and silver coins—to England, and of strictures on the colonial issuance of paper money. The shortage of money hampered business and curtailed growth, throwing the colonists back on barter and artifices like land scrip in lieu of cash. Franklin had advocated paper money before, and he did so again, with a twist. The British government should issue loans to merchants and other applicants; the loans would be represented by paper notes, which could be transferred to others and would serve as money. The holders of the notes would pay interest on the loans the notes represented.

Besides allaying the colonists' money problem, Franklin's scheme would solve Grenville's revenue problem in an elegant manner. Franklin said of the interest on the notes, "It will operate as a general tax on the colonies, and yet not an unpleasing one, as he who actually pays the interest has an equivalent or more in the use of the principal." The tax would be voluntary, in that anyone who objected to it could simply avoid the use of the paper notes. And it would fall most heavily on those best able to pay. "The rich who handle most money would in reality pay most of the tax."

The scheme might have worked. And had it worked, it could have prevented much anguish between the American colonists and the British government. But Grenville demurred. His supporters included British bankers and other creditors who objected to anything that rendered money more plentiful and therefore less valuable. Equally to the point, Grenville wanted to show the Americans who made laws for them: Parliament, not their own legislatures. He pressed ahead with his stamp scheme, which became law as the Stamp Act.

Franklin was disappointed. But having done all he could to prevent the passage of the act, he resolved to make the best of the situation. "I think it will affect the printers more than anybody, as a sterling halfpenny stamp on every half sheet of a newspaper, and two shillings sterling on every advertisement, will go near to knock up one half of both," he wrote to David Hall, his managing partner in the printing business. Franklin preempted the law by purchasing a large quantity of printing paper ahead of the effective date and sending it to Philadelphia.

In the event, Franklin's effort at economy failed. The law, as enforced, required newsprint to receive its stamp in England, *after* the law took effect. The paper Franklin bought had to be sent back to London.

ANOTHER MISSTEP WAS more serious. The Stamp Act required the appointment of stamp agents, or stamp-tax collectors. The British government would determine who the stamp agents would be, and Grenville, as a consolation prize to Franklin, let him nominate the agent for Pennsylvania. Grenville might have had another motive as well: to make Franklin seem complicit in the Stamp Act. If such was Grenville's plan, it worked. Franklin nominated a friend, John Hughes, of Philadelphia, and Grenville confirmed the appointment.

It was a fateful error. The Stamp Act provoked a much stronger reaction in America than Franklin had imagined. In nearly every city riots broke out. The stamp agents were threatened with violence; property of individuals thought to support the Stamp Act was damaged or destroyed. John Hughes soon feared for his life. "You are now from letter to letter to suppose each may be the last that you will receive from your old friend, as the spirit or flame of rebellion is got to a high pitch," he wrote to Franklin from Philadelphia. "A sort of frenzy or madness has got such hold of the people of all ranks that I fancy some lives will be lost before this fire is put out." A few days later, Hughes wrote again. "Our clamours run very high," he said. "And I am told my house shall be pulled down and the stamps burnt." Yet Hughes said he wouldn't be intimidated. "I for my part am well-armed with fire-arms, and am determined to stand a siege. If I live till tomorrow morning I shall give you a farther account." Franklin, receiving these letters in London, awaited the next post with grave concern, and no small feeling of responsibility for what his friend was experiencing. With relief he read Hughes's next installment: "We are all yet in the land of the living, and our property safe. Thank God."

Franklin was far from the riots, but a new house he had built for Debbie was not. Some of those Franklin had crossed swords with in Pennsylvania politics now spread rumors that he had sold out his countrymen and gone over to the British. His fine new house was cited as evidence of the preferment he enjoyed in London; maybe he was getting a cut of the stamp-tax collections. The same mob that threatened John Hughes's house set its sights on Franklin's.

Debbie took her own stand. She wasn't going to surrender her home without a fight. "I sent to ask my brother to come and bring his gun," she wrote to Franklin afterward. She summoned a cousin to do the same. "We made one room into a magazine. I ordered some sort of defence upstairs as I could manage myself." The mob approached, and it sent a delegate to demand that Debbie evacuate, lest she be harmed personally. She would do no such thing. "I had not given any offence to any person at all," she told Franklin she had responded. "Nor would I be made uneasy by anybody, nor would I stir or show the least uneasiness. But if anyone came to disturb me, I would show a proper resentment."

Debbie's determination encouraged Franklin's friends in Philadelphia to rally around her. A small militia mobilized and compelled the mob to disperse. As soon as Franklin learned the outcome he sang his wife's praises in a letter home. "I honour much the spirit and courage you showed, and the prudent preparations you made in that time of danger," he told her. "The woman deserves a good house that is determined to defend it."

THOMAS HUTCHINSON DIDN'T FARE so well. Hutchinson had continued his careful climb up the ladder of Massachusetts life and politics; in 1765 he was the lieutenant governor of the province. His boss, Governor Francis Bernard, was a king's man, a British-born royal appointee, but Hutchinson still hewed to his Boston roots. Nonetheless his loyalties, like Franklin's, were called into doubt amid the tumult over the Stamp Act.

Hutchinson first sensed trouble when Jared Ingersoll returned from London. Ingersoll had gone further than Franklin in bending to the ill wind of the act; he got himself appointed stamp agent for Connecticut. His ship landed in Boston, and he consulted with friends in the city before heading overland for Hartford. Among his friends was Andrew Oliver, the stamp agent for Massachusetts. Oliver rode out of Boston with Ingersoll, to keep his friend company. "This occasioned murmuring among the people, and an inflammatory piece in the next Boston Gazetteer," Hutchinson recalled. The expressed concern was that Oliver was conspiring with Ingersoll against the interests of the people. "A few days after, early in the morning, a stuffed image was hung upon a tree, called the great tree of the south part of Boston," Hutchinson continued. "Labels affixed denoted it to be designed for the distributor of the stamps." Such a public death threat inevitably piqued local curiosity. "People who were passing by stopped to view it, and the report caused others to gather from all quarters of the town, and many from the towns adjacent."

Governor Bernard considered how to respond. He couldn't let this threat against a government official go unanswered, but neither did he want to provoke violence. Hutchinson urged caution. "The people were orderly and, if left alone, would take down the image and bury it without any disturbance," Hutchinson summarized his reasoning. "But an attempt to remove it would bring on a riot, the mischief designed to be prevented."

Sure enough, the effigy came down. Yet rather than being buried, it was paraded about the city, even into the chamber where the governor and his council were meeting. A larger demonstration ensued. "Forty or fifty tradesmen, decently dressed, preceded, and some thousands of the mob followed down King Street to Oliver's dock, near which Mr. Oliver had lately erected a building which, it was conjectured, he designed for a stamp office," Hutchinson wrote. "This was laid flat in a few minutes. From thence the mob proceeded for Fort Hill, but Mr. Oliver's house being in the way, they endeavoured to force themselves into it, and being opposed, broke the windows, beat down the doors, entered, and destroyed part of his furniture, and continued in riot until midnight, before they separated."

In the morning Bernard issued a proclamation condemning the violence and offering a reward for information leading to the arrest and conviction of the leaders of the mob. Hutchinson expected little to come of the offer, as the identities of the leaders were perfectly well known. But he granted that the governor had had to say something, and this was the best he could do. Bernard considered calling out the militia, to stand guard in the town, but was persuaded not to do so, as the militia would bring arms, which would add to the danger. Besides, some of the mob were members of the militia. The governor's advisers who knew Boston best told him to forget about enforcing the Stamp Act. "The people, not only of the town of Boston, but of the country in general"—Massachusetts—"would never submit to the execution of the Stamp Act, let the consequence of an opposition to it be what it would," Hutchinson wrote. At just this time came reports from Connecticut that resisters there had vowed to hang Jared Ingersoll the moment he stepped into the province, and that he had turned aside for Rhode Island.

Andrew Oliver understandably feared for his safety, indeed his life. His family was no less afraid. He publicly announced that he was resigning his position as stamp agent and swore never to take up the position in the future.

Oliver, Hutchinson, Bernard and most residents of Boston held their breath wondering if the resignation would appease opponents of the Stamp Act. The mob assembled again the next night. The tension was greater than ever. But this time the leaders of the mob congratulated Oliver rather than threatening him. A bonfire was built on the hill near his house in celebration of the popular victory over incipient tyranny.

Hutchinson allowed himself to relax. "It was hoped that the people, having obtained all that they desired, would return to order," he remembered.

Such was not to be. The following evening the crowd came to Hutchinson's house. Hutchinson had been at Andrew Oliver's house the night before, and had tried to get the sheriff to intervene, before the mob gave Oliver its absolution. "A report was soon spread that he was a favourer of the Stamp Act, and had encouraged it by letters to the ministry," Hutchinson wrote of himself. "Upon notice of the approach of the people, he caused the doors and windows to be barred." Hutchinson remained inside, watching the mob through the windows. "After attempting to enter, they called upon him to come into the balcony, and to declare that he had not written in favour of the act, and they would retire quite satisfied." Hutchinson had not, in fact, supported the Stamp Act, but he refused to say so under duress. "This was an indignity to which he would not submit, and therefore he made no answer," Hutchinson wrote. A tradesman who had known Hutchinson for years stood up in front of the mob. He chided them for subjecting the lieutenant governor to this kind of treatment, and he vouched for Hutchinson's opposition to the Stamp Act. This satisfied most of those gathered in front of the house. "They dispersed, with only breaking some of the glass," Hutchinson remarked.

Yet they didn't stay satisfied. Hutchinson was chief justice of Massachusetts, besides being lieutenant governor. As chief justice he had acted to rein in smuggling, to the anger of the smugglers. Some of them seem to have been behind a recent campaign of denunciation against him.

Mobs continued to roam the streets of Boston. "In the evening of the 26th of August, such a mob was collected in King Street, drawn there by a bonfire and well supplied with strong drink," Hutchinson recounted. "After some annoyance to the house of the registrar of the admiralty, and somewhat greater to that of the comptroller of the customs, whose cellars they plundered of the wine and spirits in them, they came, with intoxicated rage, upon the house of the lieutenant governor. The doors were immediately split to pieces with broad axes, and a way made there, and at the windows, for the entry of the mob, which poured in and filled, in an instant, every room of the house."

The mob was upon his house almost before Hutchinson had notice. He told his wife and children to leave at once. He intended to stay and confront the rioters. One of his children had different ideas. "His eldest daughter, after going a little way from the house, returned, and refused to quit it unless her father would do the like." Refusing to put his daughter in danger, Hutchinson left with her, moments before the mob entered.

They took their time dismantling the house. "They continued their possession until daylight; destroyed, carried away, or cast into the street everything that was in the house; demolished every part of it, except the walls, so far as lay in their power; and had begun to break away the brick work." The dawn found them weary but satisfied; sobering up, they retired to their homes.

AS HUTCHINSON SURVEYED the ruins of his house, he contemplated the ruin of a career. "It is uncertain whether I shall remain here," he wrote to Franklin. "My loss is so heavy that I cannot well bear it. I should immediately or soon after I met it have gone to England to solicit a compensation if I had not been in hopes of doing some service to my country here." Those hopes had largely vanished as the strength of the animus toward the Stamp Act became clear. "I am now almost in despair, and if I should receive advice that I may hope for a compensation in England by making a voyage there, and that I should not be like to obtain it without, I think in justice to my family I must undertake it."

Hutchinson reflected on the change that had come over America. Every day brought news of protests and riots from other provinces. He himself had sampled the atmosphere in New England. "I have been in most parts of this province, and in New Hampshire and Rhode Island," Hutchinson told Franklin. "Almost everywhere I found a full dependence upon the repeal of the Stamp Act as soon as the Parliament meets." The radicals were demanding a boycott of the stamps, on pain of treatment like that doled out to himself. "In Boston it would be utterly unsafe to make the least doubt of a repeal," Hutchinson said.

"Indeed, it is not safe there to advance anything contrary to any popular opinions whatsoever. Everybody who used to have virtue enough to oppose them is now afraid of my fate."

A congress of protest against the Stamp Act had gathered at New York; delegates from nine colonies approved resolutions denouncing the act, denying the right of Parliament to tax the colonies, and insisting on speedy repeal. Hutchinson ruefully reminded Franklin how they had worked together a decade earlier to achieve a union of the colonies. "'Join or die' is the motto," Hutchinson said, recalling Franklin's epigram from that earlier effort. "When you and I were at Albany ten years ago, we did not propose an union for such purposes as these."

THE BOYCOTTS AND THREATS SPREAD. "It is difficult to describe the distress to which these distracted and violent measures have subjected the people of this province and indeed all North America," Joseph Galloway informed Franklin from Philadelphia. Galloway was an ally and protégé of Franklin in Pennsylvania politics; the same age as Franklin's son, William, Galloway had married into the wealthy Philadelphia family of Lawrence Growden and added its influence to his own powers of persuasiveness and administration. With Benjamin Franklin he opposed the prerogatives of the Penn family in Pennsylvania affairs; like Franklin he judged the Stamp Act misguided and counterproductive.

"Here are stamp papers," Galloway wrote to Franklin, "but the mob will not suffer them to be used, and the public officers of justice and of trade, being under obligation of their oaths and liable to the penalties of the statute, will not proceed in their duties without them. A stop is put to our commerce and our Courts of Justice is shut up. Our harbours are filled with vessels, but none of them, save those cleared out before the 2d. of November"—the date the Stamp Act took effect—"dare to move, because neither the governor or collector will clear them out, and if they would, the men-of-war threaten to seize them as forfeited for want of papers agreeable to the laws of trade. Our debtors are selling off their effects before our eyes, and removing to another country with innumerable other mischiefs brought on us by this fatal conduct, from which I can see no relief but from an immediate repeal of the Act."

Galloway prayed repeal would come soon. Otherwise the violent spirit that had seized America would do irreparable damage to the British empire. Galloway agreed with Franklin that the empire was a wonderful thing; like Franklin he feared that British arrogance and folly would prevent the empire from becoming even better. The government in London *must* acknowledge the Americans' right to legislate for themselves. Nothing but good could come of it. "This would form the strongest and most indissoluble bond of union that can be invented between the mother country and her foreign dominions," Galloway said. And nothing but bad would come of denying it. "Can Britain, when she duly considers the ambitious temper of human nature, without this or some theory like it, expect to retain her sovereignty over the colonies longer than they find themselves in a capacity to separate from her?" Americans were jealous of their rights. "Should it not be recollected that the first settlers of America came over possessed of the highest ideas of liberty? That their posterity have been educated in the same notions?" American theory and practice reflected this libertarian tradition. "Several of their governments are merely democratical, and consequently very liable to discontent and insurrections." Geography didn't help. "Their distance from their mother country will lessen her awe, and the idea of her power, and when in a more opulent state, and increased in numbers, will probably prompt them to throw off their subordination."

A demand for independence: this was what the present turmoil foreshadowed, Galloway judged. He shook his head at the idea. "I do not think this can possibly happen in our day," he wrote to Franklin. "God grant it never may. I am sure no good man would wish to see it. But certainly these considerations indicate the prudence, if not the necessity of uniting the colonies to their mother country by every prudential measure that can be devised."

JOHN ADAMS WAS as thrilled by the Stamp Act crisis as Galloway was distressed. Adams was the son of a stern Massachusetts Puritan who insisted that his eldest son and namesake—Adams had two younger brothers—receive the finest education the Massachusetts Bay colony could provide, in order that John enter the ministry well armed against Anglicans and other backsliders. The heavy load at the Braintree Latin School provoked a hint of rebellion in the boy, who mused of tending crops and livestock rather than souls. But Adams *père* brooked no dissent, even as he enlisted a more congenial teacher for the boy. Adams *fils* entered Harvard College at sixteen and studied the Greek and Roman classics. He continued his rebellion sub rosa, putting out of his own mind any thoughts of the ministry. Instead he would become a lawyer.

But what he *really* wanted to become was famous. During this time he developed the habit of keeping a diary. Therein he recorded his struggle with his desire to win renown among his fellows. "Men of the most exalted genius and active minds are generally perfect slaves to the love of fame," he wrote. "They sometimes descend to as mean tricks and artifices in pursuit of honour or reputation, as the miser descends to in pursuit of gold. The greatest men have been the most envious, malicious, and revengeful. The miser toils by night and day, fasts and watches, till he emaciates his body, to fatten his purse and increase his coffers. The ambitious man rolls and tumbles in his bed, a stranger to refreshing sleep and repose through anxiety about a preferment he has in view."

Yet the itch for reputation wouldn't let him go. "I sometimes, in my sprightly moments, consider myself, in my great chair at school, as some dictator at the head of a commonwealth," he confided to his journal. "In this little state I can discover all the great geniuses, all the surprizing actions and revolutions of the great world in miniature. I have several renowned generals but 3 feet high, and several deep-projecting politicians in petticoats." All bowed to him, who commanded the realm. "Is it not then the highest pleasure, my friend, to preside in this little world, to bestow the proper applause upon virtuous and generous actions, to blame and punish every vicious and contracted trick, to wear out of the tender mind everything that is mean and little and fire the new-born soul with a noble ardor and emulation? The world affords no greater pleasure."

Adams recognized the temptation in pride. He soothed his conscience by telling himself that his goals were better than what his peers aspired to. "Let others waste the bloom of life at the card or billiard table, among rakes and fools," he said. "And when their minds are sufficiently fretted with losses and inflamed by wine, ramble through the streets assaulting innocent people, breaking windows or debauching young girls." A recent instance served as warning. "About 4 months since, a poor girl in this neighbourhood, walking by the meeting house upon some occasion in the evening, met a fine gentleman with laced hat and waist coat and a sword who solicited her to turn aside with him into the horse stable. The girl relucted a little, upon which he gave her 3 guineas, and wished he might be damned if he did not have her in 3 months. Into the horse stable they went. The 3 guineas proved 3 farthings—and the girl proves with child, without a friend upon earth that will own her, or knowing the father of her 3 farthing bastard."

In time he stilled his qualms. "Reputation ought to be the perpetual subject of my thoughts and aim of my behavior," he declared forthrightly. The means, not the end, was now the question. "How shall I gain a reputation! How shall I spread an opinion of myself as a lawyer of distinguished genius, learning and virtue? Shall I make frequent visits in the neighbourhood and converse familiarly with men, women and children in their own style, on the common tittle-tattle of the town and the ordinary concerns of a family, and so take every fair opportunity of shewing my knowledge in the law? . . . Shall I endeavour to renew my acquaintance with those young gentlemen in Boston who were at college with me and to extend my acquaintance among merchants, shop keepers, tradesmen, etc. and mingle with the crowd upon change, and traipse the townhouse floor, with one and another, in order to get a character in town? . . . Shall I, by making remarks and proposing questions to the lawyers at the bar, endeavour to get a great character for understanding and learning with them? . . . Shall I look out for a cause to speak to, and exert all the soul and all the body I own, to cut a flash, strike amazement, to catch the vulgar? In short shall I walk a lingering, heavy pace or shall I take one bold determined leap? . . . A bold push, a resolute attempt, a determined enterprize, or a slow, silent, imperceptible creeping? Shall I creep or fly?"

The Stamp Act afforded Adams the chance to fly. He had returned to Braintree and hung out his shingle; his law practice crept along. And then came the attack on American rights, providing the cause he had sought to speak to. He wrote a remonstrance on behalf of his townsmen and presented it for their consideration. They were impressed, and the town council adopted it.

"In all the calamities which have ever befallen this our dear native country, within the memory of the oldest of us all," declared the twenty-nine-year-old, "we have never felt so sincere a grief and concern, or so many alarming fears and apprehensions, as at the present time. We have many of us lived to see both pestilence and scarcity, and the encroachments and hostilities of bitter, subtle and powerful enemies, but we never yet apprehended our liberties and fortunes and our very being in any real danger till now." Adams reiterated the belief behind the American complaints about the Stamp Act. "We have always understood it to be a grand and fundamental principle of the British constitution that no freeman should be subjected to any tax to which he has not given his own consent in person or by proxy." He added an objection that was more obvious to a lawyer than to some others. "The most cruel and grievous and, as we esteem it, unjust innovation of all, in the act aforesaid, is the alarming extension of the powers of courts of admiralty," he said. "In these courts one judge alone presides. No juries have any concern there." The judges, moreover, served at the pleasure of the administration in Britain, and received their pay from the fines they levied. "The judge, single and dependent as he is, is under a pecuniary temptation always against the subject." The new arrangement was a formula for oppression, guaranteed to render Americans "the most sordid and forlorn slaves who live upon the earth." Adams liked the ring of his formula equating taxes to slavery; admonishing Braintree's representatives in the state legislature to resist the Stamp Act with all their might, he concluded, "We never can be slaves."

The statement won Adams the recognition he coveted; soon he was accounted almost as ardent a defender of American rights as cousin Samuel Adams, a Boston tax collector who had become the firebrand of the Boston tax protests. In his diary a few months later, John Adams congratulated himself on his good work. "The year 1765 has been the most remarkable year of my life," he said. "The Stamp Act has raised and spread through the whole continent a spirit that will be recorded to our honour with all future generations. In every colony, from Georgia to New Hampshire inclusively, the stamp distributors and inspectors have been compelled by the unconquerable rage of the people to renounce their offices." No one dared even to speak in favor of the Stamp Act. "The people, even to the lowest ranks, have become more attentive to their liberties, more inquisitive about them, and more determined to defend them, than they were ever before."

The act remained on the books; the boycott of the stamps had cost Adams personally. "The probate office is shut, the custom house is shut, the courts of justice are shut, and all business seems at a stand," he observed. "I have not drawn a writ since 1st November." Yet he wouldn't have had Americans—himself included—do otherwise. And they must remain determined and united in opposition to Britain's unwarranted claim to tax them. "If this authority is once acknowledged and established, the ruin of America will become inevitable."

VIRGINIA'S RESPONSE TO the Stamp Act was less demonstrative and more rhetorical than the reactions of the northern colonies. To some degree this reflected the absence of cities in Virginia; without cities, the ready gathering of protest mobs was nearly impossible. It also reflected the smaller size of the merchant class in Virginia, and the closer connection between Virginia consumers like George Washington and merchants in England.

Yet Virginia protested in its own way. Leading the opposition in the Virginia house of burgesses was a twenty-nine-year-old lawyer named Patrick Henry, who was still new to the house when he presented a series of resolutions decrying the Stamp Act and the constitutional theory that underlay it. The crucial fifth resolution summarized the others: "Resolved, therefore, that the general assembly of this colony have the sole right and power to lay taxes and impositions upon the inhabitants of this colony, and that every attempt to vest such power in any person or persons whatsoever, other than the general assembly aforesaid, has a manifest tendency to destroy British as well as American freedom."

More striking than the language of his resolutions was the tone of Henry's argument in favor. The burgesses kept no regular journal of their speeches, but Henry's outpouring stuck in the memories of those present. The most widely circulated reconstruction of his speech had him likening the British king to tyrants past: "Caesar had his Brutus, Charles I his Cromwell, and George III . . ." At this point the speaker of the house shouted "Treason!" and other members joined in. Henry let them shout, then with a sly smile finished: ". . . may profit by their example." He paused before appending: "If this be treason, make the most of it."

Henry's resolutions hardly swept the house. "They were opposed by

Randolph, Bland, Pendleton, Nicholas, Wythe and all the old members whose influence in the house had, till then, been unbroken," Thomas Jefferson recalled afterward. Jefferson was several years younger than Henry and a lawyer-in-training in Williamsburg. George Wythe, his sponsor and one of the old guard, encouraged him to observe the house at work. "They did it, not from any question of our rights," Jefferson continued, regarding the action of Henry's opponents, "but on the ground that the same sentiments had been, at their preceding session, expressed in a more conciliatory form, to which the answers were not yet received."

Yet Henry and some others demanded a decision now. Henry's side won a majority on each of the first four resolutions. "The last, however, and strongest resolution was carried but by a single vote," Jefferson recounted. "The debate on it was most bloody. I was then but a student, and was listening at the door of the lobby (for as yet there was no gallery) when Peyton Randolph, after the vote, came out of the house, and said, as he entered the lobby, 'By god, I would have given 500 guineas for a single vote.'"

GEORGE WASHINGTON WAS a member of the house of burgesses, but he didn't vote on Henry's resolutions, and he didn't hear Henry's speech. Washington had left Williamsburg for Mount Vernon, to tend to the spring planting and other essential work of the farmer. His diary for the day of the vote read: "Peter Green came to me a gardener."

Washington was worried about the course of British policy, but not alarmed. Writing to one of his wife's relatives in London, he explained, "The Stamp Act imposed on the colonies by the Parliament of Great Britain engrosses the conversation of the speculative part of the colonists, who look upon this unconstitutional method of taxation as a direful attack upon their liberties, and loudly exclaim against the violation. What may be the result of this, and some other (I think I may add) ill-judged measures, I will not undertake to determine. But this I may venture to affirm, that the advantage accruing to the Mother Country will fall greatly short of the expectations of the ministry; for certain it is, our whole substance does already in a manner flow to Great Britain and that whatsoever contributes to lessen our importations must be hurtful to their manufacturers."

This was the crucial weakness of Parliament's efforts to levy taxes in America, Washington said. And it was the singular strength of the American opposition. Washington didn't like the riots; he thought violence would be counterproductive. The cumulated decisions made by the mass of ordinary people would have greater effect. "The eyes of our people, already beginning to open, will perceive that many luxuries which we lavish our substance to Great Britain for, can well be dispensed with whilst the necessaries of life are (mostly) to be had within ourselves. This consequently will introduce frugality, and be a necessary stimulation to industry. If Great Britain therefore loads her manufactures with heavy taxes, will it not facilitate these measures? They will not compel us I think to give our money for their exports, whether we will or no, and certain I am none of their traders will part from them without a valuable consideration. Where then is the utility of these restrictions?"

Washington supposed the British merchants would come to the aid of their American customers. The Stamp Act would make it impossible for creditors to collect debts. "Our courts of judicature must inevitably be shut up, for it is impossible (or next of kin to it) under our present circumstances that the act of Parliament can be complied with were we ever so willing to enforce the execution," he wrote. "We have not money to pay the stamps. . . . And if a stop be put to our judicial proceedings I fancy the merchants of Great Britain trading to the colonies will not be among the last to wish for a repeal of it."

Washington worried more about the Proclamation of 1763, but not a great deal more. He considered it a minor and temporary impediment to western settlement, and to his own speculations. Considered rightly, it might actually be an opportunity. Washington wrote confidentially to William Crawford, a potential partner in one of his schemes, "I can never look upon that Proclamation in any other light (but this I say between ourselves) than as a temporary expedient to quiet the minds of the Indians, which must fall of course in a few years especially when those Indians are consenting to our occupying the lands. Any person therefore who neglects the present opportunity of hunting out good lands and in some measure marking and distinguishing them for their own (in order to keep others from settling them) will never regain it."

Washington requested that Crawford see to the hunting out and marking. "If therefore you will be at the trouble of seeking out the lands, I will take upon me the part of securing them so soon as there is a possibility of doing it and will moreover be at all the cost and charges of surveying, patenting etc., after which you shall have such a reasonable proportion of the whole as we may fix upon." Washington let Crawford know it would be worth his while. "My plan is to secure a good deal of land," he wrote. "You will consequently come in for a very handsome quantity."

Discretion was vital. "I would recommend it to you to keep this whole matter a profound secret, or trust it only with those in whom you can confide and who can assist you in bringing it to bear," Washington told Crawford. It would be embarrassing for Washington to be seen as circumventing imperial law; it would also alert competition. "I might be censured for the opinion I have given in respect to the King's Proclamation. and then if the scheme I am now proposing to you was known it might give the alarm to others, and by putting them upon a plan of the same nature (before we could lay a proper foundation for success ourselves) set the different interests a'clashing and very probably in the end overturn the whole." Washington advised Crawford to pretend he was hunting deer and other game, rather than scouting land. He should afterward inform Washington of what he had found. "Advise me of it, and if there appears but a bare possibility of succeeding any time hence, I will have the lands immediately surveyed to keep others off and leave the rest to time and my own assiduity to accomplish."

12

THE UPROAR IN AMERICA resounded in Britain. The British government might have resisted the anti-tax violence, which, if anything, inclined the ministry to dig in its heels, but the government couldn't withstand the defection of British merchants. George Grenville tumbled from power for reasons largely unrelated to the Stamp Act; his successor, the Marquis of Rockingham, heeded the complaints of merchants that their American trade was being ruined by the Stamp Act. Rockingham readied a tactical retreat; to assist, he summoned Benjamin Franklin to testify before the House of Commons, meeting as a committee of the whole.

"What is your name, and place of abode?" was the first question put.

"Franklin, of Philadelphia."

The interrogators included allies of Rockingham, who supported repeal, but also defenders of parliamentary authority who insisted on American subordination. The former put friendly questions to Franklin; the latter were more hostile.

"Do the Americans pay any considerable taxes among themselves?" he was asked.

"Certainly many, and very heavy taxes," Franklin said.

"What are the present taxes in Pennsylvania, laid by the laws of the colony?"

Franklin was happy to delineate. "There are taxes on all estates real and personal, a poll tax, a tax on all offices, professions, trades and businesses, according to their profits; an excise on all wine, rum, and other spirits; and a duty of ten pounds per head on all Negroes imported, with some other duties," he said.

"For what purposes are those taxes laid?"

"For the support of the civil and military establishments of the country, and to discharge the heavy debt contracted in the last war," Franklin said.

"How long are those taxes to continue?"

"Those for discharging the debt are to continue till 1772, and longer, if the debt should not be then all discharged. The others must always continue." Franklin's point was that the American colonies were burdened enough with taxes, without the Stamp Act.

"Are not all the people very able to pay those taxes?"

"No," said Franklin. "The frontier counties, all along the continent, having been frequently ravaged by the enemy, and greatly impoverished, are able to pay very little tax. And therefore, in consideration of their distresses, our late tax laws do expressly favour those counties, excusing the sufferers; and I suppose the same is done in other governments."

"Are not the colonies, from their circumstances, very able to pay the stamp duty?"

Emphatically not, Franklin said. "There is not gold and silver enough in the colonies to pay the stamp duty for one year."

But the design of the Stamp Act was meant to ensure that the taxes collected remain in the colonies, a questioner said. "Don't you know that the money arising from the stamps was all to be laid out in America?"

"I know it is appropriated by the act to the American service, but it will be spent in the conquered colonies where the soldiers are"—in Canada primarily—"not in the colonies that pay it."

But was there not a balance of trade among the colonies? Wouldn't the money circulate from the new colonies to the old colonies?

"I think not," Franklin said. "I believe very little would come back. I know of no trade likely to bring it back. I think it would come from the colonies where it was spent directly to England; for I have always observed, that in every colony the more plenty the means of remittance to England, the more goods are sent for, and the more trade with England carried on." The gold and silver that paid the taxes would inevitably find their way to England, to the detriment of America.

A member wanted details: "What may be the amount of one year's imports into Pennsylvania from Britain?"

"I have been informed that our merchants compute the imports from Britain to be above 500,000 pounds," Franklin said. He knew his hearers included men with connections to the colonial trade; he wanted them to know how much this trade was worth.

"What may be the amount of the produce of your province exported to Britain?"

"It must be small, as we produce little that is wanted in Britain," Franklin said. "I suppose it cannot exceed 40,000 pounds." This was good news to the mercantilists in his audience, who favored a positive balance of trade above all else.

A skeptic demanded, "Do you think it right that America should be protected by this country, and pay no part of the expence?"

Franklin rejected the premise. "That is not the case," he said. "The colonies raised, clothed and paid, during the last war, near 25,000 men, and spent many millions."

"Were you not reimbursed by Parliament?"

"We were only reimbursed what, in your opinion, we had advanced beyond our proportion, or beyond what might reasonably be expected from us," Franklin said. "And it was a very small part of what we spent. Pennsylvania, in particular, disbursed about 500,000 pounds, and the reimbursements, in the whole, did not exceed 60,000 pounds."

The questioning turned to the politics surrounding the Stamp Act. "What was the temper of America towards Great Britain before the year 1763?"

"The best in the world," Franklin said. The colonists considered themselves good and faithful subjects of the empire. "They submitted willingly to the government of the Crown, and paid, in all their courts, obedience to acts of Parliament. Numerous as the people are in the several old provinces"—the non-Canadian provinces—"they cost you nothing in forts, citadels, garrisons or armies to keep them in subjection. They were governed by this country at the expence only of a little pen, ink and paper. They were led by a thread. They had not only a respect, but an affection, for Great Britain, for its laws, its customs and manners, and even a fondness for its fashions, that greatly increased the commerce. Natives of Britain were always treated with particular regard; to be an Old England-man was, of itself, a character of some respect, and gave a kind of rank among us."

Had things changed? "What is their temper now?"

"Oh, very much altered," Franklin said.

"Did you ever hear the authority of Parliament to make laws for America questioned till lately?"

"The authority of Parliament was allowed to be valid in all laws, except such as should lay internal taxes," Franklin said. "It was never disputed in laying duties to regulate commerce."

This matter of internal taxes versus import duties, the latter often called external taxes, would become a crux of Franklin's argument to Parliament, and of the debate between the colonies and the government in London. At the moment, a member wanted to hear more about the change of attitude in America. "In what light did the people of America use to consider the parliament of Great-Britain?" he asked.

"They considered the Parliament as the great bulwark and security of their liberties and privileges, and always spoke of it with the utmost respect and veneration," Franklin said. "Arbitrary ministers, they thought, might possibly, at times, attempt to oppress them; but they relied on it that the Parliament, on application, would always give redress. They remembered, with gratitude, a strong instance of this, when a bill was brought into parliament, with a clause to make royal instructions laws in the colonies, which the House of Commons would not pass, and it was thrown out."

"And have they not still the same respect for Parliament?"

Sadly, no, Franklin said. "It is greatly lessened."

What had caused the shift?

"The restraints lately laid on their trade, by which the bringing of foreign gold and silver into the colonies was prevented," Franklin said. "The prohibition of making paper money among themselves; and then demanding a new and heavy tax by stamps."

"Don't you think they would submit to the Stamp Act, if it was modified, the obnoxious parts taken out, and the duty reduced to some particulars, of small moment?"

"No," said Franklin. "They will never submit to it." There was a principle at stake.

And what was that principle?

"I never heard any objection to the right of laying duties to regulate commerce," Franklin said. "But a right to lay internal taxes was never supposed to be in Parliament, as we are not represented there."

Could Franklin elaborate on this distinction? Was the difference really that great?

"I think the difference is very great," Franklin said. "An external tax is a duty laid on commodities imported; that duty is added to the first cost, and other charges on the commodity, and when it is offered to sale, makes a part of the price. If the people do not like it at that price, they refuse it; they are not obliged to pay it. But an internal tax is forced from the people without their consent, if not laid by their own representatives. The Stamp Act says we shall have no commerce, make no exchange of property with each other, neither purchase nor grant, nor recover debts; we shall neither marry, nor make our wills, unless we pay such and such sums, and thus it is intended to extort our money from us, or ruin us by the consequences of refusing to pay it."

What if the duty were laid on necessities imported from England? Wouldn't that make it the equivalent of an internal tax?

"I do not know a single article imported into the northern colonies but what they can either do without, or make themselves," Franklin said.

Was English cloth not a necessity?

"No, by no means absolutely necessary," Franklin said. "With industry and good management, they may very well supply themselves with all they want."

Some in Parliament had suggested repealing the Stamp Act while replacing it with an affirmation of Parliament's right to legislate for the colonies. Would this satisfy the Americans?

Franklin said it would. "I think the resolutions of right will give them very little concern, if they are never attempted to be carried into practice. The colonies will probably consider themselves in the same situation, in that respect, with Ireland; they know you claim the same right with regard to Ireland, but you never exercise it. And they may believe you never will exercise it in the colonies, any more than in Ireland, unless on some very extraordinary occasion."

What if Parliament insisted on retaining the law as it was? "Can anything less than a military force carry the Stamp Act into execution?"

"I do not see how a military force can be applied to that purpose," Franklin said.

Why not?

"Suppose a military force sent into America," Franklin said. "They will find nobody in arms. What are they then to do? They cannot force a man to take stamps who chooses to do without them. They will not find a rebellion; they may indeed make one."

If the act remained in effect, what would be the consequences?

"A total loss of the respect and affection the people of America bear to this country," Franklin said, "and of all the commerce that depends on that respect and affection."

Franklin was asked to elaborate on the commercial consequences of retention of the act. This was a matter of great concern to the merchants.

"You will find that if the act is not repealed, they will take very little of your manufactures in a short time," Franklin said of the Americans. "The goods they take from Britain are either necessaries, mere conveniences, or superfluities. The first, as cloth etc., with a little industry they can make at home; the second they can do without, till they are able to provide them among themselves; and the last, which are much the greatest part, they will strike off immediately. They are mere articles of fashion, purchased and consumed, because the fashion in a respected country, but will now be detested and rejected. The people have already struck off, by general agreement, the use of all goods fashionable in mournings, and many thousand pounds worth are sent back as unsaleable."

But could this boycott be sustained? Wouldn't the Americans eventually tire, and return to the better materials they could import?

Franklin thought the boycott could be sustained, and would be extended. "People will pay as freely to gratify one passion as another, their resentment as their pride," he said.

But weren't Americans mostly farmers, rather than manufacturers?

They were at present, Franklin said, but they needn't remain so. "They would manufacture more, and plough less."

But what about people engaged in commerce? Wouldn't they require the stamps to conduct their business?

Franklin shared his own sentiments on the subject. "I can only judge what other people will think, and how they will act, by what I feel within myself," he said. "I have a great many debts due to me in America, and I had rather they should remain unrecoverable by any law than submit to the Stamp Act. They will be debts of honour."

Franklin took pains to dispel some confusion he detected in Britain regarding the colonies. "The proceedings of the people in America have been considered too much together," he said. "The proceedings of the assemblies have been very different from those of the mobs, and should be distinguished, as having no connection with each other. The assemblies have only peaceably resolved what they take to be their rights; they have taken no measures for opposition by force; they have not built a fort, raised a man, or provided a grain of ammunition, in order to such opposition." The mobs had nothing to do with the majority of law-abiding colonists. "Every sober sensible man would wish to see rioters punished; as otherwise peaceable people have no security of person or estate." The colonists as a group had nothing but good will toward Britain. "They consider themselves as a part of the British empire, and as having one common interest with it," Franklin said. "They may be looked on here as foreigners, but they do not consider themselves as such. They are zealous for the honour and prosperity of this nation, and, while they are well used, will always be ready to support it, as far as their little power goes." The interests of Britain were the deemed the interests of America. "They consider themselves as a part of the whole."

And for precisely this reason they stood on the venerable English principle that people could not be taxed without their consent, Franklin said. The recent actions of Parliament, in particular the Stamp Act, failed this test. "They think the Parliament of Great Britain cannot properly give that consent till it has representatives from America."

Franklin was asked whether the Americans would ever change their minds on the taxing authority of Parliament.

"No, never," he said.

Never? Was there no power on earth that could move the Americans?

None, said Franklin. "No power, how great soever, can force men to change their opinions."

13

FRANKLIN'S PERFORMANCE GRATIFIED his friends and vexed his enemies. For the moment at least, Rockingham counted as a friend, and the prime minister couldn't have been more pleased. "The Marquis of Rockingham told a friend of mine a few days after, that he never knew truth make so great a progress in so very short a time," William Strahan reported to David Hall, Franklin's business partner, about Franklin's testimony. "From that day, the repeal was generally and absolutely determined, all that passed afterwards being merely form."

Indeed, Parliament repealed the Stamp Act a short while later, and Strahan credited Franklin. "To this very examination, more than to anything else, you are indebted to the speedy and total repeal of this odious law," he told Hall. Strahan couldn't say enough good about Franklin. "Happy man! In truth, I almost envy him the inward pleasure, as well as the outward fame, he must derive from having it in his power to do his country such eminent and seasonable service." Strahan had heard that Franklin had enemies in America who spread rumors about his continued attachment to his homeland; this should shut them up. "So striking and so indubitably authentic a proof of his patriotism must, I imagine, forever silence his enemies with you, and must afford you and his other friends the greatest pleasure."

THE VICTORY WASN'T as complete as Strahan claimed. The repeal of the Stamp Act was accompanied by the passage of a measure called the Declaratory Act, which affirmed the right of Parliament to legislate for the colonies. Nonetheless, many in America, and in Britain as well, assumed that the self-interest that had brought British merchants to the Americans' side on the stamp issue would persist, and would deter Parliament from trying to tax the Americans again.

Franklin declined to take anything for granted. He made the case for the colonies in meetings with government ministers, in conversations with friends, and in the journals and gazettes of London. Writing as "Benevolus," a putative English friend of the Americans, he corrected misconceptions he thought were confusing the readers of the *London Chronicle*. One was that the American colonies had been founded at the expense of the British government. Nothing could be more incorrect, Franklin said. "If we examine our records, the journals of Parliament, we shall not find that a farthing was ever granted for the settling any colonies before the last reign, and then only for Georgia and Nova Scotia, which are still of little value. But the colonies of New-Hampshire, Massachusetts, Rhode-Island, Connecticut, New-York (as far as the English were concerned in it), New-Jersey, Pennsylvania, Maryland, Virginia, North and South Carolina, etc. were settled at the private expence of the adventurers."

Another erroneous belief, similarly cited in justification of Parliament's power to tax the colonies, was that they had received their charters from Parliament. "The charters themselves shew that they were granted by the King," Franklin rejoined. "And the truth is, that Parliament had no participation in these grants, and was not so much as consulted upon them."

The pro-tax group asserted that Parliament had long been paying for colonial defense. Wrong again, said Franklin. "No grants for that purpose appear on our records, and the fact is, that they protected themselves, at their own expence, for near 150 years after the first settlement, and never thought of applying to Parliament for any aid against the Indians."

But what about defense against the French? Hadn't Britain's recent wars been triggered by events in North America?

Again not so, said Franklin. The next-to-last war he traced to Spanish depredations on British shipping on the high seas. "It was, therefore, a war for the protection of our commerce, and not for the protection of the people of America." As for the latest war against France, this too was for the protection of British trade, namely the Indian trade of Ohio. "It was, therefore, a British interest, that was to

be defended and secured by that war. The colonies were in peace, and
the settlers had not been attacked or molested in the least, till after the
miscarriage of Braddock's expedition to the Ohio."

But the Americans paid no taxes, or not taxes enough, said the
critics.

"There cannot be a greater mistake than this," replied Franklin.
The colonists paid taxes aplenty. They paid for their governments,
their militias, their postal service. "They are besides under great burthens that we are free from. Our ancestors in Britain have long since
defrayed the expence of most of our public buildings, churches, col-
leges, highways, bridges, and other conveniences, which are left to us
as an inheritance. These our people who remove to America cannot
enjoy, but as they extend their settlements, are obliged to tax themselves anew for all such public works."

Yet didn't the Americans imperil the integrity of the empire by
rejecting the authority of Parliament?

Once more no, said Franklin. "The truth is that all acts of the
British legislature expressly extending to the colonies have ever been
received there as laws and executed in their courts, the right of Parliament to make them being never yet contested, acts to raise money upon
the colonies by internal taxes only and alone excepted." This was an
important exception, to be sure. But it was no more than Englishmen
had long claimed as a right. "In granting their money to the crown,
they think their assent is constitutionally necessary," Franklin said.
"And they think it hard that a Parliament in which they have no representative should make a merit to itself by granting *their money* to the
crown without asking their consent." This was the sole point in dispute
between the Americans and Parliament.

Franklin returned to an argument he had made in his testimony in
the House of Commons—and thereby risked revealing the identity of
"Benevolus." The Americans, he said, distinguished between internal
and external taxes. "An internal tax to be raised in the colonies by
authority of Parliament forces the money out of my purse without the
consent of my representative in assembly. An external tax or duty is
added to the first cost and other charges of the commodity on which
it is laid, and makes a part of its price. If I do not like it at that price,
I refuse it. If I do like it, I pay the price, and do not need to give my

consent by my representative for the payment of this tax, because I can consent to it myself in person."

FRANKLIN SOON DISCOVERED that his distinction between internal and external taxes wasn't universally shared in America. The new chancellor of the exchequer, Charles Townshend, took the Americans at Franklin's word and crafted a program of external taxes, in the form of duties on paper, glass, lead, pigments and tea. The duties were accompanied by measures that punished New York for that province's failure to comply with an earlier act demanding payments for the quartering of British troops; that specified that revenues from the duties would go toward the salaries of British officials in the colonies; and that gave preference to the British East India Company in the American tea trade.

The Townshend duties, far from being accepted by the Americans, provoked a new uproar. Non-importation agreements were crafted in the various colonies, often by the same people who had been at the front of the protests against the Stamp Act, and were enforced with a vigor approaching that which the Stamp Act had evoked.

The boycott strongly suggested that the Americans rejected not simply internal taxes but taxes of any sort, and it left Franklin hanging. He had misrepresented the American view, possibly because he had misunderstood it from the start, or, more likely, because it had changed. If there had never been a Stamp Act to galvanize American opposition, perhaps the provincials would have accepted the Townshend duties. But there *had* been the hated act, and Americans had resisted it effectively. They intended to resist the new duties, with what they hoped would be equal effect.

Franklin had some explaining to do. In early 1768 he again took to the pages of the *London Chronicle*, where he pointed out that the colonial assemblies had been accustomed to receiving requisitions from the king, which they were pleased to supply. "Had this happy method of requisition been continued . . . ," he said, "there is no doubt but all the money that could reasonably be expected to be raised from them in any manner might have been obtained, without the least heart-burning, offence, or breach of the harmony, of affections and interests, that so long subsisted between the two countries." Instead, the ministry in London had attempted a novel method of extracting revenues from America by force. The Americans, as good Englishmen, could not but resist. "The colonies universally were of opinion that no money could be levied from English subjects but by their own consent given by themselves or their chosen representatives." Parliament had prudently repealed the Stamp Act, but subsequent measures signaled a continued disregard for American rights. The act punishing New York evoked alarm and objection throughout the colonies. "The language of such an act seemed to them to be: Obey implicitly laws made by the Parliament of Great Britain to raise money on you without your consent, or you shall enjoy no rights or privileges at all."

And then there were the duties on glass, paper and so on. What made the duties most onerous, Franklin wrote, was that much of the revenue they produced would be employed to pay the salaries of colonial governors and other imperial officials. This was a break with tradition, and a further attack on the rights of the Americans. "They are generally strangers to the provinces they are sent to govern, have no estate, natural connection, or relation there, to give them an affection for the country," Franklin said of the governors. "They come only to make money as fast as they can; are sometimes men of vicious characters and broken fortunes, sent by a minister merely to get them out of the way. . . . As they intend staying in the country no longer than their government continues, and purpose to leave no family behind them, they are apt to be regardless of the good will of the people, and care not what is said or thought of them after they are gone." Until lately, the lone check the people of a province had upon misadministration by a governor was the power of the purse. Suddenly this check was removed.

The American resistance to the new duties took a different form than the resistance to the Stamp Act, Franklin explained. He depicted the Americans saying to themselves: "Let us unite in solemn resolutions and engagements with and to each other, that we will give these new officers as little trouble as possible by not consuming the British manufactures on which they are to levy the duties. Let us agree to consume no more of their expensive gewgaws. Let us live frugally, and let us industriously manufacture what we can for ourselves. Thus we shall be able honourably to discharge the debts we already owe them, and after that we may be able to keep some money in our country, not only for the uses of our internal commerce, but for the service of our gracious sovereign, whenever he shall have occasion for it, and think proper to require it of us in the old *constitutional* manner."

Franklin was again writing pseudonymously; his alter ego didn't profess to accept these views. Indeed, he called them "the wild ravings of the at-present half distracted Americans." Yet the sentiments needed to be aired in Britain, and taken into account, for Britain's interest as much as America's. "I sincerely wish, for the sake of the manufactures and commerce of Great Britain, and for the sake of the strength which a firm union with our growing colonies would give us, that these people had never been thus needlessly driven out of their senses."

IN WRITING FOR PUBLICATION, even if not under his own name, Franklin shaped his message to influence his audience. The American boycott had undercut his distinction between internal and external taxes, compelling him to justify the American opposition to the Townshend duties in other terms. The one he chose—that the use of the duties to pay British colonial officials would make the officials less concerned about the welfare of the Americans—was weak. Of course the officials had to be paid, and why not from taxes paid by the Americans? But it was the best he could come up with.

It wasn't what he really believed. Franklin had competition in trying to furnish a principled basis for the American resistance. John Dickinson had sparred with Franklin in Pennsylvania politics, taking the side of the Penn family against Franklin and the Pennsylvania assembly. Amid the reaction to the Townshend duties, Dickinson wrote a series of essays subsequently gathered as *Letters from a Farmer in Pennsylvania*. In the letters Dickinson rejected Franklin's distinction between internal and external taxes, offering instead a distinction between taxes for revenue and taxes for regulation. London might legitimately tax the colonies for regulation of their commerce, Dickinson said. Such authority had always been inherent in the administration of the empire. But taxing for revenue was novel and illegitimate. The colonies were not cows to be milked for the benefit of the mother country.

Franklin thought enough of the *Farmer* letters to arrange their publication in Britain. But he took issue with their central argument. Writing to son William, Franklin said he couldn't tell "what bounds the Farmer sets to the power he acknowledges in Parliament to 'regulate the trade of the colonies,' it being difficult to draw lines between duties for regulation and those for revenue." Franklin added, "If the Parliament is to be the judge, it seems to me that establishing such principles of distinction will amount to little." This was the rub: who would determine where the authority of Parliament ended? "The more I have thought and read on the subject the more I find myself confirmed in opinion that no middle doctrine can be well maintained," Franklin said. "Something might be made of either of the extremes: that Parliament has a power to make *all laws* for us, or that it has a power to make *no laws* for us. And I think the arguments for the latter more numerous and weighty than those for the former. Supposing that doctrine established, the colonies would then be so many separate states, only subject to the same king, as England and Scotland were before the union. And then the question would be, whether a union like that with Scotland would or would not be advantageous to *the whole*. I should have no doubt of the affirmative, being fully persuaded that it would be best for *the whole*, and that though particular parts might find particular disadvantages in it, they would find greater advantages in the security arising to every part from the increased strength of the whole. But such union is not likely to take place while the nature of our present relation is so little understood on both sides the water, and sentiments concerning it remain so widely different."

Part IV

Can a Virtuous Man Hesitate?

THE BOYCOTT OF IMPORTS from Britain imperiled the profits of American merchants; for this reason many of the merchants were skeptical if not flatly opposed. A boycott might also reduce the standard of living of wealthy individuals like George Washington. In the spring of 1768, Washington wrote to Robert Cary, his London agent, about acquiring a new carriage. "My old chariot, having run its race and gone through as many stages as I could conveniently make it travel, is now rendered incapable of any further service," Washington said. "The intent of this letter, therefore, is to desire you will bespeak me a new one, time enough to come out with the goods (I shall hereafter write for) by Captain Johnston, or some other ship. As these are kind of articles that last with care against number of years, I would willingly have the chariot you may now send me made in the newest taste, handsome, genteel and light; yet not slight and consequently unserviceable; to be made of the best seasoned wood, and by a celebrated workman." Washington liked green as the color for a carriage, because green was tasteful and green paint tended not to fade in the Virginia sun. "I would give it the preference, unless any other color more in vogue and equally lasting is entitled to precedency. In that case I would be governed by fashion." He specified other features: "a light gilding on the mouldings (that is, round the panels) and any other ornaments, that may not have a heavy and tawdry look (together with my arms agreeable to the impression here sent) . . . a lining of a handsome, lively colored leather of good quality . . . a pole (not shafts) for the wheel horses to draw by, together with a handsome set of harness." He added, "On the harness let my crest be engraved."

Washington watched as the non-importation strategy took hold, at first in the northern colonies. "In my opinion it is a good one, and must be attended with salutary effects, provided it can be carried pretty generally into execution," he wrote to George Mason, a neighbor and fellow burgess. But time would tell whether the boycotters could stick with it. "That there will be difficulties attending the execution of it everywhere, from clashing interests and selfish, designing men (ever attentive to their own gain, and watchful of every turn that can assist their lucrative views, in preference to every other consideration) cannot be denied."

Elsewhere the boycott might develop differently, Washington supposed. "In the tobacco colonies, where the trade is so diffused, and in a manner wholly conducted by factors for their principals at home"— that is, in London—"these difficulties are certainly enhanced," he said. Boycotters in Boston could squeeze Boston merchants, effectively curtailing offensive imports, but southern planters, including Washington himself, often dealt directly with Britain. Even so, said Washington, the boycott could work "if the gentlemen in their several counties will be at some pains to explain matters to the people and stimulate them to a cordial agreement to purchase none but certain enumerated articles out of any of the stores after such a period, nor import nor purchase any themselves."

Like Benjamin Franklin, Washington saw merit in a boycott even if it didn't compel a policy change by Parliament. "The more I consider a scheme of this sort, the more ardently I wish success to it, because I think there are private as well as public advantages to result from it," he said. "That the colonies are considerably indebted to Great Britain is a truth universally acknowledged. That many families are reduced almost, if not quite, to penury and want from the low ebb of their fortunes, and estates daily selling for the discharge of debts, the public papers furnish but too many melancholy proofs of, and that a scheme of this sort will contribute more effectually than any other I can devise to emerge the country from the distress it at present labors under, I do most firmly believe, if it can be generally adopted."

Enforced thrift could be beneficial to all classes. "I can see but one set of people (the merchants excepted) who will not, or ought not, to wish well to the scheme, and that is those who live genteelly and hospitably on clear estates," Washington told Mason. "Such as these, were they not to consider the valuable object in view, and the good of others, might think it hard to be curtailed in their living and enjoyments." Men like Washington himself, in other words, would have to be motivated by civic virtue to forgo their fancy carriages. But everyone else would be materially better off for a boycott. "For as to the penurious man, he saves his money and he saves his credit, having the best plea for doing that which before, perhaps, he had the most violent struggles to refrain from doing. The extravagant and expensive man has the same good plea to retrench his expenses. He is thereby furnished with a pretext to live within bounds, and embraces it. Prudence dictated economy to him before, but his resolution was too weak to put it in practice."

Washington deemed the boycott an apt response to British presumption, in that it charted a middle ground between unprincipled acquiescence and unlawful violence. "At a time when our lordly masters in Great Britain will be satisfied with nothing less than the deprivation of American freedom, it seems highly necessary that something should be done to avert the stroke and maintain the liberty which we have derived from our ancestors," he told Mason. Some hotheads were talking about taking up arms against Britain. Washington, the former soldier, had nothing against armed resistance in principle. "That no man should scruple, or hesitate a moment, to use a—ms in defence of so valuable a blessing, on which all the good and evil of life depends, is clearly my opinion," he wrote (though he scrupled to spell out the full word). "Yet a—ms, I would beg leave to add, should be the last resource, the *dernier resort*. Addresses to the throne, and remonstrances to Parliament, we have already, it is said, proved the inefficacy of. How far, then, their attention to our rights and privileges is to be awakened or alarmed, by starving their trade and manufactures, remains to be tried."

And it *should* be tried. "Upon the whole, therefore," Washington concluded, "I think the scheme a good one, and that it ought to be tried here, with such alterations as the exigency of our circumstances renders absolutely necessary."

THE BOYCOTT SCHEME *WAS* TRIED, and it failed in Virginia. The merchants complained that it killed their business, and other Virginians found their consumptive urges too powerful to resist. The burgesses revised the boycott downward. "A new Association is formed, much upon the old plan, but more relaxed, to which the merchants then in town acceded," Washington reported to George Fairfax after the 1770 session. "Committees in each county are to be chosen to attend to the importations and see if our agreements cannot be more strictly adhered to."

Washington hoped they would be. "That there should be a dissatisfaction and murmuring at the Virginia Association (by those who are more strictly bound) I do not much wonder at, but it was the best that the friends to the cause could obtain here," he remarked to a friend in Maryland. "And though too much relaxed from the spirit with which a measure of this sort ought to be conducted, yet will be attended with better effects (I expect) than the last, inasmuch as it will become general, and adopted by the trade." Again Washington distinguished between the northern and southern colonies. "Upon the whole I think the people of Virginia have too large latitude, and wish that the inhabitants of the North may not have too little." The key was how much the people could bear. "What I would be understood by it is that their public virtue may not be put to too severe a trial to stand the test much longer if their importations are not equal to the real necessities of the people."

He had his doubts. "Whether it is or is not I cannot undertake to judge, but suppose they are not, by the defection of New York and attempts (though unsuccessful as yet) in other places to admit a general importation of goods, tea only excepted."

FRANKLIN HAD GREATER FAITH, not least because he had a closer look at British politics. "The public affairs of this nation are at present in great disorder," he wrote to Joseph Galloway from London. "Parties run very high, and have abused each other so thoroughly that there is not now left an unbespattered character in the kingdom of any note or importance." The squabbling might serve America's interest. The boycott had convinced nearly everyone in England that a change in policy was in order. Lord Hillsborough, the colonial secretary and president of the board of trade, had circulated a letter advocating partial repeal of the duties. "For some time," Franklin told Galloway, "there was nearly an equal balance in the cabinet between those who were for repealing only the duties mentioned in Lord H.'s circular letter, and those who were for giving America complete satisfaction, and getting rid of the dispute forever." The proponents of the harder line predicted a weakening of American resolve; some said the boycott was already crumbling. News from the colonies showed this to be untrue. "A ship arrived at Bristol from Boston with a returned cargo of those very goods that country was supposed most to want, and least able to subsist without, bringing also authentic advices that the resolutions of non-importation continued in full force."

The hardliners were set back, but they weren't defeated, Franklin said. "Lord H. and the Bedford faction"—a group associated with the Duke of Bedford—"have confidently always predicted that our agreements would not hold, that the known self-interestedness of merchants would soon overcome their pretended patriotism, that the distresses of the people for want of British goods, without which they could not subsist, would compel an importation; that the different colonies were a rope of sand, and could not long hold together for any one purpose; and that a little firmness shewn by government here would infallibly break us all to pieces. On this principle they have acted." Continued American resistance became all the more necessary, Franklin said. "If we give way, they and their friends will exult; their judgment and foresight will be admired; they will be extolled as able statesmen, worthy to hold the reins in governing America." And America would be permanently diminished. "We, if we break through the agreement, can never promise ourselves any effect from like agreements hereafter, for it will always be said here: Be firm and their associations will come to nothing. Therefore I should be for adhering at all events."

WHILE MODERATES LIKE FRANKLIN and Washington discussed the merits of the boycott, radicals in Massachusetts
took their arguments into the street. Boston remained the hotbed of
resistance to British authority, and although the monthly temperature
rose or fell according to the mood of the ministry in London and the
policies of Parliament, the trend was decidedly in a warming direction.
Samuel Adams and his allies pushed against the boundaries demarked
by the British government, and the British government pushed back.
London sent a warship to Boston for the nominal purpose of capturing
smugglers; the unspoken purpose was to awe the populace. London
sent British troops to ensure the safety of British colonial officials, and
to deter violators of the peace and British law.

Neither tactic worked; the Boston mob grew more unruly than
ever. In February 1770 a riot threatened the home of a Boston resident
conceived to be too partial to the British. "Having been a landwaiter,
or inferior custom-house officer, and before that an informer against
illicit traders, he was particularly obnoxious to the people," Thomas
Hutchinson recalled of the man and the rioters. "The mob surrounded
his house, threw stones and brickbats through the windows, and, as
it appeared upon trial, were forcing their way in when he fired upon
them, and killed a boy of eleven or twelve years of age."

Hutchinson was officially lieutenant governor still, but he was the
acting governor in the absence of Frances Bernard, who had been
summoned to Britain. Hutchinson watched the events in Boston with
the sympathy of a native but the skepticism of a servant of the British crown. "The boy that was killed was the son of a poor German
immigrant," he continued. "A grand funeral was, however, judged very
proper for him. Young and old, some of all ranks and orders, attended
in a solemn procession from liberty tree"—by now a landmark—"to the

town-house, and then to the common burying ground." The funeral served to solidify the position of the radicals in Boston; their movement had its first martyr.

It soon acquired more. All winter Bostonians and British soldiers had glared at each other, with the former often taunting and provoking the latter, who occasionally responded but never with lethal force. The killing of the German boy ratcheted tensions higher. Things seemed near a breaking point on March 5. "Early in the evening, clusters of the inhabitants were observed in different quarters of the town," Hutchinson recalled. "Parties of soldiers were also driving about the streets, as if the one, and the other, had something more than ordinary upon their minds. About eight o'clock, one of the bells of the town was rung in such manner as is usual in case of fire. This called people into the streets. A larger number assembled in the market-place, not far from King Street, armed with bludgeons, or clubs."

Hutchinson witnessed part of this personally; other information he gathered from court testimony afterward. "A small fray between some of the inhabitants and the soldiers, at or near the barracks at the west part of the town, was of little importance, and soon over," Hutchinson recorded. "A sentinel, who was posted at the custom-house, not far from the main guard, was next insulted, and pelted with pieces of ice, etc., which caused him to call to the main guard to protect him. Notice was soon given to Captain Preston, whose company was then on guard. A sergeant, with six men, was sent to protect the sentinel, but the captain, to prevent any rash, precipitate action, followed them himself."

The arrival of the reinforcements caused a larger crowd to gather. "The guards were more insulted than the sentinel had been, and received frequent strokes from snowballs, lumps of ice, etc.," Hutchinson said. "Captain Preston thereupon ordered them to charge; but this was no discouragement to the assailants, who continued to pelt the guard, daring them to fire. Some of the people who were behind the soldiers, and observed the abuse, called on them to fire. At length, one of them received a blow with a club, which brought him to the ground; but, rising again, he immediately fired, and all the rest, one excepted, followed the example."

Three men were killed at once, and two more were fatally wounded. Several members of the crowd received lesser wounds. One of those who died on the spot was Crispus Attucks, a mixed-race man whom Hutchinson described as "among the most active in this attack." A man named Carr offered a striking perspective on the evening's events, Hutchinson related. "Carr, one of the mortally wounded, acknowledged upon his death bed that he had seen mobs in Ireland, but never knew troops bear so much without firing, as these had done."

Witnesses to the shooting ran to Hutchinson's house, a half-mile away, and "begged, for God's sake, he would go to King Street, where, they feared, a general action would come on, between the troops and the inhabitants," according to Hutchinson. The lieutenant governor sought out Captain Preston to learn why the troops had fired without orders. The shooting had silenced the crowd briefly, but now they were shouting so loudly Hutchinson couldn't make himself understood. He eventually inferred that they wanted him to order the troops to retire to their barracks. "He refused to comply," Hutchinson said of himself, "and calling from the balcony"—of the town house, or city hall—"to the great body of people which remained in the street, he expressed his great concern at the unhappy event, assured them he would do everything in his power in order to a full and impartial inquiry, that the law might have its course, and advised them to go peaceably to their several homes."

Most in the crowd complied, to Hutchinson's relief. At that point he turned to the commander of the troops and requested they also retire. "If the companies in arms were ordered to their barracks," Hutchinson reasoned, "the streets would be cleared and the town in quiet for that night." The commander consented, the troops retired, and the rest of the crowd went home too.

Hutchinson made good on his promise in the following days, and several British soldiers were arrested and scheduled for trial. But already the events of the night of March 5 were being portrayed in pamphlets, broadside posters, editorials and speeches as the "Boston massacre." The five men killed were cast as martyrs to American liberty. The rift between the Americans and the British yawned wider.

JOHN ADAMS WAS A LAWYER, not a pamphleteer. And as a lawyer, devoted to the common-law heritage of the British people, he determined that the soldiers who fired the shots deserved a sturdy defense.

"The evening of the fifth of March, I spent at Mr. Henderson Inches's house at the South End of Boston, in company with a club with whom I had been associated for several years," Adams recalled. "About nine o'clock we were alarmed with the ringing of bells, and supposing it to be the signal of fire, we snatched our hats and cloaks, broke up the club, and went out to assist in quenching the fire or aiding our friends who might be in danger." Once in the street they learned that the alarm signaled no fire but something more shocking. "We were informed that the British soldiers had fired on the inhabitants, killed some and wounded others near the town house. A crowd of people was flowing down the street to the scene of action. When we arrived we saw nothing but some field pieces placed before the south door of the town house and some engineers and grenadiers drawn up to protect them." The Adamses were living not far from the Common, and Abigail Adams was pregnant. "I was apprehensive of the effect of the surprise upon her, who was alone, excepting her maids and a boy in the house." He hurried toward the house. "I walked down Boylston's Alley into Brattle Square, where a company or two of regular soldiers were drawn up in front of Dr. Cooper's old church with their muskets all shouldered and their bayonets all fixed. I had no other way to proceed but along the whole front in a very narrow space which they had left for foot passengers. Pursuing my way, without taking the least notice of them or they of me, any more than if they had been marble statues, I went directly home to Cold Lane."

He found Abigail as unflappable as usual. She had heard the commotion but soon perceived in it no threat. The house was calm. "We had nothing but our reflections to interrupt our repose," he wrote. But these were worry enough. "Endeavours had been systematically pursued for many months by certain busy characters to excite quarrels, rencounters"—run-ins—"and combats single or compound in the night between the inhabitants of the lower class and the soldiers, and at all risks to enkindle an immortal hatred between them. I suspected that this was the explosion which had been intentionally wrought up by designing men who knew what they were aiming at better than the instrument employed. If these poor tools should be prosecuted for any of their illegal conduct, they must be punished. If the soldiers in self defence should kill any of them, they must be tried, and, if truth was respected and the law prevailed, must be acquitted."

Besides being a lawyer, Adams was known throughout the city as an honest man. The next morning he received a visit at his office, mere steps from the town house, from an acquaintance named Forrest. The fellow was agitated. "With tears streaming from his eyes, he said I am come with a very solemn message from a very unfortunate man, Captain Preston, in prison. He wishes for counsel, and can get none." Forrest had approached some other attorneys, who had either declined outright or conditioned their acceptance on Adams's willingness to head the defense.

Adams frowned at the timidity of his colleagues. "I had no hesitation in answering that counsel ought to be the very last thing that an accused person should want in a free country. That the bar ought in my opinion to be independent and impartial at all times and in every circumstance. And that persons whose lives were at stake ought to have the counsel they preferred." Yet Adams wanted to be sure Preston knew what he was getting into. "This would be as important a cause as ever was tried in any court or country of the world, and that every lawyer must hold himself responsible not only to his country but to the highest and most infallible of all tribunals for the part he should act. He must therefore expect from me no art or address, no sophistry or prevarication in such a cause; nor anything more than fact, evidence and law would justify."

Forrest relayed the message and brought a reply. "Captain Preston he said requested and desired no more, and that he had such an opinion, from all he had heard from all parties of me, that he could cheerfully trust his life with me upon those principles."

The murder trial of Preston and the other British soldiers was a sensation second only to the incident that prompted it. The Boston mob howled for their necks, and some of its members—and not a few other Bostonians—bawled at Adams for defending them. Yet Adams didn't flinch, and he gave Preston everything he had promised. He depicted for the jury the danger the soldiers had faced from the rioters. "When the multitude was shouting and huzzaing, and threatening life, the bells all ringing, the mob whistle screaming and rending like an Indian yell, the people from all quarters throwing every species of rubbish they could pick up in the street, and some who were quite on the other side of the street throwing clubs at the whole party, Montgomery"—one of the soldiers—"in particular smote with a club and knocked down, and as soon as he could rise and take up his fire-lock, another club from afar struck his breast or shoulder, what could he do?" demanded Adams. "Do you expect he should behave like a stoic philosopher lost in apathy?" Of course not. "You must suppose him divested of all human passions if you don't think him at the least provoked, thrown off his guard and into the *furor brevis*"—momentary madness—"by such treatment as this."

Crispus Attucks was the most provocative, Adams said. Brandishing a large club, Attucks led the mob pell-mell at the soldiers. "When the soldiers pushed the people off, this man with his party cried, 'Do not be afraid of them, they dare not fire. Kill them! Kill them! Knock them over! And he tried to knock their brains out."

Adams took a moment to lecture the jury on the philosophy of law in the culture of English liberty. "We find in the rules laid down by the greatest English judges, who have been the brightest of mankind, that we are to look upon it as more beneficial that many guilty persons should escape unpunished than one innocent person should suffer. The reason is, because it's of more importance to the community that innocence should be protected than it is that guilt should be punished; for guilt and crimes are so frequent in the world that all of them cannot be punished, and many times they happen in such a manner that it is not of much consequence to the public whether they are punished or not. But when innocence itself is brought to the bar and condemned, especially to die, the subject will exclaim, 'It is immaterial to me whether I behave well or ill, for virtue itself is no security.' And if such a sentiment as this should take place in the mind of the subject, there would be an end to all security whatsoever."

Reverting to the facts of the present case, Adams declared, "Facts are stubborn things, and whatever may be our wishes, our inclinations, or the dictates of our passions, they cannot alter the state of facts and evidence." Nor was the law less stubborn than the facts. "If an assault was made to endanger their lives, the law is clear: they had a right to kill in their own defence. If it was not so severe as to endanger their lives, yet if they were assaulted at all, struck and abused by blows of any sort, by snow-balls, oyster-shells, cinders, clubs, or sticks of any kind, this was a provocation for which the law reduces the offence of killing, down to manslaughter, in consideration of those passions in our nature which cannot be eradicated."

The jury agreed. Six of the eight defendants were acquitted of all charges; the other two were convicted of manslaughter and punished by branding on the thumb.

Adams wasn't the kind to understate his accomplishments, but even he thought he had done well. "The part I took in defence of Captain Preston and the soldiers procured me anxiety and obloquy enough," he observed later. "It was, however, one of the most gallant, generous, manly and disinterested actions of my whole life, and one of the best pieces of service I ever rendered my country. Judgment of death against those soldiers would have been as foul a stain upon this country as the executions of the Quakers or witches anciently."

THE TURBULENCE IN AMERICA was mirrored by turmoil in Britain. Indeed, the troubles were twins, for the turnover in the British government and the accompanying reversals of British policy toward the colonies encouraged the Americans to think their protests were working, and therefore to continue them. The Americans weren't wholly wrong, but neither were they quite right. Had American affairs gone smoothly, British ministers would have had an easier time holding their jobs. But the American resistance raised the hackles of ministers and members of Parliament who demanded that the Americans be made to feel their subordination to Britain.

Lord Hillsborough was one whose hackles rose readily. The colonial secretary considered the American protesters seditionists, and he judged the Bostonians to be the worst of the bunch. A letter drafted by Sam Adams and James Otis denouncing the Townshend Acts had been approved by the Massachusetts assembly and distributed among the colonies; it urged a united front against this latest despotism. Hillsborough condemned the circular as revolutionary and ordered the Massachusetts assembly to disavow it. If it refused, it would be dissolved.

The assembly did refuse, but before the dissolution took effect, Parliament reversed course once more. Again the worries of British merchants won out. Hillsborough took the reversal personally. Massachusetts had defied him and gotten away with it.

He was still angry when Benjamin Franklin requested an interview at the beginning of 1771. The Massachusetts assembly had named Franklin its agent in London, a post he could fill without giving up his same job for Pennsylvania. Franklin desired to present his new credentials to Hillsborough.

"I went this morning to wait on Lord Hillsborough," Franklin recorded after the meeting. "The porter at first denied his lordship, on which I left my name, and drove off. But before the coach got out of the square, the coachman heard a call, turned, and went back to the door, when the porter came and said: His lordship will see you, sir."

Franklin was intrigued at the apparent change of mind, which Hillsborough shortly explained. "His lordship came towards me, and said 'I was dressing in order to go to court, but hearing that you were at the door, who are a man of business, I determined to see you immediately.'"

Franklin thanked Hillsborough and said his present business wasn't much. He merely wish to convey that he had been appointed by Massachusetts to be its agent in London. He began to say he hoped he could offer good service in that post. But Hillsborough cut him off. "His lordship, whose countenance changed at my naming that province, cut me short by saying, with something between a smile and a sneer, 'I must set you right there, Mr. Franklin. You are not agent.'"

"Why, my lord?" Franklin responded.

"You are not appointed."

"I do not understand your lordship," said Franklin. "I have the appointment in my pocket."

"You are mistaken," said Hillsborough. "I have later and better advices. I have a letter from Governor Hutchinson. He would not give his assent to the bill."

"There was no bill, my lord. It is a vote of the house."

"There was a bill presented to the governor," Hillsborough insisted, "for the purpose of appointing you, and another, one Dr. Lee, I think he is called"—Arthur Lee—"to which the governor refused his assent."

"I cannot understand this, my lord. I think there must be some mistake in it. Is your lordship quite sure that you have such a letter?"

"I will convince you of it directly," Hillsborough said. He rang for his secretary. The man arrived. Hillsborough asked abruptly, "Have not you at hand Governor Hutchinson's letter mentioning his refusing his assent to the bill for appointing Dr. Franklin agent?"

"My lord?"

"Is there not such a letter?"

"No, my lord." The secretary said there was a letter from Hutchinson, but it didn't mention Franklin.

"Is there nothing in that letter to the purpose I mention?"

"No, my lord."

Franklin spoke up. "I thought it could not well be, my lord, as my letters are by the last ships and mention no such thing," he said. "Here is an authentic copy of the vote of the house appointing me, in which there is no mention of any act intended. Will your lordship please to look at it?"

Hillsborough grumpily took the letter but didn't read it. He told Franklin it must be presented to the board of trade.

Franklin offered to take it there. The board would enter the letter into its records.

Hillsborough grew flustered. "It shall not be entered there," he said. "No such paper shall be entered there while I have anything to do with the business of that board." Hillsborough also chaired the trade board. "The house of representatives"—of Massachusetts—"has no right to appoint an agent. We shall take no notice of any agents but such as are appointed by acts of assembly to which the governor gives his assent."

"I cannot conceive, my lord, why the consent of the *governor* should be thought necessary to the appointment of an agent for the *people*," Franklin said. "It seems to me, that—"

Hillsborough cut him off. "I shall not enter into a dispute with you, sir, upon this subject," he said contemptuously.

"I beg your lordship's pardon," Franklin said. "I do not presume to dispute with your lordship. I would only say that it seems to me that every body of men who cannot appear in person where business relating to them may be transacted should have a right to appear by an agent. The concurrence of the governor does not seem to me necessary. It is the business of the people that is to be done; he is not one of them. He is himself an agent."

Hillsborough waved this off. "No agent can be appointed but by an act," he reiterated. "Besides, this proceeding is directly contrary to express instructions."

"I did not know there had been such instructions," Franklin said. "I am not concerned in any offence against them, and—"

"Your offering such a paper to be entered is an offence against them," Hillsborough said. "No such appointment shall be entered." He folded Franklin's letter in half, still without reading it. "When I came into the administration of American affairs," he continued, "I found them in great disorder. By my firmness they are now something mended, and while I have the honour to hold the seals"—of his office—"I shall continue the same conduct, the same firmness. I think my duty to the master I serve and to the government of this nation require it of me. If that conduct is not approved, they may take my office from me when they please. I shall make them a bow, and thank them. I shall resign with pleasure."

Franklin decided to end the interview. He reached out for his letter, which Hillsborough returned to him. "I beg your lordship's pardon for taking up so much of your time," Franklin said. "It is I believe of no great importance whether the appointment is acknowledged or not, for I have not the least conception that an agent can at present be of any use, to any of the colonies. I shall therefore give your lordship no farther trouble."

FRANKLIN NEVER GOT anywhere with Hillsborough, but fortunately for him and the other American opponents of Hillsborough's policies, the colonial secretary lost his job in 1772. The turmoil in British politics continued, and Hillsborough gave way to Lord Dartmouth, who at first appeared inclined toward conciliation with the Americans.

Yet appearances deceived, and they deceived Franklin most fatefully of all. About the time Dartmouth took up the portfolio for America, the Massachusetts assembly sent a petition to Franklin for delivery to King George. The petition declared the decided belief of the assembly that paying the salary of the Massachusetts governor was the prerogative of the assembly and not of the king; for the king to pay infringed the rights of the people of Massachusetts. George was known to take the opposite view, and Franklin supposed that delivering the petition might provoke him to measures even less acceptable to Massachusetts. He also supposed that provocation was part of the purpose of the petition. Franklin still sought reconciliation between Britain and America, and he hoped the new colonial secretary might help.

Dartmouth gave Franklin reason for hope. Franklin called on Dartmouth, who wasn't in, and left the petition for his perusal. A few days later Dartmouth requested that Franklin come and discuss it. Franklin did so, and argued the case for Massachusetts' position. "After a long audience he was pleased to say that notwithstanding all I had said or that could be said in support of the petition, he was sure the presenting it at this time could not possibly produce any good," Franklin reported to Thomas Cushing, the speaker of the Massachusetts assembly. "The king would be exceedingly offended." He might ask Parliament for new sanctions against the Americans. "The most favourable thing to be expected was a severe reprimand to the assembly by order of his majesty, the natural consequence of which must be more discontent and uneasiness in the province." Dartmouth declared that he didn't want this to happen. "Possessed as he was with great good-will for New-England, he was extremely unwilling that one of the first acts of his administration with regard to the Massachusetts should be of so unpleasant a nature," Franklin paraphrased. "Minds had been heated and irritated on both sides the water, but he hoped those heats were now cooling, and he was averse to any addition of fresh fuel."

Dartmouth urged Franklin to explain the situation to the Massachusetts assembly, and to refrain from delivering the petition to the king until he heard back. He promised he would not then stand in the way of delivery. Indeed, he assured Franklin he did not now stand in the way. If Franklin insisted, the petition would go forward at once. "But from motives of pure good will to the province, he only wished me not to insist on it till I should receive fresh orders," Franklin wrote.

Franklin consented. "Upon the whole I thought it best not to disoblige him in the beginning of his administration by refusing him what he seemed so desirous of," he told Cushing.

Franklin knew the delay would not sit well with the radicals in Boston. They might well ask themselves why the assembly was paying Franklin if he refused to do the assembly's bidding.

Franklin anticipated the complaints, and sought to blunt them— for his own sake and that of reconciliation—by including in his letter to Cushing a packet the speaker would find most interesting. The packet contained letters written by Thomas Hutchinson, among a few others, to a friend in England. Hutchinson's steadfastness in the face of the destruction of his home and sundry threats to his person had prompted his promotion from lieutenant governor of Massachusetts to governor, and his letters carried greater weight on that account. How the letters came into Franklin's possession, Franklin declined to say to Cushing. Nor did he ever tell anyone. Franklin felt obliged to explain to Cushing why he was trafficking in others' correspondence, a practice inconsistent with the code of an honorable man, let alone the post-master of the American colonies. The letters were crucial, Franklin said, to understanding how matters between America and Britain had reached their current nadir; they "laid the foundation of most if not all our present grievances."

In one such letter, written in early 1769, Hutchinson lamented the irresolution of the British government in the face of the popular resis-tance in Massachusetts. The province must be made to recognize and acknowledge its dependence on the mother country, he said. "If no measures shall have been taken to secure this dependence, or nothing more than some declaratory acts or resolves, *it is all over with us*. The friends of government will be utterly disheartened, and the friends of anarchy will be afraid of nothing, be it ever so extravagant." The gov-ernment must not falter; its next moves must be stern. "There must be an abridgement of what are called English liberties." Hutchinson understood what he was asking, but the crisis demanded no less. "I relieve myself by considering that in a remove from the state of nature to the most perfect state of government there must be a great restraint of natural liberty. I doubt whether it is possible to project a system of government in which a colony 3000 miles distant from the parent state shall enjoy all the liberty of the parent state. I am certain I have never yet seen the projection. I wish the good of the colony when I wish to see some further restraint of liberty rather than the connexion with the parent state should be broken, for I am sure such a breach must prove the ruin of the colony."

Franklin asserted, in his explanation to Cushing, that the Hutchin-son letters had opened his eyes. "My resentment against this country for its arbitrary measures in governing us, conducted by the late minis-ter, has, since my conviction by these papers that those measures were projected, advised and called for by men of character among ourselves, and whose advice must therefore be attended with all the weight that was proper to mislead, and which could therefore scarce fail of mis-leading—my own resentment, I say, has by this means been consid-erably abated." Franklin hoped that the resentment of Cushing and others in the Massachusetts assembly might be abated too.

Franklin expanded on this point. The fault, he said, lay not with the British government, but with Hutchinson and a handful of other British appointees in Boston. Franklin said he had tried to put himself in the shoes of Hutchinson, and imagine what things looked like to him. "A man educated in prepossessions of the unbounded authority of Parliament, etc., may think unjustifiable every opposition even to its unconstitutional exertions," Franklin wrote. But the actions of Hutchinson and the others had gone beyond principled difference. "When I find them bartering away the liberties of their native country for posts, and negotiating for salaries and pensions, for which the money is to be squeezed from the people; and, conscious of the odium these might be attended with, calling for troops to protect and secure the enjoyment of them; when I see them exciting jealousies in the crown and provoking it to wrath against a great part of its faithful subjects, creating enmities between the different countries of which the empire consists; occasioning a great expence to the new country for the payment of needless gratifications to useless officers and enemies; and to the old for suppressing or preventing imaginary rebellions in the new, I cannot but doubt their sincerity even in the political principles they profess, and deem them mere time-servers, seeking their own private emolument through any quantity of public mischief, betrayers of the interest, not of their native country only, but of the government they pretend to serve, and of the whole English empire."

Franklin told Cushing the letters were for his eyes only, and the eyes of others he trusted. They must not be shared more broadly. They must not be published.

FRANKLIN'S INSTRUCTIONS WERE followed for several months. Cushing showed the letters to a few others, and then a few more. Word circulated of their contents, and discontent grew against Hutchinson, as Franklin intended. Indeed, his ban on publication rendered the letters more damaging than publication might have been, for in the absence of the letters themselves, suspicious minds in Massachusetts could conjure no end of evil coming from the dark heart of the governor.

Franklin was pleased at the effect of his coup. "You mention the surprise of gentlemen to whom those letters have been communicated, at the restrictions with which they were accompanied, and which they suppose render them incapable of answering any important end," he wrote to the Reverend Samuel Cooper, a minister to some of the Boston radicals, in the summer of 1773. "The great reason of forbidding their publication was an apprehension that it might put all the possessors of such correspondence here upon their guard, and so prevent the obtaining more of it. And it was imagined that showing the originals to so many as were named, and to a few such others as they might think fit, would be sufficient to establish the authenticity, and to spread through the province so just an estimation of the writers, as to strip them of all their deluded friends, and demolish effectually their interest and influence. The letters might be shown even to some of the governor's and lieutenant governor's partisans; and spoken of to everybody; for there was no restraint proposed to talking of them, but only to copying. And possibly, as distant objects seen only through a mist appear larger, the same may happen from the mystery in this case."

Thomas Hutchinson learned about the circulation of his letters secondhand, from the nasty things said in the assembly about him. He grew angry, and frustrated at his impotence. Until the letters were published, he couldn't rebut the charges made against him, for he didn't know which letters had been pilfered. So he seethed in silence while the assembly approved resolutions denouncing him for his designs against their liberties. "It was not in the power of the governor to put a stop to the proceedings of the house, by a prorogation or dissolution, without a worse consequence than what would follow from their continuing to sit," Hutchinson wrote afterward. "The construction would have been that a consciousness of guilt had induced him to take that measure."

In time the secret proved too good to keep. Hutchinson's defenders denied he had said what was imputed to him; his detractors felt obliged to show he had. The letters were published, and though most of what they contained was innocuous or explainable, his assertion that "there must be an abridgement of what are called English liberties," especially when taken out of context, as it immediately was, made the governor's position even less tenable than it had been. It seemed only a matter of time before the king felt obliged to replace him.

FRANKLIN'S ROLE IN the affair remained unknown to all but Cushing and a few others. Franklin congratulated himself on a job well done. If he reminisced about the time he and Hutchinson had collaborated on a plan for colonial union, he doubtless observed that much had happened since then, and much had drawn them apart. Franklin had little against Hutchinson personally; he might well have judged Hutchinson less culpable than the governor's critics in Massachusetts made him out to be. But there was the larger issue of the empire. Franklin hadn't given up on reconciliation between America and Britain, and if Hutchinson had to lose his job to bring the two back together, Franklin wouldn't weep for his old collaborator.

While the discord he had sown in Boston spread, Franklin preached unity in London. He continued to meet with ministers of the government and members of Parliament, to whom he made straightforward arguments for colonial rights. He meanwhile wrote for the popular press, in which he cast the America case satirically. An essay titled "Rules by which a Great Empire may be reduced to a Small One" chaffed recent administrations for their policies toward America. "In the first place, gentlemen, you are to consider, that a great empire, like a great cake, is most easily diminished at the edges," Franklin wrote anonymously. "Turn your attention therefore first to your remotest provinces; that as you get rid of them, the next may follow in order. That the possibility of this separation may always exist, take special care the provinces are never incorporated with the mother country, that they do not enjoy the same common rights, the same privileges in commerce, and that they are governed by *severer* laws, all of *your enacting*, without allowing them any share in the choice of the legislators." Unfounded suspicion would aid the dismantling of the empire. "However peaceably your colonies have submitted to your government,

shewn their affection to your interest, and patiently borne their grievances, you are to *suppose* them always inclined to revolt, and treat them
accordingly. Quarter troops among them, who by their insolence may
provoke the rising of mobs, and by their bullets and bayonets *suppress*
them. By this means, like the husband who uses his wife ill *from suspicion*, you may in time convert your *suspicions* into *realities*." Maladmin-
istration was essential, particularly in the choice of colonial officials.
"If you can find prodigals who have ruined their fortunes, broken
gamesters or stock-jobbers, these may do well as *governors*, for they
will probably be rapacious and provoke the people by their extortions."
Financial impositions must not be overlooked. "Harass them with
novel taxes." Finally, arrogance and superciliousness should inform
all dealings with the colonists. "They will petition for redress. Let
the Parliaments flout their claims, reject their petitions, refuse even to
suffer the reading of them, and treat the petitioners with the utmost
contempt. Nothing can have a better effect, in producing the alien-
ation proposed, for though many can forgive injuries, *none ever forgave
contempt*."

FRANKLIN WASN'T THINKING of himself when he wrote that last
line, but it soon applied to him. The fuss over the Hutchinson letters
spilled from Boston back to London, provoking appalled or amused—
depending on one's view of the American question—surmise as to who
had sent the letters to Massachusetts. Charges were leveled at this person and that; the charges were indignantly denied. In one case the
finger-pointing caused pistols to be pointed, and then fired, in a duel
over the matter.

Franklin at last felt obliged to break his silence. "Finding that two
gentlemen have been unfortunately engaged in a duel, about a transaction and its circumstances of which both of them are totally ignorant
and innocent, I think it incumbent on me to declare (for the preven-
tion of farther mischief, as far as such a declaration may contribute to
prevent it) that I alone am the person who obtained and transmitted
to Boston the letters in question," he declared in the *London Chronicle*.
He justified his action on the ground that the letters were not private
correspondence between friends. "They were written by public officers
to persons in public station, on public affairs, and intended to procure

public measures." The influence of the letters could only be injurious to the harmony of the empire. "Their tendency was to incense the mother country against her colonies, and, by the steps recommended, to widen the breach, which they effected."

Political London gasped on reading Franklin's admission. His rationalization seemed weak; whatever the motive, his violation of the seal of correspondence put him beyond the pale of honorable discourse. Franklin's friends shook their heads in disappointment, while his enemies rubbed their hands in hope of capitalizing on his misstep.

Before they had the chance, another report from Boston provoked new outrage. The American boycott had persuaded Parliament to repeal most of the Townshend duties, leaving only the tax on tea. In 1773 the tax was reduced by a measure that simultaneously awarded a monopoly on the American tea trade to the British East India Company, a pet of influential members of Parliament. "When the intelligence first came to Boston, it caused no alarm," Thomas Hutchinson recalled of the new arrangement. "The threepenny duty had been paid the last two years without any stir, and some of the great friends of liberty had been importers of tea. The body of people were pleased with the prospect of drinking tea at less expense than ever." Boston's tea merchants alone registered discontent, at losing their business.

The first concerted opposition arose not in Boston but in Philadelphia, where recipients and consumers of tea were denounced as foes of liberty. By this time committees of correspondence efficiently relayed news from one colony to the next regarding the fell designs of the British government and the best methods of foiling them. Boston received news of the Philadelphia tea boycott, and radicals there adopted the same approach. A meeting was held at the Liberty Tree, and the merchants to whom the East India Company's tea was consigned were summoned, in order that they be forced to refuse the tea. They declined the summons and were branded enemies of the people.

Additional meetings were held. Resolves were adopted declaring that none of the noxious tea would be allowed to land on Boston's soil. Three vessels were approaching the harbor just then; the attention of the town focused on these. Again the consignees were pressured to swear they would not accept the shipments. They pleaded their contractual commitments to take delivery, and again they were threatened.

They appealed to Hutchinson. "He foresaw that this would prove a more difficult affair than any which had preceded it," Hutchinson wrote of himself. Heretofore his differences with the radicals had been political, and such damage as had been done him had been confined to his property. But the mood of the town had changed. "He was now to encounter with bodies of the people collected together, and a great proportion of them the lowest part of the people, from whom, when there is no power to restrain them, acts of violence are to be expected." His council of advisers refused to come to his aid. They urged him not to resist the popular will but instead to order the tea ships back to Britain. He refused their recommendation.

The tea ships reached the wharf. Immediately the radicals circulated a notice: "Friends! Brethren! Countrymen! That worst of plagues, the detested tea, shipped for this port by the East India Company, is now arrived in this harbor. The hour of destruction, or manly opposition to the machinations of tyranny, stare you in the face. Every friend to his country, to himself, and posterity is now called upon to meet at Faneuil Hall at nine o'clock this day, at which time the bells will ring, to make an united and successful resistance to this last, worst and most destructive measure of administration."

Thousands of Bostonians attended the meeting. When Hutchinson called upon the justices of the peace to prepare measures to prevent violence, he was condemned as a tool of the British government. "The conduct of Governor Hutchinson, in requiring the justices of the peace in the town to meet and use their endeavours to suppress routs, riots etc., carried a designed reflection upon the people there met together, and was solely calculated to serve the views of administration," the meeting resolved, to loud cheers.

Hutchinson again feared for his personal safety, and grew frustrated at his official impotence. The radicals had taken control of the city, despite lacking any legal authority. He decided he had to make a statement, if only for the record. "He knew he could say nothing which would check the usurpers," he wrote. But he did what he could. He sent the sheriff to the meeting with a proclamation declaring it an unlawful assembly and demanding that those in attendance disperse. Many at the meeting desired to prevent the sheriff from reading the proclamation, but Samuel Adams said they should hear it. It was read and immediately denounced.

The resistance escalated and ramified, with runners sent to the villages around Massachusetts Bay to ensure that none of them receive the ships and circumvent the boycott. Meanwhile the owner of one of the tea ships applied to Hutchinson for protection for his property. "His concern was not for his ship, which he did not believe was in any danger, but he could not tell what would be the fate of the tea on board," Hutchinson recounted. The governor confessed he could offer him little.

That evening a segment of the mob, clothed and painted as Indians to disguise their identities, descended on the wharf where the vessels were tied. They boarded the ships, entered the holds and returned to the decks with the chests of tea. One by one the chests were opened and the tea dumped into the harbor. More than two hours were required to empty more than three hundred tea chests.

Hutchinson learned of the looting as it happened. He held himself blameless. "It was out of his power to have prevented this mischief without the most imminent hazard of much greater mischief," he wrote. "The tea could have been secured in the town in no other way than by landing marines from the men-of-war"—British naval vessels in the harbor—"or bringing to town the regiment which was at the castle, to remove the guards from the ships and to take their places." The memory of the Boston Massacre was fresh in Hutchinson's mind, and he knew it was fresh in the minds of others as well. "This would have brought on a greater convulsion than there was any danger of in 1770," he said of summoning the troops.

Hutchinson felt isolated. Respect for order and the rule of law had all but vanished in Boston; he alone held fast. "The house of representatives openly avowed principles which implied complete independency," he said of the provincial assembly. "The council, appointed by charter to be assisting to him, declared against any advice from which might be inferred an acknowledgment of the authority of Parliament in imposing taxes. The superior judges were intimidated from acting upon their own judgment by the censure of the house of representatives, and by the threats of impeachment of all who shall receive their salaries under the authority of an act of Parliament which had enabled the king to grant them. There was not a justice of peace, sheriff, constable or peace officer in the province who would venture to take cognizance of any breach of law, against the general bent of the people."

The militia was equally cowed. "When he required the colonel of the regiment of militia in the town to use the powers with which by law he was entrusted, he excused himself by urging the hazard to which he would be exposed, and the inefficacy of any attempt." The merest efforts by Hutchinson to protect himself were held against him. "He could not take any measures for his security without the charge of needless precaution in order to bring an odium against the people, when they meant him no harm."

Hutchinson sensed that a divide had been crossed. "This was the boldest stroke which had yet been struck in America," he said. The radicals had succeeded in drawing the masses into their struggle against British authority. Samuel Adams and some others had previously crossed the line, placing themselves outside British law, but their ultimate goal, which Hutchinson identified as independence, required more company. "There was no way of attaining to it but by involving the body of the people in the same circumstances they were in themselves. And it is certain that, ever after this time, an opinion was easily instilled, and was continually increasing, that the body of the people had also gone too far to recede, and that an open and general revolt must be the consequence." Hutchinson shuddered at the thought.

18

THE NEWS OF the Boston Tea Party, as the affair was blithely dubbed in America, reached London shortly after the imperial capital learned that Franklin had been the purveyor of the filched Hutchinson letters. Such sympathy as had survived his admission was all but obliterated by the mass vandalism of the tea cargo. The government wanted someone to blame, and Franklin seemed just the man.

He was summoned to appear before the king's Privy Council, in a building called the Cockpit, after the rooster matches once held on the site. Of the preening politicians who had replaced the feisty gamecocks, none strutted more arrogantly than Alexander Wedderburn, the king's solicitor general. Wedderburn's razor tongue made him feared as a prosecutor and valued as an entertainer; connected Londoners crowded his performances to watch him torment witnesses. On this day the crowd in the Cockpit was larger than usual. Franklin had demonstrated in his session with Parliament that he could handle examination adeptly; the impending battle of wits and words between the two men set the audience abuzz hours ahead of the start.

Wedderburn at once seized the initiative, and never let go. The Massachusetts assembly had cited the Hutchinson letters in petitioning to have Hutchinson and his deputy removed from office for want of confidence; Wedderburn now made those letters, and Franklin's theft of them, the basis for the Crown's rejection of the petition and its condemnation of him. Wedderburn defended Hutchinson's performance as beyond reproach, and adduced earlier evidence from the assembly of its previous confidence in the governor. The members' subsequent loss of confidence was all the work of Franklin, he declared. "Dr. Franklin therefore stands in the light of the first mover and prime conductor of this whole contrivance against his majesty's two governors, and having by the help of his own special confidents and party leaders, first made the assembly *his* agents in carrying on his own secret designs, he now appears before your lordships to give the finishing stroke to the work of his own hands."

Wedderburn asked the council to consider how Franklin must have acquired the correspondence. "The letters could not have come to Dr. Franklin by fair means," he said. "The writers did not give them to him, nor yet did the deceased correspondent, who from our intimacy would otherwise have told me of it. Nothing then will acquit Dr. Franklin of the charge of obtaining them by fraudulent or corrupt means, for the most malignant of purposes—unless he stole them from the person who stole them. This argument is irrefragable."

Wedderburn leveled an accusing finger at Franklin. "I hope, my lords, you will mark the man, for the honour of this country, of Europe, and of mankind," he said. "Private correspondence has hitherto been held sacred, in times of the greatest party rage, not only in politics but religion. He has forfeited all the respect of societies and of men. Into what companies will he hereafter go with an unembarrassed face, or the honest intrepidity of virtue. Men will watch him with a jealous eye; they will hide their papers from him, and lock up their escrutoires. He will henceforth esteem it a libel to be called *a man of letters—homo trium literarum!*" This was a reference to a line from a Roman play in which the three letters were *fur*: thief.

Wedderburn's audience got the reference, and gave him the laugh he sought, at Franklin's expense. The solicitor piled on. He reminded the council that Franklin had concealed his role for months. And his belated explanation, after the duel, had been self-serving in the extreme. "It is impossible to read his account, expressive of the coolest and most deliberate malice, without horror. Amidst these tragical events, of one person nearly murdered, of another answerable for the issue, of a worthy governor hurt in his dearest interests, the fate of America in suspense; here is a man, who with the utmost insensibility of remorse, stands up and avows himself the author of all."

Wedderburn rejected Franklin's assertion that the purloined letters were public because they were written by public men. "Can then a man in a public station have no private friends, and write no private letters?" he demanded. "Will Dr. Franklin avow the principle that he has a right to make all private letters of your lordships his own, and to apply them to such uses as will best answer the purposes of party malevolence? Whatever may have been the confidence heretofore placed in him, such a declaration will surely not contribute to increase it."

Wedderburn argued that Franklin intended nothing less than the dissevering of the empire, whatever he might profess to the contrary. "My lords, Dr. Franklin's mind may have been so possessed with the idea of a great American republic that he may easily slide into the language of the minister of a foreign independent state," the solicitor said. "A foreign ambassador when residing here, just before the breaking out of a war, or upon particular occasions, may bribe a villain to steal or betray any state papers; he is under the command of another state, and is not amenable to the laws of the country where he resides; and the secure exemption from punishment may induce a laxer morality." Franklin gravely mistook things, and he would pay for his error. "Dr. Franklin, whatever he may teach the people at Boston, while he is *here* at least is a subject; and if a subject injure a subject, he is answerable to the law. And the court of chancery will not much attend to his new self-created importance."

Why were Franklin and his friends in the Massachusetts assembly so bent on destroying Governor Hutchinson? asked Wedderburn. Because the governor understood their seditious designs. "He stopped the train which Dr. Franklin's constituents had laid, to blow up the province into a flame, which from thence was to have been spread over the other provinces. This was the real provocation: and for this they have been seeking for some ground of accusation against him."

Wedderburn said more than this, much more. Some of it was so personally scurrilous that the secretaries who recorded his speech declined to reproduce it. But the gist of it all was that Franklin was beneath consideration and unfit to call himself a Briton.

FRANKLIN SAID NOTHING while Wedderburn's barrage persisted. And he said nothing after it ended, choosing not to dignify the solicitor's insults with a reply. The ostensible purpose of the session—to have the Privy Council rule on the Massachusetts petition to remove Hutchinson—admitted but one plausible outcome: denial. The government wasn't going to set a precedent that royally appointed governors could be removed at the whim of colonials. Franklin would be wasting his breath to argue against such inevitability. As for the actual purpose of the Cockpit session—to condemn the Massachusetts assembly by destroying the reputation of its agent—Franklin chose to play no part in that.

He realized that his strategy in transmitting the Hutchinson letters had failed. Indeed, it had done worse than fail: it had produced the opposite result from what he had intended. His goal had been to bring the colonies and the home country closer together by blaming their differences on a few bad actors who might be removed, allowing comity to be restored. Wedderburn had turned this strategy on its head. The solicitor had framed matters as though the Americans were in revolt already, with Franklin the arch-rebel. And by the appreciative laughter that rolled through the Cockpit at Wedderburn's jibes, and the knowing nods that accompanied his insults, his construction had carried the day.

There was the personal element as well—the utter contempt displayed by Wedderburn and mirrored by the Privy lords. Franklin could bear contradiction with equanimity; contradiction was no more than difference of opinions. But contempt was another matter. The contempt in the Cockpit told Franklin that his hope for American equality in an enlightened British empire was a foolish dream. The contempt told him he could never be fully British. "None ever forgave contempt," he had written in his satire on the deconstruction of an empire. What he now felt had nothing of satire in it; he was deadly earnest in silently vowing he would never forgive the contempt directed at him that day.

19

L ORD NORTH, prime minister since 1770, was more respectful in speech and manner than Alexander Wedderburn, but he was no less determined to put the Americans in their place. The outrage in Massachusetts required a swift response, he judged. Summarizing the sins of the colonists from the Stamp Act riots to the dumping of the Boston tea, North demanded rhetorically of Parliament, "Will this country sit still when they see the colony proceeding against your own subjects, tarring and feathering your servants, denying your laws and authority, refusing every direction and advice which you send? Are we, sir, seeing all this, to be silent and give the governor"—Thomas Hutchinson—"no support?" Patience had its virtues, and mercy its merits, but both had their limits. "So clement and so long forbearing has our conduct been that it is incumbent on us now to take a different course." Borrowing a line from Hutchinson, North declared, "Whatever may be the consequence, we must risk something; if we do not, all is over."

What North proposed and Parliament accepted was a set of acts that closed the port of Boston, pending payment for the tossed tea; suspended the Massachusetts charter, and with it the troublesome assembly; mandated that colonial officials charged with crimes be tried in England rather than America; and required the colonies to furnish housing for British troops posted there.

The British called the measures the Coercive Acts; in America they became the Intolerable Acts. Americans, and not just in Massachusetts, judged the measures a direct assault on liberties they had long taken for granted. But what to do? Some in the colonies recommended another petition. If the government in London understood America's whole-hearted opposition to the new laws, they reasoned, the acts would be rescinded.

George Washington judged a petition a waste of time. "Have we not tried this already?" he wrote to Bryan Fairfax, a brother of George Fairfax. "Have we not addressed the Lords, and remonstrated to the Commons? And to what end? Did they deign to look at our petitions? Does it not appear, as clear as the sun in its meridian brightness, that there is a regular, systematic plan formed to fix the right and practice of taxation upon us? Does not the uniform conduct of Parliament for some years past confirm this?" The new measures allowed no other interpretation. "Is there anything to be expected from petitioning after this?" The laws hit Boston hardest, but the rights of all Americans were in jeopardy. Petitions were mere talk, and talk had yielded nothing. "Ought we not, then, to put our virtue and fortitude to the severest test?"

But *what* test? That was the question. Washington suggested reviving the boycott; Bryan Fairfax spoke of withholding payment of debts to British merchants. Others had different ideas. Yet most of those alarmed by the British coercion concluded that a unified American response was essential. Previous attempts at colonial unification, starting with Benjamin Franklin's effort in the 1750s, had yielded only sporadic success; the current crisis demanded something more enduring. The committees of correspondence had started trading views while the Intolerable Acts were still being debated in Parliament; no sooner had the measures been adopted than a call went out for a congress of delegates from the various colonies. Centrally located Pennsylvania volunteered Philadelphia as the site of the congress, which convened in September.

Washington was selected as one of Virginia's delegates. The post was his for the asking; no one in the province matched his combination of wealth and public accomplishment. The only question was whether he would ask. He had never been a leader in Virginia politics, preferring to let others do the debating and drafting of legislation. To the degree he engaged with policy issues, he focused on the land question. The Proclamation of 1763 had been modified by a series of treaties between the British government and the Iroquois and other tribes that had the effect of opening parts of the Ohio Valley to settlement. Washington was among the first to press claims to the region, on his own behalf and that of soldiers who had served with him in the French and Indian War. As compensation for their service, the government of Virginia had promised the soldiers grants of land in the West. The Proclamation had stayed the promise, but the new treaties raised the prospect that the veterans would finally receive their land. Washington pressed the Virginia government on the matter; as success came into view, in the autumn of 1770 he made a long tour of the Ohio country to select parcels for himself and his men.

He wound up with 20,000 acres; the rest of the 200,000-acre grant was allotted in smaller parcels to junior officers and enlisted men. Washington took pride in what his persistence had produced. He explained the slow process to one of his fellow officers, and said, "I might add without much arrogance, that if it had not been for my unremitted attention to every favorable circumstance, not a single acre of land would ever have been obtained."

Some of the soldiers intended to settle on their land; Washington sought tenants to settle on his. "TWENTY THOUSAND Acres of LAND on the *Ohio* and *Great Kanhawa*," he advertised. He offered to divide the land into parcels of any size and to lease said parcels on "moderate terms," contingent on the lessee's clearing, fencing and tilling of the land. The improvements would benefit the improvers; they would also benefit Washington, by raising the land's value. "As these lands are among the first which have been surveyed in the part of the country they lie in, it is almost needless to premise that none can exceed them in luxuriance of soil, or convenience of situation, all of them lying upon the banks either of the Ohio or Kanhawa, and abounding with fine fish and wild fowl of various kinds, as also in most excellent meadows, many of which (by the bountiful hand of nature) are, in their present state, almost fit for the scythe," Washington declared. Interested parties should contact his agent—and cousin— Lund Washington at Alexandria.

When tenants failed to appear in sufficient numbers to suit his ambitions, Washington hatched another plan: to import tenants from abroad. Germans from the Rhine region called the Palatinate had settled in New York and Pennsylvania; Washington supposed Palatines might be drawn to his Ohio lands. As they were often poor, he would pay their transport in exchange for an indenture of their services. "To make matters as easy and agreeable as possible to these emigrants, I will engage, on my part, that the indentures shall be considered in no other light than as a security for reimbursing to me every expense

I am under, with interest, in importing them, removing them to the land, and supporting them there, till they can raise a crop for their own subsistence," he explained to a potential partner in the project. "I can also engage to set them down upon as good land as any in that country, and, where there is neither house built, nor land cleared, I will allow them an exemption of rent four years, and, where there is a house erected, and five acres of land cleared and fit for cultivation, two years." Some of the Palatines were Protestant and others Catholic, but none were Anglicans, the majority in Virginia. Yet this would not be an issue. "I see no prospect of these people being restrained in the smallest degree, either in their civil or religious principles; which I take notice of, because these are privileges which mankind are solicitous to enjoy, and upon which emigrants must be anxious to be informed."

THE TUMULT IN AMERICA following passage of the Intolerable Acts interrupted Washington's colonization scheme, and drew him more deeply into politics. He joined forces with George Mason to draft resolves for their Fairfax County neighbors to vote on, and he chaired the meeting where the votes were cast. The resolves were numerous and wordy; they denounced the Intolerable Acts, rejected the supremacy of Parliament, endorsed the Continental Congress, recommended a renewed boycott of British imports, and proposed an embargo of exports to Britain. Washington and Mason forswore any desire to separate from Britain, but added, "Though we are its subjects, we will use every means which Heaven hath given us to prevent our becoming its slaves."

Washington gathered with the other members of the house of burgesses to protest the Intolerable Acts; when the Virginia governor dissolved the house, they relocated to Williamsburg's Raleigh Tavern and chose delegates to the Continental Congress. Washington decided he must be one. "An innate spirit of freedom first told me that the measures which administration hath for some time been and now are most violently pursuing are repugnant to every principle of natural justice," he wrote to Bryan Fairfax, "whilst much abler heads than my own hath fully convinced me that it is not only repugnant to natural right but subversive of the laws and constitution of Great Britain itself in the establishment of which some of the best blood in the kingdom hath been spilt." The British had demonstrated their unfitness to rule America. "The acts of a British Parliament are no longer governed by the principles of justice," Washington said. "It is trampling upon the valuable rights of Americans, confirmed to them by charter and the constitution they themselves"—the British—"boast of." At an earlier stage of the dispute, an honest man might have dismissed Britain's intrusions on American rights as inadvertent; no longer. "These measures are the result of deliberation, and attempted to be carried into execution by the hand of power," Washington said.

The time had come to make a stand. "For my own part, I shall not undertake to say where the line between Great Britain and the colonies should be drawn," Washington conceded to Fairfax. "But I am clearly of opinion that one ought to be drawn, and our rights clearly ascertained. I could wish, I own, that the dispute had been left to posterity to determine, but the crisis is arrived when we must assert our rights, or submit to every imposition, that can be heaped upon us, till custom and use shall make us as tame and abject slaves, as the blacks we rule over with such arbitrary sway." The scheduled congress was the right first step to foil the plot of the British against America. "Nothing but unanimity in the colonies (a stroke they did not expect) and firmness can prevent it."

UNANIMITY CAME HARD at the Continental Congress. Twelve of the thirteen colonies sent delegates; Georgia abstained, being involved in a war with Indians and loath to lose the help of the British army. Some states chose delegates by vote of their assemblies; others followed Virginia in giving the task to special conventions.

Washington left Mount Vernon on August 31, accompanied by fellow delegates Patrick Henry and Edmund Pendleton. They reached Philadelphia on September 4, in time for the next day's opening session of the Congress.

Washington was a presence in the deliberations, but a silent one. "He never spoke in public," John Adams recalled of the Congress. Washington reserved his views for the dinners that followed each session, and for other informal gatherings. "In private he advocated a non-exportation as well as a non-importation agreement," Adams wrote. "With both, he thought, we should prevail. Without either, he thought it doubtful."

Non-importation was something all the delegates could agree on, for it had worked in the past. Non-exportation—an embargo—was untested. And it was potentially painful, if not ruinous, for commercial farmers like Washington. If he couldn't sell his tobacco to Britain, his revenue stream would dry up and his operations would be in jeopardy. Yet he was willing to give an embargo a try. Other measures the Congress considered ranged from fresh petitions to new statements of constitutional philosophy. After weeks of debate, often heated and occasionally bitter, the Congress approved a set of resolves declaring that the Americans were entitled to "life, liberty and property"; that the first settlers of America had possessed "all the rights, liberties, and immunities of free and natural-born subjects within the realm of England," and that their descendants had never relinquished these rights; that the foundation of English liberty was the right of the people to legislate for themselves, and that since the Americans were not and could not be represented in Parliament, they were entitled to "a free and exclusive power of legislation in their several provincial legislatures"; that Britain might regulate imperial commerce but that such regulation must exclude "every idea of taxation internal or external, for raising a revenue on the subjects, in America, without their consent." The resolutions decried the transfer of trials to England, the peacetime positioning of troops in America, and the dissolving of any colonial legislature.

Joseph Galloway proposed a plan Franklin might have put forward had he been in Philadelphia. Galloway urged the creation of an American council comprising delegates from all the colonies; it would be to America what Parliament was to Britain. And as Parliament stood to the king, so the American council would stand to a president-general appointed by the king. The plan certainly would have been rejected by Parliament and the king, but they never had the opportunity, for the plan was rejected by the Continental Congress, in a close vote.

Besides approving the resolutions, the Congress set a deadline for the revival of the boycott—December 1, 1774—unless Parliament by then had repealed the Intolerable Acts. An embargo of colonial exports was held in abeyance. And the Congress agreed to convene again, in the spring of 1775, if satisfaction had not been achieved.

The result was less than the radicals at the Congress had hoped for, and more than the conservatives desired. John Adams, closer to the radicals than to the conservatives, wondered if anything, truly, had been accomplished. As the delegates were departing, Adams compared thoughts with Patrick Henry. "I expressed a full conviction that all our resolves, declarations of rights, enumeration of wrongs, petitions and remonstrances and addresses, associations and non-importation agreements, though they might be expected by the people of America and necessary to cement their union, would be but waste water in England," Adams recalled afterward.

Henry disagreed only slightly. "He thought they might be of some use among the people of England but would be totally lost upon the government," Adams wrote. Adams continued his recollection: "I had just received a hasty letter written to me by Major Joseph Hawley of Northampton"—Massachusetts—"containing 'A few broken hints' as he called them, of what was proper to be done, and concluding with these words: 'After all, we must fight.' This letter I read to Mr. Henry, who listened to it with great attention, and as soon as I had pronounced the words 'After all, we must fight,' he erected his head and with an energy and vehemence that I can never forget, broke out with '*By God, I am of that man's mind.*' I put the letter into his hand, and when he had read it he returned it to me with an equally solemn asseveration that he agreed entirely in opinion with the writer."

Henry was less hopeful for reconciliation than most of his Virginia colleagues. Richard Henry Lee brimmed with confidence that Britain would change its policies. "We shall infallibly carry all our points," Lee told Adams, according to Adams's recollection. "You will be completely relieved; all the offensive acts will be repealed, the army and fleet will be recalled and Britain will give up her foolish project." Most of the other Virginians concurred.

"Washington only was in doubt," Adams said. Adams recalled Washington's judgment that an embargo would have to accompany a boycott before Britain would pay attention. Summarizing, Adams wrote, "Henry was clear in one opinion, Lee in an opposite opinion, and Washington doubted between them."

WASHINGTON WAS MORE ASSERTIVE in private letters. Robert Mackenzie was a British officer Washington knew from the French and Indian War; he was also a skeptic on the good faith of the Bostonians. Washington undertook to change Mackenzie's mind. "Permit me with the freedom of a friend (for you know I always esteemed you) to express my sorrow that fortune should place you in a service that must fix curses to the latest posterity upon the contrivers and, if success (which, by the by, is impossible) accompanies it, execrations upon all those who have been instrumental in the execution," Washington wrote to Mackenzie. He acknowledged that a soldier like Mackenzie had to do his duty. "But I conceive when you condemn the conduct of the Massachusetts people, you reason from effects, not causes; otherwise you would not wonder at a people who are every day receiving fresh proofs of a systematic assertion of an arbitrary power, deeply planned to overturn the laws and constitution of their country, and to violate the most essential and valuable rights of mankind, being irritated, and with difficulty restrained from acts of the greatest violence and intemperance. For my own part, I confess to you candidly that I view things in a very different point of light from the one in which you seem to consider them; and though you are led to believe by venal men—for such I must take the liberty of calling those new-fangled counsellors who fly to and surround you, and all others, who, for honors or pecuniary gratifications, will lend their aid to overturn the constitution and introduce a system of arbitrary government—although you are taught, I say, by discoursing with such men, to believe that the people of Massachusetts are rebellious, setting up for independency and what not, give me leave, my good friend, to tell you, that you are abused, grossly abused."

Massachusetts wasn't rebellious, Washington said; it was merely determined. It wasn't seeking independence. And neither were the other colonies. "I can announce it as a fact that it is not the wish or interest of that government, or any other upon this continent, separately or collectively, to set up for independence." Lest Mackenzie have any doubts on this subject, Washington reiterated: "I am well satisfied that no such thing is desired by any thinking man in all North America; on the contrary, that it is the ardent wish of the warmest advocates for liberty, that peace and tranquillity, upon constitutional grounds, may be restored, and the horrors of civil discord prevented."

Yet the American colonies *would* insist on their constitutional rights, Washington said. "None of them will ever submit to the loss of those valuable rights and privileges which are essential to the happiness of every free state, and without which, life, liberty and property are rendered totally insecure." They would fight for their rights, if it came to that. Britain would bear the blame, which might be very great. "More blood will be spilled on this occasion, if the ministry are determined to push matters to extremity, than history has ever yet furnished instances of in the annals of North America, and such a vital wound will be given to the peace of this great country, as time itself cannot cure, or eradicate the remembrance of."

BENJAMIN FRANKLIN OBSERVED the Philadelphia proceedings from afar. In the immediate aftermath of his ordeal in the Cockpit, he thought he would be heading for America soon; he inferred from his treatment by the king's solicitor that further efforts to change opinions in London would be a waste of energy. He wrote to William, "This line is just to acquaint you that I am well, and that my office of Deputy-Postmaster is taken from me." The government had lost no time depriving Franklin of the job in which he had served the American colonies and the empire very well. The dismissal seemed further reason for despairing of reasonable policies from the government as it was currently constituted.

William himself held a government post, an important one. When Franklin was in the favor of the British government, in the early 1760s, he had helped William win appointment as royal governor of New Jersey. Franklin was proud of the boy—by this time a man in his thirties. Yet William lacked his father's facility with money, and he had a wife who expected more than Deborah ever asked of Franklin. Between one thing and another, the governorship proved a drain on William's finances and caused him to turn to his father to cover the difference between revenues and expenses. William had sometimes talked of retiring to a farm he owned, musing that he would do better there.

Franklin suggested now might be the time. He supposed the Crown and ministry would visit the alleged sins of the father upon the son. "There is no prospect of your being ever promoted to a better government," Franklin told William flatly, referring to a more remunerative governorship than New Jersey's. "That you hold has never defrayed its expences." He added, "I wish you were well settled in your farm. 'Tis an honester and a more honourable, because a more independent, employment." At the time of Franklin's writing, William could not have received word of the Cockpit session. "You will hear from others the treatment I have received," Franklin said. "I leave you to your own reflections and determinations upon it, and remain ever—Your affectionate Father."

William would indeed reflect on his father's experience, and make his own determination. What that should be was hard to know. Franklin himself couldn't quite decide. Although his first letter after the Cockpit suggested resignation for William, his second took the opposite view. Franklin had been talking to men with connections in the government. "Some tell me that it is determined to displace you likewise, but I do not know it as certain," he reported to William. There seemed to be some reluctance to fire William outright. "Perhaps they may expect that your resentment of their treatment of me may induce you to resign, and save them the shame of depriving you whom they ought to promote." Franklin urged William not to give them the satisfaction. "Let them take your place if they want it, though in truth I think it scarce worth your keeping, since it has not afforded you sufficient to prevent your running every year behind hand with me." Franklin shared with William a rule he had devised: "One may make something of an injury, nothing of a resignation."

As for himself, Franklin judged that his public service was at an end. His youngest sister, Jane Franklin Mecom, had long been a confidante; at this point she was sixty-two and he sixty-eight. "You will hear before this comes to hand that I am deprived of my office," he wrote to her in Boston. "Don't let this give you any uneasiness. You and I have almost finished the journey of life; we are now but a little way from home, and have enough in our pockets to pay the post chaises." Franklin judged that he had gotten the better of his enemies. "Intending to disgrace me, they have rather done me honour. No failure of duty in my office is alleged against me; such a fault I should have been ashamed of. But I am too much attached to the interests of America, and an opposer of the measures of administration. The displacing me therefore is a testimony of my being uncorrupted."

Franklin watched the political storm that produced the Coercive Acts. "It is yet unknown what measures will be taken here on the occasion," he wrote to the committee of correspondence of the Massachusetts assembly following his receipt of their account of the Boston Tea Party. "But the clamour against the proceeding is high and general."

Franklin thought the destruction of the tea would do Massachusetts no good. "I am truly concerned, as I believe all considerate men are with you, that there should seem to any a necessity for carrying matters to such extremity as, in a dispute about public rights, to destroy private property." Franklin shared the objection to the East India Company's monopoly, but he thought the mob had misidentified the enemy. "The offensive measure of sending their teas did not take its rise with them, but was an expedient of the ministry." Franklin hoped Massachusetts would demonstrate its devotion to the rule of honest law, and by that means stave off worse. "I cannot but wish and hope that before any compulsive measures are thought of here, our General Court"—the Massachusetts General Court—"will have shewn a disposition to repair the damage and make compensation to the company." It was crucial for Massachusetts, and America, to be in the right in their dispute with British government, so that "if war is finally to be made upon us, which some threaten, an act of violent injustice on our part, unrectified, may not give a colourable pretence for it."

Massachusetts refused to repent, and the mood in London grew worse. "I suppose we never had since we were a people so few friends in Britain," Franklin told Thomas Cushing. "The violent destruction of the tea seems to have united all parties here against our province." Franklin once more urged that the tea be paid for. "Such a step will remove much of the prejudice now entertained against us, and put us again on a fair footing in contending for our old privileges as occasion may require."

After Parliament went ahead with the Coercive Acts, Franklin observed the American reaction, and was gratified by the unity the colonies displayed. "I rejoice to find that the whole continent have so justly, wisely, and unanimously taken up our cause as their own," he wrote to Cushing. The convening of the Continental Congress was especially praiseworthy. "This is an unexpected blow to the ministry, who relied on our being neglected by every other colony: this they depended on as another circumstance that must force our immediate submission, of which they were likewise perfectly sure." Yet the government was in no mood to back down. "The language of those about the court rather is that the king must now go on, whatever may be the consequence."

Franklin informed Cushing that he was doing what he could to educate America's remaining friends in Parliament. "I have been taking pains among them to show the mischief that must arise to the whole from a dismembering of the empire, which all the measures of the present mad administration have a tendency to accomplish." Yet he had to be discreet. "I must not now relate to you with whom I have conferred, nor the conversations I have had on this subject, lest my letter fall into wrong hands," Franklin told Cushing. This remark might have been oblique chastisement of Cushing for letting the Hutchinson letters be published; Franklin wasn't going to make that same mistake again.

He allowed himself some hope. "I may say, I have reason to think a strong push will be made at the very beginning of the session to have all the late acts reversed, and a solemn assurance given America that no future attempts shall be made to tax us without our consent," he wrote.

THE BOSTON TEA RIOT convinced Thomas Hutchinson that his usefulness as Massachusetts governor was at an end. "I see no prospect, my Lord, of the government of this province being restored to its former authority without the interposition of the authority in England," he wrote to Lord Dartmouth, the colonial secretary. "I rather think the anarchy will continually increase until the whole province is in confusion." The radicals behind the destruction of the tea had captured the popular imagination. "The people, my Lord, in every colony, more or less, have been made to believe that by firmly adhering to their demands, they may obtain a compliance in every one of them."

Hutchinson observed that until but a few years before, no one in America had questioned the authority of Parliament. Now nearly everyone did. The government faced a hard task. "A conviction of this authority, or a persuasion that, at all events, the Parliament will maintain it against all opposition, will restore order," Hutchinson said. "But how this conviction or persuasion is to be effected, I must humbly submit to your Lordship." He did offer one suggestion, which coincided with what Benjamin Franklin had recommended. Rather than impose taxes directly upon the Americans, the government should set revenue quotas for the colonies and let their own assemblies levy the taxes. "I beg leave to suggest that it would greatly tend, if it is not absolutely necessary, to conciliate the affections of the colonies to the parent state."

Hutchinson's advice, like that of Franklin, had no effect on a Parliament bent on coercing the Americans, rather than conciliating them. In the bargain, the administration in London replaced Hutchinson with Thomas Gage, who also served as commander of British military forces in America. The message was clear: the Americans would be compelled to acknowledge the authority of Parliament, by force if need be.

Hutchinson took leave of his post, and of his native land. He sailed for England at the beginning of the summer of 1774, and reached London a month later. His ship had scarcely tied up at the dock when Lord Dartmouth whisked him away to brief the king.

"How do you do, Mr. Hutchinson, after your voyage?" asked George politely.

"Much reduced, sir, by sea-sickness, and unfit on that account, as well as my New England dress, to appear before your Majesty," Hutchinson replied.

Dartmouth interjected that he himself was to blame for Hutchinson's unconventional appearance. But he thought it vital that the king hear from one fresh from the front, so to speak.

George agreed. "How did you leave your government, and how did the people receive the news of the late measures in Parliament?" he asked.

"When I left Boston, we had no news of any act of Parliament except the one for shutting up the port, which was extremely alarming to the people," Hutchinson said.

Dartmouth offered that Boston had asked the other colonies to close their own ports in solidarity with Boston. Some had agreed, but Virginia had refused.

George looked at Hutchinson. "Do you believe that the account from Virginia is true?" he asked.

"I have no other reason to doubt it except that the authority for it seems to be only a newspaper, and it is very common for articles to be inserted in newspapers without any foundation," Hutchinson replied.

Dartmouth complimented Hutchinson by saying that merchants, clergy and lawyers had written expressing support for the governor's handling of affairs.

George nodded approval and agreement. "I do not see how it could be otherwise," he said. "I am sure his conduct has been universally approved of here by people of all parties."

Hutchinson accepted the compliment. "I am very happy in your Majesty's favorable opinion of my administration," he said.

"I am entirely satisfied with it," George reiterated. "I am well acquainted with the difficulties you have encountered, and with the abuse and injury offered you." He singled out the actions of Benjamin Franklin. "Nothing could be more cruel than the treatment you met with in betraying your private letters."

Hutchinson explained the origin of the letters. "The correspondence, sir, was not of my seeking," he said. "It was a mere matter of friendly amusement, chiefly a narrative of occurrences, in relating of which I avoided personalities as much as I could, and endeavored to treat persons, when they could not be avoided, with tenderness, as much as if my letters were intended to be exposed." He added at once, "I had no reason to suppose they ever would be exposed."

George asked if Hutchinson knew how the letters wound up in New England.

"Doctor Franklin has made a public declaration that he sent them," Hutchinson gently reminded. "And the Speaker"—Thomas Cushing—"has acknowledged to me that he received them." Hutchinson went on to say that Cushing had told him Franklin had insisted that the letters be shown to no more than a handful of people.

George asked who these handful were.

Hutchinson listed them, including "the two Mr. Adamses."

"I have heard of one Mr. Adams," the king said, referring to Samuel Adams. "But who is the other?"

"He is a lawyer, sir," Hutchinson said.

"Brother to the other?"

"No, sir, a relation. He has been of the House"—the assembly—"but is not now."

Hutchinson described how the letters came to be published, despite Franklin's insistence that they be closely held. Hutchinson had put the matter to Cushing. "I asked him how he could be guilty of such a breach of trust as to suffer them to be made public. He excused it by saying that he was against their being brought before the House, but was overruled; and when they had been read there, the people abroad compelled their publication, or would not be satisfied without it." Afterward, the letters were returned to Franklin.

"Where *is* Dr. Franklin?" the king inquired.

Dartmouth spoke up. "I believe, sir, he is in town. He was going to America, but I fancy he is not gone."

"I heard he was going to Switzerland, or to some part of the Continent," said George.

Dartmouth said he too had heard such reports but didn't think they were true.

George returned to the mistreatment the governor had suffered. "In such abuse, Mr. Hutchinson, as you met with, I suppose there must have been personal malevolence as well as party rage."

Hutchinson replied that no one had attacked his personal character. "The attacks have been on my public conduct, and for such things as my duty to your Majesty required me to do, and which you have been pleased to approve of. I don't know that any of my enemies have complained of a personal injury."

"I see that they threatened to pitch and feather you," George said.

"*Tar* and feather, may it please your Majesty. But I don't remember that I was ever threatened with it."

"What guard had you, Mr. Hutchinson?"

"I depended, sir, on the protection of Heaven. I had no other guard. I was not conscious of having done anything of which they could justly complain or make a pretence of offering violence to my person. I was not sure, but I hoped they only meant to intimidate. By discovering that I was afraid, I should encourage them to go on. By taking measures for my security, I should expose myself to calumny."

George nodded. He said he heard that Hutchinson lived in the country, outside of Boston. Presumably he was safer there.

"I have lived in the country, sir, in the summer for twenty years," Hutchinson replied. "But except the winter after my house was pulled down, I have never lived in the country in winter until the last." It was part of his refusing to be intimidated.

George asked about the leaders of the assembly. He'd heard of Speaker Cushing. "Is he not a great man of the party?"

"He has been many years speaker, but a speaker, sir, is not always the person of the greatest influence," Hutchinson said. Samuel Adams was the true leader of the opposition.

"What gives him his importance?" asked George.

"A great pretended zeal for liberty, and a most inflexible natural temper," Hutchinson said. "He was the first that publicly asserted the independency of the colonies upon the kingdom, or the supreme authority of it."

George realized that some of the trouble with America owed to its growing strength and self-confidence. "Does population greatly increase in your province?" he asked.

"Very rapidly, sir. I used to think that Dr. Franklin, who has taken much pains in his calculations, carried it too far when he supposed the inhabitants of America, from their natural increase, doubled their number in 25 years. But I rather think now that he did not." Massachusetts was doubling every generation, and it was one of the slower-growing colonies. Immigrants liked warmer winters than New England offered.

George asked about the Indians. How many were left in Massachusetts?

"They are almost extinct," Hutchinson said. "Perhaps there are 50 or 60 families at most upon the eastern frontier, where there is a small fort maintained, though I conceive the inhabitants would not be in the least danger. It looks, sir, as if in a few years the Indians would be extinct in all parts of the Continent."

"To what is that owing?"

"I have thought, sir, in part to their being dispirited at their low despicable condition among the Europeans who have taken possession of their country and treat them as an inferior race of beings," Hutchinson said. "But more to the immoderate use of spirituous liquors."

Dartmouth called a halt to the conversation, saying he feared, after the governor's difficult journey, that he must be tired.

"I observed that so gracious a reception made me insensible of this," Hutchinson remarked in his diary.

Hutchinson departed impressed with the king's mastery of detail in the politics of the colonies. "It is surprising that he should have so perfect a knowledge of the state of his dominions," he wrote to a friend.

A S DARTMOUTH SURMISED, Benjamin Franklin was indeed still in London. Angry though he was at his treatment by Alexander Wedderburn and the Privy Council, Franklin continued to hope for reconciliation between America and Britain. And as long as he could hope, he would continue to work to bring the two sides back together.

For the few months after the Cockpit session, he kept "a cool, sullen silence," as he told William, awaiting a more propitious moment for raising the American question with potentially helpful members of Parliament. His chance seemed to come at the end of the summer of 1774. Franklin received an invitation to speak with Lord Chatham, who as William Pitt, leader of the House of Commons, had helped turn the tide in the Seven Years' War and now held a seat in the House of Lords. "That truly great man Lord Chatham received me with abundance of civility, enquired particularly into the situation of affairs in America, spoke feelingly of the severity of the late laws against Massachusetts, gave me some account of his speech in opposing them and expressed great regard and esteem for the people of that country, who he hoped would continue firm and united in defending by all peaceable and legal means their constitutional rights," Franklin told William after the fact. Franklin assured Chatham that the people of Massachusetts would do just as he advised. Chatham said he was pleased to hear it.

"I then took occasion to remark to him that in former cases great empires had crumbled first at their extremities from this cause: that countries remote from the seat and eye of government, which therefore could not well understand their affairs for want of full and true information, had never been well governed, but had been oppressed by bad governors on presumption that complaint was difficult to be made and supported against them at such a distance," Franklin wrote to William. For many decades Britain had avoided this error by allowing the colonies to govern themselves, he observed to Chatham. Britain's hands-off policy had yielded great benefits to the empire. "Hence had arisen such satisfaction in the subjects, and such encouragement to new settlements, that had it not been for the late wrong politics (which would have Parliament to be *omnipotent*, though it ought not to be so unless it could at the same time be *omniscient*) we might have gone on extending our western empire adding province to province as far as the South Sea"—the Pacific Ocean. "I lamented the ruin which seemed impending over so fine a plan, so well adapted to make all the subjects of the greatest empire happy, and I hoped that if his lordship with the other great and wise men of this nation would unite and exert themselves; it might yet be rescued out of the mangling hands of the present set of blundering ministers, and that the union and harmony between Britain and her colonies so necessary to the welfare of both might be restored."

Chatham seemed quite taken by Franklin's vision of an enlightened, expanded empire. "He replied with great politeness that my idea of extending our empire in that manner was a sound one and worthy of a great, benevolent and comprehensive mind," Franklin reported to William. Yet Chatham asked whether the other Americans shared Franklin's vision. "He mentioned an opinion prevailing here that America aimed at setting up for itself as an independent state."

Franklin said this wasn't so. "I assured him that having more than once travelled almost from one end of the continent to the other and kept a great variety of company, eating, drinking and conversing with them freely, I never had heard in any conversation from any person, drunk or sober, the least expression of a wish for a separation, or hint that such a thing would be advantageous to America."

Chatham appeared pleased with the conversation. "He expressed much satisfaction in my having called upon him, and particularly in the assurances I had given him that America did not aim at independence," Franklin recorded. Chatham said he hoped they might speak again; Franklin answered that he would be delighted.

At about this time, Franklin received an unexpected message. An intermediary brought a challenge to a chess match from Caroline Howe, sister of Lord Richard Howe, an admiral and political figure known to be friendly toward the Americans. Franklin had played chess as a young man, but hadn't pursued the pastime. He said he was out of practice. Yet if the lady insisted, he would oblige. The intermediary accompanied him to the home of Mrs. Howe (who had married a man named Howe, sparing her the inconvenience of a name change). The chess went well, and Franklin agreed to a rematch, unaware that more was envisioned. "I had not the least apprehension that any political business could have any connection with this new acquaintance," he recounted.

On the second visit, though, the conversation turned political. "What is to be done with this dispute between Britain and the colonies?" asked Mrs. Howe. "I hope we are not to have a civil war."

"They should kiss and be friends," Franklin replied. "What can they do better? Quarrelling can be of service to neither, but is ruin to both."

"I have often said that I wished government would employ you to settle the dispute for them," Mrs. Howe said. "I am sure nobody could do it so well. Don't you think that the thing is practicable?"

"Undoubtedly, madam, if the parties are disposed to reconciliation, for the two countries have really no clashing interest to differ about. It is rather a matter of punctilio, which two or three reasonable people might settle in half an hour." Yet Franklin had little confidence it would happen. "I thank you for the good opinion you are pleased to express of me," he said. "But the ministers will never think of employing me in that good work. They choose rather to abuse me."

"Aye, they have behaved shamefully to you," said Mrs. Howe. "And indeed some of them are now ashamed of it themselves."

In Franklin's recounting to William, he said he considered this conversation to be more an accident than otherwise, and gave it little thought. Yet on a subsequent visit, on Christmas Day, Mrs. Howe's brother appeared. Lord Howe knew Franklin and struck up a conversation. "After some extremely polite compliments as to the general motives for his desiring an acquaintance with me, he said he had a particular one at this time, namely the alarming situation of our affairs with America," Franklin told William. Howe said it was the opinion of his friends that no one was better placed than Franklin to conduct a reconciliation between Britain and the colonies, if he would undertake it. "He was sensible I had been very ill treated by the ministry, but he hoped that would not be considered by me in the present case." Howe said he was certain some ministers regretted the way Franklin had been treated and were looking for a way out of the present impasse. "If he were himself in administration, he should be ready to make me ample satisfaction."

Franklin said he wouldn't let the injuries done him personally stand in the way of reconciliation. "Those done my country were so much greater that I did not think the others at this time worth mentioning," he paraphrased to William. "That, besides, it was a fixed rule with me not to mix my private affairs with those of the public; that I could join with my personal enemy in serving the public, or, when it was for its interest, with the public in serving that enemy."

Howe nodded in satisfaction, and asked Franklin to draw up terms on which he thought a reconciliation might be reached. He hoped to present such terms to the appropriate ministers in due course. For the time being, they should be kept secret, as should the fact that he and Franklin were meeting. His sister's house could be their point of rendezvous, as she was known to play chess with Franklin, and she was of course his sister. Each could visit her without attracting attention.

Franklin initially declined to draft the paper Howe requested, saying the position of the Americans had been made quite clear. He had no authority to go beyond this. But on second thought he said he would try.

While he did, he heard once more from Lord Chatham. News of the resolves of the Continental Congress had just arrived, and Chatham wanted to discuss them. Franklin went to Chatham's home. "He received me with an affectionate kind of respect that from so great a man was extremely engaging," Franklin recorded. "But the opinion he expressed of the congress was still more so. They had acted, he said, with so much temper, moderation and wisdom that he thought it the most honourable assembly of statesmen since those of the ancient Greeks and Romans in the most virtuous times." Chatham didn't agree with every point the Congress made. He thought the government had a right to keep an army in the colonies. "The rest he admired and honoured. He thought the petition decent, manly and properly expressed." He asked Franklin about the perseverance of the colonies and their ability to maintain their united front. Franklin replied that America was serious and determined. "He seemed well satisfied," Franklin told William. "He expressed a great regard and warm affection for that country, with hearty wishes for their prosperity, and that government here might soon come to see its mistakes and rectify them."

When Parliament resumed business in the new year, Chatham invited Franklin to come with him to the House of Lords. Attendance was a rare honor for an Englishman, and rarer still for an American. Franklin understood that Chatham was making a point, and accepted at once. As it happened, even Chatham was challenged by the door-keeper, who said the particular entrance Chatham was approaching was reserved for peers, their brothers and their eldest sons. Franklin could not enter. Taking Franklin by the arm, Chatham guided him to another door and announced loudly, "This is Dr. Franklin, whom I would have admitted." The door opened and Franklin walked through.

Chatham had been ill and not in the habit of attending the sessions of the Lords. His presence created a stir. His solicitude toward Franklin amplified the effect. Ears bent toward the old hero as he offered a motion to remove the troops from Boston as a gesture of reconciliation.

"I was quite charmed with Lord Chatham's speech in support of his motion," Franklin recounted. "He impressed me with the highest idea of him as a great and most able statesman." Other peers supported Chatham's motion.

But they didn't have the votes. "All availed no more than the whistling of the winds," Franklin wrote. "The motion was rejected."

Yet hope remained, or so Chatham and Howe told Franklin. During the following weeks Franklin continued to discuss American affairs with them, helping prepare a new set of proposals, which Chatham presented to the House of Lords. Franklin, once more in attendance, observed the reaction. "When he sat down, Lord Dartmouth rose and very properly said, it contained matter of such weight and magnitude as to require much consideration, and he therefore hoped the noble earl did not expect their lordships to decide upon it by an immediate vote, but would be willing it should lie upon the table for consideration," Franklin recounted. Chatham said he wished for nothing more.

This didn't suit others in the chamber. "Lord Sandwich rose, and in a petulant, vehement speech opposed its being received at all, and gave his opinion that it ought to be immediately REJECTED with the contempt it deserved," Franklin wrote to William. "That he could never believe it the production of any British peer. That it appeared to him rather the work of some American; and turning his face towards me, who was leaning on the bar, said he fancied he had in his eye the person who drew it up, one of the bitterest and most mischievous enemies this country had ever known." The gaze of the lords turned to Franklin, who feigned not to notice. "I kept my countenance as immoveable as if my features had been made of wood."

Chatham denounced the insinuation that he had presented another man's work as his own. And he came to Franklin's defense. "He made no scruple to declare that if he were the first minister of this country, and had the care of settling this momentous business, he should not be ashamed of publicly calling to his assistance a person so perfectly acquainted with the whole of American affairs as the gentleman alluded to and injuriously reflected on—one, he was pleased to say, whom all Europe held in high estimation for his knowledge and wisdom, and ranked with our Boyles and Newtons, who was an honour not to the English nation only but to human nature." Franklin remarked to William, "I found it harder to stand this extravagant compliment than the preceding equally extravagant abuse, but kept as well as I could an unconcerned countenance, as not conceiving it to relate to me."

Once more Chatham's effort failed. He was willing to try yet again, and received support from Howe and others. Howe informed Franklin that there was talk in the ministry of having him—Howe—travel to America as a commissioner to negotiate with the colonies on behalf of the government. He inquired whether Franklin, who knew so much more about America than he did, would be willing to go along. "What he now wished was to be authorized by me to say that I consented to accompany him and would cooperate with him in the great work of reconciliation," Franklin recorded. Howe added "that the influence I had over the minds of people in America was known to be very extensive, and that I could, if any man could, prevail with them to comply with reasonable propositions."

"I replied that I was obliged to his lordship for the favourable opinion he had of me, and for the honour he did me in proposing to make use of my assistance; that I wished to know what propositions were intended for America," Franklin told William. "If they were reasonable ones in themselves, possibly I might be able to make them appear such to my countrymen, but if they were otherwise, I doubted whether that could be done by any man and certainly I should not undertake it."

Howe was satisfied with the response. "His lordship then said that he should not expect my assistance without a *proper consideration*," Franklin wrote. "That the business was of great importance, and if he undertook it, he should insist on being enabled to make generous and ample appointments for those he took with him, particularly for me, as well as a firm promise of subsequent rewards."

"My lord," responded Franklin, "I shall deem it a great honour to be in any shape joined with your lordship in so good a work, but if you hope service from any influence I may be supposed to have, drop all thoughts of procuring me any previous favour from ministers. My accepting them would destroy the very influence you propose to make use of; they would be considered as so many bribes to betray the interest of my country. Only let me see the propositions, and if I approve of them, I shall not hesitate a moment, but will hold myself ready to accompany your lordship at an hour's warning."

The idea that Howe might travel to America stalled at this point, for reasons Franklin couldn't determine. Franklin continued to speak with potential friends in Parliament. Howe urged him to visit Lord Hyde, formerly the postmaster general, who knew Franklin from that position. Franklin did so. Hyde asked Franklin's opinion of a proposal by Lord North under which the colonies would voluntarily pay taxes, as they had before, but that the British government would reserve the right to say how much they should pay and to employ force if they fell short.

Franklin said this would never do. "The proposition was similar to no mode of obtaining aids that ever existed except that of a highwayman who presents his pistol and hat at a coach window, demanding no specific sum, but if you will give all your money or what he is pleased to think sufficient, he will civilly omit putting his own hand into your pockets," he summarized. "If not, there is his pistol."

Hyde intimated that Franklin was allowing personal resentment of his harsh treatment at the hands of the ministry and its friends to stand in the way of a compromise solution. He hoped Franklin could get past that. Like Howe, he said there would be something in it for Franklin. "I was, as he understood, highly esteemed among the Americans," Franklin recorded. "That if I would bring about a reconciliation on terms suitable to the dignity of government, I might be as highly and generally esteemed here, and be honoured and rewarded perhaps beyond my expectation."

Franklin told Hyde he had things very wrong. "That I was not the reserved man imagined, having really no secret instructions to act upon; that I was certainly willing to do everything that could reasonably be expected of me. But if any supposed I could prevail with my countrymen to take black for white and wrong for right, it was not knowing either them or me. They were not capable of being so imposed on, nor was I capable of attempting it."

As warrant of his personal good faith, Franklin offered to pay for the ruined tea out of his own pocket, in exchange for the repeal of the Coercive Acts. He said he had no instruction to do so, nor any assurance that he would be reimbursed. "I must have risqued my whole fortune, which I thought few besides me would have done," Franklin remarked afterward.

IT WAS ALL in vain. The government had planted its banner. It was not going to repeal the Coercive Acts until Massachusetts yielded on the basic point at issue: that Parliament ruled America as surely as it ruled Britain. Massachusetts would *not* yield that point, and Franklin definitely wouldn't yield it on Massachusetts' behalf.

He finally bowed to the weight of the evidence he had seen and felt. Parliament was terminally pigheaded; reason had lost its power. In annoyance and anger, Franklin drafted a memorial to Lord Dartmouth calling not for payment by Massachusetts for the ruined tea, but for payment *to* Massachusetts for the damages the colony had suffered as a result of the Coercive Acts. "The blockade of Boston, now continued nine months, hath every week of its continuance done damage to that town equal to what was suffered there by the India Company," Franklin asserted. "It follows that such exceeding damage is an *injury* done by this government"—the British government—"for which reparation ought to be made."

Franklin wasn't serious. Or rather, he didn't seriously think the British government would entertain such a proposal. He simply wanted to show that justice, not to mention the British constitution, lay on the side of the colonists. He shared his draft with Thomas Walpole, a cousin of Horace Walpole and a Franklin ally, who warned him against delivering it. Doing so would inflame the situation, Walpole said, and might place Franklin at risk of arrest and imprisonment.

Franklin grudgingly conceded the point. "I had no desire to make matters worse, and, being grown cooler, took the advice so kindly given me," he told William. He filed the draft memorial away, out of sight of Dartmouth or anyone else.

And he boarded a ship sailing to America. For a decade he had spared no effort trying to keep the rift between the colonies and the British government from becoming irreparable. He had done all he could; he could do no more. The Atlantic was growing wider by the week; better to cross it while he still could.

WITH US HERE, things wear a disagreeable aspect," George Washington in Virginia wrote to a friend while Franklin was packing his bags to leave London. "The minds of men are exceedingly disturbed at the measures of the British government." Not knowing what Franklin had just experienced, Washington still clung to hope that a separation might be avoided, but he had little confidence Parliament would make this possible. If anything, it seemed to be pushing for a confrontation. "Matters are drawing to a point," he said.

Washington would be ready. And so would Virginia. Young men of the province mustered with their militia units even as a new convention of Virginia leaders pondered how to make best use of them. "A great number of very good companies were raised in many counties in this colony, before it was recommended to them by the convention, and are now in excellent training," Washington observed.

The Virginians weren't alone in bracing to defend themselves. Militia in Massachusetts stockpiled weapons in towns and villages west of Boston. Governor and general Thomas Gage got wind of the caching and sent a column of soldiers to seize the arms. The minutemen, as the Massachusetts militia called themselves, refused to yield. At Lexington on April 19, the colonials and the British regulars exchanged fire. Eight of the militiamen were killed; one British regular was wounded.

The British column, commanded by Lieutenant Colonel Francis Smith, proceeded to Concord. But the shooting had aroused the neighborhood, and more militia turned out. Additional shots were exchanged. Smith reversed field and led his troops back toward Boston. The militia followed the British and harassed them with sporadic fire from behind fences and trees. The tactic was maddening to the British, who deemed it uncivilized; it was also quite effective. By the time the redcoats reached the safety of Boston, they had lost more than two hundred killed or wounded, and the militia were proclaiming a brilliant victory.

When Washington heard of the events in Massachusetts, he tried to parse their political motivation and military consequence. "General Gage acknowledges that the detachment under Lieutenant-Colonel Smith was sent out to destroy private property, or, in other words, to destroy a magazine, which self-preservation obliged the inhabitants to establish," he wrote to George William Fairfax. A plainer violation of American rights was hard to imagine. "And he also confesses, in effect at least, that his men made a very precipitate retreat from Concord." Washington judged that Gage and the British had been lucky to escape a more thorough manhandling by the minutemen. "From the best accounts I have been able to collect of that affair, indeed from every one, I believe the fact, stripped of all coloring, to be plainly this, that if the retreat had not been as precipitate as it was, and God knows it could not well have been more so, the ministerial troops must have surrendered, or been totally cut off. For they had not arrived in Charlestown (under cover of their ships) half an hour before a powerful body of men from Marblehead and Salem was at their heels, and must, if they had happened to be up one hour sooner, inevitably have intercepted their retreat to Charlestown. Unhappy it is, though, to reflect, that a brother's sword has been sheathed in a brother's breast, and that the once happy and peaceful plains of America are either to be drenched with blood or inhabited by slaves."

The political events of the previous decade had pushed Washington ever closer to a decision about America's fate. The resort to arms now forced his hand. With fighting under way, America's foremost soldier could not stand aside. "Sad alternative!" he observed to Fairfax about the choice between slavery and war. "But can a virtuous man hesitate in his choice?"

WASHINGTON WAS WRITING from Philadelphia, where the Continental Congress had reconvened. The previous year he had kept in the background; this year he stood front and center. He arrived in Philadelphia wearing his Virginia military uniform of buff and blue; without saying a word he let the Congress know he was ready to take the field on behalf of his countrymen. The first order of business of the

Congress was to embrace Massachusetts' fight as America's fight, and to call for the creation of an army drawing from all the colonies. This was swiftly done.

The second order of business was to appoint a commander for the Continental Army. Washington was the obvious choice but not an automatic one. His experience and reputation placed him ahead of the alternative candidates; the fact that he was a Virginian would emphasize the continental character of the army, which currently consisted of Massachusetts men mostly and some other New Englanders.

Yet this geographical element caused certain delegates to object to Washington's appointment. Massachusetts was leading the armed resistance with singular success, they said; Massachusetts should lead the new army. John Hancock of Boston thought the command ought to be his. Hancock had played a key role in readying the Massachusetts militia, and although lacking in command experience, he thought he deserved the job. Or at least he deserved an offer, which he might decline in favor of someone else.

John Adams refused to flatter Hancock's vanity. Adams decided, on geographical grounds as well as military ones, that the command must go to Washington. "Accordingly," he recalled later, "when Congress had assembled I rose in my place and in as short a speech as the subject would admit, represented the state of the colonies, the uncertainty in the minds of the people, their great expectations and anxiety, the distresses of the army, the danger of its dissolution, the difficulty of collecting another, and the probability that the British army would take advantage of our delays, march out of Boston and spread desolation as far as they could go. I concluded with a motion in form that Congress would adopt the army at Cambridge and appoint a general, that though this was not the proper time to nominate a general, yet as I had reason to believe this was a point of the greatest difficulty, I had no hesitation to declare that I had but one gentleman in my mind for that important command, and that was a gentleman from Virginia who was among us and very well known to all of us, a gentleman whose skill and experience as an officer, whose independent fortune, great talents and excellent universal character, would command the approbation of all America, and unite the cordial exertions of all the colonies better than any other person in the union."

Adams observed the effect of his nomination on the two men most interested. "Mr. Washington, who happened to sit near the door, as soon as he heard me allude to him, from his usual modesty darted into the library room. Mr. Hancock, who was our president, which gave me an opportunity to observe his countenance, while I was speaking on the state of the colonies, the army at Cambridge and the enemy, heard me with visible pleasure, but when I came to describe Washington for the commander, I never remarked a more sudden and sinking change of countenance. Mortification and resentment were expressed as forcibly as his face could exhibit them."

Adams's argument carried the hour, and Washington won the unanimous approval of the Congress. Even Hancock came around, conceding the strength of the case for Washington. "Mr. Hancock, however, never loved me so well after this," Adams noted.

Washington accepted the appointment with due humility. "Though I am truly sensible of the high honor done me in this appointment, yet I feel great distress from a consciousness that my abilities and military experience may not be equal to the extensive and important trust," he declared to the gathered delegates. "However, as the Congress desire it, I will enter upon the momentous duty and exert every power I possess in the service and for support of the glorious cause."

He broke the news to his wife, Martha, that he wouldn't be coming home. "You may believe me, my dear Patsy, when I assure you, in the most solemn manner, that, so far from seeking this appointment, I have used every endeavor in my power to avoid it, not only from my unwillingness to part with you and the family, but from a consciousness of its being a trust too great for my capacity, and that I should enjoy more real happiness in one month with you at home than I have the most distant prospect of finding abroad, if my stay were to be seven times seven years. But as it has been a kind of destiny that has thrown me upon this service, I shall hope that my undertaking it is designed to answer some good purpose."

To his brother-in-law he declared, "I am now embarked on a tempestuous ocean." Washington wasn't sure where he might find a safe harbor, if such a harbor existed. He couldn't promise results, only an honest effort. "I can answer but for three things: a firm belief of the justice of our cause, close attention in the prosecution of it, and the strictest integrity." These would have to suffice.

Part V

Rebellion to Tyrants

I ARRIVED HERE on Friday evening," Benjamin Franklin wrote from Philadelphia to David Hartley, an English friend, on Monday, May 8, 1775, "and the next morning was unanimously chosen by the general assembly a delegate for the ensuing congress, which is to meet on Wednesday." The congress was the Continental Congress, for which Washington and the other delegates were just then arriving. "You will have heard before this reaches you of the commencement of a civil war," Franklin continued to Hartley. "The end of it perhaps neither myself, nor you, who are much younger, may live to see." Franklin had learned of the fighting in Massachusetts only on his arrival in America. "I find here all ranks of people in arms, disciplining themselves morning and evening, and am informed that the firmest union prevails throughout North America." Hartley much admired Franklin and sympathized with the Americans; Franklin wanted him to know how the commencement of hostilities had galvanized the colonies.

Franklin had left London in an attitude of discouragement, convinced that his dream of an Anglo-American empire would never come to pass. His spirits mellowed on the six-week voyage to America, which featured fair weather and easy sailing, and allowed time for scientific observation of the weather and the ocean currents. But his mental climate grew dark again after he arrived in America and heard of the outbreak of fighting. The more he learned about the actions of General Gage in Massachusetts before and after Lexington, the angrier he grew. "The governor had called the assembly to propose Lord North's pacific plan," Franklin wrote to Joseph Priestley, another English friend and admirer, "but before the time of their meeting, began cutting of throats. You know it was said he carried the sword in one hand, and the olive branch in the other; and it seems he chose to give them a taste of the sword first." Gage's treachery would cost Britain dearly, Franklin said. "All America is exasperated by his conduct, and more firmly united than ever. The breach between the two countries is grown wider, and in danger of becoming irreparable."

Franklin realized it wasn't like him to feel as he did. "You see I am warm," he wrote to Jonathan Shipley, an English friend of America. "And if a temper naturally cool and phlegmatic can, in old age, which often cools the warmest, be thus heated, you will judge by that of the general temper here, which is now little short of madness." Franklin blamed Gage for commencing the current crisis at Lexington. "Gage's perfidy has now made him universally detested." But Gage's actions were encouraged and endorsed by groups in Britain that treated Americans as inferior beings. Citing some men Shipley knew well, Franklin went on, "The humane Sir W. Draper, who had been hospitably entertained in every one of our colonies, proposes, in his papers called *The Traveller*, to excite the domestic slaves you have sold us to cut their master's throats. Dr. Johnson"—Samuel Johnson, the lexicographer—"a court pensioner, in his *Taxation no Tyranny* adopts and recommends that measure, together with another of hiring the Indian savages to assassinate our planters in the back settlements. They are the poorest and most innocent of all people, and the Indian manner is to murder and scalp men, women and children. His book I heard applauded by Lord Sandwich in Parliament, and all the ministerial people recommended it." Shipley had remarked that if war had to come between America and Britain, he hoped it would be carried on as by nations that once had been friends and hoped to be friends again. Franklin answered that the administration in London and its allies seemed not to share his view. "This is making war like nations who never had been friends, and never wish to be such while the world stands." He spoke again of his own reaction: "When I consider that all this mischief is done my country, by Englishmen and Protestant Christians, of a nation among whom I have so many personal friends, I am ashamed to feel any consolation in a prospect of revenge." He struggled to find his consolation elsewhere. "I choose to draw it rather from a confidence that we shall sooner or later obtain reparation. I have proposed therefore to our people that they keep just accounts and never resume the commerce or the union till satisfaction is made."

Franklin's anger turned him against some of his oldest friends. William Strahan had championed Franklin from before Franklin's arrival in London as colonial agent; for decades the two men were as close as friends could be. But Strahan was siding with the British government against the American colonies. Franklin declared their friendship at an end. "You are a member of Parliament, and one of that majority which has doomed my country to destruction," he wrote. "Look upon your hands! They are stained with the blood of your relations! You and I were long friends; you are now my enemy, and I am yours."

Franklin held this letter for a day, as was his custom when he felt emotion getting the better of him. He decided against sending it, not because he changed his mind about Strahan, but because he prided himself on keeping emotion out of his work.

Although Franklin's Pennsylvania allies had immediately voted him a delegate to the Continental Congress, some other delegates eyed him with suspicion. He had been in England for most of the previous two decades, and was known to have formed close relationships with powerful people. His son, moreover, was the king's man in New Jersey. Samuel Adams openly questioned Franklin's devotion to the colonies' cause, and few rose to defend him.

Franklin did himself no favors by seeking out Joseph Galloway, his longtime collaborator in Pennsylvania politics. Galloway still hoped the empire could be saved, yet, concluding that the independence men had taken control of the Congress, he had retired from politics. In his absence, Sam Adams and the other radicals branded him an enemy of American freedom. Franklin nonetheless visited Galloway at his country home outside Philadelphia, and shared the latest news from London. He read to Galloway the journal he had written summarizing his efforts on behalf of American rights.

During one session at Galloway's, William Franklin joined the other two men. Franklin knew William held the government in London in higher esteem than he did; in the office William held, he could do no less.

The question was whether he should continue to hold that office. William had deflected Franklin's written suggestions that he should resign his governorship; now that they were meeting face-to-face, each assumed the topic would come up again.

It did. Galloway plied his guests with wine, which loosened their tongues. "The glass having gone about freely, the Doctor at a late hour opened himself and declared in favor of measures for attaining to independence," Thomas Hutchinson later wrote in his diary, having just heard the story from Galloway. Franklin "exclaimed against the corruption and dissipation of the kingdom, and signified his opinion that from the strength of opposition, the want of union in the ministry, the great resources in the colonies, they would finally prevail. He urged Galloway to come into the Congress again."

Galloway declined, repeating that the Congress was no longer an honestly deliberative body. It was, in its own way, as biased as Parliament. Beyond this, Galloway didn't support independence. He still took the view Franklin had taken until recently: that the British empire, for all its faults, was a powerfully positive force in the world. From what he had seen of Sam Adams and the Sons of Liberty, American freedoms were in greater danger from them than from anything London had done. He told Franklin of the death threats he himself had received; these included a hangman's noose left on his doorstep.

William Franklin sided with Galloway against his father. Radicals in New Jersey had attacked him for simply trying to uphold the law. William shared his own stories of threats and attempts at intimidation; he agreed with Galloway that American liberties would succumb sooner at the hands of radicals like Sam Adams than from the legitimate acts of Parliament. William made clear he would not be intimidated; he would not resign his office.

As the evening waned, Franklin realized he had lost his son. He shouldn't have been surprised; William was simply proving as independent-minded as Franklin himself. William's beliefs and interests were no longer his father's, and now he didn't hesitate to say so.

FRANKLIN WAS GROWING resigned to American independence, even while lending his support to an effort that appeared to affirm the opposite. "The Congress met at a time when all minds were so exasperated by the perfidy of General Gage and his attack on the country people that propositions of attempting an accommodation were not much relished," Franklin explained to Joseph Priestley. "And it has been with difficulty that we have carried another humble petition to the crown, to give Britain one more chance, one opportunity more of recovering the friendship of the colonies; which however I think she has not sense enough to embrace, and so I conclude she has lost them forever."

The petition came to be called the Olive Branch Petition. It avowed the colonies' continued loyalty to the British crown, blaming the bad policies of the recent years on Parliament. Those policies had included attacks on the persons and property of colonists; hence the fighting, which on the American side was nothing more than self-defense. The petition asked the king to reverse the evils done and restore the comity that had existed between the colonies and the mother country before all the troubles began.

Many of those supporting the petition, including Franklin, who helped draft it, understood that the petition's distinction between the policies of Parliament and those of the king was a political fiction. Not for a century had the Crown governed independently of Parliament. The primary audience for the petition was not King George, who would certainly reject it, but fence-sitters in America, who clung to the hope that the old relationship between America and Britain might be restored. For Franklin and others who increasingly saw no alternative to independence, the purpose of the petition was to force the king to embrace the policies the Americans found so hateful. By driving him publicly into the arms of Parliament, which the independence party had already written off, the petition would make independence inevitable.

NOT ALL THE DELEGATES thought the petition a good idea. "The Congress is not yet so much alarmed as it ought to be," John Adams wrote in secret to James Warren. The secrecy was required by the pledge of confidence all the delegates had taken, which Adams hereby violated. "There are still hopes that ministry and Parliament will immediately recede as soon as they hear of the battle of Lexington, the spirit of New York and Philadelphia, the permanency of the union of the colonies etc.," he continued derisively. "I think they are much deceived and that we shall have nothing but deceit and hostility, fire, famine, pestilence and sword from administration and Parliament." Yet Adams judged it necessary to humor those who demanded the petition. "You will see a strange oscillation between love and hatred, between war and peace, preparations for war, and negotiations for peace," he told Warren. "We must have a petition to the King, and a delicate proposal of negotiation etc. This negotiation I dread like death. But it must be proposed. We can't avoid it. Discord and total disunion would be the certain effect of a resolute refusal to petition and negotiate."

Adams was counting on the rejection of the petition by the British government. "My hopes are that ministry will be afraid of negotiation as well as we, and therefore refuse it," he told Warren. "If they agree to it, we shall have occasion for all our wit, vigilance and virtue to avoid being deceived, wheedled, threatened or bribed out of our freedom." Adams urged moving boldly toward independence. "We ought immediately to dissolve all ministerial tyrannies and custom houses, set up governments of our own, like that of Connecticut"—the most self-governing of the colonies—"in all the colonies, confederate together like an indissoluble band for mutual defense, and open our ports to all nations immediately." Referring to himself, Adams concluded, "This is the system that your friend has aimed at promoting from first to last, but the colonies are not yet ripe for it."

London responded as Adams hoped and Franklin expected. King George refused to receive the petition, having, by the time it arrived, declared the colonies to be in rebellion. His judgment was confirmed by another letter from Adams to James Warren, which was intercepted by British intelligence. "In confidence, I am determined to write freely to you this time," Adams began, once more violating the pledge of confidence. "A certain great fortune and piddling genius, whose fame has been trumpeted so loudly, has given a silly cast to our whole doings." Warren knew that Adams was referring to John Dickinson, the "American Farmer" and the principal drafter of the Olive Branch Petition. Dickinson himself, and others who read Adams's letter when it was promptly published, inferred the identification. "We are between hawk and buzzard," Adams continued. "We ought to have had in our hands a month ago the whole legislative, executive and judicial of the whole continent, and have completely modeled a constitution, to have raised a naval power and opened all our ports wide, to have arrested every friend to government on the continent and held them as hostages for the poor victims in Boston"—where General Gage had entrenched his army upon the people. "And then opened the door as wide as possible for peace and reconciliation. After this they might have petitioned and negotiated and addressed etc., if they would. Is all this extravagant? Is it wild? Is it not the soundest policy?"

George and the British government's principal ministers were already convinced the Americans were a pack of ungrateful rebels; Adams's intercepted letter, in conjunction with the Olive Branch Petition, suggested they were liars as well. Adams was projecting an independent government for the colonies. The letter's chief effect was to sabotage the British friends of America, who had been arguing that the Americans merely wanted their old rights back. The effort at reconciliation, whether sincere, as Dickinson intended it, or cynical, as Franklin and Adams deemed it, fell flat.

FRANKLIN COMMENCED work on the national constitution Adams recommended. He drafted a charter for what he called "The United Colonies of North America." Franklin's use of "colonies" was a nod to the Olive Branch Petition, which was still en route to England; to have employed a term like "states" would have given away the game entirely. But the draft otherwise described a confederation independent of Britain. The separate provinces would bind themselves into a "firm league of friendship" for the purpose of promoting "the security of their liberties and properties, the safety of their persons and families, and their mutual and general welfare." Autonomy would be the guiding principle. "Each colony shall enjoy and retain as much as it may think fit of its own present laws, customs, rights, privileges, and peculiar jurisdictions within its own limits; and may amend its own constitution as shall seem best to its own assembly or convention." A "general congress" would coordinate the efforts of the separate colonies; the congress would have the power of determining war and peace, of forming alliances with other countries, of settling disputes among the colonies, of planting new colonies, and of making "such general ordinances as, though necessary to the general welfare, particular assemblies cannot be competent to."

Franklin's proposed constitution won enough support that he was allowed to read it to the Continental Congress and to leave his draft on the table for others to examine. But its implicit endorsement of independence made a mockery of the Olive Branch Petition, whose supporters refused to countenance a vote on Franklin's constitution and insisted that any mention of it be kept out of the journal of the Congress.

Even so, the Congress authorized Franklin to make a separate start toward a national government. The interception of Adams's letter, along with the seizure of other correspondence, convinced the Congress that a postal system independent of Britain was essential to even a narrow defense of American rights. And who better to create the new system than the man who had built the old system? Franklin got the job, and set to work.

He had other duties as well. The united colonies, whether independent or not, required representation to the Indian tribes, if only to keep them from siding with the British in the event of full war. Franklin, while a member of the Pennsylvania assembly, had negotiated with the Indians of Pennsylvania and won their trust; he was assigned the task of establishing relations with the Indians of Ohio. He meanwhile presided over a committee of public safety for Pennsylvania, distinct from the Continental Congress. In this capacity he reprised his work organizing and arming the Pennsylvania militia two decades earlier.

A S PRESIDENT OF THE COMMITTEE of public safety, Franklin corresponded regularly with George Washington, who was busy trying to meld the colonial militias gathered before Boston into the Continental Army the Congress had authorized. The British retreat from Concord left Thomas Gage's force bottled up in Boston, which in those days occupied a peninsula connected to the mainland by a narrow neck. The Patriot forces—as those resisting British authority called themselves—had gained confidence from the punishment they had inflicted on the retreating British, but they were untrained, unorganized and utterly inexperienced in anything like siege warfare. Moreover, they lacked artillery with which to bombard the British position in Boston. Yet they managed to keep Gage and the British within the city.

On one occasion before Washington's arrival, the British had sallied out. North of Boston, across a channel, lay the peninsula of Charlestown, commanded by the heights of Bunker Hill and Breed's Hill. The rebels hadn't occupied the hills, but Gage appreciated that if they did, and if they acquired artillery, they could fire down on Boston and make it uninhabitable. He determined to take the heights before the rebels did. But they got wind of the British plans through sympathizers in the city, and the British force dispatched across the channel met stiff resistance. In the first set battle of the developing war, the British succeeded in taking the heights, but at sobering cost. The Bunker Hill victory disabused Gage and the British of any idea that the Americans could be easily scattered.

Washington arrived two weeks later. He surveyed the situation he inherited, and wasn't encouraged. "I found a mixed multitude of people here, under very little discipline, order, or government," he wrote to his brother John. "I found the enemy in possession of a place called

Bunker's Hill, on Charles Town Neck, strongly entrenched, and forti-
fying themselves. I found part of our army on two hills (called Winter
and Prospect Hills) about a mile and a quarter from the enemy on
Bunker's Hill, in a very insecure state; I found another part of the
army at this village"—Cambridge, where Washington established his
headquarters—"and a third part at Roxbury, guarding the entrance in
and out of Boston."

Washington set to work rationalizing these haphazard positions.
"My whole time since I came here has been employed in throwing
up lines of defence at these three several places, to secure, in the first
instance, our own troops from any attempts of the enemy, and, in the
next place, to cut off all communication between their troops and the
country," he told John. "To do this, and to prevent them from penetrat-
ing into the country with fire and sword, and to harass them if they do,
is all that is expected of me; and if effected, must totally overthrow the
designs of administration, as the whole force of Great Britain in the
town and harbor of Boston can answer no other end than to sink her
under the disgrace and weight of the expense."

Even at this early moment, Washington understood that the key to
victory was avoiding defeat. He didn't have to beat the British; he simply had to outlast them. The weight of a long and distant war would
eventually undo the British effort to deprive Americans of their liberty.

Not that avoiding defeat would be easy. "Their force, including
marines, Tories, etc., are computed, from the best accounts I can get, at
about twelve thousand men; ours, including sick absent, etc., at about
sixteen thousand," Washington told John. "But then we have a semicircle of eight or nine miles to guard, to every part of which we are
obliged to be equally attentive; whilst they, situated as it were in the
center of the semicircle, can bend their whole force (having the entire
command of the water), against any one part of it with equal facility.
This renders our situation not very agreeable, though necessary." Even
so, things were improving. "By incessant labor (Sundays not excepted),
we are in a much better posture of defence now than when I first came."

Washington had an advantage over Gage in the form of a largely
friendly populace. Many of the Tories, or Loyalists, in the region
around Boston had fled into the city and taken shelter with the British
army there, leaving the outskirts to Washington and the Patriots. At
the same time, enough Patriots remained within the city that Gage

had difficulty keeping secrets from them, and when they ventured out, as they managed to do, they carried valuable information to Washington at Cambridge, three miles to the west. "By very authentic intelligence lately received out of Boston from a person who saw the returns, the number of regulars (including I presume the marines) the morning of the action on Bunker's Hill amounted to 7533 men," Washington told John. "Their killed and wounded on that occasion amounted to 1043, whereof 92 were officers. Our loss was 138 killed, 38 missing, and 276 wounded." The situation of the British appeared to be deteriorating. "The enemy are sickly, and scarce of fresh provisions. Beef, which is chiefly got by slaughtering their milk cows in Boston, sells from one shilling to eighteen pence sterling per pound; and that it may not get cheaper or more plenty I have drove all the stock, within a considerable distance of this place, back into the country, out of the way of the men-of-war's boats." The British had employed the boats to snatch cows from the countryside. "In short, I have done, and shall continue to do, everything in my power to distress them."

Would this be enough? Washington couldn't tell. "I can see no reason why they should not, if they ever attempt it, come boldly out and put the matter to issue at once," he said. With his own army still unorganized, he wasn't sure he could prevent a British breakout and the scattering of his force. "If they think themselves not strong enough to do this," Washington continued, "they surely will carry their arms (having ships of war and transports ready) to some other part of the continent." Such a move would put the conflict, and Washington's challenge, in a whole new light.

WASHINGTON AND GAGE SHARED a military culture both had learned under British arms. Part of that culture dictated decent treatment of prisoners and exchanges where possible. But the issue was complicated in the present conflict by the fact that in British eyes, the Patriots were not legitimate combatants but rebels and traitors. They were entitled to nothing but the harshest treatment should they be captured.

Washington raised the prisoner issue with Gage, following reports from Boston that captured Americans were being treated badly. "I understand that the officers engaged in the cause of liberty and their country, who by the fortune of war have fallen into your hands, have been thrown indiscriminately into a common gaol appropriated for felons," he wrote; "that no consideration has been had for those of the most respectable rank, when languishing with wounds and sickness; that some have been even amputated in this unworthy situation." This was intolerable, Washington said. "Let your opinion, sir, of the principle which actuates them be what it may, they suppose they act from the noblest of all principles, a love of freedom and their country. But political principles, I conceive, are foreign to this point. The obligations arising from the rights of humanity and claims of rank are universally binding and extensive, except in case of retaliation."

Washington mentioned the retaliation exception deliberately. "My duty now makes it necessary to apprize you, that, for the future, I shall regulate my conduct towards those gentlemen who are or may be in our possession exactly by the rule you shall observe towards those of ours now in your custody. If severity and hardship mark the line of your conduct, painful as it may be to me your prisoners will feel its effects. But if kindness and humanity are shown to ours, I shall with pleasure consider those in our hands only as unfortunate, and they shall receive from me that treatment to which the unfortunate are ever entitled."

Gage refused to take instructions on the obligations of a British commander from a rebel provincial. In a letter pointedly addressed to "George Washington, Esq.," Gage replied, "To the glory of civilized nations, humanity and war have been compatible, and compassion to the subdued is become almost a general system. Britons, ever preeminent in mercy, have outgone common examples, and overlooked the criminal in the captive. Upon these principles your prisoners, whose lives by the law of the land are destined to the cord"—the hangman's noose—"have hitherto been treated with care and kindness, and more comfortably lodged than the king's troops in the hospitals, indiscriminately it is true, for I acknowledge no rank, that is not derived from the king."

Gage threw the charge of mistreatment back at Washington. "My intelligence from your army would justify severe recrimination," he said. "I understand there are of the king's faithful subjects some taken by the rebels laboring like negro slaves to gain their daily subsistence, or reduced to the wretched alternative, to perish by famine, or take arms against their king and country." Washington was either misinformed or a liar, Gage said. "Those who have made the treatment of the prisoners in my hands, or of your other friends in Boston, a pretence for such measures, found barbarity upon falsehood." Gage dismissed Washington's threats; should he inflict the harm on prisoners he threatened, he would gain nothing. "British soldiers, asserting the rights of the state, the laws of the land, the being of the constitution, will meet all events with becoming fortitude. They will court victory with the spirit their cause inspires, and, from the same motive will find the patience of martyrs under misfortune."

Washington realized he was wasting his time debating Gage. Yet the charge Gage had leveled about the mistreatment of British prisoners required a reply. "I have taken time, sir, to make a strict inquiry, and find it has not the least foundation in truth," he answered. If anything, the prisoners had been treated more charitably than their actions deserved. "Even those execrable parricides whose counsels and aid have deluged their country with blood"—American Tories— "have been protected from the fury of a justly enraged people." Gage should take a lesson in the meaning of military rank. "You affect, sir, to despise all rank not derived from the same source with your own. I cannot conceive one more honorable than that which flows from the uncorrupted choice of a brave and free people, the purest source and original fountain of all power." Speaking for that brave and free people, Washington warned again about mistreatment of prisoners. "If your officers, our prisoners, receive a treatment from me different from that which I wished to show them, they and you will remember the occasion of it."

WASHINGTON COMMANDED the Continental Army, but he didn't dictate American strategy. The Continental Congress, headed by the disappointed John Hancock, presumed to keep overall direction of the war in its own hands. While Washington was shoring up the siege of Boston, the Congress ordered an invasion of Quebec. The operation was cast as a liberation of "the oppressed inhabitants of Canada," as the Congress addressed the northerners in a letter encouraging their cooperation. "You and your wives and your children are made slaves," the letter said, referring to the same acts of Parliament the lower thirteen colonies were resisting. "You have nothing that you can call your own, and all the fruits of your labour and industry may be taken from you whenever an avaricious governor and a rapacious council may incline to demand them." The American army came in friendship, and hoped for friendship in return. "We presume you will not, by doing us injury, reduce us to the disagreeable necessity of treating you as enemies."

Command of the invasion was given to Philip Schuyler, a prominent New Yorker, a veteran of the French and Indian War, and a member of the Continental Congress until commissioned as major general and placed in charge of the Northern Department in the Continental Army. Schuyler's army would ascend the Hudson River and continue north along Lakes George and Champlain to Montreal and thence to Quebec City, still the military stronghold of the province.

Washington proposed to complement Schuyler's force with a second column, moving more directly upon Quebec. "It is to penetrate into Canada by way of Kennebec River, and so to Quebec by a route ninety miles below Montreal," Washington explained to Schuyler. Washington guessed Schuyler might not welcome this backup, reading it as a vote of little confidence; he assured Schuyler otherwise.

He explained that the second column would complicate the British defense of Quebec. "It would make a diversion that would distract Carleton"—General Guy Carleton, the governor of Quebec province, who was then thought to be at Montreal. "He must either break up and follow this party to Quebec, by which he will leave you a free passage, or he must suffer that important place to fall into our hands, an event that would have a decisive effect and influence on the public interests."

TO COMMAND THE SECOND COLUMN Washington chose Benedict Arnold, an erstwhile merchant from Connecticut. Arnold was nine years younger than Washington, and not yet thirty when the troubles that led to the war began. A great-grandfather bearing his name had been governor of Rhode Island; Arnold's father built a thriving mercantile business based in Norwich, Connecticut. But fate turned against the Arnold family, and four of Benedict's five siblings died in childhood. His father applied alcohol to the wounds the children's deaths did his soul, and the business suffered. By the time Benedict was old enough to inherit it, there was nothing left to inherit. Instead he caught on with some kin of his mother, likewise merchants, and with them he learned the arts of buying and selling. By his early twenties he had formed a business of his own. His intelligence and native ambition, the latter perhaps piqued by a need to regain the respect his father had cost the family, set the business on the path to solid success.

The British government had other plans. The anti-smuggling provisions of the Sugar Act threatened Arnold's business, and the Stamp and Declaratory Acts, by provoking non-importation agreements, deprived him of customers. Arnold's hopes for the business had prompted him to borrow heavily against future revenues; when these failed, the business verged on collapse.

A reversal like this might have made a rebel of anyone. But it particularly irked Arnold, who internalized setbacks and affronts and, more readily than most people, spun rationales of principle to justify actions based on self-interest. He joined the protests against the new laws and accounted himself a defender of American liberty. He managed to save the business, but only by working harder than ever. The news of the Boston Massacre caught him in the West Indies chasing commercial leads; he fired off an indignant letter to a New Haven associate. "I am now in a corner of the world where you can expect no news of consequence," he wrote, by way of explaining his slowness to react to the news. "Was very much shocked the other day on hearing the accounts of the most cruel, wanton and inhuman murders committed in Boston by the soldiers. Good God! Are the Americans all asleep and tamely giving up their liberties, or all they all turned philosophers that they don't take immediate vengeance on such miscreants? I am afraid of the latter and that we shall all soon see ourselves as poor and as much oppressed as ever heathen philosopher was."

When the fighting broke out at Lexington and Concord, Arnold exchanged his ledgers for a sword. He joined the Connecticut militia and marched with his comrades, who elected him a company captain, to partake in the siege of Boston. But siege work was boring, and he proposed a strike against a British fort at Ticonderoga, at the southern end of Lake Champlain. His arguments persuaded the Massachusetts committee of safety, which commissioned him a colonel in their provincial militia and gave him permission to raise troops in western Massachusetts on the way to his target.

The expedition proved a brilliant success. Arnold met a column of Vermont militia under Ethan Allen who had decided on their own to attack Ticonderoga; together the groups caught the British garrison by surprise and captured the fort. The Patriot militias proceeded to take another British fort, at Crown Point on Champlain's western shore, giving the rebels control of the route to Canada, and making possible the Schuyler invasion, which followed shortly. As a bonus, the capture of the British forts yielded more than a hundred cannons, of which George Washington's Continental Army was dangerously short. Arnold at once arranged their transport to Washington's camp.

Washington was mightily impressed by the energetic young colonel, and when Arnold suggested the second line of attack against Quebec, Washington pronounced it a splendid idea and said Arnold must lead it. "You are entrusted with a command of the utmost consequence to the interest and liberties of America," he told Arnold. "Upon your conduct and courage, and that of the officers and soldiers detached on this expedition, not only the success of the present enterprise, and your own honor, but the safety and welfare of the whole continent may depend." Arnold and his men were not simply soldiers but ambassadors. They must win the support of the Canadians and the Indians of the region. To this end, Arnold must enforce strict discipline. "Should any American soldier be so base and infamous as to injure any Canadian or Indian, in his person or property, I do most earnestly enjoin you to bring him to such severe and exemplary punishment as the enormity of the crime may require. Should it extend to death itself, it will not be disproportioned to its guilt, at such a time and in such a cause."

Washington suspected that Arnold's audacity might cause him to question the wisdom of others. Arnold had squabbled with Ethan Allen over rank and precedence. Washington made clear that Schuyler would have overall command in Canada. "In case of a union with General Schuyler, or if he should be in Canada upon your arrival there, you are by no means to consider yourself as upon a separate and independent command, but are to put yourself under him and follow his directions," Washington wrote. "Upon this occasion, and all others, I recommend most earnestly to avoid all contention about rank. In such a cause every post is honorable in which a man can serve his country."

Arnold's capacity for resentment would emerge in time, but for now he nodded and headed north. His kit bag carried copies of Washington's own manifesto to the Canadian people. "Friends and brethren," Washington declared: "The unnatural contest between the English colonies and Great Britain has now risen to such a height that arms alone must decide it." Washington boasted that the war was going well; the British were locked up in Boston. Yet they had the temerity to cast scorn upon the provincials, among whom they specifically included the Canadians. "They have even dared to say that the Canadians were not capable of distinguishing between the blessings of liberty and the wretchedness of slavery." Washington believed they were wrong, and that the Canadians would prove them so. "Unite with us in an indissoluble union," he urged. "Let us run together to the same goal."

27

BENJAMIN FRANKLIN JUST MISSED Arnold on the latter's departure to the north. The Continental Congress had dispatched Franklin and two other members—Thomas Lynch and Benjamin Harrison—to Massachusetts to determine the needs of Washington and his army. Joining them for what turned out to be a six-day conference were the deputy governors of Connecticut and Rhode Island, and four representatives of the council of Massachusetts.

The discussions covered all aspects of mustering, provisioning, training and disciplining what was referred to as the "new army," to distinguish it from the militias Washington had inherited. The men of those militias had terms of service that were running out, compelling replacements. No less important, the new army was to answer directly to Washington and the Continental Congress, rather than to the governors of the separate colonies. To his own army Washington could issue orders; to the militias he often had to route requests through the governors.

Washington and his staff had worked up estimates of the size of the force he would require; the figure they presented to Franklin and his colleagues was a remarkably precise 20,372 men. The breakdown of this number into companies and regiments accounted for the precision. The soldiers in the new army were to be volunteers, motivated by patriotism but also requiring to be paid, to support wives and children, in many cases. Retention had been a problem due to low pay; Washington sought to have the pay increased. The Congress, on the other hand, had instructed Franklin and his colleagues to discover whether the pay might be *de*creased, to save money. The committee, after listening to Washington, rejected any decrease, saying, "Under the present circumstances, the proposition of lowering the pay of the troops would be attended with dangerous consequences."

Washington and Franklin had learned during the French and Indian War how crucial provisions were to the maintenance of an army. Most of one day's discussion was devoted to the nature and quantity of rations. The committee concluded that each soldier should receive a pound of beef or salted fish or three-quarters of a pound of pork each day, a pound of bread or flour, and a pint of milk. He should get three pints of peas or beans or vegetables each week, along with a pint of corn meal or a half pint of rice. Liquid rations should take the form of a quart of spruce beer or cider per man per day, or nine gallons of molasses per company of one hundred men per week, for making rum. Twenty-four pounds of soft soap or eight pounds of hard soap per week would keep each hundred-man company clean; three pounds of candles would light the company's evenings.

A problem with the militia was the variety of weapons the men brought to their service. Franklin's committee, on Washington's recommendation, urged standardization in the arms of the new army. The Congress commanded no armory and didn't expect to build one; the manufacture of weapons would remain with the separate colonies. But the colonies' gunsmiths should be instructed to manufacture "good firelocks with bayonets, each firelock to be made with a good bridle lock, ¾ of an inch in the bore and of good substance at the breech, the barrel to be 3 feet 8 inches in length and a bayonet of 18 inches in the blade, with a steel ramrod the upper loop to be trumpet mouthed."

Washington raised questions of discipline and loyalty. He needed to be able to punish his soldiers when they misbehaved, and he wanted to be able to punish civilians who abetted the misbehaving. The committee agreed that offenses against property—embezzlement of funds, theft or destruction of arms or provisions—should result in forfeiture of pay, reduction of rank, or whipping. Desertion to the "enemy"— the British—should be punishable by death. The committee allowed Washington to extend his authority to the surrounding populace. Civilians harboring deserters might be fined; if unable to pay the fine, they should be whipped. On the other hand, any person who apprehended a deserter and returned him to camp should receive a bounty of five dollars, deducted from the pay of the deserter.

The most sweeping authority Franklin's committee allowed Washington was to monitor and punish civilians who cooperated with the British. "All persons convicted of holding an unwarrantable correspondence with or giving intelligence to the enemy shall suffer death or such other punishment as a general court martial shall think proper," the committee declared. In other words, loyalty to Britain could now be construed as a capital crime.

Some matters were referred to the Congress. Washington had captured property of Tories; should he use it? Sell it? Destroy it? Franklin's committee judged that this was for the Congress to decide. Likewise for Congress was the choice of a surgeon general for the army.

What should be done with the British prisoners? The committee accepted Washington's recommendation that they be treated "as prisoners of war but with humanity." Should they be exchanged for colonials captured by the British? The committee answered positively, but any exchange must be on a basis of strict equality: "citizens for citizens, but not officers and soldiers of the regular army for citizens." Should Negroes, including slaves, be allowed to enlist in the army? The committee determined that Negroes should be "rejected altogether."

For the most part the discussions avoided issues of military strategy per se. Washington was the expert, and Franklin and the committee were pleased to leave the military decisions to him. But Washington himself sought guidance on a military question that had powerful political overtones. The actions of the British had convinced him they intended to remain in Boston for the winter. This would leave Washington and his army, camped in the open outside the town, at a serious disadvantage when the cold weather set in. He had considered trying to drive the British out of Boston before that happened. A frontal assault would be costly, and would have the greatest chance of success only if preceded by a bombardment of British positions in the town. But such a bombardment might well destroy much of the town. Should he go ahead anyway?

The committee discussed the matter, eliciting further detail from Washington as to how such a bombardment and attack might unfold. The committee decided not to decide. "This is a matter of too much consequence to be determined by them," the minutes of the conference recorded. Franklin would refer it to the Congress.

Washington impressed upon Franklin and the other committee members the need for money. Money paid the soldiers; it fed them;

it clothed and housed and shod them; it purchased weapons for them to fire and ammunition for the weapons. Without money "constantly and regularly sent," Washington said, the army could not be raised and retained. The struggle would be lost, and with it America's freedom.

28

FRANKLIN'S VISIT TO the front encouraged him about the prospects of a war against Britain. The vicinity of Boston, the center of the fighting so far, was holding up well. "There are as many cheerful countenances among those who are driven from house and home at Boston or lost their all at Charlestown as among other people," Franklin wrote to his son-in-law, Richard Bache. "Not a murmur has yet been heard that if they had been less zealous in the cause of liberty they might still have enjoyed their possessions." The war would be costly, in terms of property destroyed and resources required, but not beyond America's ability to sustain. "Though I am for the most prudent parsimony of the public treasure, I am not terrified by the expence of this war, should it continue ever so long," he said. "A little more frugality, or a little more industry in individuals, will with ease defray it. Suppose it £100,000 a month or £1,200,000 a year: If 500,000 families will each spend a shilling a week less, or earn a shilling a week more, or if they will spend 6 pence a week less and earn 6 pence a week more, they may pay the whole sum without otherwise feeling it. Forbearing to drink tea saves three fourths of the money; and 500,000 women doing each threepence worth of spinning or knitting in a week will pay the rest." Franklin hoped things wouldn't come to this; he told Richard Bache he wished "most earnestly for peace, this war being a truly unnatural and mischievous one." But not peace on Britain's terms. "We have nothing to expect from submission but slavery and contempt."

Just before Franklin sent this letter he heard of the burning of the seaport town of Falmouth, Massachusetts—modern Portland, Maine—by British naval forces. A British warship fired incendiary shells into the town, and marines from the ship followed up with torches. Franklin was outraged by the news and what it portended. "We have just received advice of the burning of Falmouth Casco Bay, and are assured that orders are come over to burn, ravage and destroy all the sea coast," he told Bache. "Such is the government of the best of princes!"

Franklin dashed off an angry essay to the *London Chronicle*, in response to an article about the cost to Britain of the American war. "Tell our good friend, Dr. P——e, not to be in any pains for us (because I remember he had his doubts)," he wrote. "We are all firm and united. As I know he is a great calculator, I will give him some data to work upon: ministry have made a campaign here, which has cost two millions; they have gained a mile of ground; they have lost half of it back again, they have lost fifteen hundred men, and killed one hundred and fifty Yankees. In the mean time we have had between sixty and seventy thousand children born. Ask him how long it will take for England to conquer America?"

To his remaining London friends, Franklin was equally direct. "Your nation must stop short and change its measures, or she will lose the colonies forever," he told David Hartley. "The burning of towns, and firing from men-of-war on defenceless cities and villages filled with women and children; the exciting the Indians to fall on our innocent back settlers, and our slaves to murder their masters, are by no means acts of a legitimate government. They are of barbarous tyranny and dissolve all allegiance. The insolence of your captains of men-of-war is intolerable. But we suppose they know whom they are to please." In another letter to Hartley, who was pleading for calm and hoping for reconciliation, Franklin declared, "I wish as ardently as you can do for peace, and should rejoice exceedingly in cooperating with you to that end. But every ship from Britain brings some intelligence of new measures that tend more and more to exasperate. And it seems to me that until you have found by dear experience the reducing us by force impracticable, you will think of nothing fair and reasonable. We have as yet resolved only on defensive measures. If you would recall your forces and stay at home, we should meditate nothing to injure you. A little time so given for cooling on both sides would have excellent effects." Yet Franklin didn't think this could happen. "You will goad and provoke us. You despise us too much; and you are insensible of the Italian adage, that *there is no little enemy.*" Franklin thought the majority of the British people probably favored the American cause, which was, after all, the cause of ordinary Britons. "But they are changeable, and by your lying gazettes may soon be made our enemies. Our respect for them will proportionally diminish; and I see clearly we are on the high road to mutual enmity, hatred, and detestation. A separation will of course be inevitable."

William Strahan, the Scottish friend whom Franklin now considered an enemy, wasn't giving up on the Anglo-American connection. In a series of letters Strahan expressed hope that the troubles between the colonies and the mother country might be resolved, and that Franklin one day would return to London. Yet Strahan defended the policies of the British government and cautioned Franklin against unleashing a whirlwind in America. "May it not be justly apprehended that the people of property in America, after having put arms into the hands of the inferior class and taught them the use of them, will one day find it no easy matter to persuade them to lay them down again?" he said. "In my opinion, you have much more reason to dread being enslaved by some of your own citizens than by the British senate. You will smile at my folly, perhaps, but I am fully persuaded that this contest will not only give a deadly check to your growing power and prosperity, but greatly endanger those very liberties you have now taken up arms to defend."

Franklin would have none of it. He impugned the motives behind Strahan's letters. "If you have shewn them to your friends the ministers, I dare say they have done you credit," Franklin replied. He himself would not respond at such length. "I am too fully engaged in actual business to write much, and I know your opinions are not easily changed." Franklin said he would not be returning to Britain; the government's policies had made that impossible. "I shall certainly be imprisoned if I appear again in England." Strahan had suggested that Franklin was letting his personal feelings color his assessment of public policy; Franklin assured Strahan this was not true. "Send us over hither fair proposals of peace, if you choose it, and nobody shall be more ready than myself to promote their acceptation."

Though his anger continued to mount, Franklin never lost his sense of mischief. In characteristic fashion, he turned it in a useful direction. Franklin had long been attracted to the epitaph as a literary form; early in his career as a printer he wrote one for himself, likening a human being to the first edition of a book, which might be revised in an afterlife. Now he presented to the publisher of the *Penn-*

sylvania Evening Post an epitaph he said had been found on a cannon near the gravesite of John Bradshaw, the presiding judge on the court that had condemned Charles I to death as a tyrant and traitor to the English constitution. The paper printed Franklin's faux memorial to this defender of liberty, which concluded:

> *O, reader,*
> *Pass not on till thou hast blessed his memory*
> *And never, never forget*
> *THAT REBELLION TO TYRANTS IS OBEDIENCE TO GOD.*

BENEDICT ARNOLD'S MARCH to Canada became the stuff of legend while it was still under way. Arnold started from Washington's camp at Cambridge with more than a thousand men well suited to a trek through the wilderness. Frontier types from Pennsylvania and Virginia, they could shoot, snare or angle their supper where game and fish were available, and tighten their belts where they weren't. They could make canoes from the bark of birch trees and beds from boughs of pine. They laughed at rain and shrugged at snow. They didn't take orders that affronted their common sense, but neither did they abandon a task they deemed worthy.

The route ran up the south-flowing Kennebec River, to a place where but a dozen miles separates it from the north-bound Chaudiere River. The going was slow. "We have had a very fatiguing time," Arnold reported to Washington. "We have been obliged to force up against a very rapid stream, where you would have taken the men for amphibious animals, as they were great part of the time under water." Yet they didn't complain. "The men are in high spirits. I make no doubt of reaching the River Chaudiere in eight or ten days, the greatest difficulty being, I hope, already past."

They weren't so lucky. "Excessive heavy rains and bad weather have much retarded our march," Arnold wrote to Washington in late October. The local deer and moose had taken shelter, out of sight of Arnold's hunters, and provisions were running short. They grew shorter still when some of the cargo boats—bateaus—overturned in rapids and the cargoes were lost. The constantly wet men lacked the calories to keep themselves warm. Sickness set in, increasing the demands on those still healthy enough to push the boats forward. The portage between the Kennebec and the Chaudiere was nearly impassable from the mud.

And winter was coming. "The season may possibly be severe in a few days," Arnold said.

He wondered if he had promised more than he could deliver. "Our march has been attended with an amazing deal of fatigue," he wrote. "I have been much deceived in every account of our route, which is longer and has been attended with a thousand difficulties I never apprehended." Yet the men endured the hardship, and so would he. "If crowned with success, and conducive to the public good, I shall think it but trifling."

Once the men and boats reached the Chaudiere River, gravity worked in their favor, for a time. Arnold decided to go ahead with the first boats and reach territory inhabited by French Canadians, who were expected to be friendly. He would purchase provisions to send back to those in the rear, including the sick who couldn't travel. "I accordingly set out the 28th early in the morning and descended the river, amazingly rapid and rocky for about twenty miles, where we had the misfortune to stave three of our bateaus and lose their provisions." Fortunately, no one drowned. "I then divided the little provisions left and proceeded on with the two remaining bateaus and six men, and very fortunately reached the French inhabitants the 30th at night, who received us in the most hospitable manner." From the French, Arnold purchased flour and other foodstuffs, which he sent back up the river.

Arnold's leadership on the march to the St. Lawrence won him the love and respect of his men. It wasn't lost on them that he shared their hardships without complaint, often covering twice or thrice the distance they did, scouting ahead and coming back to offer encouragement. One of Arnold's officers, writing at the journey's end, declared, "Our commander is a gentleman worthy of the trust reposed in him; a man, I believe, of invincible courage, of great prudence; ever serene, he defies the greatest danger to affect him, or difficulties to alter his temper; in fine, you will ever find him the intrepid hero and the unruffled Christian."

Washington was equally impressed. "It is not in the power of any man to command success, but you have done more—you have deserved it," he wrote Arnold. "My thanks are due, and sincerely offered to you, for your enterprizing and persevering spirit. To your brave followers I likewise present them."

GETTING TO QUEBEC was one thing; taking the city was something else. Richard Montgomery had succeeded to the command of the Canadian expedition when sickness incapacitated Philip Schuyler. Montgomery captured Montreal, and in early December linked up with Arnold before Quebec. They pondered a siege of the city but felt the time pressure of year's end, when the terms of service of many of their militia would be up. On New Year's Eve, amid a blizzard, Montgomery and Arnold ordered an attack.

It stumbled at once when a load of grapeshot took off Montgomery's head, unnerving his men. Arnold, leading a separate charge, was wounded in the leg. He remained on the battlefield, giving orders and encouragement, until his loss of blood threatened his life. The men responded with energy, but their lack of experience told, and the attack dissolved into a fiasco, with somewhat less than half the American force killed, wounded or captured. The Canadian defenders were hardly scathed.

"I make no doubt you will soon hear of our misfortune on the 31st," Arnold reported to Washington. He didn't disguise things. "Our loss and repulse struck an amazing panic into both officers and men, and had the enemy improved their advantage, our affairs here must have been entirely ruined. . . . Upwards of one hundred officers and soldiers instantly set off for Montreal, and it was with the greatest difficulty I could persuade the rest to make a stand. The panic soon subsided. I arranged the men in such order as effectually to blockade the city and enable them to assist each other if attacked. . . . Our present force is only seven hundred. I am in daily expectation of a reinforcement from Montreal of two or three hundred men." But this was far too few to take Quebec. He would continue the blockade yet couldn't promise anything more, without major reinforcements.

The bad news hit Washington hard. "This unhappy affair affects me in a very sensible manner," he wrote to Arnold. Washington had expected to hear of the capture of Quebec, which figured centrally in his strategy for the war. "I need not mention to you the great importance of this place, and the consequent possession of all Canada, in the scale of American affairs. To whomsoever it belongs, in their favor probably will the balance turn. If it is in ours, success I think will most certainly crown our virtuous struggles. If it is in theirs, the contest at best will be doubtful, hazardous, and bloody."

Washington ordered Arnold to try again. "The glorious work must be accomplished in the course of this winter," he said. "Otherwise it will become difficult, most probably impracticable; for administration"— the British government—"knowing that it will be impossible ever to reduce us to a state of slavery and arbitrary rule without it, will certainly send a large reinforcement there in the spring."

Arnold did his best. Awaiting reinforcements from the south, he recruited among the Indians of the north. "Brothers, we are the children of those people who have now taken up the hatchet against us," he told a group of Indian leaders inquiring why he had invaded their territory. He recited a brief history of the English colonies. "More than one hundred years ago, we were all as one family. We then differed in our religion, and came over to this great country by consent of the king." The colonists bought land from the Indians. They tilled the soil and grew numerous—"even as the stars in the sky." Of late, things had changed. "A new king and his wicked great men want to take our lands and money without our consent. This we think unjust, and all our great men, from the river St. Lawrence to the Mississippi, met together at Philadelphia, where they all talked together and sent a prayer to the king that they would be brothers and fight for him, but would not give up their lands and money." The king had refused their prayer and sent his soldiers against them. The colonists had fought the soldiers and had trapped them in Boston.

But the king had forts and troops in Canada, and these might join the soldiers at Boston. Arnold was trying to prevent this. He also hoped to enlist the aid of the people of Canada. "We hear the French and Indians in Canada have sent to us, that the king's troops oppress them and make them pay a great price for their rum etc., press them to take up arms against the Bostonians, their brethren, who have done them no hurt. By the desire of the French and Indians, our brothers, we have come to their assistance, with an intent to drive out the king's soldiers. When drove off, we will return to our own country and leave this to the peaceable enjoyment of its proper inhabitants."

The impassive faces of the Indians left Arnold wondering whether they believed his account or his promise. He nonetheless proceeded, offering them a deal. "If the Indians, our brethren, will join us, we will be very much obliged to them, and will give them one Portuguese per months, two dollars bounty, and find them their provisions, and the liberty to choose their own officers."

Arnold's argument won him some fifty Indian allies, who stuck with him the rest of the Quebec campaign. Arnold's persuasiveness also brought two hundred French Canadians to the siege of Quebec. Through the winter, while Arnold's leg, shattered by a musket ball, slowly mended, he and his small force kept watch on the city, hoping for the reinforcements from New York or New England that would enable them to take it.

Washington's own siege of Boston wasn't going much better. "We are now without any money in our treasury, powder in our magazines, arms in our stores," he wrote to Joseph Reed, his adjutant general. "Our enlistments are at a stand; the fears I ever entertained are realized: that is, the discontented officers (for I do not know how else to account for it) have thrown such difficulties or stumbling-blocks in the way of recruiting that I no longer entertain a hope of completing the army by voluntary enlistments, and I see no move or likelihood of one, to do it by other means." Officers and men treated orders to return to their regiments as mere suggestions. "Another is now gone forth, peremptorily requiring all officers under pain of being cashiered, and recruits as being treated as deserters, to join their respective regiments by the 1st day of next month, that I may know my real strength." Whether this order would be more effectual, Washington couldn't say.

Lack of men was only half the problem. "With regard to arms I am yet worse off," Washington told Reed. "Before the dissolution of the old army, I issued an order directing three judicious men of each brigade to attend, review, and appraise the good arms of every regiment; and finding a very great unwillingness in the men to part with their arms, at the same time not having it in my power to pay them for the months of November and December, I threatened severely that every soldier who carried away his firelock without leave should never receive pay for those months; yet so many have been carried off, partly by stealth, but chiefly as condemned, that we have not at this time one hundred guns in the stores." Where new weapons would come from, Washington couldn't say with any confidence. "I have applied to this and the neighboring colonies, but with what success time only can tell."

He struggled to remain hopeful. "The reflection on my situation, and that of this army, produces many an uneasy hour when all around me are wrapped in sleep," Washington wrote. "Few people know the predicament we are in, on a thousand accounts; fewer still will believe, if any disaster happens to these lines, from what causes it flows. I have often thought how much happier I should have been if, instead of accepting of a command under such circumstances, I had taken my musket on my shoulder and entered the ranks, or, if I could have justified the measure to posterity and my own conscience, had retired to the back country and lived in a wigwam." With no one else cooperating, Washington looked to heaven. "If I shall be able to rise superior to these and many other difficulties which might be enumerated, I shall most religiously believe that the finger of Providence is in it to blind the eyes of our enemies; for surely if we get well through this month, it must be for want of their knowing the disadvantages we labour under."

HE DECIDED TO GIVE Providence an assist. He would take the fight to the British and drive them out of Boston. Washington shared his idea with his council of war—his general officers. "The late freezing weather had formed some pretty strong ice from Dorchester to Boston Neck, and from Roxbury to the Common, which would have afforded a less dangerous approach to the town than through the lines or by water," he explained afterward. But the generals demurred. "They thought, and perhaps rightly, that such an enterprise in our present weak state of men (for the militia are not yet half arrived) and deficiency of powder would be attended with too much hazard and therefore that we had better wait."

Washington would learn to override counsels of caution, but at this point, having won no battles, he felt obliged to heed his advisers' reservations. Yet he didn't wait long. In early March, following the arrival of more men and powder, he put his plan in motion. Under cover of night, and with his cannons providing cover and distraction, he sent troops to seize and reinforce positions on Dorchester Heights that commanded the city and its southern approaches. William Howe, brother of Richard Howe, had replaced Thomas Gage in command of the British at Boston; Howe discovered Washington's move too late to prevent it.

Washington hoped to lure Howe into attacking the new American positions. He aimed to have it out with the British then and there. He initially thought Howe was taking the bait. "When the enemy first discovered our works in the morning, they seemed to be in great confusion and, from their movements, to have intended an attack," Washington recounted to John Hancock. "It is much to be wished that it had been made." Washington had readied an amphibious force to assault Boston from the north and west while the British were fighting on the Dorchester Hills to the south and east. "The event, I think, must have been fortunate and nothing less than success and victory on our side, as our officers and men appeared impatient for the appeal, and to possess the most animated sentiments and determined resolution."

Washington tried to force Howe's hand by turning his cannons loose on the city. The Congress had deferred to Washington's judgment on using artillery, and he concluded that it had become necessary. "Our bombardment and cannonade caused a good deal of surprise and alarm in town, as many of the soldiery said they never heard or thought we had mortars or shells," Washington reported to John Hancock, relying on information from a Patriot who had sneaked out of the city. "The cannon shot for the greatest part went through the houses, and he"—the informant—"was told that one took off the legs and arms of six men lying in the barracks on the Neck." The informant said the bombardment had especially unnerved the naval commander of the British force. "Admiral Shuldham, discovering the works our people were throwing up on Dorchester Heights, immediately sent an express to General Howe to inform him that it was necessary they should be attacked and dislodged from thence, or he would be under the necessity of withdrawing the ships from the harbour which were under his command."

Howe decided to attack. He loaded three thousand troops onto transports for an assault against the American positions on Dorchester Heights. But a sudden storm blew in, making the crossing impossible. The British soldiers, already unenthusiastic, became morose, as Washington learned from his informant. "He heard several of the privates and one or two sergeants say as they were embarking that it would be another Bunker Hill affair," Washington told Hancock.

Howe reconsidered. He concluded that Boston was untenable. Washington could bombard the city far more effectively than he—

Howe—could return Washington's fire. And his own supplies were running short. Rations had to be cut, until the troops grew weak from hunger and susceptible to disease, including smallpox, which had broken out in the city. Howe decided it was better to evacuate his army than to watch it dwindle and die.

He ordered his troops onto ships, and piled arms in with them. When the wind turned fair the British flotilla, numbering more than a hundred vessels and carrying ten thousand troops, sailed away from Boston and out of sight.

WASHINGTON ENTERED THE CITY shortly after the British departure. "The town, although it has suffered greatly, is not in so bad a state as I expected to find it," he wrote to Hancock. "And I have a particular pleasure in being able to inform you, sir, that your house has received no damage worth mentioning. Your furniture is in tolerable order, and the family pictures are all left entire and untouched." Obviously the British had been in a hurry. "They have left their barracks and other works of wood at Bunker's Hill all standing, and have destroyed but a small part of their lines. They have also left a number of fine pieces of cannon, which they first spiked up, also a very large iron mortar; and, as I am informed, they have thrown another over the end of your wharf. I have employed proper persons to drill the cannon, and doubt not I shall save the most of them."

As Washington's troops occupied Boston, they carried their commander's instructions against mistreating the residents of the city. "All officers and soldiers are hereby ordered to live in the strictest peace and amity with the inhabitants," Washington declared. "No inhabitant or other person employed in his lawful business in the town is to be molested in his person or property, on any pretence whatever."

The order was necessary, for resentments ran deep in Washington's army against Americans who had collaborated with the British. Many of the Loyalists had sailed away with Howe's fleet, but others remained. And questions arose about the allegiance of anyone who had lived under British rule during the eleven months of the siege. Collaboration must have taken place at some level, or if not collaboration, then acquiescence. In either case, those soldiers who spent the winter in the open had often wondered about their compatriots snug in their Boston houses. Whose side were they on? Violence had been a part of Boston politics from the first protests over the Stamp Act; there was ample reason to think it might continue. And if inflicted by soldiers bearing arms, it might be worse than ever.

Washington understood his men's bitterness about the Loyalists, for he felt it himself. On entering Boston he learned of the departure of the Loyalists, and of the fate of some who hadn't found room on the crowded ships. "One or two have done what a great number ought to have done long ago, committed suicide," he wrote to John Washington. As for those who had left, they were reaping the grim harvest they deserved. "By all accounts, there never existed a more miserable set of beings than these wretched creatures now are. Taught to believe that the power of Great Britain was superior to all opposition, and, if not, that foreign aid was at hand, they were even higher and more insulting in their opposition than the regulars. When the order issued, therefore, for embarking the troops in Boston, no electric shock, no sudden explosion of thunder, in a word, not the last trump could have struck them with greater consternation. They were at their wits' end, and, conscious of their black ingratitude, they chose to commit themselves, in the manner I have above described, to the mercy of the waves at a tempestuous season, rather than meet their offended countrymen."

IN PUBLIC WASHINGTON CAST the flight of the British as a victory for Patriot arms. The city had been under the boot of the British government since the arrival of British troops nearly a decade before; it finally breathed free once more.

In private he felt quite otherwise. He had had Howe at a disadvantage, and nearly lured him into a pitched battle. But then came the storm that put Howe off. "Much blood was saved, and a very important blow, to one side or the other, was prevented," Washington conceded to brother John. He didn't presume to gainsay heaven. "That this most remarkable interposition of Providence is for some wise purpose, I have not a doubt." Yet he regretted it still. His plan had been a sound one, and must have succeeded. "I can scarcely forbear lamenting the disappointment."

Howe and his army had escaped, and Washington couldn't tell their destination. "Whither they are bound and where their tents will be next pitched, I know not," he told John. But he did know where *he* would have gone, had he been Howe. "New York and Hudson's River are the most important objects they can have in view, as the latter secures the communication with Canada at the same time that it separates the northern and southern colonies." He said he had already taken appropriate steps. "As soon as they embarked, I detached a brigade of six regiments to that government"—New York—"and when they sailed, another brigade composed of the same number. And tomorrow another brigade of five regiments will march. In a day or two more, I shall follow myself."

WHILE WASHINGTON WAS MOVING south, Benjamin Franklin trekked north. With the military campaign in Canada at a standstill, the Continental Congress launched a political campaign. "You are with all convenient dispatch to repair to Canada, and make known to the people of that country the wishes and intentions of Congress with respect to them," Franklin was charged, along with Samuel Chase and Charles Carroll. "Represent to them that the arms of the United Colonies having been carried into that province for the purpose of frustrating the designs of the British court against our common liberties, we expect not only to defeat the hostile machinations of Governor Carleton against us but that we shall put it in the power of our Canadian brethren to pursue such measures for securing their own freedom and happiness as a generous love of liberty and sound policy shall dictate to them." Franklin and his colleagues should preach the parallelism of interests of all the North American colonies. "Inform them that in our judgment their interest and ours are inseparably united," the instructions said. "It is impossible we can be reduced to a servile submission to Great Britain without their sharing in our fate." The Congress promised the Canadians full equality in a union with the older colonies. "The people of Canada may set up such a form of government as will be most likely, in their judgment, to produce their happiness." Most of the Canadians were Catholics; they would be guaranteed freedom of worship. "We hold sacred the rights of conscience."

The late-winter journey proved arduous. Franklin had turned seventy several weeks earlier, and suffered from gout and kidney stones. The winter travel over rough roads made him wince at every jolt, and the cold got into his lungs and bones. He kept his troubles to himself as long as he could, but after several weeks admitted, "I grow daily more feeble."

Yet he soldiered on in the face of the winter, and of Canadian skepticism. The American assertions that they were defending English liberties were lost on the mostly French Canadians. The Canadians had no particular complaints against London, and little reason to think the Americans would win their contest against the British army and government. At the moment, the Canadians' principal complaint was against the American army that had invaded their country.

And against the promissory notes the army tried to use to pay for the provisions it purchased. "It is impossible to give you a just idea of the lowness of the Continental credit here from the want of hard money, and the prejudice it is to our affairs," Franklin wrote from Montreal to John Hancock. "Not the most trifling service can be procured without an assurance of instant pay in silver or gold. The express we sent from St. John's to inform the General"—Benedict Arnold—"of our arrival there, and to request carriages for La Prairie, was stopped at the ferry till a friend passing changed a dollar for him into silver." The Canadians were keeping their wallets closed and their powder dry. "The general apprehension that we shall be driven out of the province as soon as the king's troops can arrive concurs with the frequent breaches of promise the inhabitants have experienced, in determining them to trust our people no farther." Franklin told Hancock to send hard money—he suggested £20,000 to start—at once. "Otherwise it will be impossible to continue the war in this country, or to expect the continuance of our interest with the people here, who begin to consider the Congress as bankrupt and their cause as desperate."

The shortage of money made the success of the army all but impossible. "We have tried in vain to borrow some here for the immediate occasions of the army, either on the public or our own private credit," Franklin told Hancock. "We cannot even sell sterling bills of exchange, which some of us have offered to draw." The poverty of the American cause had political consequences. "The Tories will not trust us a farthing, and some who perhaps wish us well, conceiving that we shall through our own poverty or from superior force be soon obliged to abandon the country, are afraid to have any dealings with us, lest they should hereafter be called to account for abetting our cause." If money didn't arrive soon, said Franklin, the Congress might as well terminate the campaign.

His pleas produced the desired effect. Two weeks later Hancock sent a letter and a package. "I have forwarded to General Schuyler by this conveyance the sum of Sixteen Hundred and Sixty-two Pounds, One Shilling and Three Pence hard money, which was all that was in the treasury," Hancock wrote.

But the money arrived too late. British reinforcements got to Quebec first. "Two men-of-war, two frigates and one tender arrived there early on Monday the 6th," Franklin wrote to Hancock on May 10. The ships carried a thousand fresh troops, who attacked the weary Americans. The result was a rout. "All our cannon, five hundred muskets, and about two hundred sick unable to come off have fallen into their hands," Franklin related. "The retreat, or rather flight was made with the utmost precipitation and confusion."

Franklin recognized that the defeat at Quebec killed any present hopes of attaching Canada to the American struggle against Britain. It also precluded any usefulness for Franklin and his fellow commissioners. They headed home.

Franklin barely survived the journey. "My dear brother and the whole world's friend is returned," wrote his sister Jane Mecom, who had fled her Boston home for Philadelphia. "The cause and circumstances are melancholy but thank God he is again safe here. He suffered many difficulties in going, was taken sick in a day or two after his arrival, and has never had a well day since."

Yet even to his sister, Franklin didn't exactly complain. "All that he himself says about it is, it is a time of life with him to expect infirmities."

A LETTER FROM GEORGE WASHINGTON caught up with Franklin at Philadelphia. Washington had been counting on the combined efforts of Franklin and Benedict Arnold—and the other soldiers and diplomats sent north—to bring Canada into the fold, or at least deny it to British forces. To Franklin he now wrote of his "concern and surprise" at the American defeat at Quebec. He wasn't quite clear about what had gone wrong, but he would take a lesson. "Hence I shall know the events of war are exceedingly doubtful, and that capricious fortune often blasts our most flattering hopes."

Franklin replied that there was no reason to despair. Reports suggested that a new British force, larger than the one that dislodged the American army from Quebec, was headed for America. Franklin welcomed the army, and the larger the better. The British could send such forces, but they couldn't send them forever, he told Washington. "I see more certainly the ruin of Britain if she persists in such expensive distant expeditions, which will probably prove more disastrous to her than anciently her wars in the Holy Land."

In this letter, written on June 21, Franklin shared with Washington that he hadn't been well. "I am just recovering from a severe fit of the gout, which has kept me from Congress and company," he said. He had fallen behind political developments. "I know little of what has passed there, except that a Declaration of Independence is preparing."

FRANKLIN SOON CAUGHT UP. The continued refusal of the British to entertain anything like the reforms the Continental Congress demanded as a basis for reconciliation—which was to say, Britain's refusal to grant the American colonies effective home rule—was augmenting the number of those in the Congress prepared to admit that reconciliation would never come. The success of Washington in replacing the militia army he inherited with a regular army of Continental soldiers, of holding the new army together through the winter, and of finally driving the British from Boston encouraged the independence-minded to think they could make their goal a reality. Thomas Paine's pamphlet *Common Sense* put the argument for independence in succinct and powerful form and gave it broad circulation among Americans at large.

The separate colonies moved toward independence at different tempos. In mid-May a Virginia convention strongly endorsed a resolution instructing the colony's delegates to the Continental Congress to put forward a motion for independence. Washington got the word at Philadelphia, to which he had traveled from his new headquarters in New York to consult with the leaders of the Congress. "I am very glad to find that the Virginia Convention have passed so noble a vote, with so much unanimity," he wrote to brother John, who was a delegate to the convention. "Things have come to that pass now as to convince us that we have nothing more to expect from the justice of Great Britain." Washington hoped the Congress would reach the same conclusion shortly.

It did. Just days later Richard Henry Lee, Washington's old colleague from the Virginia house of burgesses and now a member of the Continental Congress, heeded the instructions of the Virginia convention and introduced an independence measure: "Resolved: That these

United Colonies are, and of right ought to be, free and independent States, that they are absolved from all allegiance to the British Crown, and that all political connection between them and the State of Great Britain is, and ought to be, totally dissolved."

Delegates from several of the colonies supported Lee's resolution, but others weren't willing to take the final step. Recognizing that unanimity of the colonies, or something close to it, was more important than swiftness in the decision process, the supporters agreed to postpone a vote. Meanwhile the Congress appointed a committee to draft a declaration of the causes that had carried the colonies to the point of believing independence necessary and right. Franklin was chosen, as were John Adams, Thomas Jefferson, Robert Livingston of New York, and Roger Sherman of Connecticut.

Adams later recalled how Jefferson happened to write the first draft of the declaration. "Mr. Jefferson came into Congress in June 1775 and brought with him a reputation for literature, science and a happy talent at composition," Adams explained. "Writings of his were handed about, remarkable for the peculiar felicity of expression. Though a silent member in Congress, he was so prompt, frank, explicit and decisive upon committees—not even Samuel Adams was more so—that he soon seized upon my heart, and upon this occasion I gave him my vote"—to be on the drafting committee—"and did all in my power to procure the votes of others."

The question then emerged as to who should do the initial drafting. "Jefferson proposed to me to make the draught," Adams recalled. "I said I will not. You shall do it."

"Oh, no!" said Jefferson.

"Why will you not?" said Adams.

"You ought to do it."

"I will not."

"Why?"

"Reasons enough."

"What can be your reasons?"

"Reason first: You are a Virginian, and Virginia ought to appear at the head of this business. Reason second: I am obnoxious, suspected and unpopular; you are very much otherwise. Reason third: You can write ten times better than I can."

"Well," said Jefferson, "if you are decided, I will do as well as I can."

Franklin approved the choice of Jefferson as drafter, citing an additional reason for not seeking the task himself. "I have made it a rule," he confided to Jefferson, "whenever in my power, to avoid becoming the draughtsman of papers to be reviewed by a public body. I took my lesson from an incident which I will relate to you. When I was a journeyman printer, one of my companions, an apprentice hatter, having served out his time, was about to open shop for himself. His first concern was to have a handsome sign-board, with a proper inscription. He composed it in these words 'John Thompson, Hatter, makes and sells hats, for ready money,' with a figure of a hat subjoined. But he thought he would submit it to his friends for their amendments. The first he shewed it to thought the word 'Hatter' tautologous, because followed by the words 'makes hats,' which shewed he was a hatter. It was struck out. The next observed that the word 'makes' might as well be omitted, because his customers would not care who made the hats. If good and to their mind, they would buy, by whomsoever made. He struck it out. A third said he thought the words 'for ready money,' were useless as it was not the custom of the place to sell on credit; everyone who purchased expected to pay. They were parted with, and the inscription now stood 'John Thompson sells hats.' '*Sells* hats?' says his next friend. 'Why, nobody will expect you to give them away. What then is the use of that word? It was stricken out. And 'hats' followed it, the rather as there was one painted on the board. So his inscription was reduced ultimately to 'John Thompson' with the figure of a hat subjoined."

Jefferson wrote his draft. He sent it to Franklin. "Will Doctor Franklin be so good as to peruse it and suggest such alterations as his more enlarged view of the subject will dictate?" he asked. Franklin recognized talent in writing when he saw it, and the changes he offered were few and modest. Jefferson's "reduce them to arbitrary power," referring to what the British crown was trying to do to the Americans, was sharpened to "reduce them under absolute despotism." Jefferson's "amount of their salaries," regarding the pay of British officials in America, was made more specific as "amount and payment of their salaries." Jefferson's "taking away our charters and altering fundamentally the forms of our government" was expanded to "taking away our charters, abolishing our most valuable laws, and altering fundamentally the forms of our government." Jefferson's "to invade and deluge us with blood" was rendered less gory as "to invade and destroy us."

Somewhere in the revision process, Jefferson's "sacred and undeniable" truths became "self-evident" truths. Though the evidence is inconclusive, this suggestion might well also have been Franklin's; it seems the kind of tightening a longtime editor like Franklin would have made, besides being more in keeping with the rationalistic philosophy of Franklin than the Christian orthodoxy of Adams, for instance.

The Continental Congress took greater liberties with Jefferson's prose. Before its editing had ceased, large pieces of Jefferson's prose had been excised or altered beyond recognition. Jefferson squirmed under the treatment, which was what prompted Franklin's story about John Thompson and his hat sign. At length the Declaration was accepted by the Congress and signed by the delegates present. At the signing John Hancock, the president of the Congress, urged every member to attach his name. "We must be unanimous," he said, according to an oft-repeated version of the event. "There must be no pulling different ways. We must all hang together."

To which Franklin replied, according to the same account: "Yes, we must all hang together, or most assuredly we shall all hang separately."

Part VI

A Scene of Horror and Distress

ALTHOUGH FRANKLIN HAD little time and less inclination to correspond with his former friends and associates in London, *they* continued to write to *him*. David Hartley assured Franklin that hope was not lost for a reconciliation between Britain and America. Hartley feared that Franklin and the Americans were getting a skewed view of British opinion. "The stoppage of communication between the two countries seems to have had the very worst of consequences, as it has given the ministry the opportunity of sending their own irritating information to America and of withholding the knowledge of all the good dispositions which there are in this country towards their fellow subjects in America," Hartley wrote. "Angry addresses have been sent with all the parade of authority to America while the petitions in favour of peace have not been suffered to appear in the gazettes." The British people didn't share the opinions of the government. "The ministry have certainly not been able to raise any national spirit of resentment against America. The generality of the people are cold upon the subject. Nine men in ten content themselves with an indolent wish for peace, but there are many zealous and principled friends to America. The only bitter enemies are the ministry and their dependents, jobbers, contractors etc. etc. *quibus utile bellum*"—to whom the war is profitable. Hartley hoped Franklin could keep this in mind. "I make all allowances for the sufferings of America. Yet still I think reconciliation and peace the best bargain to both sides." The government was talking of sending one or more commissioners to America. Hartley didn't know who they were or what their charge, but he urged Franklin to greet them with an open mind. "Peace is the general wish of this country. I hope it is the same in America."

The one commissioner turned out to be Lord Richard Howe, Franklin's erstwhile collaborator in London. Howe received command of Britain's naval forces in American waters, giving him standing in America comparable to that of his younger brother General William Howe. Richard Howe hoped to revive the cooperation between himself and Franklin, with positive effects for the relation between Britain and America. "You will learn the nature of my mission from the official dispatches which I have recommended to be forwarded," he wrote to Franklin. "Retaining all the earnestness I ever expressed to see our differences accommodated, I shall conceive, if I meet with the same disposition in the colonies which I was once taught to expect, the most flattering hopes of proving serviceable in the objects of the king's paternal solicitude, by promoting the re-establishment of lasting peace and union with the colonies."

Franklin at once let Howe know that things had changed on the American side, even as they remained stuck on the British end. "The official dispatches to which you refer me contain nothing more than what we had seen in the act of Parliament, viz. offers of pardon upon submission, which I was sorry to find, as it must give your lordship pain to be sent so far on so hopeless a business," Franklin replied. Parliament put things just backward, he said. "Directing pardons to be offered the colonies, who are the very parties injured, expresses indeed that opinion of our ignorance, baseness, and insensibility which your uninformed and proud nation has long been pleased to entertain of us. But it can have no other effect than that of increasing our resentment. It is impossible we should think of submission to a government that has with the most wanton barbarity and cruelty burnt our defenceless towns in the midst of winter, excited the savages to massacre our farmers, and our slaves to murder their masters, and is even now bringing foreign mercenaries to deluge our settlements with blood. These atrocious injuries have extinguished every remaining spark of affection for that parent country we once held so dear."

British memory would be no less intractable, Franklin said. "Were it possible for *us* to forget and forgive them, it is not possible for *you* (I mean the British nation) to forgive the people you have so heavily injured. You can never confide again in those as fellow subjects, and permit them to enjoy equal freedom, to whom you know you have given such just cause of lasting enmity. And this must impel you, were we again under your government, to endeavour the breaking our spirit by the severest tyranny, and obstructing by every means in your power our growing strength and prosperity."

Franklin allowed that if the British government paid compensation for the damages it had done to the Americans, Britain might regain some of the regard in which it had been held in America. But he asserted that Britain would never do any such thing. "I know too well her abounding pride and deficient wisdom to believe she will ever take such salutary measures. Her fondness for conquest as a warlike nation, her lust of dominion as an ambitious one, and her thirst for a gainful monopoly as a commercial one (none of them legitimate causes of war) will all join to hide from her eyes every view of her true interests, and continually goad her on in these ruinous distant expeditions, so destructive both of lives and treasure that must prove as pernicious to her in the end as the Crusades formerly were to most of the nations of Europe." Franklin didn't expect Howe or his sponsors to listen. "I have not the vanity, my lord, to think of intimidating by thus predicting the effects of this war, for I know it will in England have the fate of all my former predictions, not to be believed till the event shall verify it."

Howe, of all people, should understand the disappointment Franklin suffered at the blasting of his hopes for an enlightened empire. "Long did I endeavour with unfeigned and unwearied zeal to preserve from breaking that fine and noble China vase the British Empire, for I knew that being once broken, the separate parts could not retain even their share of the strength or value that existed in the whole, and that a perfect reunion of those parts could scarce even be hoped for," Franklin wrote. "Your lordship may possibly remember the tears of joy that wet my cheek when, at your good sister's in London, you once gave me expectations that a reconciliation might soon take place. I had the misfortune to find those expectations disappointed, and to be treated as the cause of the mischief I was labouring to prevent."

Even then, Franklin said, he had taken consolation in the friendship of wise and good men like Howe. He still did, which made the current conflict the more hurtful. "The well-founded esteem, and permit me to say affection, which I shall always have for your lordship makes it painful to me to see you engaged in conducting a war, the great ground of which, as expressed in your letter, is, 'the necessity of preventing the American trade from passing into foreign channels.'

To me it seems that neither the obtaining or retaining of any trade, how valuable soever, is an object for which men may justly spill each other's blood; that the true and sure means of extending and securing commerce is the goodness and cheapness of commodities; and that the profits of no trade can ever be equal to the expence of compelling it, and of holding it, by fleets and armies. I consider this war against us, therefore, as both unjust and unwise, and I am persuaded cool dispassionate posterity will condemn to infamy those who advised it." Franklin didn't asperse Howe's intentions, but he advised him to reconsider and act accordingly. "I know your great motive in coming hither was the hope of being instrumental in a reconciliation, and I believe when you find *that* impossible on any terms given you to propose, you will relinquish so odious a command and return to a more honourable private station."

Howe wouldn't be put off so easily. "I am sorry, my worthy friend, that it is only on the assurances you give me of my having still preserved a place in your esteem, that I can now found a pretension to trouble you with a reply," he wrote. "I can have no difficulty to acknowledge that the powers I am invested with were never calculated to negotiate a reunion with America under any other description than as subject to the crown of Great Britain." Yet Howe pointed out that the most recent petition from the Continental Congress—the Olive Branch Petition—had affirmed the colonies' loyalty to the British crown. He added that diplomatic discretion prevented him from saying more in a letter that might be read by others—"not conceiving it could be understood to refer to peace on any other conditions but those of mutual interest to both countries, which could alone render it permanent." In other words, he seemed to be saying, he would be open to proposals from Franklin and his associates.

Howe's hint came too late. "The temper of the colonies as professed in their several petitions to the crown was sincere," Franklin replied. "The terms they proposed should then have been closed with, and all might have been peace. I dare say your lordship, as well as myself, laments they were not accepted. I remember I told you that better would never be offered." The refusal of the British government to entertain the American proposals had contributed to the events that followed. "The contempt with which those petitions were treated, none of them being vouchsafed an answer, and the cruel measures since taken, have

George Washington, Patriot.
Library of Congress.

John Adams, Patriot.
Massachusetts Historical Society.

Benjamin Franklin, Patriot.
National Portrait Gallery, Smithsonian Institution; gift of the Morris and Gwendolyn Cafritz Foundation.

William Franklin, Loyalist. *Wikimedia Commons.*

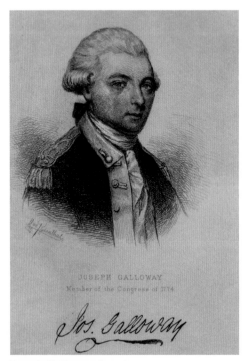

Joseph Galloway, Loyalist.
New York Public Library.

Thomas Hutchinson, Loyalist.
Massachusetts Historical Society.

Benedict Arnold, Patriot who turned
Loyalist. *Library of Congress.*

Joseph Brant, Loyalist and Mohawk.
Library of Congress.

William Johnson, Joseph Brant's sponsor.
Wikimedia Commons.

Abigail Adams, Patriot scandalized by America's French allies. *Massachusetts Historical Society.*

Banastre Tarleton, British leader of Loyalists and scourge of Patriots. *Library of Congress.*

"GIVE ME LIBERTY, OR GIVE ME DEATH !"

Patrick Henry in full voice. *Library of Congress.*

Boston Massacre, per Paul Revere. *Library of Congress.*

Thomas Jefferson delivering the Declaration of Independence to the Continental Congress, while Benjamin Franklin (seated in front of the table) and John Adams (standing, with hand in waistcoat) look on. *Library of Congress.*

Burning of New York upon Washington's evacuation, 1776. *New York Public Library.*

Washington crossing the Delaware. *Metropolitan Museum of Art.*

Franklin's reception at the court of Louis XVI. *Library of Congress.*

Washington,
with Lafayette,
at Valley Forge.
Wikimedia Commons.

Inside the British prison ship *Jersey*. *Library of Congress.*

Yorktown. *Wikimedia Commons.*

Signing of the Treaty of Paris. Seated, from left, are John Adams, Benjamin Franklin, and William Temple Franklin. The British delegation refused to be portrayed. *Wikimedia Commons.*

changed that temper. It could not be otherwise. To propose now to the colonies a submission to the crown of Great Britain would be fruitless. The time is past."

FRANKLIN'S BACK-AND-FORTH with Howe consumed several weeks during the summer of 1776. The duration owed a bit to the difficulties of communication across military lines, but more to the fact that Howe's brother was hoping for a decisive battlefield victory over George Washington, which presumably would incline Franklin and the other American rebels to reconsider their recalcitrance. Immediately upon the British evacuation of Boston, Washington had moved the bulk of his army to New York, which he deemed the logical point of British re-entry into the American theater. By early August all signs pointed to the aptness of his surmise. "This morning two deserters have come in," Washington wrote to John Hancock on August 7. They told of a British fleet heading Washington's way. General Howe had gone from Boston to Halifax to rest and regroup; his army was now descending on New York. A smaller army was coming from South Carolina, where Patriot militia had repelled an attack on Charleston. German Hessians and Scottish Highlanders were crossing the Atlantic. The first contingents of the combined force had already landed on Staten Island. "The attack will soon be made, if the other troops arrive," Washington told Hancock, relying on his informants. "They will lay the Jerseys waste with fire and sword. The computed strength of their army will be 30,000 men."

To oppose this army Washington had scarcely a third as many troops. He did what he could to even the odds. In a letter to Jesse Root, of the Connecticut council of safety, he described the size of the British army that was approaching, and said, "An attack is now therefore to be expected which will probably decide the fate of America." Root and his Connecticut friends must send all the militia they could. "I cannot doubt but a sense of public duty and the imminent dangers to which everything that is dear to us is exposed will induce every true friend and lover of his country to exert his utmost powers for its salvation and defence." To the commander of Pennsylvania militia, Washington issued a similar call to patriotic duty. "Brave men who love their country and are resolved to defend it will go where the service requires at so critical and dangerous a period as this," he said. "I flatter myself therefore when the brave officers and soldiers under your special command reflect that the time is fast approaching which is to determine our fate and that of our posterity, they will most cheerfully persevere and comply with such request respecting their march and destination as the state of things requires."

To his own men, Washington issued a directive to gird up. "The General exhorts every man, both officer and soldier; to be prepared for action; to have his arms in the best order; not to wander from his encampment or quarters; to remember what their country expects of them, what a few brave men have lately done in South Carolina, against a powerful fleet and army; to acquit themselves like men and with the blessing of heaven on so just a cause." Washington expressed his confidence in his men and their cause. "We cannot doubt of success."

YET HE *DID* DOUBT of success, and for good reason. His men were few and untested; many were sick. His pleas for reinforcements yielded promises but few men so far. Worse, General Howe had turned the tables on him by giving up Boston. There, Washington had known exactly where Howe was and could plan accordingly. In New York, he had no such certain knowledge. He relied on rumor, informants and intuition—uncertain guides all. The strength of New York as a harbor and point of entry to the American continent—the numerous waterways that converged in the estuary of the Hudson—became Washington's weakness in trying to defend the place. The British might land on Staten Island, on Long Island, on Manhattan, in New Jersey, or somewhere up the Hudson. No matter where he placed his army, the British might find a way around it by land or by water. Washington didn't even know the intentions of the Howe brothers. Did they aim to destroy his army in a pitched battle? To elude his army and strike to the interior? To establish a base for Loyalist forces? To sap the morale of American Patriots?

Washington had time to ponder these questions, for the attack his intelligence had led him to expect didn't come. Days passed, then a week. He felt obliged to warn his men against letting their guard down. "The enemy's whole reinforcement is now arrived, so that an attack must and will soon be made," he declared on August 13. "The

General therefore again repeats his earnest request that every officer and soldier will have his arms and ammunition in good order; keep within their quarters and encampment as much as possible; be ready for action at a moment's call; and when called to it, remember that liberty, property, life and honor are all at stake; that upon their courage and conduct rest the hopes of their bleeding and insulted country; that their wives, children and parents expect safety from them." Washington told his men to stay calm. "The enemy will endeavour to intimidate by shew and appearance," he said. "But remember how they have been repulsed on various occasions by a few brave Americans. Their cause is bad; their men are conscious of it, and if opposed with firmness, and coolness, at their first onset, with our advantage of works and knowledge of the ground, victory is most assuredly ours." Washington readied his men for the moment of battle. "Every good soldier will be silent and attentive, wait for orders and reserve his fire till he is sure of doing execution. The officers to be particularly careful of this." Courage was expected, its opposite condemned. "If any infamous rascal, in time of action, shall attempt to skulk, hide himself or retreat from the enemy without orders of his commanding officer; he will instantly be shot down as an example of cowardice. On the other hand, the General solemnly promises that he will reward those who shall distinguish themselves by brave and noble actions."

Still the Howes refused to engage. Washington employed the time to construct defenses, while knowing they might be useless. Indeed, the very construction of forts and batteries would encourage the British to attack elsewhere.

What Washington needed most—knowledge of where the blow would fall, and when—he didn't have. "Very unexpectedly to me, another revolving Monday is arrived before an attack upon this city or a movement of the enemy," he wrote to his cousin Lund on August 19. "The reason of this is incomprehensible to me. True it is (from some late informations) they expect another arrival of about 5000 Hessians. But then, they have been stronger than the army under my command; which will now, I expect, gain strength faster than theirs." The British delay had allowed militia troops to join Washington's Continentals.

It didn't make sense. "There is something exceedingly mysterious in the conduct of the enemy," Washington told Lund. Were things less settled among the British forces than he knew? Or was there something in British or European politics that was giving the Howe brothers second thoughts about a major new campaign? "What this can be the Lord knows," Washington said. He himself surely didn't. "We are now past the middle of August, and they are in possession of an island only"—Staten Island—"which it never was in our power or intention to dispute their landing on. This is but a small step towards the conquest of this continent."

Washington eventually concluded that the British delay was deliberate. Richard Howe cast the prospect of peace upon the waters of the rebellion, in hope of diminishing the resolve of Washington's soldiers and prompting desertions.

Washington answered by ordering the deserters arrested, when they could be located, and punished by up to thirty-nine lashes. Soldiers so beaten were of little use for much of anything for a week or more afterward, but Washington's point was to let prospective imitators know they ran greater danger from disobeying their general than from following him into battle.

FINALLY THE BRITISH TIPPED their hand. In the last week of August, William Howe sent half his troops from Staten Island across the Hudson to Long Island, landing at Gravesend Bay. From there they marched toward lines Washington had established on Long Island closer to the East River. The British approached to within about three miles of the American lines, and camped near the village of Flatbush.

Washington was relieved that the suspense was ending. But he wished the engagement had begun better. His troops watching the shore had fallen back ahead of the British and burned barns and killed cattle, ostensibly to deny them to the invaders but in some cases apparently to please themselves. Washington winced on news of this, fearing it would make Loyalists of many who hadn't yet chosen sides. He sent off a sharply worded dispatch to Israel Putnam, his general in charge of the offending soldiers. "The distinction between a well-regulated army and a mob is the good order and discipline of the first, and the licentious and disorderly behaviour of the latter," Washington said. "Men, therefore, who are not employed as mere hirelings"—like the Hessians—"but have stepped forth in defence of everything that is dear and valuable not only to themselves but to posterity, should take uncommon pains to conduct themselves with uncommon propriety and good order."

Washington nonetheless looked forward to fighting the enemy at last. "I have no doubt but a little time will produce some important events," he wrote to John Hancock on August 23. "I hope they will be happy." If his men's spirits were any guide, he had cause to be optimistic. "The reinforcement detached yesterday went off in high spirits, and I have the pleasure to inform you that the whole of the army that are effective and capable of duty discover the same and great cheerfulness."

Although the British were moving, Washington couldn't tell just where they might strike. Current evidence suggested Long Island. "Almost the whole of the enemy's fleet have fallen down to the Narrows, and from this circumstance—the striking of their tents at their several encampments on Staten Island from time to time previous to the departure of the ships from thence—we are led to think they mean to land the main body of their army on Long Island and to make their grand push there," he wrote to Hancock on August 26 from his Manhattan headquarters. But he couldn't be sure. "This may possibly be only a feint, to draw over our troops to that quarter, in order to weaken us here."

Washington hedged his bets. He bolstered his Long Island positions on Brooklyn Heights but held back sufficient men to answer British thrusts elsewhere. His caution reflected his present tactical uncertainty but also his abiding strategy in the broader war. He could afford to give up territory; America was a large continent. He could *not* afford to lose his army. Whatever happened on Long Island, he must live to fight another day.

And so he did, but barely. Local Loyalists informed William Howe of a way around the American lines on Brooklyn Heights, and British generals Henry Clinton and Lord Cornwallis led their men on a night march through the pass. They caught American forces under Israel Putnam by surprise and on August 27 delivered a stinging defeat. Two thousand Americans were killed, wounded or captured in the battle. The losses included nearly all of a unit called the Maryland 400, which covered the retreat of the larger army into Brooklyn Heights, at the cost of the lives of all but some dozen.

The damage might have been greater had Howe pressed the attack into the Heights. But he paused to let his troops catch their breath, and to allow Washington and the Americans to reconsider their position. His brother, Richard Howe, sincerely sought peace, albeit on Britain's terms, and judged that the less blood spilled, the sooner peace might come. Washington and the Americans now knew what war against Britain entailed. The Howes hoped they would decide against continuing it.

Washington never entertained giving up the war, but he did decide, after consulting his generals, to yield the battle. The American position on Long Island was too precarious, with a heartened British army in front and the threat of British ships behind. The ships might cut off any retreat and enable the capture of the rest of the army there. Even if the Americans held Brooklyn Heights, by doing so they would be prevented from opposing a British landing elsewhere in the region.

Managing the retreat to Manhattan was no small chore. The men were dispirited by their defeat but couldn't be allowed to dwell on it, at least not until the churning East River lay between them and the British army. Washington commandeered all the boats his men could find and put them into service ferrying the surviving nine thousand troops in Brooklyn over to Manhattan. Rain, fog and darkness cloaked the crossing, which Washington himself supervised, taking passage only on the last boat to leave.

The demands of the operation kept Washington from writing to John Hancock and the Continental Congress, who were left wondering whether the war was about to end in defeat. Not until August 31, a Saturday, was he able to explain. "The extreme fatigue which myself and family have undergone, as much from the weather since as the engagement on the 27th, rendered me and them entirely unfit to take pen in hand," he said. "Since Monday, scarce any of us have been out of the lines till our passage across the East River was effected yesterday morning; and, for forty-eight hours preceding that I had hardly been off my horse, and never closed my eyes, so that I was quite unfit to write or dictate till this morning."

But the army was saved. The fight continued.

IN THE GLOW of the British victory on Long Island, Richard Howe approached Benjamin Franklin once more. He proposed a face-to-face meeting. Franklin still doubted that Howe had anything significant to offer, but the Congress insisted on hearing him out. It appointed Franklin, with Edward Rutledge and John Adams, to a commission charged with meeting Howe. Adams was even more skeptical than Franklin; when Howe's formal proposal for the meeting was delivered to the Congress by General John Sullivan, captured on Long Island and paroled for the purpose, Adams muttered to Benjamin Rush that he wished "that the first ball that had been fired on the day of the defeat of our army had gone through his head." To the whole Congress, Adams declared Sullivan a "decoy duck whom Lord Howe has sent among us to seduce us into a renunciation of our independence." Adams nonetheless accepted appointment to the commission, believing he was the one most likely to resist Howe's blandishment.

He was still feeling cranky when he and Franklin and Rutledge set out from Philadelphia. His mood didn't improve on the journey. "On the road and at all the public houses we saw such numbers of officers and soldiers straggling and loitering as gave me at least but a poor opinion of the discipline of our forces and excited as much indignation as anxiety," Adams wrote. "Such thoughtless dissipation at a time so critical was not calculated to inspire very sanguine hopes or give great courage to ambassadors." They spent the first night in New Brunswick, New Jersey. "The taverns were so full we could with difficulty obtain entertainment. At Brunswick but one bed could be procured for Dr. Franklin and me, in a chamber little larger than the bed, without a chimney and with only one small window. The window was open, and I, who was an invalid and afraid of the air in the night, shut it close. 'Oh!' says Franklin, 'don't shut the window. We shall be suffocated.' I answered I was afraid of the evening air. Dr. Franklin replied, 'The air within this chamber will soon be, and indeed is now worse than that without doors. Come! open the window and come to bed, and I will convince you. I believe you are not acquainted with my theory of colds.' Opening the window and leaping into bed, I said I had read his letters to Dr. Cooper in which he had advanced that nobody ever got a cold by going into a cold church, or any other cold air: but the theory was so little consistent with my experience, that I thought it a paradox. However, I had so much curiosity to hear his reasons, that I would run the risk of a cold. The Doctor then began an harangue upon air and cold and respiration and perspiration, with which I was so much amused that I soon fell asleep and left him and his philosophy together. But I believe they were equally sound and insensible, within a few minutes after me, for the last words I heard were pronounced as if he was more than half asleep."

Adams remained distrustful as the party reached the spot on the New Jersey shore from which they would embark to Staten Island. "Lord Howe had sent over an officer as an hostage for our security," Adams wrote. "I said to Dr. Franklin, it would be childish in us to depend upon such a pledge, and insisted on taking him over with us, and keeping our surety on the same side of the water with us." Franklin and Rutledge assented. "We all embarked in his lordship's barge. As we approached the shore, his lordship, observing us, came down to the water's edge to receive us, and looking at the officer, he said, 'Gentlemen, you make me a very high compliment, and you may depend upon it, I will consider it as the most sacred of things.'"

The meeting place was a private home commandeered by the British army. "We walked up to the house between lines of guards of grenadiers, looking as fierce as ten furies and making all the grimaces and gestures and motions of their muskets with bayonets fixed, which I suppose military etiquette requires but which we neither understood nor regarded," Adams wrote. "The house had been the habitation of military guards, and was as dirty as a stable: but his lordship had prepared a large handsome room by spreading a carpet of moss and green sprigs from bushes and shrubs in the neighbourhood, till he had made it not only wholesome but romantically elegant, and he entertained us with good claret, good bread, cold ham, tongues and mutton."

Once the dining was done, Howe turned to business. He opened the discussion by remarking his history of good feelings toward the Americans. He acknowledged Franklin's observation that the Olive Branch Petition was now a dead letter, but he hoped the sentiments it expressed might yet be the basis for a reconciliation. This said, he explained that he could not treat with the three as representatives of the Congress of an independent country. The king had not recognized either the legitimacy of the Congress or the independence of America, and what the king had not recognized, neither could he, as representative of the king. All the same, he wished to speak to them as gentlemen of great ability and influence among the Americans. "They were now met to converse together and to try if any outline could be drawn to put a stop to the calamities of war, and to bring forward some plan that might be satisfactory both to America and to England," he said of the entire group, in the paraphrasing words of the notes of the meeting.

Franklin replied that Howe might think of the three of them however he wished, but they would consider themselves in their real character, as delegates of the Congress of the independent United States of America. Franklin was willing for the conversation to proceed, but Howe must know this.

Adams, speaking for himself, said he had "no objection to Lord Howe's considering him, on the present occasion, merely as a private gentleman, or in any character except that of a British subject."

Howe reiterated that he could not acknowledge American independence. Yet he kept talking. "His majesty's most earnest desire was to make his American subjects happy, to cause a reform in whatever affected the freedom of their legislation, and to concur with his Parliament in the redress of any real grievances," Howe declared. He said that his powers, as the king's agent, were "to restore peace and grant pardons, to attend to complaints and representations, and to confer upon means of establishing a reunion upon terms honorable and advantageous to the colonies as well as to Great Britain." He reiterated again his desire to end the armed conflict. "It is desirable to put a stop to these ruinous extremities, as well for the sake of our country as yours," he said to Franklin and the others. "When an American falls, England feels it. Is there no way of treading back this step of independency, and opening the door to a full discussion?"

No, there was not, Franklin said at once, his temper rising. Hadn't Howe been listening? Britain's reply to America's petitions had been contempt and violence; the British government had sent out armies and burned American towns. The decision for independence was irrevocable. "All former attachment"—to Britain—"was *obliterated*," Franklin said. "America could not return again to the domination of Great Britain."

Adams and Rutledge seconded Franklin's view, and the meeting soon ended. "Lord Howe said that if such were their sentiments, he could only lament it was not in his power to bring about the accommodation he wished," the meeting notes recorded. "That he had not authority, nor did he expect he ever should have, to treat with the colonies as states independent of the crown of Great Britain, and that he was sorry the gentlemen had had the trouble of coming so far, to so little purpose. That if the colonies would not give up the system of independency, it was impossible for him to enter into any negotiation."

Adams later recalled a part of the conversation between Howe and Franklin that summarized the distance that now separated Britain and America. Howe expressed gratitude for a statue Massachusetts had paid to have erected in London's Westminster Abbey to honor his brother George Howe, who had been killed in the French and Indian War. So great was his affection toward America as a result of this that he felt for America as for a brother, and if America should fall, he would lament it like the loss of a brother.

Adams described the response: "Dr. Franklin, with an easy air and a collected countenance, a bow, a smile and all that naïveté which sometimes appeared in his conversation and is often observed in his writings, replied 'My lord, we will do our utmost endeavours to save your lordship that mortification.'"

H OWE RESPONDED, in a rueful tone, "I suppose you will endeavour to give us employment in Europe."

This was exactly what the Congress had in mind. The refusal of the British government to recognize American independence meant that the war would continue, and that allies in the war were more important to America than ever. In late September the Congress appointed Franklin, Silas Deane and Arthur Lee commissioners to France. Their job was to negotiate a treaty with the French government that would help America win the war against Britain.

When Franklin sailed from Philadelphia for Paris at the end of October 1776, two of his grandsons accompanied him. Benjamin Franklin Bache was the seven-year-old son of Sally and Richard Bache; worried about the war, and with Franklin's encouragement, they decided to send Benny to Europe to be educated. Franklin would enroll him in boarding school in Paris.

William Temple Franklin was the sixteen-year-old son of William Franklin. Temple, as the lad was called, had been born out of wedlock in England, when William was studying law while his father served as colonial agent. Unlike Franklin, who was about to be married to Deborah when William was similarly born out of wedlock, William had no obvious female caregiver who could help with the boy's upbringing. So he placed the infant in a foster home. Franklin paid for Temple's support, and eventually brought him into his own London household. When Franklin returned to America in 1775, Temple traveled with him. The following year, Franklin took Temple to Paris.

Temple's decision to join his grandfather wasn't automatic, and it wasn't easy, for it required him to choose not simply between his father and his grandfather, but between America and Britain. By this time William Franklin was the senior royal governor in North America, and he unsurprisingly interpreted matters from the point of view of the British crown. He thought the radicals in Massachusetts had been foolishly stubborn in refusing to pay for the tea tossed overboard in the Boston Tea Party. "I cannot but think it very extraordinary that neither the assembly of Massachusetts Bay nor the town of Boston have so much as intimated any intention or desire of making satisfaction to the East India Company and the officers of the customs, when by doing those two things, which are consistent with strict justice, and by declaring that they will not hereafter attempt to hinder the landing at Boston any goods legally imported they might get their port opened in a few months," William had written to Franklin. "They ought first to do justice before they ask it of others." The first Continental Congress was about to meet; William guessed it would do more harm than good. "There is no foreseeing the consequences which may result from such a congress."

Franklin, taking the opposite view, refused to grant the sincerity of his son's position. He had replied that the Massachusetts men were right not to pay; the British government was not to be trusted. "As to 'doing justice before they ask it,' that should have been thought of by the legislature here"—in London—"before they demanded it of the Bostonians. They have extorted many thousand pounds from America unconstitutionally, under colour of acts of Parliament, and with an armed force. Of this money they ought to make restitution. They might first have taken out payment for the tea, etc., and returned the rest." But Franklin didn't expect William to understand. "You, who are a thorough courtier, see everything with government eyes," he said dismissively.

The quarrel between father and son grew more personal, and more poignant. After the difficult early years between William and Deborah, as he matured and she aged, he showed her the loving concern of any natural son. Debbie suffered a stroke in 1774, and William relayed to Franklin that his wife was calling for her husband to come home from England. Franklin tarried, overestimating his ability to reconcile America and Britain and underestimating the gravity of Debbie's decline. He was still in London when she died in December 1774. William helped bury her, and in reporting the funeral he chided his father for inattention to his spouse. "I heartily wish you had happened to have come over in the fall, as I think her disappointment in that respect preyed a good deal on her spirits."

William proceeded to criticize his father for inordinate self-importance. Franklin was wasting his time in England, William said. "If there was any prospect of your being able to bring the people in power to your way of thinking, or of those of your way of thinking's being brought into power, I should not think so much of your stay. But as you have had by this time pretty strong proofs that neither can be reasonably expected, and that you are looked upon with an evil eye in that country, and are in no small danger of being brought into trouble for your political conduct, you had certainly better return, while you are able to bear the fatigues of the voyage, to a country where the people revere you and are inclined to pay a deference to your opinions." In America, Franklin might have an actual calming effect. It was certainly needed, William said. "However mad you may think the measures of the ministry are, yet I trust you have candor enough to acknowledge that we are no ways behindhand with them in instances of madness on this side the water." Having said all this, William knew his father wouldn't agree. "It is a disagreeable subject, and I'll drop it."

The correspondence between father and son ceased, not to be resumed for a decade. But one matter of common concern couldn't be ignored: the education of Temple Franklin. Temple had spent most of his boyhood with his grandfather, and Franklin took the lead in planning his future. "Methinks 'tis time to think of a profession for Temple (who is now upwards of 14), that the remainder of his education may have some relation to it," Franklin wrote in one of his last letters to William. "I have thought he may make an expert lawyer, as he has a good memory, quick parts, and ready elocution. He would certainly make an excellent painter, having a vast fondness for drawing, which he pursues with unwearied industry, and has made great proficiency. But I do not find that he thinks of it as a business. The only hint of inclination that he has given is that of being a surgeon, but it was slightly mentioned." Franklin wanted Temple to learn self-reliance. "It is indeed my wish that he might learn some art by which he could at any time procure a subsistence." After that, if a better calling emerged, all to the good. Franklin said he would steer Temple away from government work. With an edge William couldn't have missed, Franklin said, "Posts and places are precarious dependencies. I would have him a free man."

THE SAGA OF THE FRANKLINS grew sadder with each passing month. The outbreak of fighting at Lexington had converted the political debate between radicals and conservatives into a mortal struggle between Patriots and Loyalists. As the Patriots gained the upper hand in the Continental Congress, they outlawed actions by the Loyalists that obstructed the war effort. Loyalists who kept their heads down might go about their daily lives largely unbothered by the growing radicalization of American politics, but those who stubbornly upheld the prerogatives of Crown and Parliament, or who held important office, found themselves with targets on their backs.

William Franklin, as New Jersey governor, held important office; he also upheld British prerogatives with all the stubbornness Franklins were capable of. William Franklin had made enemies in the New Jersey assembly in the way every strong-minded governor made enemies in his colony; these foes now took the opportunity to oust him from power. In early 1776 they met in an extra-legal body they called the Provincial Congress and sent a band of militia to arrest him.

William Franklin disdainfully rejected their authority, resented their intrusion upon his home, and refused to go quietly, though he was outnumbered and outgunned. The Patriot soldiers, flummoxed by his resistance, contented themselves with placing him under house arrest. A stalemate ensued. Franklin sneered at the Provincial Congress, contending it had not been authorized under British law; moreover, the congress and its adherents prevented the gathering of the existing New Jersey assembly, which he *did* recognize and tried to summon.

William Franklin reported the incident to Lord Germain, the colonial secretary, with his interpretation as to what it meant. "It has long appeared to me that they, or some of them at least, wanted to have the king's governors to quit the colonies, that they might have a pretence for forming them into separate republics," he said. "This consideration determined me to remain here as long as possible." Other governors had retreated to British vessels anchored in rivers or bays, within the boundaries of the colonies but beyond the physical reach of the radicals. "Perhaps if there had been a king's ship stationed in the harbour at Amboy, on board of which I might have resided as Governor Tryon"—of New York—"had done, and yet still consider myself as in my province, and execute the powers of government, I might, during the time I was so ill treated, have contrived to have gone on board. But as that was not the case, my language has constantly been: You may force me, but you shall never frighten me out of the province."

It was vital for Germain and the government in London to know the strength of the conservatives in New Jersey, compared with that of the radicals, William Franklin explained. It was greater than it seemed. "I am convinced that there are some members of the Council who reprobate most of the measures which have been adopted by the congress as much as I do, though they have at times been under a necessity, for the preservation of themselves and families in these times of violence, to appear to entertain sentiments of a different nature." And some who sincerely approved the measures of the congress did so under false pretenses. "I have no doubt but that their approbation was founded on a full persuasion they had that the congress meant what they professed: a reconciliation with the mother country on the principles of the English Constitution. Nor do I imagine they would have given any countenance to the proceedings of the congress had they suspected a design in them or their leaders of widening the breach for the sake of a more easy admission of independency." Most of the congress was averse to independence, Franklin said, although one would never guess it. "The majority have incautiously suffered themselves to be led by some designing men among them into a system of measures which, if successful, can have no other effect."

William Franklin had heard about the commissioners coming out from London. He hoped the gesture would have a good effect. "I most sincerely wish that so wise and lenient a measure as the sending out commissioners may effect a lasting reconciliation and union between the two countries." Yet he wasn't counting on anything. "If we may judge from the temper manifested in some late publications"—Franklin included examples with his letter—"nothing in the power of some of our artful and designing men will be omitted to counteract the merciful and benevolent intentions of the supreme legislature"—Parliament—"in this respect. They already, as your Lordship will see, represent reconciliation and ruin as nearly related."

In a postscript, William Franklin added some breaking news about members of the Continental Congress, including his father. "I have just heard that two of the delegates (Dr. Franklin and Mr. Chace) have passed through Woodbridge this morning in their way to Canada, accompanied by a Mr. Carrol, a Roman Catholic gentleman of great estate in Maryland, and a Romish priest or two. It is suggested that their principal business is to prevail on the Canadians to enter into the confederacy with the other colonies, and to send delegates to the Continental Congress." The diplomats were following in the wake of troops heading north. The latter were encountering difficulties. "It is likewise reported that a great number of the Continental troops have returned to Albany, not being able to cross the lakes—several soldiers, carriages, etc. having fallen in, and some lives lost, by the breaking of the ice."

WHETHER WILLIAM FRANKLIN INTENDED that his reporting on his father's movements and destination would assist in his father's arrest by British forces is hard to tell. As he himself languished in detention, he might well have wished the same on his father, who, in William's view, was guilty of far more than he himself was.

Meanwhile he castigated his tormentors, those designing men who presumed to dispute the authority he derived from the British crown. From house arrest he smuggled out a statement he managed to have printed; in it he addressed the members of the provincial assembly, moribund though it now was. "Having by proclamation summoned you to attend a meeting of the General Assembly of the province on the 20th instant, in order that I might communicate to you matters of great importance to the public welfare," William Franklin said, "and as there now seems little probability that I shall have it in my power to meet you, agreeable to my intentions, it is necessary that I should acquaint you with the cause of the disappointment that you may act such a part on the occasion as you may think the nature and exigency of the case requires."

For those who hadn't heard, he told how his home had been violated by orders of the illegal Provincial Congress, whose minions had arrested him. He had demanded to know the charges, and was informed that he had been branded "an enemy to the liberties of this country."

The idea was outrageous. "To be represented as an enemy to the liberties of my country merely for doing my duty in calling a meeting of the legal representatives of the people, to lay before them matters of the utmost concern to their future happiness and safety, was, as you may imagine, sufficient to rouse the indignation of any man not dead to human feelings, and occasion him to express his resentment in terms suitable to such unmerited provocation," Franklin said. The members of the assembly, of all people, should know the utter untruth of the charge. "To you, gentlemen, and to every individual in the province, can I safely appeal to vouch for me, that in no one instance have I ever manifested the least inimical disposition towards this colony. Your journals and minutes will shew that from the first commencement of the present unhappy disputes, I have been uniformly for having them accommodated by negotiation and treaty; from a full conviction that America might thereby obtain a fixed constitution which would afford every reasonable security for the enjoyment of British liberties."

The so-called congress had also ordered that payment of his salary be halted. This action, besides being illegal, manifested the pettiness of his opponents. "The stoppage of my salary is, I must say, an instance of meanness which I never expected to have experienced from any body of men in New Jersey." The action was rationalized on grounds that the governor had enriched himself on the job. Nothing could be further from the truth. "Those who best know me and my affairs know that if I were to quit this province tomorrow I should not retire one farthing the richer for anything acquired by means of my office. The income has at no time been more than sufficient to barely support the dignity of the station, and of late years it has been by no means adequate to the increased expences of living." To date the action of the congress had not been endorsed by the people of New Jersey. Should that happen, he would be truly hurt. "If the people at large should approve of this unworthy treatment of a man who has done his duty faithfully by them during a thirteen years administration, I own it would give me a concern infinitely greater than the loss of my salary."

For all his defiant tone, the governor realized he was at the mercy of his enemies. "I shall take my leave of you, and the good people you represent—perhaps for the last time," he said. But he couldn't go without offering advice and a warning. "Defend your constitution in all its branches. . . . Avoid, above all things, the traps of independency and republicanism now set for you, however temptingly they may be baited." The people must consider what they were being asked to give up. "You can never place yourselves in a happier situation than in your ancient constitutional dependency on Great Britain. No independent state ever was or ever can be so happy as we have been, and might still be, under that government." He repeated what he had said before. "I have early and often warned you of the pernicious designs of many pretended patriots, who, under the mask of zeal for reconciliation, have been from the first insidiously promoting a system of measures purposely calculated for widening the breach between the two countries, so far as to let in an independent republican tyranny—the worst and most debasing of all possible tyrannies. They well know that this has not even a chance of being accomplished but at the expence of the lives and properties of many thousands of the honest people of this country—yet *these*, it seems, are as nothing in the eyes of such desperate gamesters! But remember, gentlemen, that I now tell you that should they, contrary to all probability, accomplish their baneful purpose, yet their government will not be lasting."

He hoped the people, and their representatives, would come to their senses before it was too late. "I most heartily wish you, gentlemen, and the people of this once happy province may again enjoy peace and prosperity, and I shall ever particularly honour and esteem such of you and them as have dared, with an honest and manly firmness, in these worst of times, to avow their loyalty to the best of sovereigns, and manifest their attachment to their legal constitution."

For himself, he remained steadfast. "No office or honour in the power of the Crown to bestow will ever influence me to forget or neglect the duty I owe my country, nor the most furious rage of the most intemperate zealots induce me to swerve from the duty I owe His Majesty."

WILLIAM FRANKLIN'S FORCED JOURNEY to Connecticut became an act of political theater. His Patriot captors paraded their Loyalist prisoner—the highest-ranking one in Patriot hands—as a trophy and a caution to other Loyalists as to what might become of them. Franklin fell sick with a fever and was miserable the whole march, yet he managed to summon the dignity he thought he owed his office and the

British crown. He continued to reject the legitimacy of his detention; he was a prisoner of force, not of any real authority.

Along the way he was reviled and cursed. Not without reason, he feared that his guards wouldn't risk their own safety to protect him from a beating or worse by Patriot rowdies. Yet he reached Hartford whole, if not hale, and Connecticut governor Jonathan Trumbull offered him residence in an ordinary house if he would give his parole—his word not to escape or to engage in activities detrimental to the Patriot cause. Until now William Franklin had resisted all such offers, sticking to his assertion that an official of the British crown didn't negotiate with rebels. But from illness, weariness and a growing recognition of the hopelessness of the situation, he gave the required pledge.

For some weeks, his existence was tolerable. He was allowed the freedom of the small town of Wallingford, east of Hartford, and could even ride horseback outside the village. He knew no one in Wallingford, and the residents, Patriots almost to a person, shunned him. Some made a point of challenging him; one confrontation turned physical and he was pushed to the ground. He requested transfer to Middletown, a community that had more Loyalists and felt safer. His request was granted.

During his captivity he never heard from his father. Benjamin Franklin took pains to avoid anything that looked like favoritism for a Loyalist who happened to be his son, seeking neither William's release nor special terms for his incarceration. Ben's compunction had political grounds: as a leader of the Patriot cause he couldn't afford to be seen as consorting with a Loyalist leader. Personal pique doubtless figured as well, for Ben knew that if he were captured by William's British sponsors, he might expect much worse than William was enduring. A man made his decisions and had to live with the consequences.

Ben's diffidence extended to Elizabeth Franklin, William's wife. She was distraught by William's arrest and detention, and she was impoverished by the seizure of William's assets. With no relatives of her own in America, she turned to her in-laws, Benjamin Franklin in particular. He sent her sixty dollars but also a reminder that in these difficult times many people were suffering more than she was.

She responded in a tone of obvious hurt. "My troubles do indeed lie heavy on my mind, and though many people may suffer still more than I do, yet that does not lessen the weight of mine, which are really more than so weak a frame is able to support," she said. "I will not distress you by enumerating all my afflictions, but allow me, dear sir, to mention that it is greatly in your power to relieve them." The money was welcome, yet what she really needed was her husband. "Suppose that Mr. Franklin would sign a parole not dishonorable to himself and satisfactory to Governor Trumbull. Why may he not be permitted to return into this province and to his family? Many of the officers that have been taken during the war have had that indulgence shewn them, and why should it be denied to him?"

The answer was that William Franklin was deemed more dangerous than other officers. Yet she didn't get this from Ben Franklin. She had to infer it from others, including William Temple Franklin, whose efforts to get to know his father had been abruptly curtailed by William's arrest and deportation. Temple's grandfather erected additional obstacles. Ben recognized that Temple was not an American but a Briton, having lived nearly his whole life in England. Temple's devotion to the Patriot cause would be questioned, the more so given the Loyalism of his father. Ben Franklin didn't strictly refuse Temple permission to visit his stepmother, yet he warned Temple to be careful in doing so, and he sought to make the visits as short as possible.

Ben threw even more hurdles in the way of Temple's traveling to Connecticut to see William. All the cautions that applied to visits to Elizabeth were multiplied in the case of William. More than that, Ben seems to have worried that William would come to have more influence over Temple than he—Ben—did. William would be persuasive in the British cause; he might make a Loyalist out of Temple. Ben feared for Temple's political soul, as it were. But he also feared for his own personal feelings. The crisis between Britain and America had already deprived Benjamin Franklin of his son; he couldn't bear to think it might deprive him of his grandson too.

"Dear Billy," Franklin wrote to Temple, employing the same nickname he had long used with William. Temple was visiting Elizabeth and had written to Ben, who now replied. "I received yours of the 16th, in which you propose going to your father, if I have no objection. I have considered the matter, and cannot approve of your taking such a journey at this time, especially alone, for many reasons which I have not time to write." Elizabeth had asked Temple to carry a letter to William. Other means would suffice, Ben said. "I am persuaded that if your mother should write a sealed letter to her husband, and enclose it under cover to Gov. Trumbull of Connecticut, acquainting him that it contains nothing but what relates to her private family concerns, and requesting him to forward or deliver it (opening it first if he should think fit), he would cause it to be delivered safe without opening." Franklin couched his aversion to Temple's going to Connecticut in terms of concern for the lad's education. The autumn session would be starting soon. "I hope you do not feel any reluctance in returning to your studies. This is the time of life in which you are to lay the foundations of your future improvement, and of your importance among men. If this season is neglected, it will be like cutting off the spring from the year."

True to Franklin family form, Temple resisted his elder's advice. "Honoured sir," he replied, "I am very sorry to find that my intended visit to my father does not meet with your approbation." But he was going to go anyway. His stepmother's letter needed to get through. "The method you mention of enclosing her letters sealed to Gov. Trumbull, she has tried with Col. Hamlen in her two last letters, but has had no account of their being received, either opened or unopened, tho' there has been sufficient time for that purpose," he explained.

Temple was insightful enough to realize that his grandfather's expressed concern about the school term wasn't his real reason for opposing the trip to Connecticut. "In my going, you might perhaps imagine I should give such intelligence to my father as would not be thought proper for him to know," he said. "But I can assure you, sir, that I am entirely ignorant of everything relating to public affairs except the petty news, which is talked of by everybody, and is in all the public prints." Temple said he had to go now or risk not being able to go at all. "The winter is approaching so fast"—he exaggerated: it was still September—"and the present troubles not likely to end." This last was true enough. "There is no time to be lost."

Ben Franklin said he'd been misunderstood. "You are mistaken in imagining that I am apprehensive of your carrying dangerous intelligence to your father," he told Temple. "For while he remains where he is, he could make no use of it were you to know and acquaint him with all that passes." He continued, "You would have been more in the right if you could have suspected me of a little tender concern for your welfare, on account of the length of the journey, your youth and inexperience, the number of sick returning on that road with the infectious camp distemper, which makes the beds unsafe, together with the loss of time in your studies, of which I fear you begin to grow tired." He suggested that Temple wasn't leveling with him, or didn't know his own mind. "I rather think the project takes its rise from your own inclination to a ramble, and disinclination for returning to college, joined with a desire I do not blame of seeing a father you have so much reason to love."

Franklin offered to send franked—postage prepaid—stationery for Elizabeth to use in writing the letters she could send via Governor Trumbull. And in what amounted to a large concession, he added a scheme for return mail: "She may desire her husband to send his letters to her under cover to me." He signed the letter, "Your affectionate Grandfather."

In the end, Temple's plan to visit William was foiled by the Continental Congress as much as by Franklin. Days after Franklin's latest letter, the Congress appointed him commissioner to France. On the alliance he was charged with seeking, the success of the revolution might depend, and time was of the essence. "I hope you will return hither immediately, and that your mother will make no objection to it, something offering here that will be much to your advantage if you are not out of the way," Franklin wrote to Temple. "I am so hurried that I can only add, Ever your affectionate Grandfather."

Temple heeded the peremptory summons, and discovered that his grandfather wanted to take him along to France. Ben Franklin's suspicion that an itch to ramble was part of Temple's desire to visit William appeared to be corroborated when Temple decided that a ramble to Paris justified forgoing a trip to Connecticut. In any event, Ben was his sole means of support, and when Ben insisted, Temple had little choice but to accede.

By this means Ben got what he wanted. Temple chose Ben and America over William and Britain. William learned of his father's coup only after it was too late to object.

BEFORE LONG, Temple wouldn't have been able to visit his father even if he wanted to. Watchers of William reported that he had violated the terms of his parole. Governor Trumbull received the news from George Washington, who had it from William Livingston, William's successor as governor of New Jersey. "Governor Livingston informed me a few days ago that he understood that Governor Franklin, by some means or other, continued to carry on a correspondence with Mr. Hugh Wallace of New York," Washington told Trumbull. "And a gentleman of the name of Livingston who went into New York and took protection, but not liking his situation, returned again, informed upon oath, that he heard that Governor Franklin granted protections to such as would take them." The protections were letters signed by William Franklin authorizing safe passage through British lines. Washington conceded that he was relating hearsay. "I don't know that the foregoing amounts to positive proof against Governor Franklin," he told Trumbull. "But it ought, at least, to put you upon your guard, and have him narrowly watched."

Washington apparently received additional evidence of William's misbehavior, for a month later he wrote again to Trumbull to say, "Mr. Franklin's conduct is truly reprehensible, and I am amazed that men under such engagements should not be more regardful of the ties of honor."

The Continental Congress agreed that the deposed governor had acted reprehensibly. It sent Trumbull an order mandating that William Franklin be closely confined, forbidden communication with others, and denied access to paper and pen.

Perhaps relieved to have the decision taken out of his hands, Trumbull directed that William Franklin be taken to Litchfield, thirty miles west of Hartford, and held there, alone, in a cell above a tavern. He was allowed no visitors and no time outside the cell, which was infested with fleas, rats and other vermin. His food was meager and scarcely palatable; the noise from the tavern kept him awake. But worst was the solitary nature of his confinement. "I suffer so much from being thus buried alive, having no one to speak to day or night, and for the want of air and exercise, that I should deem it a favor to be immediately taken out and shot," he wrote to Trumbull.

Elizabeth Franklin suffered, too. After her husband was carted off to Connecticut, she fled Patriot-controlled New Jersey for British-occupied and Loyalist-dominated New York City. She had no money, their property having been confiscated, and had no friends in New York. In poverty and solitude she soon fell ill. William heard of her distress and wrote to George Washington requesting a furlough to see her. He acknowledged that the Continental Congress had ordered his imprisonment and that Washington might feel a need to defer, but he appealed to Washington's humanity. "All I request is to be allowed to visit my poor dying wife, and to endeavour to recover her, or, if that should not be possible, to at least contribute all in my power to comfort her in her last moments," he said.

Washington refused. "I heartily sympathise with you in your distressing situation," he said, "but however strong my inclination to comply with your request, it is by no means in my power to supersede a positive resolution of Congress, under which your present confinement took place." With what William Franklin must have taken for cold comfort, Washington added, "I sincerely hope a speedy restoration of Mrs. Franklin's health may relieve you from the anxiety you must naturally feel from her present declining condition."

Mrs. Franklin did not recover. She died alone and uncomforted.

BRITISH GOVERNORS OF THE PROVINCES were becoming an endangered species. Against the rising tide of resistance to Parliament, they had little recourse. Thomas Hutchinson had had British troops, but they wound up simply inflaming the situation, to the point where his replacement was General Gage. The Patriots were quicker off the mark than the Loyalists to bring provincial militias to their side, not least since the rhetoric of defending American rights was more inspiring than calls to defend the British crown.

John Murray, Lord Dunmore, had been governor of Virginia since 1771. He soon ran athwart Patrick Henry and the radicals in the house of burgesses, and when the administration in Britain ordered the governors to prevent their provinces from sending delegates to the Continental Congress, he tried. But it was an impossible task, given the state of public opinion, and the effort simply made him less liked in Virginia than he had already been.

At almost the same moment when Thomas Gage was attempting to disarm the Massachusetts militia at Lexington, Dunmore tried a similar neutralization of the Virginia militia. He ordered royal marines from a British warship anchored near Williamsburg to carry off a supply of gunpowder from its storage site on land to the ship, where it would be beyond the reach of the militia.

Patrick Henry learned of the seizure and rallied the militia. An armed confrontation ensued. The battles of Lexington and Concord had just been fought, but the news hadn't reached Virginia. If it had, there might well have been a southern reprise of the same. As it was, Dunmore and Henry reached an accommodation whereby the governor paid Henry and the militia for the powder. Violence was averted, but its specter hung over the province. Fearing for his safety, Dunmore took refuge on another warship, in the York River.

He called on Loyalists to defend him and the authority of the king. They did so in numbers sufficient to annoy the Patriot party yet insufficient to restore his authority much beyond his ship. Seeing little chance of improving his position by ordinary means, in November 1775 Dunmore took what he called a "most disagreeable but now absolutely necessary step." He proclaimed martial law, suspending civil government in Virginia, and went on to state, "To the end that peace and good order may the sooner be restored, I do require every person capable of bearing arms to resort to his Majesty's standard or be looked upon as traitors to his Majesty's Crown and government and thereby become liable to the penalty the law inflicts upon such offences, such as forfeiture of life, confiscation of lands, etc. etc." And then came the really shocking part: "And I do hereby farther declare all indentured servants, Negroes, or others (appertaining to rebels) free that are able and willing to bear arms."

Dunmore's proclamation raised the stakes of the struggle in Virginia dramatically. Martial law contravened what Virginians conceived to be their most basic rights as Britons. Dunmore's branding as traitors, subject to execution, not simply those in arms against him but those who refused to take arms *for* him left no room for moderates and scarce hope for accommodation. His threat of confiscation of land made even Loyalist-minded planters wonder if their holdings were safe.

But it was the promise of freedom to slaves who fled their masters and joined the British army that really got the attention of Virginians, of all races. Since the arrival of the first African slaves in the English colonies in America—in Virginia in 1619—slaveholders had taken pains to keep weapons out of the hands of slaves. A slave uprising haunted slaveholders' dreams. Dunmore was bringing that nightmare to life.

The slaveholders responded with outrage and threats of their own. A Virginia convention defying the martial-law declaration warned slaves not to be seduced by Dunmore's "base and insidious arts." It reminded slaves of an existing Virginia law decreeing that "all negro or other slaves conspiring to rebel or make insurrection shall suffer death." At the same time, it offered amnesty to those "unhappy people already deluded" who now saw the error of their ways. If they turned in their weapons and returned to their masters, they would be forgiven. But only if they did so at once.

THE RESPONSE OF THE SLAVES varied from region to region, plantation to plantation, and person to person. Far from the camps of the British, the balance of risk against benefit disposed most slaves to stay put, at least for the time being. Even for those close to British lines, the slaves had to calculate the trustworthiness of Dunmore and his British backers. Would he change his mind and leave them at the mercy of angry masters? Beyond trustworthiness was the question of war-worthiness. Would the British win? If they didn't, their best intentions toward the slaves might count for nothing, or worse.

The choice before the slaves was the choice before all Americans once the fighting began: which side to bet on. Yet for slaves the stakes were higher. It was hard to imagine many white Loyalists being executed by victorious Patriots. But it was *not* hard to imagine black Loyalists, erstwhile slaves, being executed, if only as an example to other slaves not to try anything similar. Or if the slave-owners balked at seeing their property destroyed, the captured slaves might be sold to the West Indies, where death would come more slowly but almost as certainly.

Despite the dangers, slaves took up Dunmore's offer. They arrived in ones and twos at first, then in dozens and scores. Before long he had enough to fill out an "Ethiopian Regiment" of three hundred armed black men, under the command of (white) British officers. They came from the largest plantations and from modest farms; they stole themselves away from wealthy masters and from those just scraping by.

George Washington worried they would leave Mount Vernon. His plantation manager, cousin Lund Washington, apprised him of the situation there. "Our Dunmore has at length published his much dreaded proclamation declaring freedom to all indentured servants and slaves (the property of rebels) that will repair to his Majesty's standard, being able to bear arms," Lund wrote in early December. "What effect it will have upon those sort of people I cannot tell." Lund was hopeful. "I think if there was no white servants in this family I should be under no apprehension about the slaves." He worried that the white servants, by running off to British lines, would set a bad example for the slaves. But he would do his best to counteract it. "I am determined that if any of them create any confusion to make an example of him." Yet Lund realized what he was up against. "They have no fault to find," he said of the slaves, self-servingly but, by his lights, in accord with the comparatively mild treatment of slaves at Mount Vernon. Yet still they would go. "Sears, who is at work here, says there is not a man of them but would leave us if they believed they could make their escape. . . . Liberty is sweet."

Which was what worried George Washington. "If the Virginians are wise, that arch-traitor to the rights of humanity, Lord Dunmore, should be instantly crushed, if it takes the force of the whole colony to do it," he wrote to a fellow officer. "Otherwise, like a snowball in rolling, his army will get size—some through fear, some through promises, and some from inclination joining his standard. But that which renders the measure indispensably necessary is the Negroes. For if he gets formidable, numbers of them will be tempted to join who will be afraid to do it without."

Until Dunmore could be crushed, his offer had to be answered, Washington judged. Unanswered, Dunmore's proclamation would make latent—if not patent—Loyalists of most slaves in Virginia and perhaps other provinces, who would realize that fighting for the British promised freedom, while declining to do so offered nothing but continued bondage. Consequently Washington overruled the earlier recommendation of Benjamin Franklin and the visiting committee from the Congress, against recruiting black troops, and in an order issued in January 1776 delivered a counteroffer. "As the General is informed that numbers of free Negroes are desirous of enlisting," Washington's order read, "he gives leave to the recruiting officers to entertain them, and promises to lay the matter before the Congress, who he doubts not will approve of it."

This fell far short of what Dunmore promised, applying only to *free* blacks, not to the enslaved. And the Continental Congress diluted it further, saying that blacks already in the army might *re*-enlist, but barring the recruitment of new black soldiers.

Yet it represented a concession nonetheless. Washington had wanted to enforce the color line in his army, judging free blacks under arms too tempting as examples to enslaved blacks. But Dunmore had set off what amounted to a bidding war for the support of American blacks, slave and free. On paper, Dunmore's offer was better than Washington's. How it would evolve in practice remained to be determined, and fought over.

WASHINGTON'S RETREAT FROM Long Island had salvaged his army, but the New York campaign raised serious questions about his leadership. He had been outflanked, outmaneuvered and simply outgeneraled by William Howe. Washington regained a modicum of respect in a September battle at Harlem Heights, but at White Plains in October he suffered another setback, and was put to flight once more, this time across the Hudson.

Worse was to come. An American battery at Fort Washington on northern Manhattan Island blocked British access to the Hudson River above; for this reason the Continental Congress urged Washington to hold the fort if at all possible. Washington had doubts but gave discretion to General Nathanael Greene, the local commander, and through Greene to Colonel Robert Magaw, in direct charge of the fort. Greene overestimated Magaw, who underestimated the British and their ability to cut off his avenues of retreat. By the time Magaw discovered his mistake, he was trapped. He mounted a game resistance but ultimately surrendered the fort and nearly three thousand troops.

Washington was dismayed and embarrassed. "This is a most unfortunate affair, and has given me great mortification," he wrote to his brother John. He should have been more decisive, he said. "I had given it as my opinion to General Greene, under whose care it was, that it would be best to evacuate the place; but, as the order was discretionary, and his opinion differed from mine, it unhappily was delayed too long, to my great grief." The result was the loss of a third of his army, not to mention the cannons and other arms captured at the fort.

To his men he put the best face on things, but to John he spoke candidly. "I am wearied almost to death with the retrograde motion of things," Washington said. He wondered what he had gotten himself into. "I solemnly protest that a pecuniary reward of twenty thousand pounds a year would not induce me to undergo what I do; and after all, perhaps, to lose my character, as it is impossible, under such a variety of distressing circumstances, to conduct matters agreeably to public expectation, or even to the expectation of those who employ me, as they will not make proper allowances for the difficulties their own errors have occasioned."

He had no choice but to keep retreating. He led what remained of his army across New Jersey, and didn't stop till he had put the Delaware River between his forces and Howe's. From the Pennsylvania side he assessed the damage to the Patriot cause. New York was lost, and by all evidence the British could have their way at whatever part of the American coast they chose to land. Perhaps Howe could never conquer the interior, but whether the interior could survive without the coast was a question Washington couldn't answer.

"I wish to Heaven it was in my power to give you a more favorable account of our situation than it is," he wrote to his cousin Lund. The recent travails weren't over. "I have no idea of being able to make a stand." Washington and his men had done what they could, but he had no confidence it would be enough. "We have brought over and destroyed all the boats we could lay our hands on upon the Jersey shore for many miles above and below this place; but it is next to impossible to guard a shore for sixty miles, with less than half the enemy's numbers, when by force or stratagem they may suddenly attempt a passage in many different places."

He was losing the battle for public opinion, at least locally. "A large part of the Jerseys have given every proof of disaffection that they can do, and this part of Pennsylvania are equally inimical," Washington told Lund. Recruiting was growing more difficult, even as it was more necessary than ever. "Our only dependence now is upon the speedy enlistment of a new army. If this fails, I think the game will be pretty well up."

WASHINGTON'S EVACUATION OF New York spared the city the ravages of battle, but left it vulnerable to other harm. "A little after 12 o'clock last night a most dreadful fire broke out in New York, in three different places in the south and windward part of the town," recorded Frederick Mackenzie, an officer of fusiliers in the British army. "The alarm was soon given, but unfortunately there was a brisk wind at the south, which spread the flames with such irresistible rapidity that notwithstanding every assistance was given which the present circumstances admitted, it was impossible to check its progress." At summer's end the mostly wooden buildings of the city were dry, and the progress of the conflagration was swift and implacable. "It broke out first near the Exchange, and burnt all the houses on the west side of Broad Street, almost as far as the City Hall, and from thence all those in Beaver Street, and almost every house on the west side of the town between the Broad Way and the North River, as far as the college, amounting in the whole to about 600 houses, besides several churches, particularly Trinity Church, the principal one in town," Mackenzie wrote.

The British did all in their power to stop the fire, to little avail. "On its first appearance, two regiments of the 5th Brigade went into town, and some time after, a great number of seamen from the fleet were sent on shore under proper officers by order of Lord Howe, to give assistance," Mackenzie said. "About daybreak the brigade of guards came in from camp, but from the absence of the regular firemen, the bad state of the engines, a want of buckets, and a scarcity of water, the efforts of the troops and seamen, though very great, could not prevent the fire from spreading in the manner it did."

The timing of the fire—just as one army was leaving, and before the other had fully arrived—was suspicious. The multiple origins caused the British to conclude that the fire was the work of arsonists, who in certain cases were discovered at work. "It is beyond a doubt that the town was designedly set on fire, either by some of those fellows who concealed themselves in it since the 15th instant"—the date of departure of Washington's army—"or by some villains left behind for the purpose," Mackenzie said. "Some of them were caught by the soldiers in the very act of setting fire to the inside of empty houses at a distance from the fire; many were detected with matches and combustibles under their clothes, and combustibles were found in several houses. . . . The Trinity Church, a very handsome, ancient building, was perceived to be on fire long before the fire reached the adjacent houses, and as it stood at some distance from any house, little doubt remained that it was set on fire willfully." Testimony from Loyalist residents seemed to confirm the identity of at least some of the firestarters. "During the time the Rebels were in possession of the town, many of them were heard to say they would burn it, sooner than it should become a nest for Tories," Mackenzie reported. "And several inhabitants who were most violently attached to the rebel cause have been heard to declare they would set fire to their own houses sooner than they should be occupied by the King's troops."

Miscreants were dealt summary justice, where possible. "One villain who abused and cut a woman who was employed in bringing water to the engines, and who was found cutting the handles of the fire buckets, was hung up by the heels on the spot by the seamen," Mackenzie said. "One or two others who were found in houses with fire brands in their hands were put to death by the enraged soldiery and thrown into the flames."

Whatever the origins of the fire, its consequences were heartrending. "It is almost impossible to conceive a scene of more horror and distress," Mackenzie wrote. "The sick, the aged, women, and children half naked were seen going they knew not where, and taking refuge in houses which were at a distance from the fire, but from whence they were in several instances driven a second and even a third time by the devouring element, and at last in a state of despair laying themselves down on the Common. The terror was increased by the horrid noise of the burning and falling houses, the pulling down of such wooden buildings as served to conduct the fire (in which the soldiers and seamen were particularly active and useful), the rattling of above 100 wagons, sent in from the army, and which were constantly employed in conveying to the Common such goods and effects as could be saved. The confused voices of so many men, the shrieks and cries of the women and children, the seeing the fire break out unexpectedly in places at a distance, which manifested a design of totally destroying the city, with numberless other circumstances of private misery and distress, made this one of the most tremendous and affecting scenes I ever beheld."

Part VII

Malignant Faction

THE ATLANTIC CROSSING OF Benjamin Franklin and William Temple Franklin was swift but rough. British warships, on the lookout for rebels like Franklin, multiplied the perils of the winter passage. But Franklin's party reached Le Havre safely, and a short time later arrived in Paris.

Franklin presented his credentials to the Comte de Vergennes, the French foreign minister. "We beg leave to acquaint your excellency that we are appointed and fully empowered by the Congress of the United States of America to propose and negotiate a treaty of amity and commerce between France and the said States," he said of himself and his fellow commissioners. The French government had indicated its openness to friendship with the United States by allowing American vessels access to French ports, and by permitting Franklin, Silas Deane and Arthur Lee to travel to Paris. Franklin and the others hoped to improve and formalize this friendship.

Franklin understood that he had some persuading to do. He needed to convince Vergennes that American independence was plausible and in the interests of France. Put otherwise, he had to show the benefits that would accrue to France from supporting American independence, and the costs France would suffer by failing to do so.

Franklin began by explaining how fully committed the American colonies were to independence. "All their humble petitions for redress of grievances being rejected, and answered only by an act of Parliament confiscating their estates and declaring their lives forfeited, and the war being carried on against them with uncommon cruelty, by burning their defenceless towns in winter, exciting slaves to rise against their masters, and savages to assassinate and massacre their inoffensive husbandmen, the several colonies, exasperated to the last degree, called loudly upon the Congress to declare an independence," he said. The Congress had done so, and the war proceeded. Meanwhile the Congress was preparing a permanent version of itself—"a general Confederation"—to coordinate the actions of the separate states, enhance the war effort, and make independence permanent.

Yet the enthusiasm for independence wasn't the whole story, Franklin told Vergennes. In each state there existed pockets of resistance to the revolution. "They consist chiefly of traders who are put out of business, of people from England and Scotland who have not been long settled in that country, or of such natives as have held offices under the former government, or are afraid of the consequences that may follow a conquest." Franklin didn't mention that his son was one such former officeholder. The number of Loyalists wasn't great, Franklin said, but it might increase if the British army won a series of victories.

Vergennes would want to know the strength of the American armed forces; Franklin told him. "The Congress have resolved 88 battalions for the ensuing campaign, each battalion to consist of about 780 men." Franklin supplied Vergennes a copy of the pertinent resolution. "They have a squadron of small ships at sea, which have greatly annoyed the English commerce. They have 13 frigates of 32 to 36 guns, just built, most of them rigged and nearly ready for sea, but some want guns and anchors. Cannon of iron are casting in different places, as large as 18 pounders; but the workmen not being yet perfect in the business, many of the pieces fail in the proof, which occasions a want of cannon from Europe. A number of privateers are also out against the enemy. Abundance of fishermen being put out of their employment by the war enter in the frigates or engage in the privateers."

Franklin supposed Vergennes would discount these figures for the optimism they embodied; Franklin would have done so had he been in Vergennes's position. Yet they were roughly right, as Vergennes could ascertain through his own sources.

Another realm was more speculative, as Franklin candidly admitted. "The number of souls in the 13 United States is commonly estimated at 3,000,000. Perhaps that estimate is too high at present; but such is the rapid increase of people there, through early marriages, that it cannot be long before that number is exceeded, the inhabitants having been generally found to double themselves by natural generation every 25 years." What did this mean for the current conflict? "Men will not be wanting to continue this war."

The treaty Franklin sought specified "amity and commerce." The commercial connection was crucial. America produced a great deal that France might want to buy. "The commerce of the 13 states has increased in a much greater proportion than that of the number of people, because at the same time that they have grown more numerous, they have also become richer, and abler to pay for richer manufactures," Franklin told Vergennes. "This commerce before the war amounted to about five millions of pounds sterling, and employed between 8 and 900 sail of ships." The British had forfeited this commerce by driving America away. "It may now, with all its future increase, be gained by France and Spain"—Spain was France's ally—"if they will protect it; and they will thereby be as much strengthened, in the vent of manufactures and produce, increase of wealth and seamen, etc., as England will be weakened, whereby the difference will be doubled. The tobacco, etc., which France and Spain cannot consume, they may vend with profit to the rest of Europe."

But the opportunity wouldn't last forever, Franklin cautioned Vergennes. "If the commerce of America is much longer obstructed, the party who dislike the war will be so strengthened as to compel the rest to accommodation with Britain. For the other party, though now by far the most numerous, and who are for continuing the war till the independence is established, until they have obliged Britain to make reparation for the injuries she has done us, will be weakened by the want of commerce, as without it taxes cannot so well be raised for supporting the war, nor the troops so easily clothed and armed." Franklin didn't expect Vergennes and the French government to make any rash decisions, but he wished them to understand that their moment might pass.

In a letter written at about the same time, Franklin, Deane and Lee sharpened the argument for swift action by promising territorial gains to France, as well as to Spain, a possible second American ally. "North America now offers to France and Spain her amity and commerce," the American commissioners said. "She is also ready to guarantee in the firmest manner to those nations all their present possessions in the West Indies, as well as those they shall acquire from the enemy in a war that may be consequential of such assistance as she requests. The interest of the three nations is the same. The opportunity of cementing them, and of securing all the advantages of that commerce, which in time will be immense, now presents itself. If neglected, it may never again return."

VERGENNES WAS INTRIGUED, and so were the people of France, to the extent Franklin and the other commissioners could ascertain. "The hearts of the French are universally for us, and the cry is strong for immediate war with Britain," Franklin reported to the Continental Congress. "Indeed everything tends that way." Yet in the next breath he added, "The court has its reasons for postponing it a little longer."

The court's reluctance was chiefly that of the French king. Louis XVI had inherited from his forebears an animus toward Britain, but also a reflexive opposition to republicanism. The Americans had thrown over their king in the name of popular sovereignty; should their example catch on, there might be no end to the mischief it could do. Louis felt reasonably secure on his throne, yet popular unrest appeared recurrently in Paris and elsewhere, involving demands that the people of France receive what the Americans had claimed for themselves. If the American war weakened Britain, so much to the good, Louis judged. But if an American victory threatened the legitimacy of monarchs, very much to the bad.

Louis's ambivalence restrained Vergennes. There would be no American treaty, not for the time being, the foreign minister told Franklin. Yet Franklin and his colleagues might seek assistance short of an official arrangement.

This they did. They negotiated purchase of firearms and warships, financed by the sale of American tobacco and other commodities. There was no lack of interest in trade with America on the part of French merchants and manufacturers. American trade with countries other than Britain had been mostly illegal as long as the colonies remained colonies; upon becoming independent states, they promised new sources of supply and new markets to France and other European powers. While the French government kept its distance from the Americans, French entrepreneurs and investors jostled to claim shares of the new business. A merchant in La Rochelle, a port on the Bay of Biscay, wrote to Franklin boasting of what his community had to offer. "This haven is safe, frequented by ships of all nations and particularly those from French America, and a good market for indigo, rice, fish oil, and furs," the merchant said. "Our brandy is almost as good as that of Cognac. We export all manufactured articles, and gunpowder is made nearby. Mr. Schweighauser"—whom Franklin had met—"and others will assure you that I deserve your trust. I should be glad to assist American ships if you will send them here."

Franklin and his colleagues negotiated trade agreements and other deals under authority granted to them by the Continental Congress, and sometimes under authority they simply granted to themselves. In a secret resolution, Franklin, Deane and Lee affirmed to one another, "In the present peril of the liberties of our country, it is our duty to hazard everything in their support and defence; therefore, resolved unanimously that if it should be necessary for the attainment of anything in our best judgment material to the defence and support of the public cause, that we should pledge our persons or hazard the censure of the Congress by exceeding our instructions, we will, for such purpose, most cheerfully risk our personal liberty or life."

Again stretching their powers, they modified the terms under which America would ally with foreign powers. France and Spain wanted guarantees that in the event of war between them and Britain, on behalf of the United States, the Americans would not suddenly reconcile with Britain. The Continental Congress had given Franklin and the others no authority to tender such a promise, but they did so anyway. "The United States shall not separately conclude a peace, nor aid Great Britain against France or Spain, nor intermit their best exertions against Great Britain during the continuance of such war," they secretly agreed. This was a weighty concession, potentially mortgaging America's future to the interests of France and Spain. But the conversations of Franklin and the others with Vergennes convinced them that nothing less would deliver the alliance America desperately needed.

FRANKLIN BECAME a recruiting agent for George Washington. Underemployed soldiers from across Europe made their way to Paris to seek the blessing of Franklin for enlistment in the American army. Some came with recommendations Franklin took seriously. "I cannot speak of the gentleman from my own knowledge but I send you enclosed the recommendation I have received of him from Monsieur Turgot, late Comptroller of the Finances, and one of the most respectable characters of this nation," Franklin wrote to Washington regarding a French cavalry officer named Cenis. "M. Turgot's judgement of men has great weight with all that have the honour of knowing him, and I am confident that an officer of his recommending will be a valuable acquisition to our army."

Some of his finds were gems. "Count Pulaski of Poland, an officer famous throughout Europe for his bravery and conduct in defence of the liberties of his country against the three great invading powers of Russia, Austria and Prussia, will have the honour of delivering this into your excellency's hands," Franklin wrote to Washington about Casimir Pulaski, who did even better work in America—enrolling, equipping and training Washington's cavalry—than he had done in his native Poland. A few months later Franklin sent Washington another recommendation: "The gentleman who will have the honour of waiting upon you with this letter is the Baron de Steuben, lately a lieutenant general in the king of Prussia's service, whom he attended in all his campaigns, being his aide camp, quarter-master general, etc. He goes to America with a true zeal for our cause, and a view of engaging in it and rendering it all the service in his power." Friedrich Wilhelm von Steuben's service proved invaluable; with Prussian thoroughness he infused military discipline into the raw recruits who enlisted in the Continental Army.

Yet another letter to Washington took a slightly different turn. The Marquis de Lafayette was a teenager when he crossed the Atlantic to fight on America's side. He was, as Franklin put it to Washington, "a young nobleman of great expectations and exceedingly beloved here." He was also rich, and innocent in the ways of the world. Franklin proposed that Washington take him under his care. "His friends here have sent him over about £500 sterling, and have proposed sending him more. But on reflection, knowing the extreme generosity of his disposition, and fearing that some of his necessitous and artful countrymen may impose on his goodness, they wish to put his money into the hands of some discreet friend who may supply him from time to time, and by that means knowing his expences may take occasion to advise him if necessary, with a friendly affection, and secure him from too much imposition." Lafayette would benefit from Washington's guidance, Franklin said, but so would the American cause, as Washington's cooperation would be "gratefully remembered and acknowledged by a number of very worthy persons here." Washington accepted Franklin's invitation, making Lafayette almost a surrogate son and winning the support of his powerful friends.

Washington was delighted with the performance of Pulaski, Steuben and Lafayette, but at times he found the European enthusiasm for the American cause to be a mixed blessing. He needed experienced officers to train his troops, but he lacked the resources to support as many as wanted to come. The result was bad feeling all around. "Every new arrival is only a new source of embarrassment to Congress and myself, and of disappointment and chagrin to the gentlemen who come over," Washington told Franklin.

Franklin got the message and discouraged those who would listen. For those who wouldn't, and who insisted on reference from the American commissioner, Franklin devised a form letter that was utterly vacuous. "The bearer of this, who is going to America, presses me to give him a letter of recommendation, though I know nothing of him, not even his name," he wrote. "This may seem extraordinary, but I assure you it is not uncommon here. Sometimes indeed one unknown person brings me another equally unknown, to recommend him; and sometimes they recommend one another! As to this gentleman, I must refer you to himself for his character and merits, with which he is certainly better acquainted than I can possibly be."

Possibly Franklin never handed this letter to anyone; it might have been a joke, meant for his eyes alone. Yet his conundrum was genuine. He couldn't simply say no to those who wished to support the American cause, for the popular goodwill in Europe for the American cause was an essential tool in his diplomatic arsenal. The wealthy kin and friends of Lafayette contributed materially to the American war effort; they and the sponsors of other prospective heroes applied political pressure that, while not decisive on its own, added to the weight of the arguments Franklin was making in the offices of Vergennes.

AND THEN THERE WERE the spies. An essential task of Franklin and his colleagues was to gather intelligence that would be of use to Washington and the Continental Congress. For this purpose they spoke to all manner of people: French men and women who knew the temperature at King Louis's court and could thereby surmise the prospects for an alliance; English travelers and expatriates who reported on the politics of Parliament and the readying of reinforcements for the war in America; Spanish nationals familiar with the mood in Madrid; Germans who related recent recruiting efforts by the British in Hesse. Franklin, especially, had lived long enough not to take at face value everything he was told, but each bit of intelligence contributed to a mosaic that furthered his mission.

Long life and experience had also taught him that others would be trying to get information out of him. Some would do so openly, others on the sly. He realized he couldn't reliably tell which inquirers were which. And so he developed an approach for dealing with all possibilities. An English female acquaintance had written to Franklin warning of agents who, she said, were reporting on his actions to the British. He responded with polite equanimity. "I am much obliged to you for your kind attention to my welfare, in the information you give me," he said. "I have no doubt of its being well founded. But as it is impossible to discover in every case the falsity of pretended friends who would know our affairs, and more so to prevent being watched by spies, when interested people may think proper to place them for that purpose, I have long observed one rule which prevents any inconvenience from such practices. It is simply this: to be concerned in no affairs that I should blush to have made public, and to do nothing but what spies may see and welcome. When a man's actions are just and honourable, the more they are known the more his reputation is increased and established. If I was sure therefore that my valet de place was a spy, as probably he is, I think I should not discharge him for that, if in other respects I liked him."

In fact it wasn't his valet but his secretary who was the spy. Edward Bancroft had been born in Massachusetts to a family of modest means. His father died when Edward was very young, and the boy had had to scramble to educate and advance himself. Franklin met Bancroft in London when Bancroft was in his early thirties, and had been favorably impressed. Bancroft was bright, with an aptitude for science and invention that echoed Franklin's; Franklin sponsored Bancroft for membership in the Royal Society. Bancroft returned the respect and admiration, defending Franklin on the Hutchinson letters when almost no one else would. Perhaps Franklin perceived his own younger self in Bancroft, perhaps a more loyal version of William Franklin. When Franklin got to Paris he sought a secretary for the American commissioners. Bancroft came to mind, and Franklin hired him.

Bancroft delivered good service in all areas but honesty. He handled the correspondence of the commissioners with dispatch and thoroughness—and shared it with his British contacts. "I went to Paris, and during the first year resided in the same house with Dr. Franklin, Mr. Deane, etc., and regularly informed this Government of every transaction of the American commissioners," Bancroft wrote in a postwar debriefing for the British government. Bancroft covered his tracks by the expedient of the double agent: while spying for the British on the Americans, he was also spying for the Americans on the British. Franklin encouraged meetings by Bancroft with British officials in Paris and London; at these meetings intelligence flowed in both directions. Sometimes Bancroft left messages in the hollow of a tree in the garden of the Tuileries Palace.

Bancroft seems to have been motivated chiefly by the money he received from both sides. The American commissioners paid his salary as a secretary, the British his stipend as a spy. His political convictions were absent or indeterminate. He told Franklin he favored American independence; the British, he favored retention of the colonies. Mostly he favored himself.

There is no evidence that Franklin realized he was being betrayed. Yet neither is there evidence that Bancroft's betrayal compromised important American interests. Franklin's rule of transparency meant that most of what Bancroft relayed to his British contacts was no more than they knew or could surmise on their own.

PHILIP GIBBES WAS more open than Bancroft about what he wanted from Franklin. But he too embodied mysteries. Gibbes held a British baronetcy and owned plantations in Barbados. He knew Franklin from before the war, and he viewed Franklin as the key to a settlement that would stop the fighting before it spread to Barbados and other parts of the British West Indies. At his own expense and apparently on his own initiative, he traveled to Paris to probe Franklin about a possible deal. Franklin couldn't tell whether Gibbes had any authorization from the British government, but he presumed that whatever he told Gibbes would be reported to authorities in London.

Gibbes recorded their conversation shortly after it took place. "My first visit, sir, was to the philosopher," he said to Franklin, referring to their initial meeting some years earlier. "I shall now address you in another style. I feel myself so much affected by this unhappy dispute between Great Britain and her colonies that I determined to avail myself of the little acquaintance I once had with you to pray you would indulge me with some conversation on the subject. I know I am not entitled to your confidence; perhaps you may think I am not entitled to your communication. I beg, sir, at once to set you at ease by assuring you that if you should judge it imprudent to answer me, or improper even to hear me, I shall rest satisfied with your caution."

Franklin said nothing, waiting for Gibbes to elaborate.

"Give me leave here to promise that this visit is not made at the request of, or even in consequence of, any communication I have had with any man whatever," Gibbes said. "I am unconnected, uninfluenced. I feel myself independent, and my conduct is directed by my own ideas of propriety. It has always been my opinion that no man is of so little consequence but that he may be useful, if he will be active. Upon this occasion I determined not to be restrained by a timid caution from offering myself as an humble instrument, if I can be used, for the general good. I have all the predilection for America that is consistent with my attachment to Great Britain. I wish to see peace established upon such constitutional principles as shall secure the permanent prosperity of both countries. United, they continue forever formidable; separated, they soon become weakened."

Gibbes paused at this point, observing Franklin's demeanor. In his notes, Gibbes recorded, "The Doctor continued silent, but I thought attentive."

Gibbes went on, to Franklin, "The work of reconciliation is become perhaps difficult, but it is far from impracticable. I cannot presume to surmise what terms the king and the Parliament of Great Britain may be inclined to grant to America. But I think I hazard nothing in assuring you that administration is sincerely disposed to conciliate with America."

Franklin still said nothing, though his distrust of the sincerity of the British government might have crept into his features.

Gibbes pressed forward. "I know your abilities sir. I know your influence in America. You owe it to your country, who confides in you; you owe it to heaven, to whom you are accountable, to employ all your powers to facilitate a reconciliation. This unfortunate business must be terminated. It must end either in absolute conquest by the sword, or in an equitable union by negotiation. The first is too horrible to think of. Let me then beseech you, sir, to devise the means of making known to administration the terms which will satisfy America, or of applying to administration to solicit the conditions which would be granted to America. I want to see a communication opened. I would by no means undertake to convey anything directly from you to any person in administration. But if I could engage so much of your confidence as to be entrusted with the great outlines of reconciliation, I think I could find the means of conveying them to Lord George Germain."

Franklin finally spoke. "I am much afraid, sir, that things are gone too far to admit of reconciliation. I am inclined to think that America would insist upon such terms as Great Britain would not be disposed to grant." Franklin reiterated what he had said to many others about Britain's unconscionable treatment of the American colonies in the last decade. "We know that the king, the ministry and the people despise and hate us; that they wish the destruction, the very extirpation of the

Americans. Great Britain has injured us too much ever to forgive us. We on our parts can place no confidence in Parliament, for we have no security for their engagements. We delayed the declaration of independency as long as we hoped for justice from Great Britain. It was the people that called for it long before it was made the act of Congress. It is made, and we must maintain it if we can."

Gibbes begged Franklin to reconsider. Did he understand what a continued war would entail? "I wish, sir, that you should be well informed of the sense of the people"—of Britain—"and the firmness of the ministry. I speak to you as a man of honour, and tell it you upon the fullest persuasion that however well inclined administration may be, it is fixed and determined to prosecute the war with vigour, unless America will submit to reasonable terms." Franklin had said the American Congress reflected the will of the American people; no less did the British government reflect the will of the British people. "The resolution is taken in conformity with the temper of the people," Gibbes said. "The ministry and people look to the end, and will not withhold the means. Knowing then the power you have to contend with, policy, humanity and every motive that ought to influence the human mind seem to conspire to direct America to sue for peace."

Hardly, said Franklin. Americans had known what they were getting into when they chose independence. "We have made up our accounts in which we have stated the loss of all our towns upon the coasts. We have already reconciled ourselves to that misfortune, but we know it is impossible to penetrate our country. Thither we are resolved to retire, and to wait events, which we trust will be favorable. We expect to be more powerfully attacked the next campaign, but we know we shall be better prepared for our defence. What we wanted in the last campaign, we shall be fully supplied with in the next. You observed, sir, that Great Britain and America united were formidable. We felt the advantages, and wished to preserve the continuance of the union, for we knew that separated both countries must become weak. But there is this difference. Great Britain will always remain weak, while America, after a time, will grow strong."

Gibbes realized he was getting nowhere. He rose to leave, saying, "I am sorry I cannot induce you to impart anything to me which I may hope to turn to the mutual advantage of the contending parties."

Franklin restated the American position. The war would end only with British recognition of American independence. "If Great Britain is disposed to grant conditions, the proposal of them must come from herself," he added. "You may be sure none will ever come from America, after the repeated contempt shewn to her petitions."

According to Gibbes, Franklin went on to describe one prospect for a postwar settlement based on American independence. "A reconciliation founded upon a federal union of the two countries may take place," Franklin allowed, in Gibbes's account. "In that union, they may engage to make peace and war as one state, and such advantages may be granted to Great Britain in the regulation of commerce as may satisfy her."

Almost certainly this part of the conversation improved in the retelling. Franklin had indeed supported a federal union between America and Britain, but that was before the China vase of his dreams had been shattered. He no longer trusted the British to treat Americans with anything but contempt. Besides, he had no authorization from the Continental Congress to say anything about what might succeed the war, and no inclination to overstep his bounds on this crucial subject, especially with one as dubious as Gibbes.

As he exited, Gibbes lamented that things had come to this. He offered Franklin and the Americans some final advice. "I hope, sir, America, pleased with the sound of independency, will not prolong the war by a vain struggle for the word. If she can enjoy the advantages without the name, I hope she will learn to be wise and to be satisfied."

41

FEARING THAT THE DEFEATS of his army would produce defeat-ism among the Patriots generally, George Washington determined to reverse the emotional tide of the war. He conceived an operation, modest in scope but demonstrating that his army could still fight. "Christmas-day at night, one hour before day, is the time fixed upon for our attempt on Trenton," he informed Colonel Joseph Reed. Washington would head a re-crossing of the Delaware and an attack on British forces on the New Jersey side. He knew the plan was risky; the size of his force remained pitifully small. Yet he had no choice. "Necessity, dire necessity, will, nay must, justify *any* attempt," he asserted to Reed. Surprise was essential. "For Heaven's sake, keep this to yourself, as the discovery of it may prove fatal to us." The goal was not to gain and hold territory but simply to show that the Continental Army remained alive. "Attack as many of their posts as you possibly can with a prospect of success," he ordered Reed. "The more we can attack at the same instant, the more confusion we shall spread, and greater good will result from it."

Washington's plan was to cross the river by midnight and reach Trenton before dawn. But the weather had other ideas. "The quantity of ice made that night impeded the passage of the boats so much that it was three o'clock before the artillery could all be got over, and near four before the troops took up their line of march," he told John Hancock afterward. "This made me despair of surprising the town, as I well knew we could not reach it before the day was fairly broke. But as I was certain there was no making a retreat without being discovered and harassed on repassing the river, I determined to push on at all events." Two other columns had worse luck than Washington's, not even getting across the river in the freezing rain and snow that night.

"I formed my detachment into two divisions, one to march by the lower or river road, the other by the upper or Pennington road," Washington continued, to Hancock. "As the divisions had nearly the same distance to march, I ordered each of them, immediately upon forcing the out-guards, to push directly into the town, that they might charge the enemy before they had time to form."

The march went smoothly, despite the bad weather, which made the roads treacherous. "The upper division arrived at the enemy's advanced posts exactly at eight o'clock," Washington said. "And in three minutes after, I found, from the fire on the lower road, that the division had also got up." The surprise, though not perfect, was good enough. While the Hessian sentries returned the American fire, the main body of the garrison seemed bewildered by the attack. Many tried to flee along the road to Princeton. "But perceiving their intention, I threw a body of troops in their way, which immediately checked them," Washington said.

It was solid work, swiftly done. The Americans suffered but a handful of casualties while killing or wounding a hundred of the enemy and capturing nine hundred. The arithmetic of the outcome was not inconsequential, but the larger effect of the Trenton attack was psychological. The British, and many Americans too, had begun to think of Washington as feckless and Howe as indomitable. Then, out of the dark and the snow, the Continentals burst on the enemy garrison, caught them unaware, and captured or killed them all. Who was feckless now?

AS PLEASED AS WASHINGTON WAS with the results of the Trenton attack, he thought he could have done better. He determined to make a second try. The Trenton raid got the attention of Howe, who gathered his forces to retake the city. Washington knew he was outnumbered. "Our situation was most critical, and our force small," he told Hancock. He had to choose: retreat again, or stand and fight. To retreat would surrender the momentum his troops had just won, and so he chose to fight.

"The enemy began to advance upon us," Washington recounted. "And after some skirmishing, the head of their column reached Trenton about four o'clock." A creek ran through Trenton; Washington's troops on one side awaited Howe's on the other. "Finding the fords guarded, they halted, and kindled their fires," Washington said. "In this situation we remained till dark, cannonading the enemy, and receiving the fire of their field-pieces, which did us but little damage."

At close range, Washington realized how badly he was outnumbered. Moreover, Howe's disposition of his troops suggested an attempt at encirclement. Washington decided to take the fight in a different direction. "I ordered all our baggage to be removed silently to Burlington soon after dark; and at twelve o'clock after renewing our fires, and leaving guards at the bridge in Trenton, and other passes on the same stream above, marched by a roundabout road to Princeton, where I knew they could not have much force left, and might have stores."

The change of plans succeeded brilliantly. Washington's troops took Princeton, killing or wounding two hundred and capturing three hundred more, while losing less than a hundred.

THE VICTORIES AT TRENTON and Princeton greatly heartened the Patriots, who once more felt independence to be possible. They also transformed Washington's outlook. From wondering whether his army could simply survive, he began to dream he could force the British back to the Hudson. "The enemy are in great consternation," he wrote. "The panic affords us a favorable opportunity to drive them out of the Jerseys." He commenced to lay plans accordingly.

But within days he reconsidered. He discovered that his men didn't all share his optimism, not least because on them the burden of winter lay most heavily. "The severity of the season has made our troops, especially the militia, extremely impatient, and has reduced the number very considerably," Washington informed John Hancock from Morristown, New Jersey. "Every day more or less leave us. Their complaints, and the great fatigue they have undergone, induced me to come to this place as the best calculated, of any in this quarter, to accommodate and refresh them."

Washington had little choice but to hunker down. The British appeared to be doing the same thing, in the comparative comfort of New York. The peace of winter fell upon the New Jersey countryside.

Word of washington's victories lent weight to Franklin's arguments to Vergennes that America was a cause deserving French support. The foreign minister congratulated Franklin on the success of American arms, and wished the Americans additional victories.

Yet he continued to deflect Franklin's proposals for a formal treaty. A career in the French diplomatic service had taught Vergennes the virtues of caution; not for him the rashness that led to avoidable missteps. In the present instance, he still required convincing that the breach between Britain and the American colonies was irreparable. With every other French patriot he recalled with pain the thrashing France took in the Seven Years' War; with others in the French government he plotted France's revenge. But he was a patient plotter, carefully reckoning the balance of forces—military, diplomatic, economic—at play between France and Britain. Watching the American war, he judged that things were moving in France's favor. And they would continue to move that way, if he exercised discretion and sound judgment. France wasn't quite ready for war with Britain again, and it certainly wasn't ready for war without allies. The worst thing imaginable was that France would embrace the American cause, thereby triggering a war with Britain, only for the Americans to abandon the conflict and leave France fighting Britain alone.

Patience, however, wasn't without risk. If the Americans *did* reconcile with Britain, perhaps on account of a failure of French support, a great opportunity would have been lost. Franklin had persuaded Vergennes of the inevitability of American growth in wealth and power; if that wealth and power remained inside the British empire, Vergennes and France might *never* have their revenge.

Vergennes did what any savvy diplomat would have done in his position: he took positions on both sides of the issue. In public, the French government kept out of the quarrel between the British and the Americans, giving London no obvious pretext for complaint. In private, Vergennes allowed Franklin and the American commissioners to buy what weapons and provisions they needed, to borrow the funds the purchases required, to take possession of the goods, and to arrange transport to America. A certain legerdemain cloaked the transactions, which were conducted by a curious cast of characters. Pierre-Augustin Caron de Beaumarchais was an inventor (of more-accurate watches, among other things), a playwright (of *The Barber of Seville* and *The Marriage of Figaro*), a social and political climber (who ingratiated himself among the courtiers of King Louis), and an arms dealer (who furnished weapons to causes and countries in need, for a price). Beaumarchais served as liaison between the French government and the American commissioners, hiding the government's role and his own percentage behind the facade of a company created for the concealment.

Beaumarchais was not alone in seeking a slice of the money the French government secretly forwarded to the Americans; others of his countrymen wanted shares for themselves. So too, apparently, did Silas Deane, Franklin's fellow commissioner, who would be charged by the Congress with profiteering, before giving up on independence and embracing Loyalism. The result of all this was a tangle of money and materiel that served the purposes of the French government and, for a time, the American cause.

But it didn't serve that cause well enough. As the war entered its third year, in the spring and summer of 1777, the Congress ordered Franklin and the commissioners to step up their efforts to fund Washington's army. Franklin and the others obliged, reiterating the American case to Vergennes and to the Count of Aranda, the Spanish ambassador in Paris. "The Commissioners received, soon after their arrival, kind assurances of the amity of France and Spain, and substantial proofs of it, which will ever be remembered with gratitude," Franklin acknowledged to Vergennes and Aranda. Yet the time had come when they needed more. Franklin made clear they were asking not for gifts but for loans. "After a settlement of their states in peace"—that is, after an American victory—"a few years will enable them to repay the aids that may now be lent them." Finance aside, such loans would be in the political interest of France and Spain, for the commerce the loans allowed would strengthen those countries in their continuing competition with Britain.

Turning specific, Franklin provided Vergennes and Aranda a list of American needs, and the prices of those needs. Thirty thousand uniforms cost one million French livres; one hundred thousand pounds of copper and tin for casting cannons, 150,000 livres; one hundred tons of saltpeter (for gunpowder), 110,000 livres; eight large warships, 7,730,000 livres; and so on. War was expensive.

Aranda took his cues from Vergennes on the American question, and Vergennes wasn't ready to give the Americans everything they asked. Without committing to anything specific, the French minister let the Americans know they wouldn't lose the war for lack of sustenance.

Franklin understood Vergennes's game, and reluctantly accepted it as the best that could be achieved for the present. "We are scarce allowed to know that they give us any aids at all, but are left to imagine, if we please, that the cannon, arms etc. which we have received and sent are the effects of private benevolence and generosity," he wrote to the Congress. "We have nevertheless the strongest reasons to consider that the same generosity will continue." And there was a potential advantage to the unofficial arrangement. "It leaves America the glory of working out her deliverance by her own virtue and bravery."

THE VIRTUE AND BRAVERY of the Continental Army were being sorely tested during this season. And so was the leadership of George Washington. After a comfortable winter in New York, William Howe tried to lure Washington into a full battle in New Jersey. When Washington declined, Howe piled his army into ships and disappeared over the horizon. "I have this moment received intelligence by express that the enemy's fleet yesterday morning about eight o'clock sailed out of the Capes"—of Delaware Bay—"in an eastern course," Washington wrote to Israel Putnam on August 1. "This surprising event gives me the greatest anxiety, and unless every possible exertion is made may be productive of the happiest consequences to the enemy, and the most injurious to us."

Washington assumed Howe would head back to land in one of

two directions. If north and up the Hudson, his goal would be to link up with General John Burgoyne, whose army of several thousand was descending the Lake Champlain–Hudson River corridor from Canada toward New York. Should Burgoyne's thrust succeed, it would sever New England from the rest of America. And should Howe provide assistance, Burgoyne's task would be much easier. "The importance of preventing Mr. Howe's getting possession of the Highlands"— overlooking the Hudson—"by a *coup de main* is infinite to America," Washington told Putnam. Every effort must be made to prevent it.

The other possibility was that Howe would return to attack Philadelphia. The city's strategic importance was modest but its symbolic importance great. To scatter the Congress and occupy the seat of government of the fledgling United States would expose the American experiment to ridicule at home and abroad. Patriots would be disheartened, Loyalists emboldened. France would withhold consent to a treaty and might withdraw the informal support it had been providing.

Washington could only guess at Howe's destination and plans. And he understood that to guess wrong might be fatal to the Patriot cause. He could reinforce the defenses on the Hudson, but in doing so would weaken his ability to protect Philadelphia. And vice versa.

"The conduct of the enemy is distressing beyond measure, and past our comprehension," Washington wrote on August 4. "On Thursday and Friday last their fleet, consisting of two hundred and twenty-eight sail, were beating off the Capes of Delaware, as if they intended to come in. From this circumstance, nobody doubted but that Philadelphia was the immediate object of their expedition, and that they would commence their operations as soon as possible." But the ships didn't enter. "They have stood out to sea again, but how far, or where they are going, remains to be known. From their entire command of the water they derive immense advantages, and distress us much by harassing and marching our troops from post to post. I wish we could fix on their destination; in such case I should hope we would be prepared to receive them."

Washington said more to his brother John. "Since General Howe's remove from the Jerseys, the troops under my command have been more harassed by marching and countermarching than by any thing that has happened to them in the course of the campaign," he wrote. "After General Howe had embarked his troops, the presumption that he would operate upon the North River"—another name for the Hudson—"to form a junction with General Burgoyne was so strong that I removed from Middle Brook to Morristown, and from Morristown to the Clove (a narrow pass leading through the Highlands) about eighteen miles from the river. Indeed, upon some pretty strong presumptive evidence, I threw two divisions over the North River." And there they waited. "We lay till about the 24th ult., when receiving certain information that the fleet had actually sailed from Sandy Hook (the outer point of New York Harbor) and the concurring sentiment of everyone (though I acknowledge my doubts of it were strong) that Philadelphia was the object, we countermarched and got to Coryell's Ferry on the Delaware (about thirty-three miles above the city) on the 27th, where I lay till I received information from Congress that the enemy were actually at the Capes of Delaware. This brought us in great haste to this place"—Germantown, Pennsylvania—"for defence of the city. But in less than twenty-four hours after our arrival, we got accounts of the disappearance of the fleet on the 31st; since which, nothing having been heard of them, we remain here in a very irksome state of suspense."

Washington was irked the more on learning of the fall of Fort Ticonderoga to Burgoyne's army. "This affair has cast a dark shade upon a very bright prospect, our accounts from that quarter being very gloomy," he told John.

Washington assumed the troubles of his army made an alliance with France less likely than before. He claimed to be comparatively unmoved. "I have from the first been among those few who never built much upon a French war," he told John. "I ever did, and still do think they never meant more than to give us a kind of underhand assistance; that is, to supply us with arms, etc. for our money and trade. This may, indeed, if Great Britain has spirit and strength to resent it, bring on a war; but the declaration, if on either side, must, I am convinced, come from the last mentioned power."

A fresh sighting of the British fleet off the Maryland coast caused Washington to conclude that both his guesses about Howe's destination had been wrong. "I am now of opinion that Charles Town is the present object of General Howe's attention," he wrote on August 20. The next day he was even more certain that the Carolinas were Howe's goal. "Had the Chesapeake Bay been his object, he would have been there long since, and the fact well established," he told John Hancock.

Another twenty-four hours prompted another reconsideration. The British fleet appeared in the Chesapeake Bay, heading north. Evidently Howe intended to take Philadelphia from the rear, the side opposite to where Washington was. Alarming though the intelligence was, at least it afforded clarity. "I have issued orders for all the troops here to be in motion tomorrow morning very early, with intention to march them towards Philadelphia," he wrote to Hancock on August 22.

Howe's threat to Philadelphia produced the general engagement with Washington that Howe had been seeking. The battle took place on Brandywine Creek, southwest of the city. The armies were evenly matched in size, each comprising about fifteen thousand men. Washington, the defender, had the advantage in position, establishing his works behind the creek and compelling Howe to cross.

But once more Washington's leadership failed. Howe's main column, under Lord Cornwallis, again informed by local Loyalists, found some unguarded fords over the creek above Washington's position and around his right flank. Washington's spies didn't detect Cornwallis's maneuver before it was too late. Washington redeployed as swiftly as he could, and fierce fighting ensued. Meanwhile another British column, capitalizing on Washington's distraction, crossed the creek and roughly treated the American left.

The fighting filled most of the day. It ended in another American defeat. "I am sorry to inform you that in this day's engagement we have been obliged to leave the enemy masters of the field," Washington reported to John Hancock. He was writing from Chester, halfway from the Brandywine battlefield to Philadelphia, at midnight. Without saying so explicitly, Washington admitted to having been outgeneraled again. "The intelligence received of the enemy's advancing up the Brandywine and crossing at a ford about six miles above us was uncertain and contradictory, notwithstanding all my pains to get the best. This prevented my making a disposition adequate to the force with which the enemy attacked us on our right; in consequence of which, the troops first engaged were obliged to retire before they could be reinforced."

Washington tried to diminish the defeat. "Although we fought under many disadvantages and were, from the causes above mentioned, obliged to retire, yet our loss of men is not, I am persuaded, very considerable; I believe much less than the enemy's," Washington said. This was quite wrong; Washington's losses were double those of Howe. "We have also lost seven or eight pieces of cannon, according to the best information I can at present obtain." In fact Washington had lost all but three of his fourteen cannons. "The baggage, having been previously moved off, is all secure, saving the men's blankets, which being at their backs, many of them doubtless were lost." Washington had withdrawn his army to a safe distance from the scene of the defeat. "Notwithstanding the misfortune of the day, I am happy to find the troops in good spirits." Even this was stretching things: in the days before and after the battle, hundreds of Washington's troops deserted. "I hope another time we shall compensate for the losses now sustained," Washington concluded his report to Hancock.

HE SOON REALIZED, if he hadn't known at the moment of writing, that such another time must be far distant. As the severity of his defeat sank in, he abandoned hope of keeping Howe from Philadelphia. After token resistance from the Americans, the British marched into Philadelphia on September 26. The Congress had fled to the interior of Pennsylvania; Washington watched from afar.

Yet he couldn't do nothing. American self-respect, and his own, required Washington to challenge Howe's hold on the capital. After Howe divided his force, sending most of troops to Germantown, northwest of the city, Washington laid plans to surprise the British there. Four columns would converge on the enemy camp and kill or capture as many troops as possible. Washington's template was the taking of Trenton the previous year; Germantown would be like that, only bigger and more impressive.

The battle commenced promisingly, and the British fell into confusion. But Washington failed to capitalize. "The morning was extremely foggy, which prevented our improving the advantages we gained so well as we should otherwise have done," he explained afterward. "This circumstance, by concealing from us the true situation of the enemy, obliged us to act with more caution and less expedition than we could have wished, and gave the enemy time to recover from the effects of our first impression. And what was still more unfortunate, it served to keep our different parties in ignorance of each other's movements and hinder their acting in concert. It also occasioned them to mistake one another for the enemy." Finding themselves under friendly fire, Washington's men became disoriented. "In the midst of the most promising appearances, when everything gave the most flattering hopes of victory, the troops began suddenly to retreat, and entirely left the field, in spite of every effort that could be made to rally them."

Once more Washington interpreted his reverse charitably. "Upon the whole, it may be said the day was rather unfortunate than injurious," he told John Hancock. "We sustained no material loss of men, and brought off all our artillery, except one piece which was dismounted. The enemy are nothing the better by the event, and our troops, who are not in the least dispirited by it, have gained what all young troops gain by being in actions."

Within forty-eight hours Washington was compelled to revise his estimate of the damage. "I have obtained a return of our loss in the action on Saturday, by which it appears to be much more considerable than I first apprehended," he told Hancock. The corrected figures put Washington's troops killed, wounded or captured at more than a thousand, roughly twice those of Howe. Nor did the distance from the battle elevate Washington's judgment of what his men had done. "It is with much chagrin and mortification I add that every account confirms the opinion I first entertained that our troops retreated at the instant when victory was declaring herself in our favor. The tumult, disorder, and even despair, which, it seems, had taken place in the British army were scarcely to be paralleled." As to why his men suddenly fell back, Washington confessed puzzlement. "I can discover no other cause for not improving this happy opportunity than the extreme haziness of the weather."

It was a lame excuse, as Washington realized. His men performed poorly because they were poorly led. It was time to reconsider and regroup. "My intention is to encamp the army at some suitable place to rest and refresh the men, and recover them from the still remaining effects of that disorder naturally attendant on a retreat," he said.

WILLIAM HOWE HAD MOVED against Philadelphia in part because he concluded that John Burgoyne didn't need help in northern New York. After taking Fort Ticonderoga, Burgoyne and his army proceeded south toward the Hudson. He called on the inhabitants of New York and New England to acknowledge that independence was a chimera; to aid their acuity he threatened to turn the Indian allies of Britain loose upon the civilian population. "I have but to give stretch to the Indian forces under my direction—and they amount to thousands—to overtake the hardened enemies of Great Britain and America (I consider them the same, wherever they may lurk)," Burgoyne proclaimed. These enemies would receive no mercy. "The messengers of justice and of wrath await them in the field, and devastation, famine and every concomitant horror that a reluctant but indispensable prosecution of military duty must occasion will bar the way to their return."

The Indian forces Burgoyne referred to were led by Joseph Brant, who in turn took cues from his sister. Molly Brant's husband, William Johnson, had died, but she was still a formidable figure among the Iroquois. "One word from her is more taken notice of by the Five Nations"—a name for the Iroquois Confederacy from an earlier time—"than a thousand from any white man, without exception," a British official responsible for relations with the Iroquois declared. Molly Brant believed that the Mohawks' future would be more secure with the British than with independent Americans, whose hunger for Mohawk land would never be satiated. Molly Brant's people would remain loyal to the British crown.

Joseph Brant carried that Loyalism onto the battlefield. Patriot forces controlled Fort Stanwix, a post on the strategic portage between the headwaters of the Mohawk, which drained into the Hudson, and the streams that flowed to Lake Ontario. As part of his drive south, Burgoyne assigned the reduction of Fort Stanwix to Barry St. Leger, who turned to the Iroquois.

"Your resolution of investing Fort Stanwix is exactly right," St. Leger wrote to a subordinate, "and to enable you to do it with greater effect, I have detached Joseph and his corps of Indians to reinforce you." St. Leger urged caution in deploying the Indians. "You will observe that I will have nothing but an investiture made; and in case the enemy, observing the discretion and judgment with which it is made, should offer to capitulate, you are to tell them that you are sure I am well disposed to listen to them. This is not to take any honor out of a young soldier's hands, but by the presence of the troops to prevent the barbarity and carnage which will ever obtain where Indians make so superior a part of the detachment."

The Indians allied to the British, like those allied to the Americans, were both a battlefield asset and a psychological weapon. They fought bravely, though as a rule they had less tolerance for casualties than the whites did. They were fewer in number and could spare fewer lost; further, they were motivated not by ideology or emotion but by a cool calculation of interest. Yet their demonstrated willingness to torture prisoners and mutilate bodies sent a shiver through nearly all the whites who found themselves arrayed against the Indians.

Some of the whites knew exactly what to expect if they fell into Indian hands. Two junior officers of a Patriot militia attached to Fort Stanwix went on a scouting mission and were ambushed by Iroquois. One was killed by rifle fire and scalped. The other was shot but merely wounded, yet badly enough that he couldn't escape or continue to resist. Fearing what awaited him if he was taken alive, he pretended to be dead. The Indians approached and pulled out their scalping knives. One grabbed the militiaman's hair and began cutting the scalp. The victim, with almost unbelievable willpower, didn't make a sound or move a muscle as the rough surgery proceeded. The Indians took their bloody prizes and left. The militiaman was saved when his dog, appreciating its master's plight, ran and summoned help. The dog became a hero, the man a walking reminder of the consequences of being caught out by unfriendly Indians.

BARRY ST. LEGER MADE the reminder more explicit. Following the lead of Burgoyne, he threatened to turn his Indians—Joseph Brant's Iroquois—loose against the Patriots. The enemies of the British crown must abandon their rebellion at once, St. Leger said. Should they fail to do so, the forces of justice would wreak "the vengeance of the state against the wilful outcasts."

The Patriots inside Fort Stanwix ignored the warning, and the siege began. Things looked grim for the defenders, outnumbered as they were, and unprepared for being cut off from resupply. Word of their predicament reached a Patriot force some distance away, and its commander summoned his men to march to the rescue of their beset compatriots.

The forests were full of spies, and Brant and the British learned they were about to be attacked from the rear. Brant laid an ambush for the approaching Patriots, where their route crossed a creek at the bottom of a ravine outside the village of Oriskany. Brant and his Indian warriors waited until the Patriots were most vulnerable, divided by the broken ground and the water, and then attacked from all sides. The Indians fired from behind trees and rocks, to draw the return fire of the Patriots. As soon as a Patriot rifleman discharged his weapon, thereby giving away his position, Indians would assault him with tomahawks before he could reload. The Patriot commander was badly wounded, and though he calmly gave orders to his men, his incapacity hindered his ability to rally them. The only thing that prevented a Patriot massacre was a sudden thundershower, which forced the combatants to seek shelter lest their powder be wetted and their rifles become useless.

When the storm eased, the fighting resumed, this time hand-to-hand. It was desperate and to the death; it was fearsome to observe, even in the aftermath. A frontiersman who came upon the battlefield days later declared, "I beheld the most shocking sight I had ever witnessed. The Indians and white men were mingled with one another, just as they had been left when death had first completed his work."

By the time the bloodletting ended, over four hundred Patriots had been killed or wounded. The losses on the British side were less than a hundred, nearly all of them Joseph Brant's Iroquois.

The Indian losses were crucial. They had joined the siege of Fort Stanwix on the understanding that there wouldn't be heavy fighting. The battle at Oriskany made some of them reconsider. Mary Jemison had been stolen as a girl by a Shawnee raiding party from a settler community on the Pennsylvania frontier. She was subsequently sold to the Senecas and forcibly adopted into the tribe. She married and had children, eventually adapting so well that when she later had the opportunity to return to the white community, she refused. The Senecas, as part of the Iroquois Confederacy, were allied with the British at the outbreak of the American Revolution. "The British sent for the Indians to come and see them whip the rebels, and at the same time stated that they did not wish to have them fight, but wanted to have them just sit down, smoke their pipes, and look on," Mary Jemison recalled of the siege of Fort Stanwix. "Our Indians went, to a man. But contrary to their expectation, instead of smoking and looking on, they were obliged to fight for their lives, and in the end of the battle were completely beaten, with a great loss in killed and wounded. Our Indians alone had thirty-six killed and a great number wounded. Our town exhibited a scene of real sorrow and distress when our soldiers returned, recounted their misfortunes, and stated the real loss they had sustained in the engagement. The mourning was excessive and was expressed by the most doleful yells, shrieks and howlings."

Governance among the Iroquois was divided, and within the tribes it was typically by consensus. The heavy losses at Oriskany caused all the tribes to reconsider their alliance with the British, and some to walk away. Joseph Brant persuaded the Mohawks to stick with the British, but other tribes, including the Oneidas, who already had doubts about the British, abandoned them and wound up fighting with the Americans, even against other Iroquois. For this reason, as well as because of the deaths suffered there, the Oriskany site was called the "Place of Great Sadness" among the Iroquois.

BENEDICT ARNOLD ARRIVED at Fort Stanwix just after the Battle of Oriskany. The failure of the Canada expedition had left Arnold chafing for another chance for distinction. The itch grew stronger when he was passed over for promotion by the Continental Congress, in favor of officers less senior and accomplished. George Washington was embarrassed by the slight, as he explained in a letter to Arnold in the spring of 1777. "I was surprized when I did not see your name in the list of major generals," Washington said. He related that a subordinate visiting the Congress had looked into the matter and been given a dubious rationale. "He was informed that the members from each state seemed to insist upon having a proportion of general officers adequate to the number of men which they furnish, and that as Connecticut had already two majors general it was their full share. I confess this is a strange mode of reasoning, but it may serve to shew you that the promotion which was due to your seniority was not overlooked for want of merit in you."

Washington had resigned a commission in the Virginia militia over a similar insult, and so understood what Arnold must be feeling. For this reason he was the more gratified that Arnold hadn't done what he himself had done as a young officer. "Your determination not to quit your present command, while any danger to the public might ensue from your leaving it, deserves my thanks and justly entitles you to the thanks of your country."

Arnold stifled his resentment and sought battlefield action, which might compel the Congress into awarding him what he thought he deserved. He received an assignment to support Philip Schuyler in the latter's effort to parry Burgoyne's thrust from Canada. It was a big job with marginally adequate materials, as Arnold explained to Washington from a camp in the wild region west of the Hudson and north of the Mohawk River. "I am stationed at this place with Nixon's and Learned's brigades of Continental troops, General TenBrooks's brigade and Colonel Ashley's battalion of militia, the former consisting of 1779 including officers, the latter about thirteen hundred, badly clad and armed," Arnold said. His tactical situation was as convoluted as the terrain. "The want of salted provisions, of which we have not one day's allowance, has prevented our sending out any considerable parties of men on scouts, by which reason we have been deprived of intelligence from the enemy, except such as is very vague and uncertain, the woods being so full of Indians, Canadians and regulars that it is almost impossible for small parties to escape them. We are daily insulted by the Indians, who on the 22d inst. attacked our picket guard, killed and scalped five men, wounded nine and took one prisoner. On the 24th they killed and scalped two officers between Fort Edward and our lines. Yesterday morning our picket at Fort Edward, where we have one hundred men advanced, was attacked by a large party of

Indians and regulars. Some of my officers were of opinion there was near one thousand men of the enemy. The advanced guard retired to the main body with the loss of one lieutenant and five privates killed and scalped and four wounded. The Indians took two women prisoners from a house near the fort, carried them to the regular troops who were paraded near the fort, where they were shot, scalped, stripped and butchered in the most shocking manner."

Arnold had responded with energy but little success. "I immediately detached a thousand men, one half to take them in rear, the other in front, who would have accomplished their purpose but for a heavy shower of rain which wet their arms and ammunition and gave the enemy time to retire," he told Washington. "Several of our small scouting parties are missing and have probably fell into the hands of the enemy. I have five or six now out but expect little from them. The regular troops are prevented from deserting by the Indians between us, so that every source of information is in a manner cut off."

Yet he wasn't discouraged. With a modest reinforcement, all would be well. "I wish Colonel Morgan's regiment would be spared to this department," Arnold wrote to Washington. "I think we should then be in a condition to see General Burgoyne with all his infernals"—Indians—"on any ground they might choose."

In a postscript, Arnold added, "Justice obliges me to observe I believe General Schuyler has done everything man could do in his situation. I am sorry to hear his character has been so unjustly aspersed and calumniated."

The aspersion Arnold referred to cost Schuyler his job as head of the Northern Department. Schuyler's subordinate Arthur St. Clair had failed to keep Fort Ticonderoga out of the hands of Burgoyne's advancing army, and Schuyler received the blame, much of which came from his successor Horatio Gates. Arnold's loyalty to Schuyler soon rankled Gates, who began aiming his criticism at Arnold.

For the moment Arnold ignored it. He led a column to the relief of Fort Stanwix, which was on the point of surrender to Barry St. Leger's force as Arnold and his men approached. Though badly outnumbered, Arnold managed to spread false word that he would soon be reinforced by a much larger column. The ruse confirmed the judgment of Joseph Brant that he had been misled by St. Leger about the role of the Indians in the fight for Fort Stanwix, and Brant led his warriors away. Without his Indian corps, and worried that Arnold's disinformation might be true, St. Leger likewise abandoned the siege.

THE VICTORY WASN'T as satisfying as Arnold wished. Winning a battle through cleverness was good, but winning by gallantry would have been better. He at once began looking for an opportunity, and he found it in battle against Burgoyne's main column.

The hardest part of the journey between Montreal and Quebec had always been the stretch south of Lakes Champlain and George and north of the Hudson River. Travelers—and armies—had to leave their boats and trek by foot through thick forests laced with innumerable streams. The Patriots opposing Burgoyne made the hard part harder by felling trees across his route and burning bridges over the streams. They attacked his supply line back to Canada. They sniped at his soldiers from behind rocks and stumps.

Burgoyne's men became confused, dispirited and hungry. The triumphal march he had projected descended into nightmare as the wagons and then the men sank in the autumn mud. Relief columns sent north from New York and east from Lake Ontario never arrived, the latter column stymied by Benedict Arnold at Fort Stanwix.

Arnold joined Horatio Gates in front of Burgoyne despite the tension between the two American generals. Arnold commanded Gates's left wing in the first of two battles near Saratoga. The outcome slightly favored the British but demonstrated the Americans' ability to hinder Burgoyne's further progress; it also aggravated the tension between Gates and Arnold. Reporting the battle to the Continental Congress, Gates ignored Arnold's part; Arnold responded angrily, causing Gates to relieve him of his command.

Arnold was tempted to leave for the camp of George Washington, who would pay him the respect he thought he deserved. By one version of the story, a petition from his men persuaded him to remain. Doubtless his own ambition played an equal part. The trap was closing on Burgoyne; Arnold wanted to be in at the finish.

He relied on the loyalty of his men, and on his own bravery. Without orders he threw himself into the thick of the second Saratoga battle, as soon as it began. He was badly wounded by a musket ball in the leg, which fractured further when his horse, felled by the same volley, rolled over on him. Yet he refused to leave the field, issuing commands and encouragement that helped ensure the devastating British defeat, including Burgoyne's surrender of his entire army of six thousand men.

THIS TIME ARNOLD'S CONTRIBUTION couldn't be denied, and it wasn't. "Enclosed you will receive a commission by which you will find that you are restored to the rank you claim in the line of the army," George Washington wrote to Arnold. "This I transmit by direction of Congress."

Washington knew of Arnold's injury. "May I venture to ask whether you are upon your legs again, and if you are not, may I flatter myself that you will be soon? There is none who wishes more sincerely for this event than I do, or who will receive the information with more pleasure." Saratoga confirmed what Washington already knew: that Arnold was the best battlefield general the Continental Army possessed. "As soon as your situation will permit, I request that you will repair to this Army, it being my earnest wish to have your services the ensuing campaign," Washington said. "I have set you down in an arrangement now under consideration, and for a command which, I trust, will be agreeable to yourself and of great advantage to the public."

BENJAMIN FRANKLIN FOLLOWED the campaigns in America as well as he could from across the Atlantic. The more worrisome initially was Howe's against Philadelphia, whose fall would be interpreted by many observers as the fall of the United States. Word arrived in early December 1777 that a ship from America had docked at Nantes, presumably bringing the latest news. Franklin and the other commissioners gathered in front of Franklin's apartment to greet the courier, who appeared shortly. "Is Philadelphia taken?" demanded Franklin at once.

"Yes, sir," the courier, a young American, replied.

Franklin frowned and turned to go inside.

"But, sir! I have greater news than that," the courier said. "General Burgoyne and his whole army are prisoners of war!"

Franklin stopped. His countenance changed at once. He understood that this was indeed greater news than the loss of Philadelphia, which had been expected. The defeat of Burgoyne and the capture of his army meant that America wouldn't be split in two. The Patriot cause—the cause of American independence—could stand the occupation of Philadelphia by enemy forces; it probably couldn't survive the loss of New England and New York.

Besides, Franklin doubted Philadelphia would be a great prize for the British. A Frenchman of Franklin's acquaintance offered condolences at the loss of the American capital; Franklin responded, "You mistake the matter. Instead of Howe taking Philadelphia, Philadelphia has taken Howe."

FRANKLIN IMMEDIATELY PRESSED Vergennes for a decision on a treaty. He reminded the French minister that America's request for a treaty with France was a year old. His American compatriots were beginning to wonder whether a treaty might ever be forthcoming, he said. The recent turn of events made the moment propitious. "The completing such a treaty at this time would have the most happy effect."

Vergennes agreed. He sent his deputy to Franklin. The deputy tendered congratulations on the American victory and declared that it removed any doubt of the ability of America to secure its independence. He invited Franklin and his fellow commissioners to put a specific treaty proposal on paper, as soon as possible.

A lesser diplomat would have seized the offer and placed a draft in Vergennes's hands the next day. But not Franklin. He interpreted Vergennes's eagerness as evidence that the balance of diplomatic power had shifted. Formerly Franklin had been the supplicant, pushing Vergennes for a treaty. The American victory at Saratoga reversed the roles. Now Vergennes wanted to press forward, causing Franklin to see merit in moving slowly. Vergennes had to worry that he'd waited too long. Burgoyne's disastrous defeat would weaken the war party in the British Parliament and bolster the accommodationists. It wasn't out of the question that the latter would take control of the government and offer to end the war on America's terms. In that event, a new form of Anglo-American union—perhaps like that of which Franklin had long spoken eloquently—might rise from the rubble of the old empire. France would be worse off than ever.

Franklin let Vergennes fret. He conspicuously visited Philip Gibbes, his interlocutor from several months before, who was again in Paris. Gibbes was delighted to see him. Gibbes told Franklin he had recounted their previous conversation to the British government. "Though I have no reason to say it has hitherto produced any effect," he said, "I would not be discouraged from requesting another conversation with you upon the same subject. I am going to England. I wish to carry with me the present ideas of America with respect to the terms of peace." He reiterated that he had no specific authorization for his request. He spoke as a private individual rather than the agent of any government. Yet he also spoke as a friend of America, and of peace. "I know I presume a great deal in this interference, unauthorized by any man. But where nothing is attempted nothing can be effected. I want to see a communication opened between Great Britain and America."

Franklin responded coyly. "I am of opinion, sir, it would do harm to communicate, even as matter of private conversation, the expectations of America," he said, according to Gibbes's account of the meeting. "Great Britain is making preparations for a vigorous campaign, with the idea of enforcing submission. While she entertains that hope, the terms which America may think just and reasonable, she may call insolent. Proposals from America, intimated even in the manner you suggest, might be supposed to arise from apprehension, and might obstruct the ends you seem desirous to promote." Yet he didn't want to leave Gibbes with nothing. "America is ready to make peace," he said. "If Great Britain desires to make peace, let her propose the terms to the commissioners here, who are empowered to treat. But I will think of the matter and give you my thoughts."

Gibbes didn't believe this would happen. "You cannot suppose, sir, that Administration will ever treat formally and openly with commissioners from the Congress," he said. And certainly not in France, Britain's historic enemy. The Americans would have to make the first proposal. Yet Gibbes went on to sketch a procedure that might appeal to Parliament: "That Parliament should pass an act to authorize the thirteen united provinces to appoint, each, one or two representatives who should be the representative body of America. That this body of representatives should appoint and send commissioners to London, empowered to conclude a definitive treaty with the legislature of Great Britain. Or that Great Britain should appoint and send commissioners to America, vested with the most ample powers that our constitution can repose in them to conclude a peace."

Franklin saw they were talking past each other. But he meant to make himself clear. "Great Britain may pass what acts she pleases," he said. "America will not think herself bound to act in conformity to them. Besides, the distance will protract the negotiation. If Great Britain cannot enforce submission she must treat. Why then delay it? If the ministry have personal objections to the present commissioners, let them state their objection. If they have an objection to Paris as the place of negotiation, let them name any town in Flanders. But whenever it shall please them to propose terms, it is hoped they will be clear and explicit; nothing concealed to create future discussion. They should be generous. You have expressed it happily. They should be such, and offered in such manner, that all the world may say, they were directed by a noble generosity and not compelled. If you should impart this conversation to your friends in England, it will be proper to acquaint them, *that whatever terms Great Britain may propose will be communicated to France.*" Franklin emphasized this point. "We are new at treaty. Advantage may be taken of our incapacity, and it is prudent to consult those upon whose experience and friendship we can depend."

Gibbes, and the British government, had hoped to preempt just such a French connection. "I am sorry, I much lament, sir, that your engagements with France oblige you to submit to her the terms of peace between Great Britain and America," he said.

Franklin corrected him. "Do not mistake me," he said. "I did not say we should *submit* them to France. I said, distrusting ourselves, we should *consult* France upon the terms that should be proposed by Great Britain. We have not engaged with France to be decided by her opinion. America considers herself as an independent state, and will decide ultimately for herself. If she approves the terms proposed, she will accept them. I am told Lord North intends to propose something conciliatory. If it be like his former proposition, it will not avail anything. But terms that come voluntarily, and shew generosity, will do honour to Great Britain and may engage the confidence of America."

Gibbes detected possibility. He brought out notes of their earlier conversation and handed them to Franklin. "It will be some satisfaction to me to know that I have faithfully represented our last conversation," he said. "I endeavoured to state it with exactness. And hope you will find I have not varied it. I pray you will take the trouble to read it."

Franklin did so. "It is accurate," he said upon finishing. "But to one part I must now except." This was the part about a federal union between America and Britain. Franklin did not dispute Gibbes's version of the previous conversation; instead he asserted that events had changed things. "At that time America would have entered into a federal union to make peace and war as one nation. Since then, it has cost her much blood and treasure to defend and strengthen her independence. I do not imagine she would now enter into such an engagement. Great Britain charges her with ingratitude for the protection she gave her at a great expence in the last war. America does not intend to involve Great Britain in wars, or to share with her in such as she may involve herself in. The system of America is universal commerce with every nation, war with none."

Gibbes nodded, then probed a particular point. "Permit me, sir, to ask you as one personally, and not inconsiderably, interested: What is the intention of America with respect to the Sugar Islands?"—the British West Indies. "They are innocent and helpless. They have given no provocation to America. And yet you have made war upon them by making captures of their property, to the injury of all and the ruin of many of the planters."

Franklin offered little comfort. "With respect to the Sugar Islands, when this matter shall be settled, we will trade with them, as with other people. But we will have no other connection with them. If we have taken their property, we have taken it as the property of the subjects of a nation who has made war upon us."

FRANKLIN NEVER SAW the notes of this second conversation. If he had seen them, he would have strengthened the statement Gibbes attributed to him merely doubting that America and Britain would form a federal union. At this late date, there was no chance of that, and Franklin wouldn't have hesitated to tell Gibbes so. In comments to Arthur Lee the next day, Franklin said he told Gibbes that any kind of dependency of America on Britain was "gone forever, like the clouds of last year."

But the meeting with Gibbes had served a purpose—two purposes, in fact. Already Franklin was looking to the peace negotiations that would end the war. Those negotiations would be with Britain, and Franklin was staking out his initial position. His other, immediate purpose was to worry Vergennes, who duly made a priority of nailing down an American alliance.

It came soon enough, established by two treaties. The first was a pact of amity and commerce. "There shall be a firm, inviolable and universal peace, and a true and sincere friendship between the most Christian King, his heirs and successors, and the United States of America," the treaty declared. It stated explicitly that the treaty should be "perpetual." It granted most-favored-nation status to trade between the two countries, meaning that whatever favorable terms of trade France observed with any third country would be granted to the United States, and vice versa.

A clause that was certain to cause trouble with Britain proclaimed, "The most Christian King shall endeavour by all the means in his power to protect and defend all vessels and the effects belonging to the subjects, people or inhabitants of the said United States . . . and the ships of war of his most Christian Majesty or any convoys sailing under his authority shall upon all occasions take under their protection all vessels belonging to the subjects, people or inhabitants of the said United States." In other words, the French navy would defend American commerce. The United States pledged to reciprocate, though this meant much less at the moment, the American navy being tiny by comparison with the French. A clause on privateering likewise favored the United States, which relied more heavily on privateers than the French did; this clause asserted, "It shall be lawful for the ships of war of either party and privateers freely to carry whithersoever they please the ships and goods taken from their enemies, without being obliged to pay any duty to the officers of the admiralty or any other judges; nor shall such prizes be arrested or seized when they come to and enter the ports of either party."

The first treaty almost guaranteed war between Britain and France; the second treaty, of military alliance, specified what that would entail. "If war should break out between France and Great Britain during the continuance of the present war between the United States and England, His Majesty and the said United States shall make it a common cause and aid each other mutually with their good offices, their counsels, and their forces," the military treaty declared. Again, America would be the greater beneficiary, as the army, as well as the navy, of France was larger and more powerful than that of the United States.

The treaty mandated a fight to the finish. "Neither of the two parties shall conclude either truce or peace with Great Britain without the formal consent of the other first obtained; and they mutually engage not to lay down their arms until the independence of the United States shall have been formally or tacitly assured by the treaty or treaties that shall terminate the war."

The treaty ambitiously specified a division of spoils in the Western Hemisphere. "If the United States should think fit to attempt the reduction of the British power remaining in the northern parts of America"—Canada—"or the islands of Bermudas, those countries or islands in case of success shall be confederated with or dependent upon the said United States," the treaty said. As for France: "If his most Christian Majesty shall think proper to attack any of the islands situated in the Gulf of Mexico, or near that Gulf, which are at present under the power of Great Britain, all the said isles, in case of success, shall appertain to the Crown of France."

The Franco-American treaty invited third parties to join the alliance. "The most Christian King and the United States agree to invite or admit other powers who may have received injuries from England to make common cause with them, and to accede to the present alliance under such conditions as shall be freely agreed to and settled between all the parties." A secret codicil to the treaty specified Spain as a third party most likely to join, in consequence of the "intimate union" that existed between France and Spain.

Franklin had cause to be pleased with himself. He had achieved the purpose for which he had been sent to Paris, obtaining the alliance with France on terms quite favorable to the United States. Though not a boaster, Franklin was never one to discount his own accomplishments, and he might well have rated this diplomatic triumph as his finest hour.

He could have been forgiven for taking the occasion to retire from public service. He was seventy-two years old, his gout was no better, and he increasingly suffered from kidney stones. No one would have begrudged his calling it a career and retiring to Philadelphia, to the bosom of his daughter's family.

Two considerations kept him from doing so. The first was that Philadelphia was occupied by the British army of William Howe. Franklin's comment that Philadelphia had captured Howe, rather than the other way around, was the sort of *bon mot* Franklin's French admirers appreciated. But it was misleading at best. Quaker-inspired Philadelphia wasn't a place that would turn the heads of Howe and his soldiers and vitiate their martial spirits. In any case, Philadelphia was proscribed to Franklin as long as the British were there, and it might remain proscribed for the duration of the war. George Washington had been unable to keep the British from occupying the city, and even with the aid of France, he might not be able to oust them. Franklin didn't intend to return to Philadelphia simply to be hanged. Paris, by contrast, was safe, especially now, and Franklin found it congenial.

Franklin's second reason for not retiring was that he believed he still had work to do. The treaty with France was a landmark of American diplomacy, but the alliance it created would require constant attention. Washington's army needed support as much as ever. And though America and France were now formal partners, their interests weren't identical. Franklin would see that America's interests were vigorously represented in the court of King Louis.

There was, moreover, the matter of how the war would end. The French alliance increased Franklin's confidence that the war would end in a victory for American independence, but the terms of peace would have to be negotiated. And those negotiations would be fully as challenging as the negotiation of the French treaties had been. The latter negotiation had been a bilateral affair of France and America. The peace negotiation would be at least trilateral: France, America and Britain. Franklin wasn't one to say he alone could manage such a negotiation, but he was self-confident enough to believe that none could do it better than he. So as long as the Congress saw fit to employ him, he would see fit to serve.

IN FACT THERE WAS yet another reason for Franklin to stay in Paris, if not necessarily to stay on the job as American commissioner. Franklin liked Paris, and Paris liked him. The break with Britain had cost Franklin London, his most satisfactory abode until then, and Philadelphia, during his eighteen months back in America, hadn't measured up. Paris became his new home, a most congenial one. Paris was sophisticated in a way even London was not, and skeptical in a manner that suited Franklin's own wry perspective. And where London finally scorned Franklin as a provincial, Paris feted him as nature's savant, the self-taught genius of the New World. His image appeared everywhere; the fur cap he chanced to be wearing on arrival in midwinter became a fashion perennial. The treaties with America completed the identification of Franklin with America in the minds of the French. America *must* be a worthy ally since Franklin was such a remarkable fellow.

John Adams joined Franklin at the height of the latter's celebrity, and thought it was entirely overblown. Adams replaced Silas Deane, whose dodgy accounting had caused the Continental Congress to remove him from the American commission to France. At the same time, the Congress promoted Franklin to minister plenipotentiary, making his ascendance over the other commissioners—Arthur Lee and now Adams—official.

Adams's service in Paris started unpromisingly. "When I arrived in France, the French nation had a great many questions to settle," he recalled. "The first was whether I was the famous Adams." Mostly through English newspapers, men and women in France knew about the firebrand who headed Boston's Sons of Liberty. Was this the man?

Adams disappointed his questioners. "It is another gentleman, whose name of Adams you have heard," he said. "It is Mr. Samuel Adams."

He wasn't believed at first. How many Adamses could there be?

In time Adams got the French to believe him, but soon began to wonder if he had succeeded too well. None went so far as to say he was "the *in*famous Adams," he joked, but the disappointment was palpable. "The consequence was settled absolutely and unalterably that I was a man of whom nobody had ever heard before, a perfect cypher, a man who did not understand a word of French, awkward in his figure, awkward in his dress, no abilities, a perfect bigot and fanatic."

Having reduced himself in the eyes of the French, Adams set about doing the same for Franklin. He conversed one day with a Monsieur Marbois; they discussed religion, and Marbois remarked on the variety of sects tolerated in America. Adams nodded agreement that, yes, religious freedom was a fundamental value in America. Marbois, noting that tolerance in France wasn't so broad, added that foreign ambassadors were allowed their own chapels. "But Mr. Franklin never had any," he said.

"No," answered Adams, "because Mr. Franklin had no—"

He caught himself. In his diary he wrote, "I was going to say what I did not say, and will not say here. I stopped short and laughed."

Marbois understood. "No," he said, "Mr. Franklin adores only great Nature, which has interested a great many people of both sexes in his favour."

"Yes," said Adams. "All the atheists, deists and libertines, as well as the philosophers and ladies are in his train—another Voltaire and Hume."

Marbois didn't see what was funny about this. "He is celebrated as the great philosopher and the great legislator of America," he said of Franklin.

"He is a great philosopher, but as a legislator of America, he has done very little," Adams rejoined. "It is universally believed in France, England and all Europe that his electric wand has accomplished all this revolution, but nothing is more groundless. He has done very little. It is believed that he made all the American constitutions, and their confederation. But he made neither. He did not even make the constitution of Pennsylvania, bad as it is. The bill of rights is taken almost verbatim from that of Virginia, which was made and published two or three months before that of Philadelphia was begun."

Marbois was perplexed. "Who made the Declaration of Independence?" he asked.

"Mr. Jefferson of Virginia was the draftsman," said Adams. Franklin was simply one of a committee of five.

Marbois didn't press the point, but Adams did, in his diary. He repeated of Franklin, "He had no title to the legislator of America." In another entry he wrote, "That he was a great genius, a great wit, a great humourist and a great satirist, and a great politician is certain. That he was a great philosopher, a great moralist and a great statesman is more questionable."

Franklin's morals caused Adams no end of concern. As he was drawn into Franklin's social circle, he was shocked by what he saw. "We were invited to dine at Monsieur Brillon's, a family in which Mr. Franklin was very intimate, and in which he spent much of his time," Adams wrote. "Here we met a large company of both sexes." The hostess stood out. "Madam Brillon was one of the most beautiful women in France," Adams observed. She and her husband made an odd pair. "Mr. Brillon was a rough kind of country squire; his lady all softness, sweetness and politeness." Two of the other guests were a gentleman, whom Adams identified as Monsieur Le Vaillant, and his wife. "She was very plain and clumsy." The second couple turned out to be closer friends with the hosts than Adams at first thought, and close in a different way than he had imagined. "I afterwards learned both from Dr. Franklin and his grandson, and from many other persons, that this woman was the amie of Mr. Brillon, and that Madam Brillon consoled herself by the amitie of Mr. Le Vaillant."

Adams didn't know what to make of this arrangement. "I was astonished that these people could live together in such apparent friendship and indeed without cutting each other's throats," he wrote. "But I did not know the world. I soon saw and heard so much of these things in other families and among almost all the great people of the kingdom that I found it was a thing of course. It was universally understood and nobody lost any reputation by it."

Adams's Puritan conscience refused to believe what his eyes saw and his ears heard. "I must say that I never knew an instance of it without perceiving that all their complaisancy was external and ostensible only: a mere conformity to the fashion: and that internally there was so far from being any real friendship or conjugal affection that their minds and hearts were full of jealousy, envy, revenge and rancour."

Adams met another of Franklin's friends, who had an arrangement, and a story, of her own. "Dined with Madam Helvetius," Adams noted. "One gentleman and one lady, besides Dr. Franklin, his grandson and myself, made the company. An elegant dinner." Adams had heard about Madame Helvetius. "This was a lady," he said, "of established reputation: the widow of the famous Helvetius, who, as Count Sarsefield once said to me, if he had made a few millions of livres the more as one of the Farmers General"—royally commissioned tax collectors—"and written a few books the less as a philosopher, it might have been better for France and the world." The widow had paid a sculptor to create a monument to her husband, showing her weeping beside his tomb. She had a smaller version in the house, which Adams saw.

But this was the extent of the mourning, as far as Adams could tell. Madame Helvetius seemed not to miss her husband. "There were three or four handsome abbes"—priests—"who daily visited the house and one at least resided there," Adams said. "These ecclesiastics, one or more of whom reside in almost every family of distinction, I suppose have as much power to pardon a sin as they have to commit one, or to assist in committing one. Oh mores! said I to myself. What absurdities, inconsistencies, distractions and horrors would these manners introduce into our republican governments in America. No kind of republican government can ever exist with such national manners as these. Cavete Americani!"

In time Adams was joined by his wife, Abigail, who was even more horrified than her husband by the habits of the French. Madame Helvetius invited Adams again for dinner, to be accompanied by Mrs. Adams. Adams warned Abigail about Madame Helvetius, whose performance exceeded the billing. "She entered the room with a careless, jaunty air," Abigail explained in letter to her niece. "Upon seeing ladies who were strangers to her, she bawled out, 'Ah! mon Dieu, where is Franklin? Why did you not tell me there were ladies here?' You must suppose her speaking all this in French. 'How I look!' said she, taking hold of a chemise made of tiffany, which she had on over a blue lute-string, and which looked as much upon the decay as her beauty, for she was once a handsome woman; her hair was frizzled; over it she had a small straw hat, with a dirty gauze half-handkerchief round it, and a bit of dirtier gauze than ever my maids wore, was bowed on behind. She had a black gauze scarf thrown over her shoulders."

Madame Helvetius ran out the room, only to return moments later in a scarcely less disheveled state. "The Doctor entered at one door," wrote Abigail Adams, "she at the other; upon which she ran forward to him, caught him by the hand, 'Helas! Franklin'; then gave him a double kiss, one upon each cheek, and another upon his forehead."

The group adjourned to the dining room. Madame Helvetius placed herself between Franklin and Adams. "She carried on the chief of the conversation at dinner, frequently locking her hand into the Doctor's, and sometimes spreading her arms upon the backs of both the gentlemen's chairs, then throwing her arm carelessly upon the Doctor's neck," wrote Abigail Adams.

Abigail struggled to maintain her composure. Franklin assisted, after a fashion. "I should have been greatly astonished at this conduct if the good Doctor had not told me that in this lady I should see a genuine Frenchwoman, wholly free from affectation or stiffness of behaviour, and one of the best women in the world." Abigail wasn't convinced. "For this I must take the Doctor's word," she said. "I should have set her down for a very bad one, although sixty years of age, and a widow. I own I was highly disgusted, and never wish for an acquaintance with any ladies of this cast. After dinner she threw herself upon a settee, where she showed more than her feet. She had a little lap-dog, who was, next to the Doctor, her favorite. This she kissed, and when he wet the floor, she wiped it up with her chemise." Abigail Adams interpreted the experience as a lesson. "Thus you see, my dear, that manners differ exceedingly in different countries," she told her niece. "I hope, however, to find amongst the French ladies manners more consistent with my ideas of decency, or I shall be a mere recluse."

AS MUCH AS JOHN ADAMS disapproved of the habits of the French, what concerned him more was that they had rubbed off on Franklin.

Adams had read the sayings of Poor Richard from Franklin's almanac; he took to heart such maxims as "Early to bed, early to rise, makes a man healthy, wealthy and wise." The Franklin that Adams encountered in Paris seemed never to have read the saying or given its wise sentiment a thought. "The life of Dr. Franklin was a scene of continual dissipation," Adams wrote. Bad enough on its own, the dissipation meant that Adams had to do all the work of the commission himself. "I could never obtain the favour of his company in a morning before breakfast, which would have been the most convenient time to read over the letters and papers, deliberate on their contents, and decide upon the substance of the answers," he remarked. Franklin slept late, and breakfasted late. And then he received visitors: philosophers, economists, men of letters. "But by far the greater part were women and children, come to have the honour to see the great Franklin, and to have the pleasure of telling stories about his simplicity, his bald head and scattering straight hairs, among their acquaintances. These visitors occupied all the time, commonly, till it was time to dress to go to dinner."

Dinner—luncheon—was the highlight of Franklin's daily schedule. "He was invited to dine abroad every day and never declined unless when we had invited company to dine with us," Adams said. "I was always invited with him, till I found it necessary to send apologies, that I might have some time to study the French language and do the business of the mission. Mr. Franklin kept a horn book always in his pocket in which he minuted all his invitations to dinner, and Mr. Lee said it was the only thing in which he was punctual." Arthur Lee shared Adams's jaundiced view of Franklin. "Mr. Lee came daily to my apartment to attend to business, but we could rarely obtain the company of Dr. Franklin for a few minutes, and often when I had drawn the papers and had them fairly copied for signature, and Mr. Lee and I had signed them, I was frequently obliged to wait several days before I could procure the signature of Dr. Franklin to them."

Franklin attended to no work after dinner. "He went according to his invitation to his dinner and after that went sometimes to the play, sometimes to the philosophers, but most commonly to visit those ladies who were complaisant enough to depart from the custom of France so far as to procure sets of tea gear, as it is called, and make tea for him," Adams said. The day was lost. "After tea, the evening was spent in hearing the ladies sing and play upon their piano fortes and other instruments of music, and in various games as cards, chess, backgammon, etc." Adams gathered that Franklin played chess and checkers but simply watched the other games. "In these agreeable and important occupations and amusements, the afternoon and evening was spent, and he came home at all hours from nine to twelve o'clock at night."

Adams granted that Franklin's routine suited Franklin, though it left him—Adams—to labor unappreciated. "This course of life contributed to his pleasure and I believe to his health and longevity," Adams said. "He was now between seventy and eighty, and I had so much respect and compassion for his age that I should have been happy to have done all the business, or rather all the drudgery, if I could have been favoured with a few moments in a day to receive his advice concerning the manner in which it ought to be done. But this condescension was not attainable. All that could be had was his signature after it was done."

WHILE FRANKLIN WAS enjoying Paris, George Washington was struggling to hold the Continental Army together outside Philadelphia. William Howe, after occupying the city, seemed in no hurry to leave. But Washington couldn't be sure the British were going to winter in Philadelphia, and in any case, the idea of leaving the American capital in control of the enemy was painful to accept. It would demoralize American Patriots and hearten the Loyalists; it would also discourage foreign governments from taking the United States seriously. Washington had yet to hear from Franklin regarding the treaty negotiations, and he couldn't take for granted that the victory at Saratoga would make the crucial difference.

He tested the British defenses around Philadelphia but found no opening. "General Howe has withdrawn himself close within his lines, which extend from the Upper Ferry upon the Schuylkill to Kensington upon the Delaware," Washington wrote to Horatio Gates in early December 1777. "They consist of a chain of strong redoubts connected by *abatis*. We have reconnoitered them well, but find it impossible to attack them while defended by a force fully equal to our own in Continental troops."

So what should be done, if Howe couldn't be dislodged? "Viewing the subject in any point of light, there was a choice of difficulties," Washington explained to John Hancock. "If keeping the field was thought of, the naked condition of the troops and the feelings of humanity opposed the measure." Supplies were already short, and winter was just beginning. "If returning to the towns in the interior parts of the state, which consistently with the preservation of the troops, from their necessitous circumstances, might have been justifiable, the measure was found inexpedient, because it would have exposed and left uncovered a large extent of country." Howe and the British could raid at will, further demoralizing the populace and exposing the Continental Army to ridicule. "If cantoning the troops in several places, divided and distant from each other, then there was a probability of their being cut off, and but little prospect of their giving security to any part." Half-measures would be worse than no measures at all.

The least bad of his options was the one Washington chose. "Under these embarrassments, I determined to take post near this place"—he was writing from Valley Forge, in the countryside northwest of Philadelphia—"as the best calculated in my judgment to secure the army, to protect our stores, and cover the country." The decision had been far from easy. "No circumstance in the course of the present contest, or in my whole life, has employed more of my reflection or consideration," Washington told Hancock. But a decision was required, and he had made it.

The advantage of Valley Forge was its location: close enough to Philadelphia to keep an eye on Howe and the British, far enough to minimize the chances of a British surprise attack on the army. Its disadvantages were nearly everything else. It was open country, affording scant shelter against the coming winter. Any shelter would have to be constructed by the troops themselves. The residents of the area were ambivalent at best, with even those leaning toward the Patriot cause lacking confidence Washington could protect them from reprisal should they conspicuously support him. And there were no stockpiles of provisions anywhere nearby.

This last was the critical issue. Washington's army was woefully short even before arriving at Valley Forge, and he had little reason to believe much was on the way. He told Hancock he had sent men out to forage, but this was no more than a stopgap. "Three or four days of bad weather would prove our destruction," Washington said. And the foraging made the army less popular than ever. "The disaffection of the people is past all belief."

As he had before, Washington felt badly used. He was being blamed for having won no victories comparable to that of General Gates, who indeed was being spoken of as Washington's replacement at the head of the Continental Army. Without mentioning Gates, Washington vented his frustration to Hancock. "It is time to speak plain in exculpation of myself," he said. "I can declare that no man in my opinion ever had his measures more impeded than I have." The Continental Congress consistently failed to furnish rations enough to keep his men fed. They lacked shirts and boots. Soap had vanished months ago. His critics in the Congress had nerve, Washington said. "I can assure those gentlemen that it is a much easier and less distressing thing to draw remonstrances in a comfortable room by a good fireside than to occupy a cold, bleak hill and sleep under frost and snow without clothes or blankets." He added, "Although they seem to have little feeling for the naked and distressed soldiers, I feel superabundantly for them"—the soldiers—"and, from my soul, I pity those miseries which it is neither in my power to relieve or prevent."

THE WEATHER THAT WINTER wasn't brutal, by the standards of Pennsylvania. But it was cold enough to leave the men shivering in the crude cabins they constructed for themselves, while they tried to stretch skimpy rations and keep from succumbing to the diseases that followed every army in those days of ignorance of basic etiology. Frostbite nipped fingers that lacked gloves and toes that stuck out of worn boots; serious cases resulted in gangrene and amputation. Simple hypothermia was a constant danger. The cold and a shortage of clean water discouraged bathing, causing lice and other parasites to flourish.

February was the worst month. "The present situation of the army is the most melancholy that can be conceived," Washington wrote. "Our supplies of provisions of the flesh kind for some time past have been very deficient and irregular. A prospect now opens of absolute want, such as will make it impossible to keep the army much longer from dissolution, unless the most vigorous and effectual measures be pursued to prevent it." Washington's men had foraged as far as they could. "Jersey, Pennsylvania and Maryland are now entirely exhausted. All the beef and pork already collected in them, or that can be collected, will not by any means support the army one month longer. Further to the southward some quantities of salt provisions have been procured, but if they were all on the spot they would afford but a very partial and temporary supply." Washington hoped New England could pitch in. "To the eastward only can we turn our eyes with any reasonable hope of timely and adequate succor." It was the army's last hope. "If every possible exertion is not made use of there to send us immediate and ample supplies of cattle, with pain I speak the alarming truth, no human efforts can keep the army from speedily disbanding."

A week later the situation had grown worse. "For some days past, there has been little less than a famine in camp," Washington wrote. "A part of the army has been a week without any kind of flesh, and the rest three or four days." He gave the men credit for steadfastness, but devotion had limits. "Naked and starving as they are, we cannot enough admire the incomparable patience and fidelity of the soldiery, that they have not been ere this excited by their suffering to a general mutiny and dispersion. Strong symptoms, however, of discontent have appeared in particular instances, and nothing but the most active efforts everywhere can long avert so shocking a catastrophe."

By this time Washington had little faith in the Congress to furnish what his men needed, and so he appealed directly to the people of the surrounding states. "Friends, Countrymen and Fellow Citizens," he wrote in a circular to the residents of New Jersey, Pennsylvania, Delaware, Maryland and Virginia. "After three campaigns during which the brave subjects of these states have contended, not unsuccessfully, with one of the most powerful kingdoms upon earth, we now find ourselves at least upon a level with our opponents." This was the good news. Next the hopeful word: "There is the best reason to believe that efforts adequate to the abilities of this country would enable us speedily to conclude the war, and to secure the invaluable blessings of peace, liberty, and safety." To this end, Washington proposed to expand the army to enable the decisive blow.

But for this he needed the people's help. "Unless the virtuous yeomanry of the states of New Jersey, Pennsylvania, Maryland and Virginia will exert themselves to prepare cattle for the use of the army during the months of May, June and July next, great difficulties may arise in the course of the campaign," Washington said. He urged the farmers to fatten their stock and offer them for sale to the army. "A bountiful price will be given," he promised, on no firm basis. Beyond this, the contributors would have done America a good turn. "They will render a most essential service to the illustrious cause of their country and contribute in a great degree to shorten this bloody contest." For the laggards among his readers, Washington added another reason for cooperating—namely, that what cattle were not offered to the Continental Army would likely be seized by the British army. To them Washington recommended his policy as one "calculated to save their property from plunder, their families from insult, and their own persons from abuse, hopeless confinement, or perhaps a violent death."

Supplies trickled in, enough to avert actual starvation—among the humans at any rate—but hardly more than that. "By death and desertion we have lost a good many men since we came to this ground, and have encountered every species of hardship, that cold, wet and hunger, and want of clothes were capable of producing," he recorded in late March. "Notwithstanding, and contrary to my expectations, we have been able to keep the soldiers from mutiny or dispersion; although, in the single article of provisions, they have encountered enough to have occasioned one or the other of these in most other armies. They have been (two or three times) days together without provisions; and once, six days without any of the meat kind. Could the poor horses tell their tale, it would be in a strain still more lamentable, as numbers have actually died from pure want."

IN WASHINGTON'S ENTOURAGE at Valley Forge was a young aide-de-camp named Alexander Hamilton. Slight of build, reddish of hair, endlessly energetic, impossibly ambitious, the West Indies orphan had landed in New York just in time for the events that led to the American Revolution. He threw himself into politics on the Patriot side, and when the war broke out he enrolled in the New York militia. He took part in Washington's failed effort to keep William Howe out of New York, and he retreated with Washington across New Jersey and into Pennsylvania. Hamilton's artillery company bombarded British positions in the Patriot victory at Princeton. He came to Washington's attention and was shortly appointed to Washington's staff.

At once a bond began to develop. Washington saw in Hamilton something of the son he never had. Hamilton perceived a posting with Washington as entrée to the highest circles of authority and power in the fledgling United States. Articulate in English and French, Hamilton quickly made himself indispensable to the commander in chief. He drafted many of Washington's letters and orders, leaving for Washington a cursory read and the signing.

Occasionally Hamilton wrote in his own voice. In one letter to George Clinton, the governor of New York, Hamilton broached a delicate topic. "You and I had some conversation when I had the pleasure of seeing you last with respect to the existence of a certain faction," he said to Clinton. He had uncovered more about this faction, and what he learned gave him cause for alarm. "I have discovered such convincing traits of the monster that I cannot doubt its reality in the most extensive sense." He supposed Clinton had sources of his own. "I dare say you have seen and heard enough to settle the matter in your own mind." Hamilton thought one moment of crisis had passed, but he expected others to come. "I believe it unmasked its batteries too soon and begins to hide its head; but as I imagine it will only change the storm to a sap, all the true and sensible friends to their country, and of course to a certain great man, ought to be upon the watch to counterplot the secret machinations of his enemies."

What Hamilton described so elliptically was what would be dubbed the "Conway cabal." Thomas Conway was of Irish descent and French upbringing, his family having fled Ireland to be free of the British harassment of Catholics there. He made a profession of arms, first in the French army and then in the Prussian. He joined the wave of soldiers of fortune who rushed to America at the start of the American Revolution, and among the inexperienced provincial officers he stood out. He made a positive first impression on Washington. "He appears to be a man of candor, and if he has been in service as long as he says he has, I should suppose him infinitely better qualified to serve us than many who have been promoted," Washington told John Hancock.

Conway's performance in the campaign for Philadelphia seemed to confirm Washington's judgment. Benjamin Rush, a Philadelphia physician, signer of the Declaration of Independence, and surgeon with the Continental Army, couldn't say enough good things about Conway after Germantown. "He is entitled to most of the glory our arms acquired in the late battle," Rush wrote to John Adams. "But his bravery and skill in war are not his only military qualifications. He is exact in his discipline, and understands every part of the detail of an army. Besides this, he is an enthusiast in our cause. Some people blame him for calling some of our generals fools—cowards—and drunkards in public company. But these things are proofs of his integrity, and should raise him in the opinion of every friend to America." Rush added, "He is, moreover, the idol of the whole army."

Conway apparently thought so, too. He blamed Washington for the defeat at Germantown, contending that Washington's hesitation had doomed the gallant effort of his troops and subordinate officers, including Conway himself. This, at any rate, was the interpretation Washington placed on a statement reportedly made by Conway to Horatio Gates: "Heaven has been determined to save your country, or a weak general and bad counsellors would have ruined it."

Had Washington been less sensitive to slights against his leadership, and less worn by the effort required to hold the army together amid the trials of the Valley Forge winter, he might have taken account of the provenance of the remark attributed to Conway. The quotation was third-hand at best, and could well have suffered in the transmittal. But Washington was already annoyed at Horatio Gates, who was being celebrated for the victory at Saratoga at the same time Washington was being questioned, if not blamed outright, for the loss of Philadelphia. Gates had a habit of sending his reports to the Congress rather than to Washington, his superior officer. Now it appeared that Conway was talking behind Washington's back to Gates, and Gates was doing nothing to discourage him.

From this Washington conjured a conspiracy against himself. "I never knew that General Conway (who I viewed in the light of a stranger to you) was a correspondent of yours," he wrote to Gates. "Much less did I suspect that I was the subject of your confidential letters." Anticipating a complaint from Gates that the confidentiality of correspondence had been betrayed, Washington declared that his informant had indicated that Gates approved of the telling. "I considered the information as coming from yourself, and given with a friendly view to forewarn and consequently forearm me against a secret enemy; or, in other words, a dangerous incendiary, in which character, sooner or later, this country will know General Conway." Washington added significantly, "But in this, as in other matters of late, I have found myself mistaken."

Gates denied the premise of Washington's complaint: that he had received a letter from Conway with the passage to which Washington had taken objection. Conway himself initially said he couldn't remember making any such statement; later, upon receiving the letter in question back from Gates, he positively denied doing so. "I find with great satisfaction that the paragraph so much spoke of does not exist in said letter nor anything like it," he wrote to Washington.

Yet this didn't end the matter. Conway had never been more than the bearer of bad news, if bearer at all. Alexander Hamilton, at Washington's right hand and sharing Washington's views, persisted in calling Conway names, declaring to George Clinton: "He is one of the vermin bred in the entrails of this chimera dire, and there does not exist a more villainous calumniator and incendiary." But Gates was the one Washington worried about. Washington feared that a faction in the Congress wanted to replace him with Horatio Gates.

From Henry Laurens, who had succeeded John Hancock as president of the Congress, Washington learned that questions were being raised about his performance. Laurens shared a paper specifying certain charges against Washington by his critics. Washington professed to be unperturbed. "I was not unapprized that a malignant faction had been for some time forming to my prejudice," he replied. Conceding "some pain on a personal account," he said his greater worries involved the effect the questioning of his leadership would have on the war effort. "My chief concern arises from an apprehension of the dangerous consequences which intestine dissentions may produce to the common cause." Patriots would be discouraged and Loyalists heartened by this break in the ranks. Washington complained to Laurens of the fix he was in. "My enemies take an ungenerous advantage of me. They know the delicacy of my situation and that motives of policy deprive me of the defence I might otherwise make against their insidious attacks. They know I cannot combat their insinuations, however injurious, without disclosing secrets it is of the utmost moment to conceal." Once more he professed to be above such things. "Why should I expect to be exempt from censure, the unfailing lot of an elevated station?"

Yet he wouldn't let the matter die. The enforced idleness at Valley Forge left Washington time to imagine what was being said and done against him. "My caution to avoid anything that could injure the service prevented me from communicating but to very few of my friends the intrigues of a faction which I know was formed against me, since it might serve to publish our internal dissentions," he wrote to Patrick Henry in March. "But their own restless zeal to advance their views has too clearly betrayed them and made concealment on my part fruitless. I cannot precisely mark the extent of their views, but it appeared in general that General Gates was to be exalted, on the ruin of my reputation and influence. This I am authorised to say from undeniable facts in my own possession, from publications the evident scope of which could not be mistaken, and from private detractions industriously circulated. General Mifflin"—Thomas Mifflin, recently quartermaster general—"it is commonly supposed, bore the second part in the cabal, and General Conway, I know, was a very active and malignant partisan."

In the event, General Gates was not exalted, and the "cabal" Washington detected never materialized. Likely it never possessed the coherence Washington ascribed to it. Soldiers always grumble, not least when things aren't going well; doubtless Conway cast aspersions on Washington's performance at one battle or another. And certainly some members of the Congress expressed impatience with Washington, quite possibly as a way of deflecting criticism of their own body for failing to support him. But nothing like an organized conspiracy, or cabal, to topple him in favor of Gates seems to have existed.

Washington's quickness to perceive a conspiracy said more about him than about the alleged conspirators. In particular it revealed aspects of his attachment to the cause of independence. He sought independence on its merits, to be sure, but also on *his* merits. He had always been touchy about his reputation, since he resigned his commission in the Virginia militia over a reduction in rank. He had been convinced of his talent at arms from the moment he and his men outperformed the British regulars at the disastrous defeat of Braddock's army. Now he felt his reputation imperiled and his talent wasted by the incompetence of the Congress, which refused to support the war effort adequately. After everything he had risked for country and its independence, such treatment was almost more than he could bear.

Washington's overreaction to Conway's criticism was of a piece with the language he employed to describe the stakes of the conflict with Britain. Repeatedly he invoked the image of slavery as the sole alternative to independence. "A period is fast approaching, big with events of the most interesting importance, when the counsels we pursue, and the part we act, may lead decisively to liberty or to slavery," he wrote to John Banister from Valley Forge. To Henry Laurens a week later he spoken in similar terms. "A most important crisis is now at hand," he said. "The result may lead to happiness or to misery, to freedom or to slavery." Washington detected a weakening of American resolve in calls for negotiations with Britain. He refused to countenance any such thing. "Nothing short of independence can possibly do," he said. The British could not be trusted; they would "attempt again to bend our necks to the yoke of slavery."

Washington wasn't alone in raising the specter of slavery; many of the Patriots indulged themselves similarly. But for the master of hundreds of real slaves, the imagery was striking. Washington knew perfectly well that the British would not reduce the Americans to chattel, bought and sold on the auction block the way African slaves were traded. He knew the Americans would not be whipped the way Washington's own slaves were whipped. He certainly recognized that his metaphor was overdrawn. But he employed it anyway. For Washington the struggle against Britain was much more than political, more than about taxes and representation. It was deeply personal, about ambition and identity.

Part VIII

Lawrence Growden's Daughter

IF JOSEPH GALLOWAY EVER READ Ben Franklin's *bon mot* about Philadelphia taking William Howe, he might have agreed, but he would have meant it differently. One reason Howe marched south toward Philadelphia rather than north to Albany—besides thinking John Burgoyne could find his way through the wilderness without getting lost—was that Galloway had been telling him for months that Philadelphia and Pennsylvania were thick with Loyalists eagerly awaiting the chance to show their support for the king.

Galloway had displayed his own colors in late 1776, as William Howe afterward recounted. "When my brother and I, in the character of His Majesty's commissioners for restoring peace, published a proclamation of indemnity for all those who had taken part in the rebellion, provided they should surrender themselves and subscribe a declaration of allegiance within a limited time, Mr. Galloway was among the first who came over to us from Philadelphia," Howe wrote. "This was in the month of December, 1776, when our great successes had intimidated the leaders of the rebellion and nearly induced a general submission."

Howe had heard of Galloway, and he thought the king's side had scored a coup by bringing him aboard. "I considered the acquisition of Mr. Galloway as a matter of some importance, because in all events I expected much assistance from a gentleman of his abilities and reputed influence in the province of Philadelphia," he said. Howe put Galloway on the army's payroll until he could find something better for him.

Galloway offered advice about rebel leaders he had worked with in the Pennsylvania assembly and the Continental Congress, about the resources of the various colonies, and about the best roads and sea lanes in the area. Above all he preached the importance of the Loyalists in any successful British strategy. He pointed out that Loyalism grew stronger the farther south one traveled in America. Loyalists were few and weak in New England, more numerous and stronger in Pennsylvania and its neighbors, and most numerous and strongest in the southern colonies. Capturing Philadelphia, Galloway explained, besides humbling and scattering the Continental Congress, would establish a durable British presence much closer to the center of gravity of American Loyalism. Galloway argued that the war would be won or lost in the hearts of Americans. Anything that encouraged the Loyalists would increase the chances of success of the British army on the battlefield.

SARAH LOGAN FISHER WAS one of those of whom Galloway spoke so glowingly. Sarah Fisher was a granddaughter of James Logan, a pillar of Pennsylvania politics who had been a mentor to Benjamin Franklin. Sarah was also a Quaker and for that reason formally neutral between the two sides in the current war, but her hopes and dreams were with the British. She had held her tongue when George Washington had briefly commandeered the estate, Stenton, she and her husband owned outside Philadelphia. "Washington appeared extremely grave and thoughtful," she wrote in her diary. But Washington's men were less restrained, and their actions didn't improve Sarah Fisher's opinion of the rebels. "Those soldiers who were encamped near Stenton did abundance of damage to the tenant in the night, destroyed his corn, potatoes, etc."

She and the other residents of Philadelphia were as mystified as Washington was during that period regarding Howe's intentions. "An express came in which brings an account that the British are landed about four miles below the Head of Elk, but where they mean to march to we remain in a state of suspense about, anxious to know, yet almost afraid to hear lest our wishes should not be answered."

The approach of the British soon touched her personally. "About 11 o'clock our new-made council sent some of their deputies to many of the inhabitants whom they suspected of Toryism, and without any regular warrant or any written paper mentioning their crime, or telling them of it in any way, committed them to the confinement," Sarah Fisher wrote on September 2. "And among their number was my dear husband." Thomas Fisher had demanded to see the warrant for his arrest. "Upon which they read over a paper which they called one, which was an order from the Congress recommending to the Executive Council to fall upon some measure to take up all such persons who had by their conduct or otherwise shown themselves enemies of the United States, and the council gave orders for the taking such persons as they thought proper." Thomas Fisher was arrested, as were a score of other Loyalists of Sarah's acquaintance. They were all men; their wives, including Sarah, were left to fend for themselves.

For ten days Thomas Fisher and the other Quakers and Loyalists were held in Philadelphia. Sarah was allowed to visit her husband. But when the men persisted in refusing to swear allegiance to the United States, they were ordered exiled to Virginia. "They were dragged into the wagons by force by soldiers employed for that purpose and drove off surrounded by guards and a mob." In her diary Sarah permitted herself a moment of satisfaction at the simultaneous misfortune of George Washington's army. "The very day our dear friends were sent away, Washington met with a great defeat"—at Brandywine.

The next week was a dark one for Sarah Fisher. "I feel forlorn and desolate, and the world appears like a dreary desert," she wrote on September 21. Since their wedding she had never been apart from her husband more than briefly; now she had no idea when or if she would see him again. The one thing that diverted her was the discomfiture of the Patriots fleeing the city ahead of the British, who drew ever closer. "Wagons rattling, horses galloping, women running, children crying, delegates flying, and altogether the greatest consternation, fright and terror that can be imagined," was how she described the chaos. "Some of our neighbors took their flight before day, and I believe all the Congress moved off before 5 o'clock." The alarm proved premature; the British were not yet at the outskirts. "Thus the guilty fly when none pursue," Sarah observed sardonically.

Having carried off the Loyalist men, the Patriots seized their movable property as well. Sarah encountered a squadron of Continental Army soldiers looting a store owned by her father-in-law. "One Captain Hamilton, by order of Lieutenant Colonel White, commander of the city, came there with armed men and forcibly broke open the store door and took away a large quantity of goods and said it was by General Washington's orders," she wrote. Captain Hamilton was in fact Lieutenant Colonel Alexander Hamilton. Sarah was incensed. The

Patriots claimed to be defending rights long cherished by Britons, but they showed no respect for the rights of those whose sole offense was their desire to continue to live as Britons. "This arbitrary conduct of theirs is I believe unprecedented before in any age or country," she said.

During the next thirty-six hours the British were reported to be getting closer and closer. Sarah Fisher could hardly wait. "Rose very early this morning in hopes of seeing a most pleasing sight," she wrote on September 26. At ten o'clock the British troops began to enter the city. "The town was still, not a cart or any obstruction in their way. The morning had before been cloudy, but nearly the time of their entrance the sun shone out with a sweet serenity, and the weather being uncommonly cool for the time of year prevented their being incommoded with the heat."

It was a perfect day for a parade, and the welcome spectacle made Sarah forget her troubles for a moment. "First came the light horse, led along by Enoch Story and Phineas Bond"—two leading Loyalists— "as the soldiers were unacquainted with the town and the different streets, nearly 200 I imagine in number, clean dress and their bright swords glittering in the sun. After that came the foot, headed by Lord Cornwallis. Before him went a band of music, which played a solemn tune and which I afterwards understood was called 'God Save Great George Our King.' Then followed the soldiers, who looked very clean and healthy, and a remarkable solidity was on their countenances, no wanton levity or indecent mirth, but a gravity well becoming the occasion seemed on all their faces. After that came the artillery and then the Hessian grenadiers, attended by a large band of music but not equal in fineness or solemnity to the other. Baggage wagons, Hessian women, and horse, cows, goats and asses brought up the rear."

Sarah Fisher was astonished that the occupation had occurred so rapidly and in such orderly fashion. "They encamped on the commons, and but for a few officers which were riding about the city, I imagine to give orders and provide quarters for their men, in 3 hours afterwards you would not have thought so great a change had taken place. Everything appeared still and quiet. A number of the inhabitants sat up to watch, and for fear of any alarm. Thus was this large city surrendered to the English without the least opposition whatever, or even firing a single gun, which I thought called for great humility and deep gratitude on our parts."

JOSEPH GALLOWAY RODE into the city beside William Howe, and was soon the most powerful civilian in Philadelphia. "I appointed him a magistrate of the police of that city, with a salary of 300 pounds sterling per annum, and six shillings a day more for a clerk," Howe explained. "I also appointed him superintendent of the port, with a salary of twenty shillings a day, making in the whole upwards of 770 pounds sterling per annum."

Galloway threw himself into his work, which included organizing shipping between New York and Philadelphia, at this point the twin headquarters of British power in America. He helped provision the British troops in Philadelphia, using his police authority to prevent price-gouging by suppliers. He conducted a census of Philadelphia, with an eye toward determining the number of males of military age who might be drawn to fight on behalf of the British. He offered to raise the troops himself. "Soon after the arrival of the army in Philadelphia, Mr. Galloway applied to me for permission to raise a troop of dragoons, which he assured me should be composed of natives of America," Howe said. The general granted permission.

But the result was less than he hoped. American Loyalists were either fewer or less enthusiastic than Galloway had said; they didn't answer the call to service in the numbers he had promised. Howe let Galloway develop a network of spies behind George Washington's lines, assuming Galloway's previous connections would produce valuable advice. "I at first paid attention to his opinions and relied upon him for procuring me secret intelligence," Howe recalled. "But I afterwards found that my confidence was misplaced. His ideas, I discovered to be visionary, and his intelligence was too frequently either ill founded or so much exaggerated that it would have been unsafe to act upon it."

By the time Howe made these remarks, he and Galloway had had a falling-out, with each blaming the other for Britain's failure to crush the rebellion. Howe thought Galloway had sold him a bill of goods by overstating the strength of the Loyalists in Pennsylvania; Galloway questioned the commitment of Howe to the war effort.

Even with the best of cooperation the occupation would have been difficult. Between the demands of Howe's army inside the city and

George Washington's nearby, the farms of the vicinity had to support more than twice the usual population. Supplies ran short and became, despite Galloway's efforts, very expensive. "Scarcely any meat in the market, nor a pound of butter or an egg at any price," wrote Sarah Fisher in October. "Sometimes by walking down to the ferry you may get a pound or two of butter that is brought over"—from New Jersey—"by stealth, but if you get it, as a favor you must pay a silver dollar. Not any wood to be had at any price. Many families of the first rank have not half a cord in the world, and know not where to get more." The military situation aggravated the problem. "Money will not procure the necessaries, for as the English have neither the command of the river nor the country, provisions cannot be brought in," Sarah Fisher said.

Things grew worse. "Low and distressed this morning, and not without reason," she wrote in November. "The prospect of suffering for want is such that it is dreadful to think what the distresses of the poor people are and must be. Everything is gone of the vegetable kind, plundered, great part of it, by the Hessians." As loyal as Loyalists like Sarah Fisher might be toward Britain, they never warmed to the German mercenaries. "Fences torn down, cows, hogs, fowls and everything gone," she continued. "Butchers obliged to kill fine milk cows for meat; mutton or veal not even heard of."

THE WORST OF THE SHORTAGES eased after British troops captured two American forts that had blocked traffic on the Delaware River, but prices remained high throughout the winter. Yet the British soldiers, lacking employment in their profession, amused themselves as soldiers often have: drinking, whoring, gambling and fighting. Joseph Galloway could do only so much to keep the roistering in check; the city built by Quakers found its sensibilities shocked.

In the spring of 1778 Galloway learned that William Howe was being replaced by Henry Clinton. The British disaster at Saratoga had convinced the British government that a change was needed in the military command. Howe's officers in Philadelphia threw him a party that offended many of the residents of the city. "This day may be remembered by many from the scenes of folly and vanity promoted by the officers of the army under the pretense of showing respect to General Howe," wrote Elizabeth Drinker, a Quaker friend of Sarah

Fisher. "How insensible do these people appear, while our land is so greatly desolated, and death and sore destruction has overtaken, and now impends, over so many!"

No less dismaying was news that the British were going to leave Philadelphia. The French alliance with America caused the British government to decide to consolidate its military position in America, and it chose New York over Philadelphia as the center of operations. Joseph Galloway vigorously opposed the decision, contending that the gains of the previous year would be lost by simply leaving the American capital. Besides, Philadelphia was closer to the Loyalist South, while New York was right next to rebellious New England. Galloway continued to argue that the war would be won by mobilizing the American Loyalists; the abandonment of Philadelphia, far from mobilizing them, would compel them to make their peace with the rebels.

Which was precisely what William Howe proposed to Galloway that the Loyalists do. "I assured him that if they chose to go with the King's army, they should be taken all possible care of, but if they rather chose to stay behind with their property and families, I could have no objection to their inquiring whether Washington and the Congress would grant them protection and security," Howe said later.

Galloway found himself in a bad spot. If he left with the British, he might lose his property; if he stayed behind, he might lose his life. Was the Congress in a mood to grant amnesty to one who had worked so visibly on behalf of the British? He doubted it. And even if the Congress waived penalties, Patriot irregulars might take matters into their own hands. Galloway had found a noose on his doorstep even before he went over to the British; he could well imagine something more than a warning now.

He chose to go, but he hedged his departure. He left his wife, Grace Growden Galloway, behind to hold on to the family property, much of which had come down from her father, a wealthy manufacturer and landowner. Joseph Galloway hoped that whatever the Patriots had against him would not be imputed to her. She was willing to give it a try, although saying goodbye to her seventeen-year-old daughter, Elizabeth, who would travel with the father to New York, especially wrenched her heart. "This evening parted with my dear husband and child," Grace wrote on June 17, in the first entry of a diary she began keeping that day.

YOU ARE IMMEDIATELY to proceed to Philadelphia and take the command of the troops there," George Washington wrote to Benedict Arnold shortly after the British evacuated the city. "You will take every prudent step in your power to preserve tranquility and order in the city, and give security to individuals of every class and description; restraining as far as possible, till the restoration of civil government, every species of persecution, insult or abuse, either from the soldiery to the inhabitants or among each other." Washington understood the delicacy of what he was asking Arnold to accomplish. Philadelphia had been a Patriot city under the Continental Congress, and then a Loyalist city under the British, and now it was a Patriot city once more. There would be powerful temptations to score-settling. Washington was relying on Arnold to negotiate the treacherous swamp Philadelphia politics would surely become. Questions of property would be crucial. "I leave it to your own discretion to adopt such measures as shall appear to you most effectual and, at the same time, least offensive for answering the views of Congress to prevent the removal, transfer or sale of any goods, wares or merchandise in possession of the inhabitants of the city till the property of them can be ascertained."

Arnold got the Philadelphia job, rather than a field command, because his wounded leg hadn't healed. Washington expected the posting to be brief. "Let me know the state of your wound," he said. As he braced for the next move of the British, now under Henry Clinton, he didn't think he could do without Arnold for long.

"My wounds are in a fair way and less painful than usual," Arnold replied. But they weren't healing as fast as he had hoped. "There is little prospect of my being able to take the field for a considerable time." Arnold spoke of perhaps transferring to the navy, where the inability to ride a horse wouldn't be a problem. His friends were urging him to consider it, he told Washington.

Washington admired Arnold's eagerness to get back into the fight. "I confess myself no competent judge in marine matters to offer advice on a subject so far out of my line," he said. And he trusted Arnold's own judgment on how he best could serve their country. But he made clear he wanted Arnold back with him. "I am very happy to learn that your wounds are less painful," Washington said. "The only drawback in the pleasure I receive is that the condition of your wounds is still such as not to admit of your active services this campaign."

GRACE GALLOWAY FORMED a favorable opinion of Arnold as soon as he took command in Philadelphia. The wife of Joseph Galloway was a distinguished figure in the city, even if her husband's politics had placed him beyond the Patriot pale. Arnold understood that respect must be paid. Grace Galloway kept a list of her visitors, who on the third day of the American reoccupation included "Major Franks with General Arnold's compliments and assurance of protection."

She soon discovered she needed protection. Among her visitors was one who identified himself as Pennsylvania's agent for confiscated estates. He had come, he said, to assume possession of her house. Grace Galloway told him it was *her* house, and she wasn't leaving. He bowed and departed, but made plain he would be back.

Taking Benedict Arnold at the general's word, Grace paid him a call. He disappointed her by saying that property questions were matters for the courts to decide. "He told me he could do nothing in the case," she wrote in her diary. Arnold said she would be safe from personal harm, but he couldn't guarantee her title to the house. She couldn't blame him, but neither did she much like him. "I thought I was received rather coolly but civilly," she recorded.

She hoped for better from her friends. She asked them for personal advice and legal counsel. She discovered that for all the Friends in the city, true friends were hard to come by. One, a man with expertise in law and insight into politics, was blunt. "He told me to do nothing but give up everything," she wrote. Rejecting this counsel, she turned to another. "He advised me to see lawyers."

This course was more helpful, but only a little. Pennsylvania law stipulated that when a woman married, her property passed to her husband, as long as he lived. Grace Galloway had no legal claim to the house she occupied. As for Joseph Galloway's title, he had forfeited it by siding with the enemy. If he died before the forfeiture was accomplished, the title might revert to her, and she might save the property.

Or she might not. The legal practice of "coverture," by which the husband got the property, also "covered" the wife against prosecution. Grace Galloway would not be prosecuted as a Loyalist as long as Joseph Galloway lived. But should he die, then the law would apply to her. And she would lose the house on that basis.

She learned all this in an excruciatingly practical form of legal education. Had she been a man, she would have been removed by force from her house and probably imprisoned. Because she was a woman, the authorities treated her more gently, albeit no less persistently. For weeks she was hounded by various representatives of the government who told her she had to get out of the house. She hired lawyers to contest the matter in court, but they never accomplished more than delaying what increasingly seemed inevitable.

Her mood alternated between anger and discouragement. "I was quite mad with Howe for betraying us to the provincials," she remarked on one particularly frustrating day. If the erstwhile British commander had displayed more nerve—and listened to her husband—he could have crushed the rebels, and she wouldn't be in her present fix. "It was quite in his power to have settled the affair." The next day she declared, "Everything wears a gloomy appearance." Several days later she lamented, "Oh, God! What shall I do?"

She continued to fight for her home. A delegation from the state arrived to take an inventory of her household items. As they finished, they said they would be advertising the house and its furnishings for auction. Grace shook her head and stood her ground. "I told them they may do as they pleased, but till it was decided by a court I would not go out unless by the force of a bayonet."

The confrontations energized her. But when the men left, the energy dissipated and the gloom gathered around her again. She longed for her husband and daughter. During the British occupation of Philadelphia, getting messages in and out of the city hadn't been difficult. But the Patriots now clamped down on communications, especially from notorious Loyalists like Joseph Galloway. Grace hoped her husband and daughter were safe in New York, but she hadn't received confirmation. The uncertainty added to her distress.

She encountered another problem. From birth she had never had to think about money; her father and then her husband had more than enough for all her needs and most of her wants. Now she was thrown onto her own devices, which weren't many. In those days before banks became common, even the wealthy often had few liquid assets; they required regular credit, secured by their property. Because Grace Galloway's property was contested, lenders wouldn't accept it as collateral. Some days she could scarcely find two pennies to rub together.

Worse than the want was the mortification it entailed. When she thought she'd run out of legal options and was about to be tossed to the curb, she visited a friend to ask for shelter. Her friend made excuses, but said there was no room. Grace Galloway was crushed. "My heart was ready to burst at the mean figure I must cut in begging to go to another person's house and be told I could not," she said.

She barricaded herself in the house, locking it against intruders. One responded by shouting at her through the door in a threatening tone. After he left she gathered her wits and appealed once more to Benedict Arnold. "Went to General Arnold and told him how exposed my house was," she wrote. "He kindly sent a guard."

THE CLIMAX CAME as the reoccupation entered its third month. A friend told her the eviction crew was coming; she should quickly bolt the doors and windows so they would have to force their way in. She did so, just in time. "A little after ten o'clock they knocked violently at the door three times," Grace Galloway wrote. She declared through the door that they would not get in. "I was in possession of my own house and would keep so," she summarized in her diary. "They should gain no admittance."

The men walked around the house and tried every door, and found them locked. "Then they went to the kitchen door and, with a scrubbing brush which they broke to pieces, they forced that open," Grace wrote.

She confronted them. She insisted that the law was on her side. She showed them a written statement to this effect by her lawyers.

The intruders waved it aside. Their leader, the government agent who had first told her she no longer owned the house, said he knew the law, and it favored them.

"I told them nothing but force should get me out of my house," Grace recounted.

A second member of the group said he knew how to remove her. They wouldn't touch her, but they would take all her clothes and put them out in the street. If she wanted to have anything to wear, she'd have to go out. He said his technique had worked with others; it would work with her. He went on to say that she couldn't expect any sympathy from her neighbors, for her husband had shown them no sympathy during the British occupation.

Grace was incensed. "I found the villain would say anything," she said. But indeed she got no support from the neighbors. "Mrs. Irwin and Smith sat and talked of the English cruelty, and Sidney Howell whined out her half-assent to the same."

The government agent, taking a softer tone, said he could find a carriage to transport her where she wanted to go.

Surrounded, outnumbered, alone, and weary from the long fight, Grace gave in. She said she would accept the carriage offer. Even so, she asked some of the onlookers to witness that she was leaving under protest.

The government agent went upstairs, threw some of Grace's clothes in a bag, and brought it down. One of the women watching asked if she could have Grace's bed.

This was too much. She turned to the agent and said she'd changed her mind. "I told him I was at home and in my own house and nothing but force should drive me out."

The agent's tone now hardened and he threatened to get physical. "He said it was not the first time he had taken a lady by the hand."

"The insolent wretch," Grace characterized the man in her diary, and perhaps to his face.

The carriage pulled to the front of the house.

"Mrs. Galloway, give me your hand," the agent said.

"I will not, nor will I go out of my house but by force," she said. "And nothing but force will make me give up my possession."

The agent sneered. "Well, madam," he said, and grasped her firmly by the arm. He pulled her out the door and onto the street. In a mockingly polite tone he asked if he could assist her into the carriage.

She shook off his arm. "You are the last man on earth I would wish to be obliged to," she said.

The carriage drove her to the house of an acquaintance. That evening she reflected on the day. "I was drove out of my house destitute and without any maintenance," she wrote. As things happened, a fire broke out just then, in a malt house behind her own house. "I was much alarmed and stood in Dr. Redman's garden, where we could see the fire plain. So many things made my head light." She hoped for rest at last. "I am just distracted but glad it is over."

IT WASN'T OVER. Grace Galloway's trials had only begun. She finally received a letter from her husband. He said he and their daughter were safe for the moment, but he feared for their future anywhere in America. They were sailing for England, and would have left by the time she received his letter.

She could hardly believe what she was reading. She had agonized over their safety when she thought they were in New York; now that they were on the high seas she began having nightmares. "I dreamed that the vessel in which Mr. G and my child were sailing was sunk and they were lost," she wrote. She woke in a cold sweat. "I went to sleep again and dreamed my dear child was going home with me to Trevose"—the family manor outside Philadelphia—"and that it rained and she was but poorly, and by the coachman's not driving right we were obliged to walk to the carriage and the roads was full of water and she got wet in her feet and I was greatly distressed but a poor fellow took her up to carry her to the carriage but I was afraid she had taken her death before. We was afterward plagued about the carriage and drove into a narrow place and was in great danger. I awoke in great terror."

Daylight eased the immediate fright but not the underlying anxiety. "What pain I feel to think my dearest child must be drove from native country, and all she has, taken from her, and I incapable of doing anything for her." Except pray: "God grant them a speedy and a prosperous voyage."

The departure of her husband and daughter, following the loss of her home, left Grace Galloway feeling utterly abandoned and woebegone. She found a cheap, shared apartment on an alley in an unsavory part of the city, and ventured out only occasionally. Once, returning, she was caught in a rainstorm. "As I was walking in the rain," she recorded that evening, "my own chariot drove by. I own then that I thought it pretty hard." Her sole comfort in the moment was that the person who had stolen her vehicle didn't recognize her. But the comfort didn't last. "My dear child came into my mind, and what would she say to see her mama walking five squares"—city blocks—"in the rain at night like a common woman and go to rooms in an alley."

Yet like some others who have lost everything, Grace Galloway discovered a certain freedom in having nothing more to lose. Gradually she reconsidered her past life, in particular her relationship with her husband. She had accepted the subservient role wives in her stratum of society were expected to play, in exchange for economic security. But the war had stolen her security and broken the bargain. She found she liked the new dispensation. "The liberty of doing as I please makes even poverty more agreeable than any time I ever spent since I married," she wrote. She still worried about her daughter, but much less about her husband. "My child is dearer to me than all nature, and if she is not happy or anything should happen to her, I am lost. Indeed I have no other wish in life than her welfare. And indeed I am concerned for her father, but his unkind treatment makes me easy, nay happy, not to be with him. . . . I want not to be kept so like a slave as he always made me in preventing every wish of my heart."

Joseph Galloway apparently had told Grace when he left that there were sums of money owed him she might count on. She now discovered this was not so. In fact *he* was the one who owed money. One of his creditors gave Grace the harsh news. "He told me Mr. G had four hundred pounds advanced on his rent," she wrote.

The knowledge that her plight was worse than she thought made her blame her husband the more. "This unhappy man has ruined himself, and I find he conceals all he can from me. Was it not for my child, I would never care anything about him, for his base conduct to me when present, and his taking no care of me in his absence, has made me quite indifferent to him."

Having lost her trust in her husband, Grace Galloway learned not to trust others. In the Patriot-controlled city, she stood out as a Loyalist. She sensed that she was watched, and talked about behind her back. She had to take care what she said. A new acquaintance dropped by, and they chatted. "I asked her if she was a Whig, in a jesting way," Grace wrote. "But I found she was a complete one by principle. I was much shocked at being so deceived." After a conversation with a man she slightly knew, she chided herself, "I fear I talked too much, as he is a Whig."

Occasionally, though, she threw caution aside. "Got my spirits at command and laughed at the whole Whig party," she wrote following another conversation. "I told them I was the happiest woman in town for I had been stripped and turned out of doors yet I was still the same, and must be Joseph Galloway's wife and Lawrence Growden's daughter." She hadn't told anyone about her disillusionment with her husband; in public she wore her Loyalist connections proudly. "It was not in their power to humble me, for I should be Grace Growden Galloway to the last."

Part IX

Treason of the Deepest Dye

WHEN THE CONTINENTAL ARMY marched out of Valley Forge in June 1778, more than the weather had changed. Washington's army had been tested in ways it had not been tested before, and the soldiers who survived that winter were more committed to the cause of freedom than they had ever been. They were also better trained. Baron von Steuben, in his capacity as inspector general of the army, educated and drilled the otherwise unoccupied men, creating a disciplined army out of a patchwork of regiments.

The bigger change, perhaps, had occurred on the side of the British. Amid the winter the whole mission of the British army in America changed. The French alliance with the United States transformed the war from a border conflict within the British empire to an ocean-spanning struggle of European powers. North America had been the central theater—the *only* theater—in the former fight; it became one theater among several, and by no means the most important. From this followed a fundamental reorientation of British strategy in the American war. Previously the British had been the aggressors, their mission to seek battle with Washington in order to destroy his army and crush the rebellion. Now the British adopted a defensive posture. They would hold key positions against Washington where they could do so without inordinate effort. They would cultivate Loyalists where convenient. But they would avoid pitched battles rather than invite them.

The change in British strategy became obvious on June 18, when Henry Clinton led his army out of Philadelphia. The symbolic importance of the American capital didn't justify the difficulty and expense of defending it against the attacks the Americans were sure to mount; knowing that reinforcements, provisions and especially naval support would be going to other theaters of the newly expanded conflict, Clinton fell back toward New York, which was both more defensible and more strategically located.

The British evacuation of Philadelphia was what prompted Washington's departure from Valley Forge. He gave chase to Clinton, not expecting to halt the northward march or even materially slow it, but to reveal to the world—including any members of the Congress who still liked Horatio Gates—that the Continental Army remained alive and able to fight.

Within ten days he proved his point. An American column under Charles Lee struck the rear of the British march at Monmouth Court House in New Jersey. Almost at once Lee discovered that he had taken on more than he could handle, for Henry Clinton reversed the direction of the main body of his troops and counterattacked. Lee ordered a retreat, which halted only when it met Washington and American reinforcements. The battle that ensued was fierce and mildly costly, more for the British than the Americans. It ended when the British broke off and resumed their northward march. This left Washington in control of the field and thereby able to claim victory.

The battle of Monmouth meant nothing to the British beyond the losses incurred that day. They proceeded to New York as planned. But it bolstered American confidence. For the first time in the war, American troops had stood firm against British regulars in open battle and given as good as they got.

In doing so they made Washington's position at the head of the Continental Army unassailable. He had held the army together during the trials of Valley Forge, and had fashioned it into an effective fighting machine. Not since the day of his appointment, three years earlier, had his reputation been so high.

BRITAIN'S RETHINKING of strategy in the war included a rekindling of interest in a negotiated peace with the Americans. No longer could even the most ardent defenders of the prerogatives of the British Parliament and crown treat the troubles in America as a matter to be resolved only after the Americans acknowledged their subordination. Put differently, until the French got involved, the worst that could happen in America was the loss of those ungrateful colonies, and there was no point conceding the worst until facts on the ground made such concession unavoidable. *After* the French got involved, the worst case grew worse. Britain could also lose some of its West Indian possessions. Britain's position in the other Indies—in particular, in India itself—likewise came into play. As Franklin had hoped, in adding the secret codicil to the treaty of alliance, Spain joined the war against Britain, putting British control of Gibraltar at risk.

Hoping to limit the damage, the British government sent peace feelers in Franklin's direction. David Hartley, Franklin's old friend, had spoken with Lord North, who was still clinging to his post as prime minister. Hartley took notes of the conversation and sent them to Franklin. The crucial portion stated, "Lord North consented to Mr. Hartley's proposition for endeavoring to procure from the American plenipotentiary or plenipotentiaries some opening that they would be willing to commence a parley on propositions of peace between Great Britain and America, and supposed the terms which Mr. Hartley had in view would be something like a tacit cession of independence to America."

This was a major concession, whether tacit or not. The British government was admitting that the American colonies were lost. Hartley's proposal went on to explain how this concession might unfold. As a first preliminary to discussions of a final settlement, which presumably would include a formal recognition of American independence, Britain and America would agree to "a suspension of hostilities by sea and land for a certain term of five or seven years." As a second preliminary, Britain would agree to "suspend the operation and effect of any and all acts of Parliament respecting America for a certain term of five or seven years." This would produce de facto independence for the United States.

Then came the catch: "It is expected, as a third preliminary, that America should be released, freed and unengaged from any treaties with foreign powers which may tend to embarrass or defeat the present negotiation."

Hartley explained these proposals in an accompanying letter to Franklin. The truce was the critical thing, he said. He quoted from a letter Franklin had written to him before the troubles between Britain and America had gotten out of hand: "A little time given for cooling might have excellent effects." Nothing would be lost by letting things be for five years, Hartley said in his own voice. "We can but fight it out at last. War never comes too late. Wisdom may step in between. These matters have stolen upon us and have risen to great and formidable consequences from small and unsuspected beginnings, but henceforward we should know by experience what to expect. If the rage of war could but be abated for a sufficient length of time for reason and reflection to operate, I think it would never revive."

Hartley understood that the French would object to any such plan as he proposed. France benefited from its alliance with America. And Hartley supposed Franklin and other Americans felt some debt of gratitude to France. But he suggested that gratitude counted for only so much in affairs among nations. The Americans could be sure France reckoned its own interest before America's interest. "There is a certain point, to France, beyond which their work would fail and recoil upon themselves. If they were to drive the British ministry totally to abandon the American war, it would become a totally French war." The French understood this; the Americans should also. "The disadvantage upon the bargain, to America, is that the efficacy of the French alliance to them presupposes their continuance in the war." But America wouldn't benefit from perpetual war; the point of the war—of *any* war—was to get to a satisfactory peace. "Peace is a *bonum in se*"—a thing good in itself—"whereas the most favourable events of war are but relatively lesser evils."

Franklin rejected Hartley's proposal out of hand. He said he was not in principle opposed to a truce. "But this is merely on motives of general humanity, to obviate the evils men devilishly inflict on men in time of war, and to lessen as much as possible the similarity of earth and hell." But better than a truce would be a permanent peace, with Britain recognizing American independence. Short of this, while it might serve the interest of Britain to halt the fighting, it did not serve the interest of Americans. "I am persuaded it is theirs to continue the war till England shall be reduced to that perfect impotence of mischief which alone can prevail with her to let other nations enjoy peace, liberty and safety."

Besides, American honor required honoring America's pledges. "America has no desire of being free from her engagements to France," Franklin said. "The chief is that of continuing the war in conjunction with her, and not making a separate peace. And this is an obligation not in the power of America to dissolve, being an obligation of gratitude and justice towards a nation which is engaged in a war on her account and for her protection, and would be forever binding, whether such an article existed or not in the treaty"—which it did. "And though it did not exist, an honest American would cut off his right hand rather than sign an agreement with England contrary to the spirit of it."

FRANKLIN WASN'T QUITE SERIOUS in asserting that France was fighting on America's account and for her protection. He knew perfectly well that France was fighting on France's account. For the time being, France's account approximated America's account; hence the alliance. But Franklin wasn't naïve enough to suppose the overlap of interest would continue forever, or to think gratitude would matter much in French reckoning when French interests diverged from American.

The time would come when Franklin would do his own recalculation; for now he was willing to affirm American solidarity with France, for the benefit of David Hartley and the British. And to let Vergennes and the French know the British had come calling. It could only benefit America for the French to realize she had suitors.

The British had better luck making overtures to other American officials. From the start of the war the British had been wooing Americans into becoming Loyalists, if they weren't Loyalists already. Their efforts involved appeals to emotion, including nostalgia for the British roots of the majority of Americans. They also involved the material self-interest of those who held office under the British, like William Franklin, or who had commercial connections to Britain, like many of the merchants in Loyalist-dominated New York.

Military coercion supplemented the appeals to emotion and material benefit. Wherever British armies went, they favored Loyalists over Patriots, thereby swelling the Loyalist ranks, at least for the duration of the British presence. The British occupation of Boston had brought out the Loyalists there; the occupation of Philadelphia had produced a similar result, and the occupation of New York continued to do so.

Britain's military coercion often included actions by its Indian allies. In the spring of 1778, while George Washington and the Continental Army were shivering at Valley Forge, and Joseph Galloway and the British were enjoying Philadelphia, Joseph Brant launched a terrifying campaign against Patriot settlements in the Mohawk Valley. During the next several months, Brant's warriors raided, killed, burned and pillaged across the richest and most fertile region of New York state.

In May, Brant's raiders descended on the hamlet of Cobleskill. Brant sent an advance squadron to lure out the defenders, who were then nearly all killed or put to flight, leaving the village defenseless. Brant's men proceeded to torch the homes in the village, destroy stored crops and kill cattle. Several of the villagers were slain; others were taken prisoners. According to one account, the prisoners were to be burned to death, in reprisal for the previous killing of some Indian prisoners, but were spared at the last moment when Brant, a Freemason from his time among the whites, recognized a Freemasonry tattoo on the arm of one of them. Brant commuted the death sentence and marched the prisoners instead to Montreal.

Some two dozen Patriots were killed in the engagement, which was described as a massacre, in the way Indian attacks on the frontier had often been described. Doubtless to the victims and their families it seemed so. To Brant and his men, it was frontier warfare: partly tactical, partly psychological, with the goal of making the region uninhabitable for the enemy.

A greater hue and cry arose after a Loyalist attack on Patriot settlements in the Wyoming Valley of western Pennsylvania. A British colonel, John Butler, led the Loyalists, who were joined by five hundred Iroquois. Joseph Brant had recruited some of the Indians, but he wasn't personally present. Butler arranged an ambush, which turned into a rout. More than three hundred Patriots, mostly untested militia, were killed. The Indians gave no quarter, taking scalps of all who fell into their hands. Stories were told that prisoners were tortured before being killed.

These stories spread when surviving settlers fled the region for safer parts. The refugees thereby did the work of Brant and the Loyalists, causing other settlers to flee and depopulating parts of a region that had been sending foodstuffs to Washington's army. Terror had been a tool of frontier warfare for generations; now it worked in favor of the Loyalists and the British.

In the autumn of 1778, Brant led another attack, on Cherry Valley in New York. The Iroquois and Loyalist militiamen surrounded and fired upon a fort garrisoned by three hundred Patriot militia, one of whom tersely recorded the assault and its outcome: "Came on 442 Indians from the Five Nations and 200 Tories under the command of one Colonel Butler and Captain Brant. Attacked headquarters. Killed Colonel Alden. Took Colonel Stacy prisoner. Attacked Fort Alden. After three hours retreated without success of taking the fort. Killed of the regulars 14 men." He listed the dead soldiers by name. Then: "Killed of the inhabitants 30 persons. Taken of the inhabitants 34 persons. Wounded 2 inhabitants, 1 of the regulars. Burnt 20 houses, 25 barns, 2 mills. N.B., a rainy day."

Joseph Brant didn't apologize for the loss of life among the noncombatants. Instead he called it a reprisal for a Patriot attack. "Your rebels came to Oughquago"—a Seneca village—"when we Indians were gone from our place, and you burned our houses, which makes us and our brothers the Seneca angry, so that we destroyed men, women and children at Cherry Valley," he explained in a letter to a Patriot commander.

Because Brant was the most visible of the Loyalist Indians, he received much of the Patriot blame for the destruction and loss of life on the frontier. "Butcher" Brant and "Monster" Brant were two of the more printable names applied to him.

The success of his campaign of terror compelled Washington to respond. He did so in kind. "The expedition you are appointed to command is to be directed against the hostile tribes of the six nations of Indians, with their associates and adherents," Washington wrote to General John Sullivan, whom Washington tasked with laying waste to the Loyalist Iroquois. "The immediate objects are the total destruction and devastation of their settlements and the capture of as many prisoners of every age and sex as possible. It will be essential to ruin their crops now in the ground and prevent their planting more."

Drawing on his own experience fighting Indians on the Virginia frontier, Washington instructed Sullivan "to make rather than receive attacks, attended with as much impetuosity, shouting and noise as possible, and to make the troops act in as loose and dispersed a way as is consistent with a proper degree of government concert and mutual support." He added, "It should be previously impressed upon the minds of the men wherever they have an opportunity, to rush on with the war whoop and fixed bayonet. Nothing will disconcert and terrify the Indians more than this." Washington directed Sullivan to employ spies and informants to determine where Brant and the Indians would strike next. "Nor need I suggest the extraordinary degree of vigilance and caution which will be necessary to guard against surprises from an adversary so secret, desultory and rapid as the Indians."

Washington would accept nothing less than total victory. Not until this had been achieved was Sullivan authorized to talk peace. "After you have very thoroughly completed the destruction of their settlements, if the Indians should show a disposition for peace, I would have you to encourage it on condition that they will give some decisive evidence of their sincerity by delivering up some of the principal instigators of their past hostility into our hands—Butler, Brandt, the most mischievous of the Tories that have joined them or any other they may have in their power that we are interested to get into ours." The Indians who weren't killed outright should be starved. Sullivan should use their hunger as leverage to get Brant and his followers to turn against the British. "They may possibly be engaged, by address, secrecy and stratagem, to surprise the garrison of Niagara and the shipping on the lakes and put them into our possession. This may be demanded as a condition of our friendship and would be a most important point gained. If they can render a service of this kind, you may stipulate to assist them in their distress with supplies of provisions and other articles of which they will stand in need." But Washington repeated: "You will not by any means listen to any overture of peace before the total ruin of their settlements is effected. . . . Our future security will be in their inability to injure us, the distance to which they are driven, and in the terror with which the severity of the chastisement they receive will inspire them."

Sullivan received the order and mounted his campaign. During the summer of 1779 he chased Brant and the Loyalist Iroquois across the northern frontier. They initially dodged battle, being badly outnumbered, but he persisted and finally forced the issue at Newtown, New York, on the Cayuga River, at the end of August. "We marched from Tioga the 26th in the afternoon," Sullivan wrote to Washington afterward. "The rains had swelled the Cayuga so as to render our march to Chemung very difficult, as we had to ford the river twice in our route.

We arrived there in the evening of the 28th and marched for the place early in the morning of the 29th." At eleven o'clock a messenger from an advance rifle corps reported that Brant, Butler and their men had prepared for battle. "The enemy had, about a mile in front of the town, a very extensive breast work erected on a rising ground which commanded the road in which we were to pass with our artillery and which would enable them to fire upon our flank and front at the same time. This breast work they had endeavoured to mask in a very artful manner; and had concealed themselves behind it in large numbers." Brant tried to lure Sullivan's force into a trap like others he had employed before, but Sullivan refused to be drawn. Relying on his heavier weapons and greater numbers, he maneuvered his cannons into position to bombard the enemy works, and arrayed his men around their flanks. When all was ready he gave the order to attack.

With the cannons pounding the Loyalist stronghold, Sullivan's troops charged the front and the sides. The result was a surprisingly rapid victory. "Our cannonade in front and I doubt not the unexpected fire from General Poor on the enemy's left occasioned them instantly to abandon their works in the utmost confusion," Sullivan told Washington. "They fled in the greatest disorder, leaving eleven of their Indian warriors and one female dead on the ground, with a great number of packs, blankets, arms, camp equippage, and a variety of their jewels, some of which are of considerable value."

Sullivan described the aftermath. "We took two prisoners, one a Tory, the other an enlisted Negro in one of the Tory companies," he said. "They both agree that there were five companies of whites and their main strength consisting of the Indian warriors of seven nations, and that this was the place where they meant to make their principal opposition and that they had been waiting here eight days. Both the Butlers, Brant and Capt. McDonald was here, each having a separate command. Brant had some time since been slightly wounded in the foot but is recovered. They further say they sent off their wounded on horseback. Many of them no doubt were carried off in canoes, and many of their dead must have been carried off or concealed, as we found many bloody packs, coats, shirts and blankets, and in short every appearance not only of havoc but of fright and confusion was left behind them. The main army pursued them about a mile and the light corps about three, but fear had given them too great speed to be overtaken." Sullivan added a note of respect for what the Indians and Loyalists had accomplished. "I cannot help saying that the disposition of the enemy's troops and the construction of their works would have done honour to much greater officers than the unprincipled wretches who commanded them."

The victory was worth the effort, Sullivan said. "This place, in English called Newtown, is a large scattered settlement abounding with extensive fields of the best corn and beans so extensive and numerous as to keep the whole army this day industriously employed in destroying, and the business yet unfinished. From the vast quantity of corn planted at this place and its vicinities, I conclude it to have been designed as their principal magazine." Sullivan reported that his men had destroyed twenty longhouses at Newtown, and another thirty in the neighborhood. It was a fitting coda to a successful summer. "The number of Indian towns destroyed since the commencement of the expedition, including those burnt by General Clinton previous to the junction, is I think fourteen, some of them considerable, others inconsiderable."

THE SCORCHED-EARTH FIGHTING on the northern frontier was matched in bitterness by partisan warfare in the South. The irregular combat resulted in the first place from the fact that neither Washington's Continental Army nor the British army of William Howe and Henry Clinton had many troops to spare for the South. Clinton had combined forces with the Royal Navy in 1776 to try to capture Charleston and gain a port and foothold on the southern coast, but the effort failed. Two years later the British managed to take Savannah, yet for many months they had their hands full simply defending it. They made little effort to penetrate inland.

In the absence of regular forces, irregular militias sprang up. Patriots and Loyalists were about evenly matched in numbers, and they inflicted comparable damage on each other. The Loyalists sometimes benefited from the assistance of Cherokee warriors who favored the British side for the same reason Joseph Brant's Mohawks did: they felt less threatened by a government based across the ocean than by one close at hand, controlled by people who coveted their territory. For their part, the Patriot opponents of the British felt threatened by the Cherokees, against whom they had been fighting for decades. The result was a running campaign of raid and reprisal, with destruction of villages and settlements, and the death or displacement of their inhabitants, an essential part of strategy.

The Loyalists took heart from the British decision, inspired by Joseph Galloway, to refocus on the South. A second attempt to take Charleston succeeded in 1780, and this time the British made clear they intended to expand their presence into the hinterland. Loyalists in the Carolinas rallied to the British banner; among them were thousands of slaves who answered the British offer of freedom in exchange for service to the Crown.

The summer and autumn of 1780 produced the murderous Battle of Waxhaws, in which the Loyalists kept killing long past the point of Patriot surrender, and the Patriots' equally brutal rejoinder at Kings Mountain. Sandwiched between was a stunning defeat of a Patriot army under Horatio Gates at Camden, South Carolina, by Lord Cornwallis, which laid the South wide open to the British and the Loyalists—besides destroying the reputation of Gates and erasing any chance he might replace Washington.

The Camden result appeared the most decisive of the outcomes that season. Cornwallis wouldn't be stopped by Patriot militia, and he had routed the regular Continental soldiers Washington sent against him. The British southern strategy was making a prophet of Joseph Galloway, who had claimed the Loyalists would provide the difference in the war; even the most ardent Patriot had to wonder if the dream of independence was slipping away.

BENEDICT ARNOLD WAS AMONG the wonderers. As Grace Growden Galloway had discovered, Arnold didn't dictate the affairs of Philadelphia during the months after the British occupation. His military stature counted less with each passing month, as civilian officials of the city and state reasserted themselves, and the members of the Congress returned from exile in York, Pennsylvania, and resumed their pre-occupation habits. Arnold's patience with politicians was scant; before long he and they were regularly trading complaints and findings of fault. Arnold was charged with misuse of authority, including schemes to enrich himself by methods that came naturally to the merchant Arnold had been before the war and might become again after, but that ill behooved a military officer of the United States. Arnold had intended to resign his Philadelphia command, but the allegations got his dander up. "The villainous attacks made on my character by the president and council of this state in their publications made it necessary for me to continue in the command until their charges were cleared up," Arnold wrote to Washington. Arnold thought he was being badly used. "Having made every sacrifice of fortune and blood, and become a cripple in the service of my country, I little expected to meet the ungrateful returns I have received of my countrymen," he told Washington.

"But as Congress have stamped ingratitude as a current coin, I must take it."

Arnold's enemies wanted to try him in state court, but Arnold insisted on a court-martial, which was duly convened. Washington, as commander in chief, had to keep clear of the case. But he let Arnold know he would be taken care of. "You will rest assured that I wish to see you in a situation where you can be of the greatest advantage, and where abilities like yours may not be lost to the public," Washington said. He deemed Arnold a friend and treated him accordingly. "Let me congratulate you on the late happy event," he wrote upon the birth of Arnold's first child.

After the court-martial delivered its slap on the wrist, Washington was pleased to place Arnold once more in a position suited to his military talents. "You are to proceed to West Point and take the command of the post and its dependencies," Washington said. The fortress guarding the Hudson River was the single most strategic spot in the entire theater of the war. Washington didn't know what Henry Clinton and the British planned for the Hudson corridor; a central part of Arnold's assignment was to find out. "You will endeavour to obtain every intelligence of the enemy's motions," Washington said.

ARNOLD ACCEPTED the assignment—and proceeded to turn Washington's order on its head. Instead of relaying intelligence about the British to the Americans, he delivered intelligence about the Americans to the British. He developed a scheme to convey crucial information about the fort and its garrison, in particular its weaknesses and the likeliest moment to capture it.

The sources of Arnold's treason were doubtless multiple. He nursed resentment about being passed over for promotion and tried for misfeasance. He had a habit of spending beyond his means, and he needed money to get out of debt. His wife, the former Margaret Shippen, leaned Loyalist and cultivated similar tendencies in him. He later claimed that the American alliance with the French, against whom he had fought in the French and Indian War, disillusioned him about the purity of the Patriot cause. In point of fact, Arnold had never been devoted to the Patriot cause; his service was more about the personal opportunity it afforded. And so, when the opportunities began to appear greater on the British side, he didn't have to turn philosophical somersaults to land there.

Arnold's discontent came to the attention of John André, a young British officer who had been one of the many admirers of Peggy Shippen during the British occupation of Philadelphia. Perhaps from Peggy, André learned of Arnold's openness to persuasion. André employed intermediaries, code names, secret ciphers and invisible ink to determine what Arnold might do for the British, and to convey what the British might do for Arnold. "In the very first instance of receiving the tidings or good offices we expect of him, our liberality will be evinced," André wrote to one of the intermediaries, for relay to Arnold. André specified the sort of tidings that would be most useful: "Contents of dispatches from foreign abettors. Original dispatches and papers which might be seized and sent to us. Channels through which such dispatches pass. Hints for securing them. Number and position of troops. Whence and what reinforcements are expected and when." Arnold's compensation would be commensurate with the value to the British of the information received. "Rewards equal at least to what such service can be estimated at will be given," André said.

Arnold responded with information about the French army Washington was expecting. He told André when he would be taking command of West Point—"a post in which I can render the most essential services, and which will be in my disposal." He asserted that the tide was shifting in Britain's direction. "The mass of the people are heartily tired of the war and wish to be on their former footing. They are promised great events from this year's exertion; if disappointed, you have only to persevere and the contest will soon be at an end. The present struggles are like the pangs of a dying man, violent but of short duration."

Arnold sought to ensure that he received his worth. "As life and fortune are risked by serving His Majesty, it is necessary that the latter shall be secured as well as the emoluments I give up, and a compensation for services agreed on and a sum advanced for that purpose," he said. He put a price on West Point. "Twenty thousand pounds sterling I think will be a cheap purchase for an object of so much importance." To close the deal, Arnold insisted on a face-to-face meeting. "A personal interview with an officer that you can confide in is absolutely necessary to plan matters."

Arnold's demand for an interview put André in a delicate position. He didn't want to risk confiding the plot to any subordinate; he must go himself. To meet Arnold, he would have to cross American lines. He couldn't do so by means of a truce flag without attracting attention, which was the last thing he wanted to do. To cross the lines in uniform would make him an easy target for American patrols or snipers. To cross the lines out of uniform would make him a spy. While captured soldiers could expect to be treated as prisoners of war, captured spies could expect to be hanged.

André hadn't quite decided which course to follow when he left New York aboard the British sloop *Vulture*. A boat sent by Arnold fetched him and carried him to shore. The two men met and sealed their agreement. André had expected to return to the *Vulture* and descend the river as he had come, but Patriot troops fired on the vessel while he was gone, forcing it to move off.

Arnold assured him he could make his way back to British lines by land. Arnold gave André a pass, made out in a false name, and André set off—in civilian clothes. He encountered three men on the road, whom he mistook for Loyalists. He explained that he was a British officer, though out of uniform, on an important mission. They thereupon informed him that they were Patriots and he was their prisoner. He changed his story and showed them his pass. They searched him, perhaps hoping to relieve him of any cash or valuables he carried. In his boot they found some papers that looked suspicious. André offered them a bribe to let him go; they declined. But even then he nearly escaped, for his captors decided to hand him over to the ranking Continental Army officer in the area, Arnold. They sent him on his way, under guard. Another Continental officer appeared, decided that transporting the prisoner was too risky, and fetched André back. The officer sent a message to Arnold explaining what had happened.

On receiving the message, Arnold realized the game was up. He instantly fled for the *Vulture*, which transported him to New York. On board he wrote a letter to Washington defending his actions. "The heart which is conscious of its own rectitude cannot attempt to palliate a step which the world may censure as wrong," Arnold declared. "I have ever acted from a principle of love to my country, since the commencement of the present unhappy contest between Great Britain and the colonies. The same principle of love to my country actuates my present conduct, however it may appear inconsistent to the world, who very seldom judge right of any man's actions." Arnold couldn't have expected Washington to believe this. He continued, more realistically: "I have no favor to ask for myself. I have too often experienced the ingratitude of my country to attempt it. But from the known humanity of your Excellence I am induced to ask your protection for Mrs. Arnold from every insult and injury that the mistaken vengeance of my country may expose her to. It ought to fall only on me."

ALEXANDER HAMILTON HADN'T BEEN thinking about Benedict Arnold or West Point. Instead he was corresponding with John Jay about improvements to the existing political structure of the United States. The powers of the Congress should be bolstered, Hamilton said, to relieve its thrall to the states. The Congress needed to have taxing authority and control over commerce between states, as well as other enhanced powers. Because the Congress, dominated by the states, would never agree to the required remedies, a special convention should be called, Hamilton said. It would craft the stronger government the nation required.

When he wasn't imagining a new constitution for the country, Hamilton wrote letters to his fiancée. Elizabeth Schuyler was the daughter of Philip Schuyler, which made her one of the most eligible young women in the state of New York. Hamilton and Elizabeth had met previously, but the romance blossomed upon her visit to a relative in Morristown, New Jersey, where Hamilton and Washington and the Continental Army were spending the winter of 1779–1780. Soon Hamilton and Elizabeth became engaged, with hopes of being wed once the campaign of the following summer ended.

Hamilton threw himself into romance as he threw himself into everything he undertook; letter after letter conveyed his undying devotion and his fervent hope that he could make himself worthy of his darling's love. He was writing another such letter when he learned of the arrest of André and the defection of Arnold. "In the midst of my letter, I was interrupted by a scene that shocked me more than anything I have met with—the discovery of a treason of the deepest dye," he told Elizabeth. The information wasn't public, so Hamilton had to explain what had happened, and his own part in it all. "The object was to sacrifice West Point. General Arnold had sold himself to André for this purpose. The latter came but in disguise and in returning to New York was detected. Arnold, hearing of it immediately fled to the enemy. I went in pursuit of him but was much too late." By chance Washington and Hamilton were in the vicinity and had intended to dine at the Arnold home near West Point; news of André's arrest and Arnold's flight jolted them into unexpected action.

Hamilton headed back to Arnold's house, where Washington already was. "On my return I saw an amiable woman"—Peggy Shippen Arnold—"frantic with distress for the loss of a husband she tenderly loved, a traitor to his country and to his fame, a disgrace to his connections. It was the most affecting scene I ever was witness to. She for a considerable time entirely lost her senses. The General went up to see her and she upbraided him with being in a plot to murder her child; one moment she raved; another she melted into tears; sometimes she pressed her infant to her bosom and lamented its fate occasioned by the imprudence of its father in a manner that would have pierced insensibility itself. All the sweetness of beauty, all the loveliness of innocence, all the tenderness of a wife and all the fondness of a mother showed themselves in her appearance and conduct."

Perhaps because he himself was in love, perhaps because Peggy Arnold was young and pretty, perhaps because she was a convincing actress, Hamilton credited her sincerity. "We have every reason to believe she was entirely unacquainted with the plan," he told Elizabeth. "Her first knowledge of it was when Arnold went to tell her he must banish himself from his country and from her forever. She instantly fell into a convulsion and he left her in that situation." Hamilton had this last part of the story from Peggy herself. As with her performance, he found it believable.

She improved overnight. "This morning she is more composed," Hamilton told Elizabeth. "I paid her a visit and endeavoured to soothe her by every method in my power, though you may imagine she is not easily to be consoled. Added to her other distresses, she is very apprehensive the resentment of her country will fall upon her (who is only unfortunate) for the guilt of her husband. I have tried to persuade her her apprehensions are ill founded; but she has too many proofs of the illiberality of the state to which she belongs to be convinced. She received us in bed, with every circumstance that could interest our sympathy. Her sufferings were so eloquent that I wished myself her brother, to have a right to become her defender. As it is, I have entreated her to enable me to give her proofs of my friendship."

Hamilton couldn't say enough about Peggy's character. "Could I forgive Arnold for sacrificing his honor, reputation and duty, I could not forgive him for acting a part that must have forfeited the esteem of so fine a woman. At present she almost forgets his crime in his misfortune, and her horror at the guilt of the traitor is lost in her love of the man. But a virtuous mind cannot long esteem a base one, and time will make her despise, if it cannot make her hate."

Hamilton's faith in Peggy Arnold spoke well of the generosity he felt toward women, but ill of his acuity in detecting falsehood. In fact Peggy had been part of Arnold's scheme all along, carrying messages between Arnold and André. The distress she showed Hamilton and Washington, if not wholly feigned, reflected the untimely discovery of the plot rather than the plot itself.

Nor was Peggy Arnold the only one who played a part well. John André charmed his captors as he had charmed most people he met, including Benedict Arnold. Arnold wrote a letter to Washington pleading André's innocence. Washington was treating André as a spy rather than a prisoner of war, in large part because André was out of uniform when taken. Arnold claimed responsibility for this. "Major André came onto shore in his uniform (without disguise), which with much reluctance at my particular and pressing instance he exchanged for another coat," Arnold said. "I furnished him with a horse and saddle and pointed out the route by which he was to return"—to British lines—"and as commanding officer in the department I had an undoubted right to transact all these matters, which if wrong Major André ought by no means to suffer for them."

Washington by now was disinclined to believe anything Arnold said. Moreover, the obvious rejoinder to Arnold's explanation was that Arnold wasn't *André's* commanding officer; André put on a civilian disguise by his own choice.

But what must have cemented Washington's decision not to give André the benefit of Arnold's explanation was Arnold's temerity, now as a *British* officer, to threaten Washington. A board of officers appointed by Washington had considered André's case, convicted him of spying, and sentenced him to death. Arnold vowed a reprisal.

"If that gentleman should suffer the severity of their sentence, I shall think myself bound by every tie of duty and honor to retaliate on such unhappy persons of your army as may fall within my power," he said. He added, "If this warning should be disregarded and he should suffer, I call heaven and earth to witness that your Excellency will be justly answerable for the torrent of blood that may be spilt in consequence."

André took a different tack. From custody he wrote to Washington describing the circumstances under which he had been taken prisoner. "I agreed to meet upon ground not within posts of either army a person who was to give me intelligence," he said. "I came up in the *Vulture* man of war for this effect and was fetched by a boat from the shore to the beach. Being there I was told that the approach of day would prevent my return and that I must be concealed until the next night. I was in my regimental"—his uniform—"and had fairly risked my person. Against my stipulation, my intention, and without my knowledge beforehand, I was conducted within one of your posts. Your Excellency may conceive my sensation on this occasion and will imagine how much more I must have been affected by a refusal to reconduct me back the next night as I had been brought. Thus become a prisoner, I had to concert my escape. I was quitted my uniform and was passed another way in the night without the American posts to neutral ground, informed I was beyond all armed parties and left to press for New York. I was taken at Tarrytown by some volunteers." André concluded, "Thus I have had the honour to relate was I betrayed (being Adjutant General of the British Army) into the vile condition of an enemy in disguise within your post." In case Washington had missed his point, André summarized: "I was involuntarily an impostor."

André's argument suffered from the same flaw as Arnold's on André's behalf: No one put a gun to André's head to make him doff his British uniform and disguise himself as an American. Beyond this, André strained plausibility in asserting that he had been taken prisoner by Arnold, the man he had succeeded in suborning.

Yet André was young—not quite thirty—and handsome; he conducted himself in captivity in a manner that impressed many of those who saw him. He never would have become Clinton's spymaster if he hadn't been persuasive. He heard his death sentence without flinching, and faced his demise with apparent equanimity.

And he might have been spared. Washington let Clinton know he would hand over André to the British if Clinton reciprocated by giving up Arnold. Clinton must have been tempted. Clinton viewed Arnold much as Washington did, and as any commanding officer would have. A turncoat was the lowest form of life in the military universe. Compared with a turncoat, a spy was almost a saint. Washington had infiltrated spies behind British lines; the most famous of these, Nathan Hale, had been captured and executed, and was indeed treated as a secular saint by Americans. Even the British had to respect his courage in facing death.

But as odious as Arnold was to Clinton, the turncoat was useful—or he would have been if the plot hadn't been discovered. In war a commander employs the weapons that come to hand. Clinton couldn't swap Arnold for André without jeopardizing the credibility of every British offer to American Loyalists. He refused the exchange.

André made a final appeal to Washington. He did not ask to be spared the death sentence; he merely requested to be shot as a soldier rather than hanged as a spy. "Sympathy towards a soldier will surely induce your Excellency and a military tribunal to adapt the mode of my death to the feelings of a man of honour," André said. "Let me hope, sir, that if ought in my character impresses you with esteem towards me, if ought in my misfortunes marks me as the victim of policy and not of resentment, I shall experience the operation of these feelings in your breast by being informed that I am not to die on a gibbet."

Washington did not reply to André's letter. Nor did he intervene to revise the sentence handed down by the board. André was hanged the next day.

Part X

Up Goes Huddy

THE ARNOLD AFFAIR LEFT a terrible taste in the mouth of every Patriot, and other events of that fighting season did little to improve it. "Do you wish to know what our army have done this campaign?" asked Samuel Shaw of his brother in late October 1780. Shaw was an aide with Washington's lieutenant Henry Knox. "The answer is easy. Nothing." Shaw explained, "The superiority of the British in our seas has rendered the assistance afforded us by our generous allies"— the French— "entirely useless, and the sanguine hopes we had of going hand and hand to New York have proved abortive. As far as depended on us, every measure was taken to induce the enemy to settle the matter genteelly in the field. Our positions were frequently made, in such a manner as gave them every advantage over us in point of situation, and could be justified on no other principle than as being designed merely as invitations to them to enter the lists. Their commander, Sir Harry"—Henry Clinton—"as often declined accepting them. Thus the campaign is drawing near to a close."

In the absence of progress—or action, even—Shaw felt the war spirit flagging. "The war is but just begun," he said, a half-decade into the fighting. Prospects favored the British. "The enemy seem determined to avail themselves of that languor which pervades and clogs our public transactions. While we are engaging levies for three and six months, they are receiving recruits which are substantial reinforcements for the war." Americans at large didn't understand what was at stake. "Our whole system of politics must be changed. It is time the country realized that an enemy is in its bowels; and experience ought to convince them of the absolute necessity there is for providing a *permanent force,* sufficient to defend its invaded rights and secure to us a happy issue of the present contest." All would hinge on the next few months. "The interval between now and the opening of another campaign is big with importance. On the improvement of it will probably depend our existence as a nation."

Far from improving, things got very much worse. "Be prepared, my dear Eliot, for a shock, and attend to an event which must sensibly affect every honest heart," Shaw wrote to a friend in January 1781. "The accumulated distresses of the army have at length produced most dreadful effects. The noncommissioned officers and privates of the Pennsylvania line, stationed at Morristown, have mutinied, broken up their cantonments, and in a body are marching to Philadelphia, to demand redress of their grievances from Congress." The lack of pay and the shortfall of provisions in a war that had no end had finally driven the Pennsylvanians over the edge.

"The particulars of this revolt, as nearly as I have been able to collect them, are as follow," Shaw continued. "On the 1st instant, the whole line, except three regiments, by a signal given for that purpose, turned out under arms, without their officers, and declared for a redress of grievances. General Wayne"—Anthony Wayne—"and the officers did everything that could be expected to quell the tumult, but in vain. Numbers of them were wounded, and one (a captain) killed. The three regiments above mentioned paraded under their officers, but, being called on by the others to join, threatened with death in case of refusal, and actually fired on, they complied. They then seized upon the field-pieces, and forcing the artillerymen, who had not yet joined them, to do it instantly, under penalty of being every man bayoneted, the mutiny became general."

The grievances of the Pennsylvanians were both common to the whole army and specific to soldiers from their state. "Besides the many and complicated injuries arising from the want of clothing, pay and provision, which the army at large have for so long a time groaned under, there was one circumstance peculiarly aggravating to the soldiers of the Pennsylvania line, and which conduced not a little to hasten the catastrophe. A deputation from the state had arrived in camp a few days before, with six hundred half-joes"—Portuguese gold coins, in contrast to the paper currency often paid to the soldiers—"to be given, three to each man, as a bounty to such of the six-months levies, whose times were then expired, as would enlist again for the war. This was too much for veterans who had borne the burden of the day to put up with. They made it the principal article of grievance, and told their officers they neither could nor would be any longer amused; that they were determined, at every hazard, to march in a body to Congress and obtain redress."

Anthony Wayne's efforts to stop them failed. "On General Wayne's cocking his pistols, there were a hundred bayonets at his breast," Shaw explained. "'We love you, we respect you,' said they, 'but you're a dead man if you fire'; and added, 'Do not mistake us; we are not going to the enemy; on the contrary, were they now to come out, you should see us fight, under your orders, with as much resolution and alacrity as ever.' They began their march that night, and the next day General Wayne forwarded after them provisions, to prevent the otherwise inevitable depredation which would be made on private property, himself and three principal officers, supposed highest in their esteem, following to mix with them, assist them with their advice, and endeavour to prevent any outrages. They were civilly received, have acquired much of the confidence of the troops, and are conducting them to Pennsylvania."

GEORGE WASHINGTON HAD NEVER been more vexed, because he had never felt so impotent. The mutiny of the Pennsylvanians violated his core tenets of military discipline; his first instinct was to mount up and crush the revolt. Yet he realized that worse than mutiny might follow such an effort. "Opposition, as it did not succeed in the first instance, cannot be effectual while the men remain together, but will keep alive resentment, and may tempt them to turn about and go in a body to the enemy," Washington wrote to Anthony Wayne. Thus far in the war, defections to the British had mostly been individual, if occasionally spectacular, as by Benedict Arnold. To lose entire regiments, especially of the state that held the seat of government, would be disastrous. The military balance would shift grievously, and the damage to the morale of the remaining troops, not to mention the country as a whole, would be even worse.

To prevent such a catastrophe, Washington ordered Wayne to proceed with caution. "Cross the Delaware with them, draw from them what they conceive to be their principal grievances, and promise faithfully to represent to Congress and to the state the substance of them, and to endeavor to obtain a redress," he said. Washington warned explicitly against what instinct urged on Wayne no less than on himself. "An attempt to reduce them by force will either drive them to the enemy, or dissipate them in such a manner that they will never be recovered."

Washington thought he could count on Wayne; he had much less confidence in the Congress. Wayne had sent word to Philadelphia of the approach of the Pennsylvania troops, hoping to focus the members' minds on doing what they should have been doing all along. Instead it simply caused them to flee, as they had fled before the British four years earlier. Washington didn't blame Wayne for sounding the alert. "It was exceedingly proper to give Congress and the state notice of the affair, that they might be prepared," he wrote to Wayne. But the result wasn't good. "The removal of Congress—waiving the indignity— might have a very unhappy influence. The mutineers, finding the body before whom they were determined to lay their grievances fled, might take a new turn and wreak their vengeance upon the persons and property of the citizens. And in a town of the size of Philadelphia there are numbers who would join them in such a business."

Washington was tempted to catch up with Wayne and confront the mutineers himself. These were his men, after all, and his responsibility. "If nothing alarming appears here, and I hear nothing farther from you, I shall tomorrow morning set out towards Philadelphia," he told Wayne. The possibility of more mutinies was real; already some New Jersey regiments had tried to emulate the Pennsylvanians, and had been dissuaded only by threat of instant death.

But after sleeping on the matter, Washington changed his mind. "Upon second thoughts I am in doubt whether I shall come down, because the mutineers must have returned to their duty, or the business be in the hands of Congress, before I could reach you, and because I am advised by such of the general officers as I have seen not to leave this post in the present situation of things, temper of the troops, and distress of the garrison for want of flour, clothing and, in short, everything."

Amid his vexation, Washington discerned an opportunity. He had been hectoring the Congress for years about the perils of shortchanging the army; now the mutineers of the Pennsylvania line were making his case for him, in a more compelling way than he ever could have. "The event I have long apprehended would be the consequence of the complicated distresses of the army has at length taken place," he wrote to John Hancock. Washington explained the events of the mutiny and described the measures taken to neutralize it. "At what point this defection will stop, or how extensive it may prove, God only knows," he went on. "At present the troops at the important posts in this vicinity remain quiet, not being acquainted with this unhappy and alarming affair. How long they will continue so cannot be ascertained, as they labor under some of the pressing hardships with the troops who have revolted." The Congress must act at once. "It is vain to think an army can be kept together much longer under such a variety of sufferings as ours has experienced," Washington said. "Unless some immediate and spirited measures are adopted to furnish at least three months' pay to the troops, in money which will be of some value to them, and at the same time ways and means are devised to clothe and feed them better (more regularly I mean) than they have been, the worst that can befall us may be expected." Washington almost never washed his hands of responsibility for matters within his purview, but now he came close. "As I have used every endeavor in my power to avert the evil that has come upon us, so will I continue to exert every mean I am possessed of to prevent an extension of the mischief, but I can neither foretell or be answerable for the issue."

EVEN AS WASHINGTON EMPHASIZED to the Congress the jeopardy in which his army stood, and with it the cause of American independence, to another audience he downplayed the peril. Almost three years after the signing of the treaty of alliance, the French government had little to show for the gamble it had taken on the Americans. The treaty had provoked hostilities with Britain almost at once, and French forces had acquitted themselves well, with French naval vessels under the Comte d'Estaing seizing various British islands in the West Indies while holding their own against the British fleet generally. Yet joint efforts with the Americans had come to naught. A French attempt to liberate Savannah in 1779 failed after Washington declined to send Continental troops from his army near New York. In the summer of 1780 French troops commanded by the Comte de Rochambeau landed at Newport, Rhode Island. Washington met with Rochambeau at Hartford to discuss common strategy, but as of early 1781 the discussions had yielded nothing concrete.

The French still hoped for good things from the American alliance, yet at times they had to wonder if their hope was well placed. Since the signing of the treaty, Washington had won no important victories over the British, and indeed had hardly engaged the enemy. Arnold's defection and the mutiny of the Pennsylvania line suggested that things were moving in the wrong direction. If the mutiny foreshadowed a dissolution of the American army, perhaps it was better that France cut its losses while it could.

Washington sought to banish such notions from French minds. He explained to Rochambeau why the mutiny of the Pennsylvanians wouldn't spread to troops from other states. The Pennsylvania troops comprised a large number of foreigners, who lacked the inherent loyalty of native-born Americans, Washington said. "The rest of our army, the Jersey troops excepted"—the ones who had tried to mutiny—"being chiefly composed of natives, I would flatter myself will continue to struggle under the same difficulties they have hitherto endured."

Events soon gave the lie to Washington's professed optimism. Although Anthony Wayne talked the Pennsylvanians into standing down, pending further discussions with the Congress, other regiments, noting the Pennsylvanians' success in having their grievances heard, embraced the tactic for themselves. The New Jersey line revolted again, and soldiers from other states grew similarly restive. "It was expected the revolt would be general," Washington informed the governors of the New England states a short while later. "The precise intention of the mutineers was not known, but their complaints and demands were similar to those of the Pennsylvanians."

Yet Washington had been expecting something like this, and he was ready. "Persuaded that without some decisive effort at all hazards to suppress this dangerous spirit, it would speedily infect the whole army, I have ordered as large a detachment as we could spare from these posts, to march under Major General Howe, with orders to compel the mutineers to unconditional submission—to listen to no terms while they were in a state of resistance, and on their reduction to execute instantly a few of the most active and most incendiary leaders." This by itself didn't solve the problem, Washington granted. "I am not certain what part the troops detached for this purpose will act." But he had had to act. "I prefer any extremity to which the Jersey troops may be driven, to a compromise."

While he again had the governors' attention, Washington made yet another pitch for the material support that would be the only true antidote to the mutiny disease. "I dare not detail the risks we run from the present scantiness of supplies," he said. "We have received few or no cattle for some time past, nor do we know of any shortly to be expected. The salted meat we ought to have reserved in the garrison is now nearly exhausted. I cannot but renew my solicitations with your state to every expedience for contributing to our immediate relief."

Washington's balance between tolerance and sternness kept the mutiny from spreading, and modest concessions from the Congress eventually brought the mutineers back into camp. Meanwhile Washington pondered his strategy against the British, and articulated it for the benefit of the French government. The occasion was the imminent departure of one of his aides, John Laurens, for Paris. Laurens was the son of Henry Laurens; in part because of this connection, Washington invited the son to join his staff. John Laurens showed great dash in the battle of Brandywine and was wounded at Germantown. When enlistments flagged in South Carolina, his home state, he recommended enrolling slaves to serve in exchange for their freedom. The Congress gave him permission to start recruiting, but opposition from slaveholders stymied the effort. Laurens returned to the field of battle, was captured by the British in their campaign against Charleston, and was returned to the American side in a prisoner swap.

In 1780 the Congress tapped Laurens to sail to France to represent Washington and explain American military strategy to the government of King Louis. Laurens resisted the appointment, preferring the battlefield to the halls of government. Perhaps he preferred, too, not to risk the fate of his father, who on a diplomatic mission of his own had been captured by the British and was languishing in the Tower of London, beyond the reach of regular prisoner exchanges. Laurens suggested sending Alexander Hamilton in his place. But Hamilton refused, and Laurens bowed to duty's call. In preparation for leaving, he asked Washington for instructions.

Washington responded with the clearest statement he ever made of the strategy he hoped would carry the United States to victory. To be sure, it was tailored to a French audience, but it said nothing Washington didn't believe. He began by stressing the importance of continued and expanded French assistance. "The efforts we have been compelled to make for carrying on the war have exceeded the natural abilities of this country, and by degrees brought it to a crisis which renders immediate and efficacious succors from abroad indispensable to its safety," Washington said. America was a wealthy country potentially, with almost limitless resources; but amid the revolution, which had overturned government and disrupted commerce, it was unable to marshal those resources sufficiently to support the war effort. "From the best estimates of the annual expense of the war and the annual revenues which these states are capable of affording, there is a large balance to be supplied by public credit." In other words, the war effort required borrowing.

Borrowing within the United States fell short. "The resource of domestic loans is inconsiderable, because there are properly speaking few moneyed men, and the few there are can employ their money more profitably otherwise," Washington wrote. The result was the recent mutiny. "The patience of the army, from an almost uninterrupted series of complicated distress, is now nearly exhausted, and their discontents matured to an extremity." Every attempt by government to alleviate the distress had failed, and likely would continue to fail. Taxes could not be increased without risking popular support for the war. "A commercial and free people little accustomed to heavy burthens, pressed by impositions of a new and odious kind, may not make a proper allowance for the necessity of the conjuncture, and may imagine they have only exchanged one tyranny for another."

From this, Washington concluded that French help was indispensable. To Laurens he asserted the "absolute necessity of an immediate, ample and efficacious succor in money, large enough to be a foundation for substantial arrangements of finance, to revive public credit, and give vigor to future operations."

Beyond money, France must supply arms. Washington stressed to Laurens "the vast importance of a decided effort of the allied arms on this continent." More than ever, French money and French soldiers and ships were essential to the success of America's revolution.

Money and arms were intimately linked, Washington said. "Without the first, we may make a feeble and expiring effort the next campaign, in all probability the period"—the end—"to our opposition. With it, we should be in a condition to continue the war as long as the obstinacy of the enemy might require. The first is essential to the latter; both combined would bring the contest to a glorious issue, crown the obligations which America already feels to the magnanimity and generosity of her ally, and perpetuate the union by all the ties of gratitude and affection, as well as mutual advantage, which alone can render it solid and indissoluble."

Ideally, French troops and ships would both become available. But ships were the more pressing need at the moment. Naval superiority on the American coast would transform the war. "This would instantly reduce the enemy to a difficult defensive, and, by removing all prospect of extending their acquisitions, would take away the motives for prosecuting the war," Washington said. "Indeed, it is not to be conceived how they could subsist a large force in this country if we had the command of the seas to interrupt the regular transmission of supplies from Europe. This superiority (with an aid in money) would enable us to convert the war into a vigorous offensive."

"A VIGOROUS OFFENSIVE"—Washington had been champing at this bit since the battle of Monmouth, when he had shown that his army could fight toe to toe with the British. But William Howe and then Henry Clinton had refused to accommodate him. They kept behind defenses in New York, refusing Washington's every effort to lure them out. Early in the war Washington had been happy not to fight; his goal had been simply to keep his army intact and in the field. He had assumed the British would eventually weary of the war and go home. But the mounting dissatisfaction in Washington's army, signaled by Arnold's treason and culminating in the Pennsylvania mutiny, revealed that it was his own soldiers who might be going home, or even going over to the enemy. Washington needed to take the offensive, to give his soldiers confidence they wouldn't be fighting forever. French assistance could make this possible. French money would hold his army together, and French ships pin down the British; with these he could attack and bring the war to a successful conclusion.

He met again with Rochambeau, to devise plans. Washington wanted to target New York, and he persuaded Rochambeau. "It was agreed that if by the aid of our allies we can have a naval superiority through the next campaign, and an army of thirty thousand men (or double the force of the enemy and its dependencies) early enough in the season to operate in that quarter, we ought to prefer it to *every* other object as the most important and decisive," Washington reported to Henry Knox after the meeting. What Washington envisioned, and Rochambeau with him, was a siege of New York, not unlike the siege of Boston with which Washington's war had begun. But this time the British wouldn't escape, on account of the French fleet. "The general idea of the plan of operations is this (if we are able to procure the force we count upon): to make two attacks, one against the works on York Island"—Manhattan—"and the other against the works of Brooklyn on Long Island," Washington told Knox.

A fallback plan, in the event something foiled operations around New York, was to take the army to the South, where the British under Cornwallis had been acting with impunity. "If we should find ourselves unable to undertake this more capital expedition"—against New York—"and if we have means equal to it, we shall attempt a secondary object, the reduction of Charles Town," Washington said. But New York was the prime objective.

HENRY CLINTON AND THE BRITISH had their own ideas. Having been unable to defeat Washington in the North, they pressed their campaign in the South. The British strategy was to build on the Loyalist base there, to the point where the southern states might abandon the American cause for a return to the British fold. At the least, Cornwallis's campaign would tempt Washington to send forces south, weakening him around New York.

The British plan succeeded in its lesser objective. "Every day convinces me that the enemy are determined to bend their force against the southern states, and that we must support them powerfully from this quarter or they will be lost," Washington wrote in early April. "Except such support is given in time, it will be ineffectual. The enemy will not only have established themselves in posts but in the affections of many of the people."

Washington was torn. Nathanael Greene commanded American forces in the South, where he and his lieutenant Daniel Morgan engaged Cornwallis and Banastre Tarleton in one battle after another. Greene and Morgan harassed the British and their American Loyalist allies, and inflicted some tactical defeats. But they were outnumbered, and without reinforcements they couldn't do much more than bother Cornwallis, who made the South the more Loyalist the longer he remained unchecked.

Through the spring of 1781 Washington wrestled with the issue of how to apportion his forces. His preference remained New York. The city was a Loyalist stronghold; retaking it would restore much of the credibility the Patriot cause had lost when Washington and his army were driven out nearly five years earlier. Moreover, a victory at New York, under Washington's direct supervision, would finally silence doubts about his command capability. Horatio Gates was no longer a serious rival, but he still had the victory at Saratoga to his credit. Washington had nothing comparable.

On the other hand, if the southern states fell under British and Loyalist control, any victory Washington won in the North would be half-complete at best. Since the entry of France into the war, politics in Britain had shifted in a direction that hinted of accommodation with America. Even if the Americans—or some of them—were no longer subjects of the British crown, they could be allies against France, by far the greater threat to British interests. Washington wasn't alone in imagining a British offer of recognition of independence to those states that clearly wanted it, as demonstrated by their support of Washington's army, but only to those states. The Loyalist-controlled southern states might remain in the empire.

The decision—New York or the South—wasn't Washington's alone. The Congress had its views, but more immediate for Washington was the position of Rochambeau and the French. The French wished the Americans well, but American independence wasn't France's greatest concern. The French wanted revenge for the settlement imposed on them by Britain in 1763, and whatever else they could wring out of a successful war. The West Indies, with their rich sugar trade, meant more to France than New York or Virginia. In much the way he could only request, rather than command, the support of the Congress and the American states, Washington could only request the support of the French for whichever strategy he pursued.

Complicating matters further was that Rochambeau didn't speak for all the French forces in and near America. In particular, he didn't command the French navy, which had its own interests and imperatives. The Comte de Grasse decided where he would sail and what he would do when he got there.

This overriding fact informed another meeting Washington held with Rochambeau, in May 1781. The two generals agreed, according to Washington's diary entry on the meeting, that the French force would march to the Hudson River "to commence an operation against New York, which in the present reduced state of the garrison it was thought would fall, unless relieved, the doing which would enfeeble their southern operations, and in either case be productive of capital advantages; or to extend our views to the southward as circumstances and a naval superiority might render more necessary and eligible." Washington could hope for the support of de Grasse and his fleet, but he couldn't rely on it. Until he could, he would continue to focus on the object near at hand: New York.

On this basis the campaign went forward. "All the French troops, except about two hundred to be left as a guard over their heavy stores and baggage at Providence, are to march as soon as circumstances will admit, and form a junction with me upon the North River," Washington reported to John Hancock and the Congress at the end of May. Washington elaborated on the decision, which he knew wouldn't be popular with the southern members of the Congress. "Upon a full consideration of affairs in every point of view, an operation against New York has been deemed preferable to making further detachments to the southward, while they can only be sent by land," Washington said. "The principal reasons, which induced to this determination, are as follows: the difficulty and expense of transportation, the lateness of the season, which would throw the troops into the extremity of the heat of summer; the *great* waste of men, which we have ever experienced in so long a march at the healthiest season; and, above all, a strong presumption, that the enemy, weakened as they now are by detachments, must either sacrifice the valuable post of New York and its dependencies, or recall a part of their force from the southward to defend them."

Washington liked the last part of this argument well enough that he emphasized it in letters to other interested parties. Thomas Jefferson had been governor of Virginia since the summer of 1779; to him Washington asserted that the campaign to recapture New York was actually a campaign in defense of the South. "The progress which the enemy are making in Virginia is very alarming, not only to the state immediately invaded but to all the rest," Washington wrote to Jefferson. "As I strongly suspect from the most recent European intelligence, they are endeavoring to make as large seeming conquests as possible, that they may urge the plea of *uti possidetis* in the proposed mediation." Jefferson was painfully aware of Virginia's vulnerability, but Washington wanted him to know that he—Washington—was, too. "Should I be supported by the neighboring states in the manner which I expect," Washington continued, "the enemy will, I hope, be reduced to the necessity of recalling part of their force from the southward to support New York, or they will run the most imminent risk of being expelled, with a great loss of stores, from that post, which is to them invaluable while they think of prosecuting the war in America; and should we, by a lucky coincidence of circumstances, gain a naval superiority, their ruin would be inevitable." Washington went so far as to say, "The prospect of giving relief to the southern states by an operation in this quarter was the principal inducement for undertaking it."

Beyond this, a southern campaign simply couldn't happen. "We found, upon a full consideration of our affairs in every point of view, that without the command of the water, it would be next to impossible for us to transport the artillery, baggage and stores of the army to so great a distance; and, besides, that we should lose at least one third of our force by desertion, sickness and the heats of the approaching season, even if it could be done," Washington said. He assured Jefferson he would attempt the impossible, if absolutely necessary. "Your Excellency may probably ask whether we are to remain here for the above reasons, should the enemy evacuate New York, and transfer the whole war to the southward. To that I answer without hesitation that we must in such case follow them at every expense and under every difficulty and loss." But until that happened, the focus would continue to be New York. "While we remain inferior at sea, and there is a probability of giving relief by diversion—and that perhaps sooner than by sending reinforcements immediately to the point in distress—good policy dictates the trial of the former."

THE GREAT IMPONDERABLE WAS de Grasse. Where was he? Where was he headed? When would he get there? Just as Washington had been forced to guess, and hedge his guesses, early in the war when William Howe had sailed out of Boston and over the horizon, so Washington now had to guess, and hedge, about de Grasse. The French admiral deliberately made himself hard to find; the British would have liked nothing better than to intercept him.

It was for this reason that Rochambeau encrypted a message he had received from de Grasse and now relayed to Washington. "It will be by the 15th of July at soonest that I will be on the coast of North America," de Grasse declared. "But is necessary, by reason of the short time that I have to stay in that country, being besides obliged to leave it by reason of the season"—the hurricane season—"that all that can be useful for the success of your projects should be ready that a moment for action may not be lost."

Washington couldn't be sure how current this intelligence was, as the letter from de Grasse was three and a half months old. Neither could Rochambeau, who appended his own commentary. "I have already wrote to the Count de Grasse that your Excellency had desired my marching to the North river to strengthen or even attack New York when the circumstances will admit of it," Rochambeau said. "I have apprised him of the number of the garrison at New York and of the considerable forces which the enemy has sent in Virginia, that the only means which seems practicable to your Excellency is a diversion upon New York which you propose to do as soon as the circumstances will allow of it. I have spoken to him of the enemy's naval forces and told him that by reason of the constant wind, I thought it would be a great stroke to go to Chesapeake Bay in which he can make great things against the naval force that will be there, and then the wind could bring him in two days before New York." Washington hadn't considered this angle: that de Grasse might do double duty. Rochambeau mentioned the troops de Grasse was transporting. "If he could bring us some moveable forces, 5 or 6 thousand men more would render our expedition much more probable."

Washington responded at once. Rochambeau had said a fast frigate was about to sail to meet de Grasse at sea; he would include a message from Washington, if it arrived in time. "You cannot, in my opinion, too strongly urge the necessity of bringing a body of troops with him, more especially as I am very dubious whether our force can be drawn together by the time he proposes to be here," Washington wrote for

Rochambeau and de Grasse. "Now *four thousand or five thousand men*, in addition to what we shall certainly have by that time, would, almost beyond a doubt, enable us with the assistance of the fleet to carry our object. It is to be regretted, that the Count's stay upon the coast will be limited. That consideration is an additional reason for wishing a force equal to giving a speedy determination to the operation."

The certainty—within the limits of war and weather—that de Grasse was coming caused Washington to weigh more carefully objectives beyond New York. "Your Excellency will be pleased to recollect that New York was looked upon by us as the only practicable object under present circumstances," he told Rochambeau. "But should we be able to secure a *naval superiority,* we may perhaps find others more practicable and equally advisable." Which others was largely up to de Grasse. "If the frigate should not have sailed, I wish you to explain this matter to the Count de Grasse, as, if I understand it, you have in your communication to him confined our views to New York alone. And, instead of advising him to run immediately into the Chesapeake, will it not be best to leave him to judge, from the information he may from time to time receive of the situation of the enemy's fleet upon this coast, which will be the most advantageous quarter for him to make his appearance in?"

Rochambeau tried to pin Washington down. It could take months to get a reply from de Grasse, and meanwhile Rochambeau had to prepare his troops for whatever they might be called on to do. "What is to be the definitive plan of operations?" he demanded. "Let us suppose that the Count de Grasse does not look on it as practicable to force Sandy Hook"—at the entrance to New York harbor—"and that he does not bring with him any land troops. In these two cases—which appear very likely, because on one hand, the seamen look on Sandy Hook bar as impossible to force, and on the other hand because the court of France makes no mention of any troops to be brought here by the Count de Grasse, in the letters that inform us of his arrival here—in these two cases, does his Excellency think that with an army, which joined to the French corps will not be much more numerous than the troops that defend New York, that it will be possible to undertake with success something against that place?" Rochambeau had no desire to launch his men on a suicide mission.

"But if His Excellency does not look on it as practicable to risk it," he continued, "could not the operations be directed against Virginia?" Washington had described the difficulties of an overland march; what if de Grasse could transport at least some of Washington's troops, along with Rochambeau's? "Would not we be then in a condition to undertake with success on Lord Cornwallis and force him to evacuate Virginia?"

Washington appreciated the arguments in favor of Virginia, but he still wanted to keep his options open. "It is next to impossible at this moment, circumstanced as we are, and labouring under uncertainties, to fix a definitive plan for the campaign," he told Rochambeau. "Definitive measures must depend upon circumstances at the time of the arrival of the Count de Grasse, particularly on the following: 1st, The situation of the enemy at that moment. 2d, On the succours he shall bring with him, or on the force we shall have collected by that time. 3d, On the operation and advantages which may be gained by the fleet in the moment of its arrival—and—4th, On the continuance of the fleet upon the coast, and the probability of its maintaining a decisive superiority whilst it is here."

Washington elaborated: "If the fleet of Count de Grasse should be late in coming to this coast, if the count should not think it prudent to attempt forcing the passage of the Hook or fail in making the attempt, if he should bring no land troops with him and the American force should not be considerably augmented—I am of opinion that under these circumstances, we ought to throw a sufficient garrison into West Point, leave some Continental troops and militia to cover the country contiguous to New York and transport the remainder, both French and American, to Virginia, should the enemy still keep a force there." Speaking from local knowledge, Washington observed, "The season and other circumstances will admit of late operations in that quarter."

Yet Virginia remained Washington's second choice. "Should the fleet arrive in season, not be limited to a short stay; should it be able to force the harbour of New York; and in addition to all these, should it find the British force in a divided state"—between New York and Virginia—"I am of opinion that the enterprize against New York and its dependencies should be our primary object."

But in mid-August, Washington suddenly scrapped the plan for assaulting New York. Word arrived that de Grasse would be on the American coast within weeks, in the vicinity of the Chesapeake. Without a French cork in the bottle of the Hudson estuary, Washington couldn't compel Henry Clinton to fight at New York. Yet if he moved swiftly, he might pin Cornwallis in Virginia.

J AMES THACHER WOULD BECOME a distinguished doctor, publishing books on medicine and medical history. In 1781 he was a
surgeon in Washington's army. He had learned on the job how to
amputate arms and legs damaged beyond repair, and how to cope with
the shortages of supply the army as a whole had suffered since the start.
He revered Washington, not least since Washington took the time to
visit the soldiers in Thacher's hospital tent and display the paternal
interest for which he was famous. "The serenity of his countenance,
and majestic gracefulness of his deportment, impart a strong impression of that dignity and grandeur which are his peculiar characteristics,
and no one can stand in his presence without feeling the ascendancy
of his mind and associating with his countenance the idea of wisdom,
philanthropy, magnanimity, and patriotism," Thacher wrote in his
journal after one such visit. "There is not in the present age, perhaps,
another man so eminently qualified to discharge the arduous duties of
the exalted station he is called to sustain, amidst difficulties which to
others would appear insurmountable, nor could any man have more at
command the veneration and regard of the officers and soldiers of our
army."

Thacher was willing to follow Washington anywhere, even when
Washington took pains to disguise the destination. "General orders
are now issued for the army to prepare for a movement at a moment's
notice," Thacher wrote on August 15. "The real object of the allied
armies in the present campaign has become a subject of much speculation. Ostensibly an investment of the city of New York is in contem-
plation; preparations in all quarters for some months past indicate this
to be the object of our combined operations. The capture of this place
would be a decisive stroke, and from the moment such event takes
place, the English must renounce all hopes of subjugating the United

States." But the British had fortified New York, and a successful attack required the help of the French fleet, which was nowhere to be seen.

The movement began. "General Washington and Count Rochambeau have crossed the North River, and it is supposed for the purpose of reconnoitering the enemy's posts from the Jersey shore," Thacher recorded. "A field for an extensive encampment has been marked out on the Jersey side, and a number of ovens have been erected and fuel provided for the purpose of baking bread for the army. From these combined circumstances we are led to conclude that a part of our besieging force is to occupy that ground. But General Washington possesses a capacious mind, full of resources, and he resolves and matures his great plans and designs under an impenetrable veil of secrecy, and while we repose the fullest confidence in our chief, our own opinions must be founded only on doubtful conjectures."

Several days brought little enlightenment. "We commenced our line of march yesterday, a party of pioneers being sent forward to clear the road towards King's bridge, and we expected immediately to follow in that direction," Thacher wrote on August 20. "But an army is a machine whose motions are directed by its chief. When the troops were paraded for the march, they were ordered to face to the right about, and making a retrograde movement up the side of the North River, we have reached King's ferry and are preparing to cross the Hudson at this ferry. Our allies are in our rear, and it is probable we are destined to occupy the ground on the Jersey side."

The mystery persisted. "Our situation reminds me of some theatrical exhibition where the interest and expectations of the spectators are continually increasing, and where curiosity is wrought to the highest point," Thacher wrote. "Our destination has been for some time matter of perplexing doubt and uncertainty; bets have run high on one side, that we were to occupy the ground marked out on the Jersey shore, to aid in the siege of New York, and on the other, that we are stealing a march on the enemy, and are actually destined to Virginia, in pursuit of the army under Lord Cornwallis."

The bets on Virginia gradually came to be seen as the winners. "Resumed our line of march, passing rapidly through Paramus, Acquackanonk, Springfield, and Princeton," Thacher recorded. "We have now passed all the enemy's posts and are pursuing our route with increased rapidity towards Philadelphia; wagons have been prepared to carry the soldiers' packs that they may press forward with greater facility. Our destination can no longer be a secret. The British army under Lord Cornwallis is unquestionably the object of our present expedition." The explanation likewise became clear. "It is now rumored that a French fleet may soon be expected to arrive in Chesapeake Bay, to cooperate with the allied army in that quarter. The great secret respecting our late preparations and movements can now be explained. It was a judiciously concerted stratagem calculated to menace and alarm Sir Henry Clinton for the safety of the garrison of New York, and induce him to recall a part of his troops from Virginia." And it had worked: some of Cornwallis's soldiers had been seen arriving in New York. Thacher admired his commander more than ever. "General Washington, having succeeded in a masterly piece of *generalship*, has now the satisfaction of leaving his adversary to ruminate on his own mortifying situation, and to anticipate the perilous fate which awaits his friend, Lord Cornwallis."

The worst of summer's heat had passed, easing Washington's worries on that count. But the march was no stroll. "In the afternoon, marched through the city of Philadelphia," Thacher wrote on September 2. "The streets being extremely dirty and the weather warm and dry, we raised a dust like a smothering snow storm, blinding our eyes and covering our bodies with it; this was not a little mortifying, as the ladies were viewing us from the open windows of every house as we passed through this splendid city." Thacher imagined what the Philadelphians were feeling. "Contemplating the noble cause in which we are engaged, they must have experienced in their hearts a glow of patriotism, if not emotions of military ardor." The army made quite a sight. "Our line of march, including appendages and attendants, extended nearly two miles. The general officers and their aids, in rich military uniform, mounted on noble steeds elegantly caparisoned, were followed by their servants and baggage. In the rear of every brigade were several field pieces, accompanied by ammunition carriages. The soldiers marched in slow and solemn step, regulated by the drum and fife. In the rear followed a great number of wagons loaded with tents, provisions and other baggage such as a few soldiers' wives and children; though a very small number of these are allowed to encumber us on this occasion. The day following, the French troops marched through the city, dressed in complete uniform of white broadcloth, faced with green, and besides the drum and fife, they were furnished with a complete band of music, which operates like enchantment."

Welcome news arrived a week later. "An express has now arrived from Virginia with the pleasing intelligence that the Count de Grasse has actually arrived at the mouth of the Chesapeake Bay, with a fleet of thirty-six ships of the line, and three thousand land forces, which are landed and have joined our troops under the Marquis de la Fayette, in Virginia," Thacher wrote.

By now the march had covered two hundred miles—in fifteen days—and deposited the army at the head of the Chesapeake Bay. The troops boarded ship for transport down the bay; the horses continued overland. "It falls to my lot to take passage on board a small schooner with four other officers and sixty men," Thacher wrote. "She is so deeply laden with cannon, mortars and other ordnance that our situation will be attended with considerable danger if rough weather should overtake us."

In fact a gale forced the flotilla of transports to seek shelter. Thacher's boat tied up at Annapolis. They had scarcely reembarked when they received word to return to port. "This is in consequence of intelligence of a naval action between the British and French fleets near the mouth of the Chesapeake Bay," Thacher observed. "Our safety requires that we should remain in port till the event of the battle is known. Should the British have obtained the victory, and should they get possession of the Chesapeake Bay, we shall be unable to proceed on our voyage, and our expedition will be entirely defeated."

Fortunately, the French were the ones who obtained the victory. De Grasse defeated the British in a close but decisive battle off the Virginia capes. The British squadron sailed away, leaving the French fleet in control of the sea lanes of the vicinity. "This event is of infinite importance, and fills our hearts with joy, as we can now proceed on our expedition," Thacher declared. Days later he and his comrades caught sight of those they had to thank. "Passed Hampton Roads, and entered James River, which is at its entrance about five miles wide. We enjoyed a distant view of the grand French fleet riding at anchor at the mouth of the Chesapeake, consisting of thirty-six ships of war, besides frigates and other armed vessels. This was the most noble and majestic spectacle I ever witnessed, and we viewed it with inexpressible pleasure, and the warmest gratitude was excited in every breast towards our great ally."

WASHINGTON SHARED THE PLEASURE, which he conveyed to de Grasse. "I take particular satisfaction in felicitating your Excellency on the glory of having driven the British fleet from the coast and taking two of their frigates," he wrote. "These happy events, and the decided superiority of your fleet, gives us the happiest presages of the most complete success in our combined operations in this bay."

Washington hastened to meet with de Grasse and coordinate what he hoped would be the end game against Cornwallis. The British general had placed his army at Yorktown, where his men were improving a port for the British ships that were supposed to provision them or rescue them in case of need. For the moment, Yorktown's peninsula had become a trap for Cornwallis, and Washington's first question to de Grasse was how long that moment would last. That is, how long did Washington have to envelop Yorktown and compel Cornwallis's surrender?

De Grasse replied that his instructions called for him to leave by October 15, so that he could meet obligations in the West Indies. "But having already taken much upon himself, he will also engage to stay the end of October," de Grasse allowed, according to the notes of the meeting.

Washington asked if he would have the use of the two thousand French troops aboard de Grasse's fleet.

"You may count upon those troops," de Grasse said.

Washington asked if de Grasse thought it practicable to force the passage of the York River—that is, to sail under fire past Yorktown to get above the British position.

"The thing is not impossible with a good wind and favourable tide," de Grasse said. "But I do not find that operation very useful. Our communication can be established, and our provisions drawn from the east side of the York River"—opposite Yorktown—"without risking the men and vessels in their passage between the batteries. But I suspend my definitive answer until I can reconnoiter the local situation and force of the enemy. I shall certainly do everything in my power."

Washington asked if de Grasse could spare any cannons and powder.

"I can give some cannon and powder," de Grasse said. But he couldn't offer very much powder, having expended a large quantity in his recent battle.

Washington was greatly encouraged by de Grasse's cooperativeness, yet he could hardly sleep for the anxiety he felt. Victory had never been so close, but events beyond his control might still snatch it away. A week after his meeting with de Grasse, while the American and French armies continued their march toward Yorktown, Washington heard a rumor that de Grasse might have changed his mind about staying through October. He dashed off a frantic letter of protest. "The enterprise against York, under the protection of your ships, is as certain as any military operation can be rendered by a decisive superiority of strength and means," Washington said. Everything would be spoiled by this sudden change of plans. "Your Excellency's departure from the Chesapeake, by affording an opening for the succor of York, which the enemy would instantly avail himself of, would frustrate these brilliant prospects; and the consequence would be not only the disgrace and loss of renouncing an enterprise upon which the fairest expectations of the allies have been founded, after the most expensive preparations and uncommon exertions and fatigues, but the disbanding perhaps of the whole army for want of provisions."

De Grasse stayed, albeit fretting about the slowness of Washington to get his troops into place. On October 1, Washington was able to report that his army had finally reached their destination. "I marched from Williamsburg with the whole army on the 28th, and approached within about two miles of the enemy at York," he wrote to John Hancock. The British made a show of resistance, but retired after a few rounds from Rochambeau's French cannoneers.

The next day Washington ordered his troops closer to the British lines. "No opposition except a few scattered shots from a small work by Moor's Mill on Wormley's Creek, and a battery on the left of Pigeon Quarter," he recorded. "A small fire all day from our riflemen and the enemy's Yagers."

Cornwallis realized his predicament, and also his opportunity. If he could hold out until de Grasse had to leave for the West Indies, his army might live to fight another day. He consolidated his defenses, pulling back to reduce his perimeter.

But in doing so, he made Washington's task easier, at least at this stage. "The enemy had evacuated all their exterior line of works, and withdrawn themselves to those near the body of the town," Washington reported to Hancock. "By this means we are in possession of very advantageous grounds, which command in a very near advance almost the whole remaining line of their defence." More progress would follow shortly, Washington predicted. "All the expedition that our circumstances will admit is using to bring up our heavy artillery and stores and to open our batteries. This work I hope will be executed in a few days, when our fire will begin with great vigor."

Standard siege technique called for the construction of trenches parallel to the lines of the defenders, from which the attackers might fire without being blasted by the enemy's guns. On the night of October 6, the American and French forces established their first parallel, some six hundred yards from the British emplacements. Losses were minor. During the next two days the allies constructed batteries within the parallel, in cannon range of Yorktown. On October 9 French and American cannons, mortars and howitzers opened fire. "We were informed"—by deserters—"that our shells did considerable execution in the town, and we could perceive that our shot which were directed against the enemy's embrasures injured them much," Washington recorded.

On October 10 four more batteries—two American and two French—joined the bombardment. "The fire now became so excessively heavy, that the enemy withdrew their cannon from their embrasures, placed them behind the merlons, and scarcely fired a shot during the whole day," Washington wrote. "In the evening the *Charon* frigate of forty-four guns was set on fire by a hot ball from the French battery on the left, and entirely consumed. . . . By the report of a deserter, our shells, which were thrown with the utmost degree of precision, did much mischief in the course of the day. Yesterday morning"—October 11—"two of the enemy's transports were fired by hot shot and burnt. This has occasioned them to warp their shipping as far over to the Gloucester shore"—opposite Yorktown—"as possible."

James Thacher had never seen such a display of destruction. "From the bank of the river, I had a fine view of this splendid conflagration," he wrote. "The ships were enwrapped in a torrent of fire, which spreading with vivid brightness among the combustible rigging, and running with amazing rapidity to the tops of the several masts, while all around was thunder and lightning from our numerous cannon and mortars, and in the darkness of night, presented one of the most sublime and magnificent spectacles which can be imagined. Some of our shells, overreaching the town, are seen to fall into the river, and bursting, throw up columns of water like the spouting of the monsters of the deep."

The British fired back, to no small effect. "The enemy were roused to the greatest exertions, the engines of war have raged with redoubled fury, and destruction on both sides, no cessation day or night," Thacher recorded. "The French had two officers wounded, and fifteen men killed or wounded, and among the Americans, two or three were wounded. I assisted in amputating a man's thigh. The siege is daily becoming more and more formidable and alarming, and his Lordship"—Cornwallis—"must view his situation as extremely critical, if not desperate. Being in the trenches every other night and day, I have a fine opportunity of witnessing the sublime and stupendous scene which is continually exhibiting. The bomb shells from the besiegers and the besieged are incessantly crossing each other's path in the air. They are clearly visible in the form of a black ball in the day, but in the night, they appear like fiery meteors with blazing tails, most beautifully brilliant, ascending majestically from the mortar to a certain altitude, and gradually descending to the spot where they are destined to execute their work of destruction. It is astonishing with what accuracy an experienced gunner will make his calculations, that a shell shall fall within a few feet of a given point, and burst at the precise time, though at a great distance. When a shell falls, it whirls round, burrows, and excavates the earth to a considerable extent, and bursting, makes dreadful havoc around. I have more than once witnessed fragments of the mangled bodies and limbs of the British soldiers thrown into the air by the bursting of our shells, and by one from the enemy, Captain White, of the seventh Massachusetts regiment, and one soldier were killed, and another wounded near where I was standing. About twelve or fourteen men have been killed or wounded within twenty-four hours; I attended at the hospital, amputated a man's arm, and assisted in dressing a number of wounds."

Yet Washington took it all in stride. "General Washington, Generals Lincoln and Knox, with their aides, having dismounted, were standing in an exposed situation," Thacher recounted. "Colonel Cobb, one of General Washington's aides, solicitous for his safety, said to his Excellency, 'Sir, you are too much exposed here, had you not better step a little back?' 'Colonel Cobb,' replied his Excellency, 'if you are afraid, you have liberty to step back.'"

THE RING WAS CLOSING. The allied forces established a second parallel, increasing the pressure on the British defenses. Only two British gun emplacements outside the main fortifications remained. "The engineers having deemed the two redoubts on the left of the enemy's line sufficiently injured by our shot and shells to make them practicable, it was determined to carry them by assault on the evening of the 14th," Washington recorded. He picked Lafayette to lead a unit of American light infantry against one; French general Baron Vioménil would direct French grenadiers against the other. The American and French soldiers were ordered to hold their fire and fight hand-to-hand, to avoid giving alarm. The action was swift, violent and successful. "Nothing could exceed the firmness and bravery of the troops," Washington said. "They advanced under the fire of the enemy without returning a shot, and effected the business by the bayonet only."

Washington was elated. "The works which we have carried are of vast importance to us," he told Hancock. Cannons mounted there could sweep the British lines and the river beyond Yorktown.

Cornwallis understood the peril he faced, and he sent troops on a sortie against the new American positions. "They entered one of the French and one of the American batteries on the second parallel, which were unfinished," Washington said. "They had only time to thrust the points of their bayonets into four pieces of the French and two of the American artillery, and break them off, but the spikes were easily extracted. They were repulsed the moment the supporting troops came up, leaving behind them seven or eight dead, and six prisoners. The French had four officers and twelve privates killed and wounded, and we had one sergeant mortally wounded."

The bombardment intensified. "The whole of our works are now mounted with cannon and mortar," James Thacher wrote. "Not less than one hundred pieces of heavy ordnance have been in continual operation during the last twenty-four hours. The whole peninsula trembles under the incessant thunderings of our infernal machines. We have levelled some of their works in ruins and silenced their guns; they have almost ceased firing. We are so near as to have a distinct view of the dreadful havoc and destruction of their works, and even see the men in their lines torn to pieces by the bursting of our shells."

Cornwallis finally waved the white flag. A courier carried a message to Washington. "Sir," Cornwallis said, dodging the question of how Washington was to be formally titled. "I propose a cessation of hostilities for twenty-four hours, and that two officers may be appointed by each side to meet at Mr. Moore's house to settle terms for the surrender of the posts of York and Gloucester."

Washington granted the truce, and the negotiations quickly produced an agreement. Cornwallis surrendered his entire army and all their weapons, except the personal arms of the officers.

JAMES THACHER RECOUNTED the surrender ceremony with no small relish. "At about twelve o'clock, the combined army was arranged and drawn up in two lines extending more than a mile in length," he wrote. "The Americans were drawn up in a line on the right side of the road, and the French occupied the left. At the head of the former the great American commander, mounted on his noble courser, took his station, attended by his aides. At the head of the latter was posted the excellent Count Rochambeau and his suite. The French troops, in complete uniform, displayed a martial and noble appearance, their band of music, of which the timbrel formed a part, is a delightful novelty, and produced while marching to the ground, a most enchanting effect. The Americans though not all in uniform nor their dress so meant, yet exhibited an erect soldierly air, and every countenance beamed with satisfaction and joy. The concourse of spectators from the country was prodigious, in point of numbers probably equal to the military, but universal silence and order prevailed. It was about two o'clock when the captive army advanced through the line formed for their reception. Every eye was prepared to gaze on Lord Cornwallis, the object of peculiar interest and solicitude; but he disappointed our anxious expectations; pretending indisposition, he made General O'Hara his substitute as the leader of his army. This officer was followed by the conquered troops in a slow and solemn step, with shouldered arms, colors cased and drums beating a British march. Having arrived at the head of the line, General O'Hara, elegantly mounted, advanced to his Excellency the Commander in Chief, taking off his hat, and apologized for the non-appearance of Earl Cornwallis. With his usual dignity and politeness his Excellency pointed to Major General Lincoln for directions, by whom the British army was conducted into a spacious field, where it was intended they should ground their arms. The royal troops, while marching through the line formed by the allied army, exhibited a decent and neat appearance, as respects arms and clothing, for their commander opened his store and directed every soldier to be furnished with a new suit complete, prior to the capitulation. But in their line of march we remarked a disorderly and unsoldierly conduct, their step was irregular, and their ranks frequently broken. But it was in the field when they came to the last act of the drama, that the spirit and pride of the British soldier was put to the severest test; here their mortification could not be concealed. Some of the platoon officers appeared to be exceedingly chagrined when giving the word 'ground arms,' and I am a witness that they performed this duty in a very unofficerlike manner, and that many of the soldiers manifested a sullen temper, throwing their arms on the pile with violence, as if determined to render them useless. This irregularity, however, was checked by the authority of General Lincoln. After having grounded their arms and divested themselves of their accoutrements, the captive troops were conducted back to Yorktown and guarded by our troops till they could be removed to the place of their destination."

The ceremony, and what it represented, made Thacher admire Washington more than ever. "In the design and execution of this successful expedition, our Commander in Chief fairly out-generaled Sir Henry Clinton, and the whole movement was marked by consummate military address, which reduced the royal general to a mortifying dilemma that no skill or enterprize could retrieve," Thacher wrote. "A siege of thirteen days, prosecuted with unexampled rapidity, has terminated in the capture of one of the greatest generals of which the English can boast, and a veteran and victorious army which has for several months past spread terror and desolation throughout the southern states. The joy on this momentous occasion is universally diffused, and the hope entertained that it will arrest the career of a cruel warfare, and advance the establishment of American independence."

WILLIAM FRANKLIN GREW LIVID when he learned of the British surrender at Yorktown. The former governor had finally been released from his Connecticut confinement, exchanged for the president of the state of Delaware, who had been captured by the British. (Chief executives in several of the newly independent states were called presidents, rather than governors.) Unlike fellow Loyalists Thomas Hutchinson and Joseph Galloway, Franklin did not sail into exile in England but instead settled in New York. "An unwillingness to quit the scene of action where I think I might be of some service, if anything is intended to be done, has induced me to remain till I can discover what turn affairs are likely to take," he wrote to Galloway.

When William Franklin heard the news from Virginia, he couldn't believe that Cornwallis had let himself be trapped. Or, once trapped, that he hadn't struggled longer. Cornwallis must have known the French ships couldn't remain on the Virginia coast; had he persisted, he and his army might have been rescued by the British fleet.

But what really rankled William Franklin, and the other Loyalists in New York, was a part of the surrender document that pertained to them. Cornwallis had proposed an article protecting Loyalists who had taken up arms for Britain. Washington had rejected the stipulation, writing, "This article cannot be assented to, being altogether of civil resort." And Cornwallis had acquiesced.

The result was that British soldiers were protected by the laws and practices of war, but American Loyalists were not. Cornwallis had handed them over to the rebels to be treated as traitors and punished as such. William Franklin and the other Loyalists seethed merely thinking about the double-cross. Besides revealing an utter lack of principle, Cornwallis's decision was the height of political folly. Potential Loyalists in the countryside would observe how Cornwallis had abandoned their brethren, and would make their peace with the rebels. "The unhappy fate of the poor Loyalists in Lord Cornwallis's army is dreadful," wrote Thomas Hutchinson's eldest son to the former Massachusetts governor. "His agreeing to that Article of Capitulation, which gives them up to the mercy of Congress, is a matter that remains to be explained."

William Franklin had an explanation for Cornwallis's betrayal. As much as he admired British institutions, Franklin saw little to like in many of the individuals who staffed the institutions. Cornwallis was the worst, for the moment, as his spineless abandonment of the Loyalists demonstrated. But Cornwallis's commander, Henry Clinton, was hardly better. And the officials who ran the British government in London were even worse. Within months of Yorktown, a sickening whiff of defeatism wafted west across the Atlantic. The new administration of Lord North seemed willing to write off the American war as a bad investment. Such a policy might make sense to a new prime minister balanced atop a shaky coalition, but it left the Loyalists in the lurch.

William Franklin briefly took heart from the replacement of Clinton by Guy Carleton, the former governor of Canada and scourge of Patriot armies there. "Were it not that our new general is restrained by the very extraordinary resolves of the House of Commons, he might easily, with the force now under his command, put an end to the rebellion in less than three months," Franklin wrote to William Strahan, his father's erstwhile friend and now enemy. "There never was a more glorious opportunity for striking a decisive stroke against Washington, who may in fact be said to have no army at all, when compared to the force that may safely be drawn out of this garrison." If not for politics in England, America might yet be saved. "But alas, your infatuated rulers have tied up the hands of your army and sent over a general not empowered to avail himself of circumstances as they arise, but on the contrary, ordered to make almost unconditional submission and prostrate the honour of Great Britain at the feet of a banditti."

WILLIAM FRANKLIN WOULDN'T STAND for it. If the British wouldn't fight for their empire, he and the Loyalists would. He had been organizing the Loyalists in New York into a force modeled on the Pennsylvania Association his father had founded three decades earlier. The "Associated Loyalists" formed an auxiliary to the British army; their agenda was the disruption of rebel activities, the running of spies and the gathering of intelligence, and the protection of Loyalists behind rebel lines. Such protection encompassed taking hostages to exchange for captured Loyalists, and mounting reprisals against rebels who had inflicted harm on Loyalists.

In practice, reprisal could be indistinguishable from revenge, and before long the Associated Loyalists, under the leadership of William Franklin, were engaged in terrorist tit-for-tat against Patriot forces. A Loyalist behind the Patriot lines would be arrested, abused or killed, and Franklin would give the order that the same be done to a rebel.

In the spring of 1782 William Franklin learned from a Loyalist that a member of the Association named Philip White had been captured and executed for treason by some Patriot irregulars. Franklin determined to retaliate. His own men had seized a Patriot named Joshua Huddy, who had boasted openly of his role in the execution of other Loyalists. Franklin gave the order to have Huddy killed, and he assigned the task to one of his Association subordinates, Richard Lippincott.

Lippincott enlisted several comrades and early one morning they took Huddy from his jail, carried him to an isolated point on the New Jersey side of the Hudson River, and hanged him. To his coat they affixed a note that was intended to be read upon discovery of the body. "We the Refugees have with grief long beheld the cruel murders of our brethren," the note explained, "and finding nothing but such measures daily carrying into execution, we therefore determine not to suffer without taking vengeance for the numerous cruelties, and having made use of Captain Huddy as the first object to present to your view, further determine to hang man for man, as long as a refugee is left existing. UP GOES HUDDY FOR PHILIP WHITE."

THE BODY WAS FOUND and the note was read. Washington condemned the execution, in a letter to Henry Clinton, as "the most wanton, unprecedented, and inhuman murder that ever disgraced the arms of a civilized people." Washington threatened reprisal of his own. "To save the innocent, I demand the guilty—Captain Lippincott, therefore, or the officer who commanded at the execution of Captain Huddy—must be given up; or, if that officer was of inferior rank to him, so many of the perpetrators as will, according to the tariff of exchange"—the formula for prisoner exchanges—"be an equivalent. To do this will mark the justice of your Excellency's character; in failure of it, I shall hold myself justifiable in the eyes of God and man for the measure to which I shall resort."

Henry Clinton considered William Franklin and his Loyalist followers a reckless cabal of bitter-enders, and he disavowed the murder of Joshua Huddy, calling it a "barbarous outrage against humanity." But he wasn't going to accede to Washington's demand. He would handle the matter himself. "When I heard of Captain Huddy's death (which was only four days before I received your letter), I instantly ordered a strict inquiry into all its circumstances, and shall bring the perpetrators of it to an immediate trial," he told Washington. Clinton went on to warn Washington against retaliating. "To sacrifice innocence under the notion of preventing guilt, in place of suppressing, would be adopting barbarity and raising it to the greatest height. Whereas if the violators of the laws of war are punished by the generals under whose powers they act, the horrors which those laws were formed to prevent will be avoided, and every degree of humanity war is capable of maintained."

Washington withheld action pending the outcome of the trial of Richard Lippincott. The problem, on the British side, became Guy Carleton's when he relieved Clinton. The court-martial went forward, and it returned a verdict of not guilty against Lippincott, who successfully argued that he was acting on the orders of William Franklin.

Carleton wasn't about to put a former royal governor on trial, especially when the evidence against William Franklin was simply the word of a man on trial for his own life. The result readily became apparent: No one was going to be punished for the killing of Huddy.

Washington had already chosen—by lot, from thirteen of comparable rank—a British officer to be executed as retaliation for Huddy's killing. He was Charles Asgill, a British captain taken prisoner earlier. Washington was in no hurry to give the odious order. Yet he couldn't ignore the outrage committed against a Patriot without inviting other such outrages in the future. He also had to worry that Patriot irregulars would escalate matters on their own. No more than Clinton and

Carleton did Washington relish a guerrilla war among civilians unanswerable to military authority.

The fate of Charles Asgill became a cause célèbre on both sides of the Atlantic. The Continental Congress weighed in, with members split between those demanding the harsh justice Washington proposed and others arguing that Asgill's execution would besmirch American honor. In Parliament the mere idea of killing a British officer for the misdeeds of criminal American Loyalists evoked outrage approaching apoplexy.

The crisis was resolved only after the king of France, claiming part ownership of prisoner Asgill, on account of his capture at Yorktown, where Cornwallis had surrendered to the combined armies of America and France, urged Washington to stay his hand. Washington, in the interest of allied comity, not to mention humanity, assented.

BY THIS TIME William Franklin was persona non grata with Guy Carleton, who wanted nothing to do with the Associated Loyalists and their vigilante activities. Nor did Franklin feel safe in New York. No one had been punished for the killing of Joshua Huddy, and with the evidence pointing at him, Franklin feared falling into the hands of the Patriots, or of Washington himself.

He decided the time had come to leave his native land. Declaring that he needed to deliver a petition personally from the Loyalists to King George, he sailed for London in August 1782.

THOMAS ANDROS WAS THRILLED to learn of the victory at Yorktown but was in no position to celebrate. Andros was the rare example of a Patriot soldier for whom fighting the British on land wasn't sufficient; after serving with Washington at Boston and New York, he took his patriotism to sea. In 1781 he joined the crew of a privateer launched from New London, Connecticut, to prey on British shipping. His heart was in the right place. "I was but in my seventeenth year when the struggle commenced, and no politician; but even a schoolboy could see the justice of some of the principles on the ground of which the country had recourse to arms," he remembered later. "The colonies had arrived to the age of manhood. They were fully competent to govern themselves and they demanded their freedom, or at least a just representation in the national legislature. For a power three thousand miles distant to claim a right to make laws to bind us in all cases whatever, and we have no voice in that legislature—this, it seemed, was a principle to which two millions of free men ought not tamely to submit."

But it was something other than principle that drew Tom Andros to sea. "In the summer of 1781, the ship *Hannah*, a very rich prize, was captured and brought into the port of New London," he continued. The richness of the prize—the vessel and its cargo—translated into wealth for the owners, officers and crew of the privateer that had caught the *Hannah*. Andros was the youngest of three brothers and had yet to discern his way in the world. Privateering promised a running start on whatever path he chose. Finding a ship wasn't easy; many others had the same idea Andros did. And the instance of the *Hannah* made the competition worse. "It infatuated great numbers of young men, who flocked on board our private armed ships fancying the same success would attend their adventures."

But Andros persisted and found a berth on the brig *Fair American*. The vessel was well armed, with sixteen carriage-guns, and well manned, with musketeers at every place on the decks. "In action she was a complete flame of fire," Andros remarked proudly.

They had hardly cleared New London before they spied their first victim—an English brig about the same size as the *Fair American*, and as well armed, but not as fast. They outmaneuvered the English ship, pulled even, and delivered a crushing broadside. The British crew, not wishing to die for the profits of the owners of the merchant ship, struck colors.

Andros and some others went aboard to take control of the vessel and sail it home. But they were detected by a frigate of the Royal Navy, which did to them what they had done to the captured vessel. Andros and the entire crew of the *Fair American* were made prisoner and consigned to chains.

Days later they were introduced to a ship—if such it still could be called—that by then struck fear into the heart of every Patriot who heard its name. The *Jersey* had been a mighty warship in its day, carrying sixty guns, but that day had passed years before the fighting in America broke out. It was used as a supply ship and then a floating storehouse, and finally a prison ship, anchored a quarter-mile off the shore of British-occupied Brooklyn. Stripped of masts and rigging, it was a shadow of its former self. "Nothing remained but an old, unsightly rotten hulk," Andros said. "Her dark and filthy external appearance perfectly corresponded with the death and despair that reigned within."

Andros and his fellow privateers encountered the *Jersey*'s death and despair almost at once. "On the commencement of the first evening, we were driven down to darkness between decks secured by iron gratings and an armed soldiery," he wrote. "And now a scene of horror which baffles all description presented itself. On every side, wretched desponding shapes of men could be seen. Around the well-room an armed guard were forcing up the prisoners to the winches, to clear the ship of water and prevent her sinking; and little else could be heard but a roar of mutual execrations, reproaches and insults. During this operation there was a small, dim light admitted below, but it served to make darkness more visible, and horror more terrific."

When Andros arrived on the *Jersey*, it held about four hundred prisoners. But during the next few months the population swelled to more than a thousand. The crowding increased the suffering already inflicted as a result of British policy. Rules of war prescribed decent accommodation of captured soldiers, and though the rules were inconsistently applied, they set outer bounds for mistreatment of prisoners. The British government, however, didn't recognize American belligerency, because it didn't recognize the United States. The Americans in arms were rebels and, in the case of the privateers, pirates. They were treated as common criminals. In those days criminals in British jails often had to provide for their own meals and clothing; the same philosophy was applied to the American prisoners. As a result, the men on board the *Jersey* suffered severe malnutrition, lacking the money to pay for food. The malnutrition made them susceptible to the infectious diseases that raged through their cramped quarters.

"All the most deadly diseases were pressed into the service of the King of Terrors," Andros observed, referring to Satan, the ally of the British here. "But his prime ministers were dysentery, smallpox and yellow fever." Two hospital ships floated near the *Jersey*, yet they were soon overwhelmed with patients, leaving most of the sick on the main ship, to spread their infections the more. They spread terror as well. "Utter derangement was a common symptom of yellow fever, and to increase the horror of the darkness that shrouded us (for we were allowed no light betwixt decks) the voice of warning would be heard: 'Take heed to yourselves. There is a madman stalking through the ship with a knife in his hand.' I sometimes found the man a corpse in the morning, by whose side I laid myself down at night. At another time he would become deranged, and attempt in darkness to rise and stumble over the bodies that everywhere covered the deck."

Clean water for bathing was nonexistent; even water for drinking was in short supply. "While so many were sick with raging fever there was a loud cry for water, but none could be had except on the upper deck, and but one allowed to ascend at a time," Andros explained. "The suffering then from the rage of thirst during the night was very great."

Come daybreak the prisoners who could move were allowed on deck, but the sight that greeted them boded grimly for their future. "The first object that met our view in the morning was a most appalling spectacle: a boat loaded with dead bodies, conveying them to the

Long Island shore, where they were very lightly covered with sand." Every night more inmates died; every morning the boat carried away the bodies.

Andros watched his own comrades succumb. "There were thirteen of the crew to which I belonged, but in a short time all but three or four were dead. The most healthy and vigorous were first seized with the fever, and died within a few hours."

Andros remarked that the British guards made one concession to humanity. "The prisoners were furnished with buckets and brushes to cleanse the ship, and with vinegar to sprinkle her inside." But the prisoners were in no position to do much with the gesture. "Their indolence and despair was such that they would not use them, or but rarely. And indeed at this time the encouragement to do so was small, for the whole ship, from her keel to the taffrail, was equally affected and contained pestilence sufficient to desolate a world. Disease and death were wrought into her very timbers. . . . A more filthy, contagious and deadly abode for human beings never existed among a Christianized people. It fell but little short of the Black Hole of Calcutta. Death was more lingering, but almost equally certain."

As bad as the British guards were, they weren't the worst. Thomas Dring was another prisoner aboard the *Jersey;* like Tom Andros, he had been captured while privateering. Dring distinguished among three categories of guards on the prison ships. "They were English, Hessians and Refugees," he said. "We always preferred the Hessians, from whom we received better treatment than from the others. As to the English, we did not complain, being aware that they merely obeyed their orders in regard to us. But the Refugees, or Royalists, as they termed themselves"—that is, Loyalists—"were viewed by us with scorn and hatred." The British knew of the hostility of the Loyalists and the Patriots for each other, and for this reason tried to keep them apart. But sometimes proximity couldn't be avoided, and it caused trouble. "Their presence occasioned much tumult and confusion," Dring remembered, "for the prisoners could not endure the sight of these men, and occasionally assailed them with abusive language, while they, in return, treated us with all the severity in their power."

The tumult turned lethal. Dring recalled a Fourth of July aboard the *Jersey.* The prisoners insisted on celebrating Independence Day, and during their fresh-air moment on the deck they produced thirteen small American flags. The guards immediately seized the flags and ordered the celebration to end. The prisoners began singing Patriot songs. The guards tried to halt the singing by breaking up the group of singers. "We were in a short time forbidden to pass along the common gangways," Dring said. "And every attempt to do so was repelled by the bayonet." The celebration persisted. "Songs were still sung, accompanied with occasional cheers." This continued into the afternoon, when the guards decided to force the prisoners below. "We received orders to descend between decks, where we were immediately driven at the point of the bayonet." The prisoners continued to express their Patriotic sentiments; the singing persisted into the evening.

When the guards made no more demands, the prisoners thought they had reconciled themselves to this modest affirmation of Patriot faith. In fact the guards were simply waiting for dark to fall. "About nine o'clock the gratings were removed and the guards descended among us with lanterns and drawn cutlasses in their hands," Dring said. "The poor, helpless prisoners retreated from the hatchways as far as their crowded situation would permit, while their cowardly assailants followed as far as they dared, cutting and wounding everyone within their reach, and then ascended to the upper deck, exulting in the gratification of their revenge."

They left below a scene of bloody chaos. "Many of the prisoners were wounded," Dring said, "but from the total darkness neither their number nor their situation could be ascertained. And if this had been possible, it was not in the power of their companions to afford them the least relief. During the whole of that tragical night, their groans and lamentations were dreadful in the extreme." Dring was an officer, a rank that had earned him quarters a bit removed from the ordinary prisoners. "But the distance was by no means far enough to prevent my hearing their continual cries, from the extremity of pain, their applications for assistance, and their curses upon the heads of their brutal assailants."

Ordinarily the prisoners filled small containers with drinking water before they were sent below for the night. Having been forced down early and suddenly, they were without water this night. "I cannot describe the horrors," Dring said. "The day had been very sultry, and the heat was extreme throughout the ship. The unusual number of hours during which we had been crowded together between decks;

the foul atmosphere and sickening heat; the additional excitement and restlessness caused by the wanton attack which had been made; above all, the want of water, not a drop of which we could obtain during the whole night, to cool our parched tongues; the imprecations of those who were half-distracted with their burning thirst; the shrieks and wailings of the wounded; the struggles and groans of the dying; together formed a combination of horrors which no pen can describe."

Dring survived the night, but many of his fellow prisoners did not. The corpse-boats had a double load the next day, carrying the dead to their shallow graves on the Brooklyn shore.

WASHINGTON'S VICTORY AT Yorktown did little at first for the prisoners on board the *Jersey*, and scarcely more for the slaves who had taken sides in the struggle between Britain and America. Boston King was the son of a slave captured in Africa and transported to South Carolina, where King was born. King remembered that his father was "beloved" by his master for the managerial skills he demonstrated, and that his mother, a seamstress, was "indulged with many privileges which the rest of the slaves were not." King benefited from his parents' comparatively high standing. He never spent a day working in the fields, and as a child became something of a pet around his master's house. As he grew older he was given a man's work, tending his master's prize racehorses. His position pleased him but inspired resentment among those he worked with. "Happening one time to lose a boot belonging to the groom," King recalled, "he would not suffer me to have any shoes all that winter, which was a great punishment to me."

King turned sixteen the year the American colonies declared their independence. He was apprenticed to a tradesman, who sometimes treated him roughly. "I had the charge of my master's tools, which being very good, were often used by the men, if I happened to be out of the way," he recounted. "When this was the case, or any of them were lost or misplaced, my master beat me severely, striking me upon my head, or any other part without mercy." Once, during a holiday season, the master's shop was broken into and some valuable items were taken. "When I came home in the evening and saw what had happened, my consternation was inconceivable," King recalled. As well it might have been. "When the master came to town, I was beat in the most unmerciful manner, so that I was not able to do anything for a fortnight."

He first felt the effect of the war indirectly. "We were employed in building a storehouse, and nails were very dear at that time, it being in the American war, so that the workmen had their nails weighed out to them," he recalled. The workmen ordered the apprentices to watch their nails while they went to dinner. When it was King's turn to eat, he assigned the task to one of the more junior apprentices. His choice proved unfortunate when the apprentice absconded with the nails of one of the journeymen, who blamed King for the theft. "For this offense I was beat and tortured most cruelly, and was laid up three weeks before I was able to do any work," he remembered. King's owner heard of the mistreatment and rebuked the master tradesman. "This had a good effect and he behaved much better to me the two succeeding years, and I began to acquire a proper knowledge of my trade."

The war came closer. As it did, the chance that the slave of a Patriot might run off to the British increased. "My master, being apprehensive that Charles Town was in danger on account of the war, removed into the country, about 38 miles off," King recalled. For obvious reasons, Patriot owners didn't announce to their slaves that the British were offering freedom in exchange for military service, but the word got around. King bided his time, doubtless weighing his options. As the lives of slaves went, his wasn't intolerable. He couldn't know if a British promise could be relied on. Indeed, to the extent masters mentioned the British offer, once it couldn't be denied, they consistently contended that it could *not* be relied on. They said the fugitives would simply be enslaved by the British for their own use, or sold to the West Indies.

King obtained leave to visit his parents, who lived a dozen miles away. His master helped him borrow a horse. King intended to return. "But a servant of my master's took the horse from me to go a little journey, and stayed two or three days longer than he ought," King said. "This involved me in the greatest perplexity, and I expected the severest punishment, because the gentleman to whom the horse belonged was a very bad man, and knew not how to shew mercy." This was the nudge King needed. "To escape his cruelty, I determined to go to Charles Town, and throw myself into the hands of the English."

They were glad to see him. They gave him food and shelter. "I began to feel the happiness, liberty, of which I knew nothing before, although I was grieved at first to be obliged to leave my friends, and among strangers," King recalled.

But then he contracted smallpox. The British commanders quarantined the infected, lest they spread the disease. King suffered, along with the other sick ones. "We lay sometimes a whole day without any thing to eat or drink," he said. But he didn't die, and he gradually began to recover.

Yet his lingering symptoms saved him from capture and re-enslavement. The British army moved on, leaving the sick behind. A Patriot army arrived and would have seized any fugitive slaves. But when the Patriots learned that the camp they had discovered was for smallpox patients, they gave it a wide berth. Two days later, the British sent back wagons for the patients, and Boston King rejoined their army.

He was abandoned again a few months later, through inadvertence. Like many other escaped slaves, King was not assigned to a combat unit but placed in a support role. He was made the personal servant of a Captain Grey. King went fishing one afternoon, seeking supper for the captain, not to mention time to himself. While King was gone, the colonel of the regiment learned that a large Patriot force was nearby. The colonel gave the order to march at once. When Boston returned from his angling, the regiment was gone.

A Captain Lewes of Loyalist militia who had been traveling with the British regulars told King not to worry. King could become *his* servant, and would be protected.

King didn't like the sound of this offer. "I answered that I was Captain Grey's servant," he recounted.

"Yes," said Lewes. "But I expect they are all taken prisoners before now." Lewes added, "I have been long enough in the English service, and am determined to leave them."

King liked the proposition even less. He said he would not go with a deserter.

Lewes replied calmly, "If you do not behave well, I will put you in irons and give you a dozen stripes every morning."

The captain's threat underscored the precariousness of King's position and that of others like him. He was still in South Carolina, where he had been a slave. He had no papers from the British showing him to be a free man. If Lewes claimed King was his slave, King's denial would count little among other South Carolina whites.

King decided he had no choice but to play along. "I now perceived that my case was desperate, and that I had nothing to trust to, but to wait the first opportunity for making my escape." It came soon enough. "The next morning, I was sent with a little boy over the river to an island to fetch the captain some horses. When we came to the island, we found about fifty of the English horses, that Captain Lewes had stolen from them at different times." Lewes was not only a deserter but a horse thief.

King and the boy delivered the horses to Lewes, who soon rode off. King waited until he had been gone some time, and then headed in the direction the British army had marched. He covered twenty miles before evening. "I came to a farmer's house, where I tarried all night, and was well used," he remembered. King didn't say what story he told the farmer; possibly the farmer didn't ask.

The next morning he continued his journey, and caught up with Captain Grey and the British. "I informed my captain that Mr. Lewes had deserted. I also told him of the horses which Lewes had conveyed to the island." Grey appreciated the intelligence and put it to use against Lewes. "Three weeks after, our light-horse went to the island and burnt his house; they likewise brought back forty of the horses. But he escaped."

King remained with Grey nearly a year. For reasons he didn't explain, he left Grey's service and sought a new niche. He found one, with the commanding officer of a small garrison guarding a ferry. He soon began to regret his trade. "Our situation was very precarious, and we expected to be made prisoners every day, for the Americans had 1600 men not far off, whereas our whole number amounted only to 250." King's boss, if captured, could expect to be accorded the customs of war. King would fare far worse.

Yet help might be had. A British regiment was camped thirty miles away, across territory held by the Patriots. "Our commander at length determined to send me with a letter, promising me great rewards if I was successful in the business," King recalled. The commander offered a horse; King refused it as too likely to draw attention.

He set off afoot at three in the afternoon. "I expected every moment to fall in with the enemy, whom I well knew would shew me no mercy," he said. The first several hours went well. Then King heard a commotion on the road ahead. He spied a band of Patriots on horseback galloping his way. "I stepped out of the road, and fell flat upon my face till they were gone by." A religious man, King thanked God for having spared him. He proceeded, his ear cocked for the return of the Patriots.

After nightfall he reached a crossroads tavern. He cautiously tapped on the door. The light inside at once went out. He tapped again, and asked the master of the place to let him in.

After a long moment, the door cracked open. To King's relief, the owner was a Loyalist. "I thought it was the Americans," the innkeeper said. "For they were here about an hour ago, and I thought they were returned again."

King asked how many the Americans were.

About a hundred, he was told.

King asked the man for a horse. The man agreed, and said he'd go with him. Likely he didn't trust King to return the animal.

In a few miles they reached the pickets at the edge of the British camp. King explained his mission, and was taken to the commander. "He received me with great kindness, and expressed his approbation of my courage and conduct in this dangerous business." The next day King was handed three shillings for his trouble, while the regiment marched to the relief of King's unit back at the ferry.

In time King once more left his boss and found a new berth, this time on a British man-of-war anchored at Charleston. The ship sailed north and captured an American merchant vessel off Chesapeake Bay. King jumped ship at New York, where he sought work in the building trade. But because he lacked tools and obvious expertise, he received no offers. He took a job as a household servant. He discovered that life in New York could be hard. "The wages were so low that I was not able to keep myself in clothes," he said. He found another job, with a different master. "I stayed with him four months, but he never paid me, and I was obliged to leave him also."

Yet in New York under British rule, King was a free man, as his ability to leave his masters demonstrated. He married, again without asking permission of anyone, besides his intended. He fell ill and languished for five weeks. "But the Lord raised me up again," he wrote.

He worked on a pilot boat out of New York harbor. "We were at sea eight days and had only provisions for five, so that we were in danger of starving," he recalled. On the ninth day they spotted an American whaleboat, which took them in. "I went on board them with a cheerful countenance, and asked for bread and water, and made very free with them," King said. But they didn't reciprocate, and he soon realized he was being enslaved once more.

Yet slavery in New Jersey, where the boat landed, wasn't like slavery in South Carolina. "My master used me as well as I could expect," King said. "And indeed the slaves about Baltimore, Philadelphia, and New York have as good victuals as many of the English, for they have meat once a day, and milk for breakfast and supper, and what is better than all, many of the masters send their slaves to school at night, that they may learn to read the Scriptures. This is a privilege indeed."

Yet it wasn't freedom. "All these enjoyments could not satisfy me without liberty," King said. "Sometimes I thought, if it was the will of God that I should be a slave, I was ready to resign myself to his will; but at other times I could not find the least desire to content myself in slavery."

He knew if he could get back to New York he would again be free. The Hudson River was wide and daunting, but a much smaller channel separated the Jersey shore from Staten Island, also under British control. In spare moments, King surveyed the locations from which a crossing might be attempted. One dark night he made his way to the water's edge, stole a boat, and rowed himself over. Presenting himself to a British sentry, he told his story. He was given a British passport and permitted to travel to New York.

"My friends rejoiced to see me once more restored to liberty, and joined me in praising the Lord for his mercy and goodness," King recounted.

AS UNCERTAIN AS THE FATE of a slave-turned-Loyalist could be at times, it was straightforward by comparison with slaves who fought for the Patriots. Jeffrey Brace—the name he adopted in America—had been born free in West Africa, captured in a slave raid, marched in chains to the coast and shipped across the Atlantic to America. He was sold from one owner to the next and often treated badly, even for a slave. He later recalled being whipped daily, sometimes more than once per day. His luck changed when he was purchased by Mary Stiles, a widow living in Woodbury, Connecticut. "This was a glorious era in my life, as widow Stiles was one of the finest women in the world," Brace wrote later. "She possessed every Christian virtue." Mary Stiles taught him to read and instructed him in the Christian gospel.

After sixteen years with Mary Stiles, Brace's luck changed again, for the worse. She died, and the American Revolution broke out. "I descended in fee simple, like real estate, to her son, Benjamin Stiles," Brace recounted. Benjamin Stiles joined the Patriot cause and took Brace with him. Brace noted the irony. "Alas!" he said. "Poor African slave to liberate freemen, my tyrants."

Brace was a large man, six feet three inches tall. He was assigned to the infantry, which valued size in soldiers. Brace participated in the New York campaign, retreating with George Washington to Manhattan and then to White Plains. Brace's superiors set him to foraging behind enemy lines. "I was one of a hundred selected for the purpose of plundering a certain British store, which was completed without the loss of a single man, but with the gain of seven loads of excellent provisions."

On the retreat from the city, Brace's regiment was overtaken by British troops. "The party that pursued us were 60 light dragoons, whom we saluted so warmly with a well aimed fire that they were obliged to return for additional force."

Brace and his comrades saw little action during the next few months, and so created their own. "The soldiers played many boyish pranks," he recalled. One named Shaw was an accomplished petty thief, who enlisted Brace's cooperation. "He with myself and some others from our camp, the day before we were to be reviewed by His Excellency General George Washington, concluded we were to have a soldier-like frolic. Accordingly we secretly stole from the lines, went to a farm not many miles distant, which was occupied by a Tory. From him we stole a shoat." They arrived back at camp just before daybreak.

They laid out their prize for all to see. But before they could butcher the animal, they heard its owner approaching. "We soon saw the frothing Tory coming for his hog," Brace recounted. Brace and Shaw covered themselves with their blankets and pretended to be asleep. The owner, spotting his property, frothed the more and insisted on seeing the colonel of the regiment. He told his story, and the colonel strode angrily to Brace's company, prepared to punish the miscreants. He demanded to know how the animal had come to the camp.

"I answered immediately that the owner had brought it for sale," Brace recounted. "But that from his manner of conversation (and knowing him to have been a Tory), we unanimously suspected him to have come as a spy, and were determined to keep the shoat until the officers might have an opportunity of being acquainted with his designs."

Brace's comrades nodded agreement with his lie, convincingly enough that the colonel turned upon the Tory and chastised him for impugning the integrity of the regiment. "The man, a little frightened at so unexpected a charge of guilt that he really had the appearance of a condemned culprit, was glad to escape with his dead pig upon his back."

Shaw was undaunted by the close call. A few days later he led Brace and some others on another foraging expedition. "Shaw went to a Dutchman's house not far distant and with artful affection of great fatigue and an ingenious representation of his sufferings excited the old lady compassion to a great degree," Brace recalled. "And she offered him a bottle of rum. He took a good draught of rum and pretended to be greatly strangled. The woman, pitying his situation, went to the well for water." Shaw exploited her absence to snatch a ham hanging in the corner by the chimney and stuff it in his knapsack. She returned and didn't miss the ham, so worried was she that he might choke to death. He drank the water and said he was all right again. She gave him bread and milk, and while she was serving him, he pocketed several pieces of her tableware. Brace and the others, observing the performance, asked Shaw on departure how he could justify treating this kind woman so badly. "He said he had long known the old Dutchman to aid and assist the British, or he could not have had a heart to do it, which account of the Dutchman we afterwards learned was correct," Brace wrote.

Theft sometimes worked in the opposite direction. A Loyalist group stole a small herd of cattle from the lines of Brace's Patriots. Brace and two other men were dispatched to retrieve the animals. They headed down the road they thought the rustlers had taken. "We came to a small hill or rise of land over which they must have passed," Brace said. "This rise being covered with bushes, it was thought prudent that I should wait upon the hither side of the hill while they went over."

But he waited too long. "I suddenly saw a man riding up to me not more than eight rods distant on full speed with a pistol in his hand," Brace wrote. The man ordered Brace to drop his weapons. Brace refused. "At first I thought he was a Jerseyman"—and fellow Patriot— "and was attempting to fool me." Black soldiers were the objects of more than their share of practical jokes.

"Therefore in return I demanded to whom I was to surrender and by what authority he demanded it," Brace wrote.

"He said I must surrender to him who demanded me in the name of the King his majesty of Great Britain."

Brace replied that he wasn't about to surrender to any lackey of the British king.

"He immediately cocked his pistol and fired. I fell flat upon the ground in order to dodge his ball." The ball missed. "I rose; he drew his sword and rode up to me so quick that I had no time to take aim before he struck my gun barrel with his cutlass, and cut it almost one third off—also cut off the bone of my middle finger on my hand." The attacker wheeled his horse to come at Brace again. But Brace fired his cut-off gun and killed the man.

"As he fell I caught his horse and sword," Brace wrote. "He was a British light horseman in disguise. I mounted immediately, and that instant discovered four men on horseback approaching me from different directions." Brace picked one of the four and galloped straight toward him, swerving only at the last second.

The British horseman fired as Brace passed, but missed. He turned, and the other three, now augmented by additional horsemen, tore after Brace. A stone wall stood in Brace's way; he urged his captured steed forward, and the animal leaped the wall. His pursuers pressed closer behind. "I drove my horse as fast as possible, stabbed him with my sword and gun, kicked my heels in his side; but having no spurs, and not being so good a horseman, they gained upon me."

Brace saw his Patriot comrades ahead, about a mile off. He kicked and jabbed his horse the more. The captain of his company ordered the men to fire at the British soldiers pursuing Brace, but to miss him. They got it barely right. "The men fired, and three balls cut my garments," Brace said. "One struck my coat sleeve, the next hit my bayonet belt, and the third went through the back side of my leather cap." The British didn't get off so easily. "The same fire killed four of the

British and five of their horses, and wounded some more." The survivors beat a hasty retreat.

Brace continued into camp. Only then did he realize he'd been wounded on the hand. "Slight fear and precipitation had turned me almost as white as my fellow soldiers," he remarked.

The wound laid him up for months. At first he thought he'd gained a horse and sword by the scrape. "But after all the poor Negro was cheated out of his horse," he observed afterward. He accepted an officer's promise to pay two hundred and fifty dollars for the horse, sword, saddle and bridle. The officer took the horse and gear, but never paid. Brace was compelled to be philosophical about the matter. "I felt more gratitude towards the horse than regret for the loss of him, as he with the assistance of divine providence saved my life."

With time to reflect, Brace pondered why the band of British horsemen had not fired at him. "I presume they chose to take me alive, which they had full faith in, as when our men fired upon them they were fast approaching me," he wrote. He surmised that the British wanted to squeeze him for intelligence about the disposition of American forces in the area. Possibly they thought that as a black man and presumptive slave, he could be enticed to talk by the British offer of freedom. On the other hand, his freedom might not have been in their minds at all. "Perhaps the soldiers thought I might be sold by them and enrich their coffers."

Brace saw action in several engagements in New York and New Jersey. His company was alerted that British forces were approaching Stanford, New York. "We marched there immediately and arrived before them," Brace remembered. "A party marched down into some meadows to watch their motion; on discovering their superior force, we fired upon them and ran off, fully believing 'That he who fights and runs away / May live to fight another day.'" He had some other close calls, including one in which a bullet pierced his knapsack but missed his flesh.

Brace remained under arms until the war's end. "Thus was I, a slave, for five years fighting for liberty," he reflected.

Part XI

Never a Good War

B ENJAMIN FRANKLIN GOT the news of Yorktown and wrote back congratulations to Washington and his army. "All the world agree that no expedition was ever better planned or better executed," he told Washington. "It has made a great addition to the military reputation you had already acquired, and brightens the glory that surrounds your name and that must accompany it to our latest posterity. No news could possibly make me more happy. The infant Hercules has now strangled the two serpents that attacked him in his cradle, and I trust his future history will be answerable."

The way forward wasn't yet clear, though. The crushing defeat of Cornwallis at Yorktown had discredited the war government of Lord North and strengthened the peace party of his opponents. But what this meant for America, or even for Britain, remained murky. "The English seem not to know either how to continue the war or to make peace with us," Franklin told Washington. "Instead of entering into a regular treaty for putting an end to a contest they are tired of, they have voted in Parliament that the recovery of America by force is impracticable, that an offensive war against us ought not to be continued, and that whoever advises it shall be deemed an enemy to his country. Thus the garrisons of New York and Charlestown"—where the British still rested securely—"if continued there, must sit still, being only allowed to defend themselves." A change of government in London was occurring, but it was far from finished. "The ministry, not understanding or approving this making of peaces by halves, have quitted their places, but we have no certain account here who is to succeed them, so that the measures likely to be taken are yet uncertain."

Franklin urged Washington to keep his powder dry. "There are grounds for good hopes," he said. "But I think we should not therefore relax in our preparations for a vigorous campaign, as that nation is subject to sudden fluctuations; and though somewhat humiliated at present, a little success in the West Indies may dissipate their present fears, recall their natural insolence, and occasion the interruption of negotiation and a continuance of the war."

A week later the prospects had become slightly clearer. The North government was replaced by one headed by Lord Rockingham, with Lord Shelburne as secretary of state for home and colonial affairs and Charles Fox as foreign secretary. Franklin relayed the news to Washington. "I have heretofore congratulated your Excellency on your victories over our enemy's *generals*," he said. "I can now do the same on your having overthrown their *politicians*. Your late successes have so strengthened the hands of opposition in Parliament that they are become the majority and have compelled the king to dismiss all his old ministers and their adherents. The unclean spirits he was possessed with are now cast out of him." This would be good for America, Franklin judged, though it would do little for Britain. "It is imagined that as soon as he has obtained a peace, they will return with others worse than themselves, and *the last state of that man,* as the Scripture says, *shall be worse than the first.*"

Franklin hoped for the best from the new ministry but let the British know that the burden was on them to show they sincerely sought peace. David Hartley shared news of the debates and votes in Parliament; Franklin read the accounts with skepticism born of experience. "I am pleased to see in the votes and parliamentary speeches, and in your public papers, that in mentioning America, the word *reconciliation* is often used," Franklin replied to Hartley. "It is a sweet expression." It meant more than peace, and certainly more than a mere cessation of hostilities, Franklin said. "Resolve in your mind, my dear friend, the means of bringing about this *reconciliation.* When you consider the injustice of your war with us, and the barbarous manner in which it has been carried on, the many suffering families among us from your burnings of towns, scalpings by savages etc. etc., will it not appear to you that though a cessation of the war may be a peace, it may not be a reconciliation? Will not some voluntary acts of justice and even of kindness on your part have excellent effects towards producing such a reconciliation? Can you not find means of repairing in some degree those injuries?"

Franklin spoke from the heart here; he still considered the British morally culpable for the war. But he also spoke for the benefit of the new government in London, to which Hartley had close ties. By introducing the issue of reparations, Franklin laid down a marker for the negotiations about to begin. Through Hartley as well, Franklin signaled that any effort by the British to drive a wedge between America and France would fail. "The project of dividing us is as vain as it would be to us injurious," Franklin said. France had stood by America in the war; America would stand by France in the peace.

Franklin's distrust of the British softened a bit after the arrival of an envoy from the new government. Richard Oswald impressed Franklin at once. "I have conversed a good deal with Mr. Oswald and am much pleased with him," Franklin wrote to Shelburne. "He appears to me a wise and honest man." Oswald had instructions to meet Franklin, sound him out, and return to London to brief the ministers. Franklin sent along a letter to Shelburne indicating a belief that the peace talks were off to a promising start. "He will be witness of my acting with all the simplicity and good faith which you do me the honour to expect from me; and if he is enabled when he returns hither to communicate more fully your Lordship's mind on the principal points to be settled, I think it may contribute much to expedite the blessed work our hearts are engaged in."

In the interests of allied solidarity, Franklin shared with Vergennes what he and Oswald had talked about. "He tells me that there has been a desire"—in Britain—"of making a separate peace with America and of continuing the war with France and Spain, but that now all wise people give up that idea as impracticable," Franklin wrote to Vergennes. "And it is his private opinion that the ministry do sincerely desire a *general peace,* and that they will readily come into it provided France does not insist upon conditions too humiliating for England, in which case she will make great and violent efforts rather than submit to them, and that much is still in her power, etc. I told the gentleman that I could not enter into particulars with him but in concert with the ministers of this court"—the French court.

But Franklin didn't tell Vergennes *everything* he and Oswald had talked about. The Continental Congress—now sometimes called the Confederation Congress, after the ratification of the Articles of Confederation in March 1781—had appointed four other men to join Franklin as peace commissioners. John Adams was currently in the

Netherlands, seeking Dutch money to cover the debts America had incurred fighting the war. John Jay was en route. Henry Laurens still languished in the Tower of London. Thomas Jefferson hadn't decided whether to accept the appointment. Franklin was closest to Adams, by geographic proximity and through prior work together. Franklin kept Adams apprised of what was happening in Paris. He sent copies of his correspondence with Shelburne and Vergennes. "These papers will inform you pretty well of what passed between me and Mr. Oswald," Franklin wrote to Adams in a cover letter, "except that in a conversation at parting I mentioned to him that I observed they spoke much in England of obtaining a *reconciliation* with the colonies; that this was more than a mere *peace;* that the latter might possibly be obtained without the former; that the cruel injuries wantonly done us by burning our towns etc. had made deep impressions of resentment which would long remain; that much of the advantage to the commerce of England from a peace would depend on a *reconciliation;* that the peace without a reconciliation would probably not be durable; that after a quarrel between friends, nothing tended so much to *conciliate* as offers made by the aggressor of reparation for injuries done by him in his passion." This was more or less what Franklin had told David Hartley. Then came something new. "I hinted that if England should make us a *voluntary offer* of Canada expressly for that purpose, it might have a good effect. Mr. Oswald liked much the idea, said they were too much straitened for money to make us pecuniary reparation, but he should endeavour to persuade their doing it in this way."

Oswald liked the idea of Canada as reparations well enough that he asked Franklin if he might take back to London a paper Franklin had composed summarizing his argument on this point. Franklin consented. "To make a peace durable, what may give occasion for future wars should, if practicable, be removed," Franklin's paper said. "The territory of the United States and that of Canada, by long extended frontiers, touch each other. The settlers on the frontiers of the American provinces are generally the most disorderly of the people, who being far removed from the eye and control of their respective governments, are more bold in committing offences against neighbours, and are forever occasioning complaints and furnishing matter for fresh differences between their states." Franklin returned to the difference between peace and reconciliation, asserting that the latter was crucial to the permanence of the former. "Nations may make a peace whenever they are both weary of making war. But if one of them has made war upon the other unjustly, and has wantonly and unnecessarily done it great injuries, and refuses reparation, though there may for the present be peace, the resentment of those injuries will remain and will break out again in vengeance when occasions offer. These occasions will be watched for by one side, feared by the other, and the peace will never be secure."

The British had committed wanton injury upon the Americans, Franklin said. "Many houses and villages have been burnt in America by the English and their allies the Indians." This was where reparations came in. "I do not know that the Americans will insist on reparation. Perhaps they may. But would it not be better for England to offer it? Nothing could have a greater tendency to conciliate. And much of the future commerce and returning intercourse between the two countries may depend on the reconciliation. Would not the advantage of reconciliation by such means be greater than the expence? If then a way can be proposed which may tend to efface the memory of injuries, at the same time that it takes away the occasions of fresh quarrel and mischief, will it not be worth considering, especially if it can be done not only without expence but be a means of saving?"

Franklin explained: "Britain possesses Canada. Her chief advantage from that possession consists in the trade for peltry. Her expences in governing and defending that settlement must be considerable. It might be humiliating to her to give it up on the demand of America. Perhaps America will not demand it: Some of her politic rulers may consider the fear of such a neighbour as a means of keeping the 13 states more united among themselves, and more attentive to military discipline. But on the minds of the people in general, would it not have an excellent effect, if Britain should voluntarily offer to give up this province; though on these conditions: that she shall in all times coming have and enjoy the right of free trade thither, unencumbered with any duties whatsoever, and that so much of the vacant lands there shall be sold as will raise a sum sufficient to pay for the houses burnt by the British troops and their Indians, and also to indemnify the royalists for the confiscation of their estates."

Shelburne was less taken with Franklin's argument than Oswald had seemed to be. "His Lordship indeed said he had not imagined reparation would be expected," Oswald told Franklin when once again in Paris. Speaking for himself, apparently, Oswald thought Franklin should drop the subject for the time being. "It seemed to have made an impression," Oswald said, in Franklin's recounting. "And he had reason to believe that matter might be settled to our satisfaction towards the end of the treaty, but in his own mind he wished it might not be mentioned at the beginning."

Oswald brought back another bit of news: that he would be joined on the British side by a second negotiator, Thomas Grenville. The family name put Franklin off; he remembered the abuse he had received at the hands of George Grenville at the time of the Stamp Act. Thomas Grenville was George Grenville's son.

The younger Grenville arrived shortly, bringing a letter of introduction from Charles Fox. The introduction increased Franklin's distrust, by suggesting that Grenville was Fox's man, in contrast to Oswald as Shelburne's. Franklin didn't like the idea of having to negotiate with two separate counterparties.

Thomas Grenville tried to ease Franklin's concerns. And he succeeded, to some extent. Grenville called on Franklin and requested an introduction to Vergennes. Franklin agreed. "I then entered into conversation with him on the subject of his mission," Franklin noted. Fox's letter had said Grenville was thoroughly acquainted with Fox's views on the peace negotiations. Grenville spoke forthrightly. "He said that peace was really wished for by everybody, if it could be obtained on reasonable terms; and as the idea of subjugating America was given up, and both France and America had thereby obtained what they had in view originally, it was hoped that there now remained no obstacle to a pacification."

Franklin invited his visitor to remain for dinner. "This gave me an opportunity of a good deal of general conversation with Mr. Grenville, who appeared to me a sensible, judicious, intelligent, good tempered and well instructed young man," Franklin observed.

Grenville—who was indeed young, a mere twenty-six—continued to impress Franklin. They went together to see Vergennes. The French minister received Grenville cordially, recalling the time he—Vergennes—had gotten to know Grenville's uncle when each had been his country's ambassador at Constantinople. Grenville reciprocated the good feeling.

He then launched into an exposition of what seemed to be Charles Fox's take on the peace negotiations. "In case England gave America independence, France it was expected would return the conquests she had made of British islands," Grenville said, in Franklin's recounting. "The original object of the war being obtained, it was supposed that France would be contented with that."

Franklin recounted Vergennes's reaction. "The minister seemed to smile at the proposed exchange, and remarked that the offer of giving independence to America amounted to little," Franklin wrote. "America, says he, does not ask it of you. There is Mr. Franklin, he will answer you as to that point."

Which Franklin did. "To be sure, I said, we do not consider ourselves as under any necessity of bargaining for a thing that is our own, and which we have bought at the expence of so much blood and treasure, and which we are in full possession of."

Vergennes resumed. "As to our being satisfied with the original object of the war," he said to Grenville, "look back to the conduct of your nation in former wars. In the last war, for example, what was the object? It was the disputed right to some waste lands on the Ohio and the frontiers of Nova Scotia. Did you content yourselves with the recovery of those lands? No, you retained at the peace all Canada, all Louisiana, all Florida, Grenada and other West-India islands, the greatest part of the northern fisheries, with all your conquests in Africa and the East Indies. It is not reasonable that a nation, after making an unprovoked, unsuccessful war upon its neighbours, should expect to sit down whole and have everything restored which she had lost in such a war."

Grenville countered that France had provoked the war by encouraging the Americans to revolt.

"On which M. de Vergennes grew a little warm," Franklin recorded, "and declared firmly that the breach was made and our independence declared long before we received the least encouragement from France, and he defied the world to give the smallest proof of the contrary. There sits, says he, Mr. Franklin, who knows the fact and will contradict me if I do not speak the truth."

Vergennes's show of temper silenced Grenville on this point, without convincing him. "On our return"—to Franklin's residence—"Mr. Grenville expressed himself as not quite satisfied with some part of M. de Vergennes' discourse, and was thoughtful," Franklin wrote.

Franklin understood the source of Grenville's dissatisfaction. Vergennes spoke a narrow truth in saying France hadn't encouraged American independence. The government of France had kept out of the Anglo-American quarrel until after the Declaration of Independence, but it had allowed, even encouraged, private individuals like Pierre Beaumarchais to offer informal assistance. Franklin declined to enlighten Grenville on the subject, leaving the young man to his unsatisfied thoughts.

Grenville subsequently met with Franklin again alone. He worked hard to draw Franklin and the Americans away from France, making the case that America's interests were no longer France's, now that America had won its independence. America must look to its own interests, for France would certainly look to *its* own.

Franklin rejoined that America's alliance with France entailed more than interest, materially construed. "I gave him a little more of my sentiments on the general subject of benefits, obligations and gratitude," Franklin recorded. "I said I thought people had often imperfect notions of their duty on those points, and that a state of obligation was to many so uneasy a state that they became ingenious in finding out reasons and arguments to prove they had been laid under no obligation at all, or that they had discharged it; and that they too easily satisfied themselves with such arguments." Franklin provided an example. "A, a stranger to B, sees him about to be imprisoned for a debt by a merciless creditor. He lends him the sum necessary to preserve his liberty. B then becomes the debtor of A, and after some time repays the money. Has he then discharged the obligation? No. He has discharged the money debt, but the obligation remains, and he is a debtor for the kindness of A in lending the sum so seasonably. If B should afterwards find A in the same circumstances that he, B, had been in when A lent him the money, he may then discharge this obligation, or debt of kindness, *in part*, by lending him an equal sum. *In part*, I said, and not wholly, because when A lent B the money, there had been no prior benefit received to induce him to it. And therefore if A should a second time need the same assistance, I thought B, if in his power, was in duty bound to afford it to him."

Grenville answered that it was carrying gratitude quite far to apply Franklin's reasoning to relations between states. French assistance to America served the interest of France as much as that of America. "It lessened the power of her rival and relatively increased her own," he said.

Franklin waved the objection aside. "I told him I was so strongly impressed with the kind assistance afforded us by France in our distress, and the generous and noble manner in which it was granted, without exacting or stipulating for a single privilege or particular advantage to herself in our commerce or otherwise, that I could never suffer myself to think of such reasonings for lessening the obligation, and I hoped and indeed did not doubt but my countrymen were all of the same sentiments."

Grenville remained dissatisfied, but now with Franklin. "We parted, however, in good humour," Franklin said. "His conversation is always polite and his manner pleasing."

IN PARIS, and in parts of America, it was possible to think the war had ended. The British had suspended combat operations in the United States, though they still occupied New York and Charleston. But the British war against France and Spain continued, sometimes fitfully, sometimes dramatically. In April 1782 the British got revenge for their defeat off the Virginia capes at the hands of Admiral de Grasse and the French navy, in a battle in the West Indies. There the British dealt de Grasse a devastating defeat, sinking one French warship, capturing four others, including de Grasse's flagship, and capturing de Grasse himself.

When the news of the French defeat reached London and Paris six weeks later, it bolstered British spirits and enervated the French. The French government came to the same conclusion the British government had reached after Yorktown: that the war had become a losing proposition, and the sooner it ended, the better.

Until this point, the French had insisted that the Americans honor their treaty with France by refusing to negotiate with Britain except in partnership with France. Franklin had accepted and defended this position to the British. Now French thinking changed. Separate agreements would come more easily than a comprehensive pact, Vergennes concluded. He informed Franklin of the shift, couching it in terms of respect for America's independence. "They want to treat with us for you," Vergennes said, referring to British diplomats who hadn't actually made such a demand. "But this the King will not agree to. He thinks it not consistent with the dignity of your state. You will treat for yourselves. And every one of the powers at war with England will make its own treaty. All that is necessary to be observed for our common security is that the treaties go hand in hand, and are signed all on the same day."

The French decision simplified Franklin's task. He could concentrate on America's interests without worrying about what any particular element of a peace deal would mean for the French. Vergennes and King Louis would still have to approve a final settlement, but a final package would be easier to defend than all the separate parts that went into it.

There remained the question, for Franklin, of who spoke for the British: Oswald or Grenville. He liked them both but found Oswald easier to deal with. "Mr. Oswald came according to appointment," Franklin wrote after a meeting in early June. He was just back from London. "He told me he had seen and had conversations with Lord Shelburne, Lord Rockingham, and Mr. Fox. That their desire of peace continued uniformly the same, though he thought some of them were a little too much elated with the late victory in the West Indies; and when observing his coolness, they asked him if he did not think it a very good thing; yes says he, if you do not rate it too high. He went on with the utmost frankness to tell me that peace was absolutely necessary for them. That the nation had been foolishly involved in four wars and could no longer raise money to carry them on." This severely crimped Britain's ability to keep fighting. "Our enemies may now do what they please with us," he told Franklin. "They have the ball at their foot. And we hope they will show their moderation and their magnanimity."

In a tone of equal candor, Oswald let Franklin know that the government in London was counting on him—Franklin—to move the negotiations forward. "They, with all the considerate people of England looked to and depended on me for the means of extricating the nation from its present desperate situation," he said, in Franklin's recounting. "Perhaps no single man had ever in his hands an opportunity of doing so much good as I had at this present."

Franklin realized he was being flattered. He hoped, and believed, he was beyond such influence. "The time has been when such flattering language as from great men might have made me vainer and had more effect on my conduct than it can at present, when I find myself so near the end of life as to esteem lightly all personal interests and concerns, except that of maintaining to the last and leaving behind me the tolerably good character I have hitherto supported," he remarked to himself.

Oswald showed Franklin a memorandum from Shelburne laying out the British government's current position on negotiations. "On our part commissioners will be named, or any character given to Mr. Oswald, which Dr. Franklin and he may judge conducive to a final settlements of things between Great Britain and America, which Dr. Franklin very properly says requires to be treated in a very different manner from the peace between Great Britain and France, which have always been at enmity with each other," Shelburne's memo said.

A second point involved the American Loyalists. "An establishment for the Loyalists must always be upon Mr. Oswald's mind, as it is uppermost in Lord Shelburne's, besides other steps in their favour, to influence the several states to agree to a fair restoration or compensation for whatever confiscations have taken place," the memo asserted. Franklin had raised the issue of reparations; Shelburne wanted him to know two could play that game.

Franklin listened attentively. He had *not* argued for separate negotiations between Britain and the United States, as Shelburne stated, but he was willing to pursue them now that Vergennes had dropped the French objection. As for restoration of the property of the Loyalists, Franklin read it as the obvious counter to his Canada demand. The serious bargaining had begun.

In response to Shelburne's memo, Franklin produced a list of American requirements, which he shared orally with Oswald. "Some he said as necessary for them to insist," Oswald reported to Shelburne; "others which he could not say he had any orders about, or were not absolutely demanded, and yet such as would be advisable for England to offer for the sake of reconciliation and her future interest."

Heading the necessary category was the obvious one: "Independence full and complete in every sense to the thirteen states, and all troops to be withdrawn from thence."

Next: "A settlement of the boundaries of their colonies, and the loyal colonies." That is, an agreement on the southern boundary of

Canada, preferably where it was located in 1763, before Canada was expanded under the 1774 Quebec Act.

Finally, an agreement on fishing rights on the banks of Newfoundland. "I own I wondered he should have thought it necessary to ask for this privilege," Oswald remarked to Shelburne. Franklin hadn't mentioned it before.

As to the advisable articles—"or such as he would as a friend recommend to be offered by England," per Oswald's description of Franklin's characterization—the first was reparations, "to indemnify many people who had been ruined by towns burnt and destroyed." Franklin suggested a figure of five or six hundred thousand pounds. "I was struck by this," Oswald remarked. "However, the Doctor said, though it was a large sum it would not be ill-bestowed, as it would conciliate the resentment of a multitude of poor sufferers who could have no other remedy and who, without some relief, would keep up a spirit of secret revenge and animosity for a long time to come against Great Britain, whereas a voluntary offer of such reparation would diffuse a universal calm and conciliation over the whole country."

Second of the advisables was "some sort of acknowledgment in some public act of Parliament or otherwise of our error in distressing those countries so much as we had done. A few words of that kind, the Doctor said, would do more good than people could imagine."

Third, free trade with Britain, as before the troubles that had produced the revolution.

Fourth and last: "Giving up every part of Canada." Franklin had already explained this, and added little more.

Oswald was encouraged. "From this conversation I have some hopes, my Lord, that it is possible to put an end to the American quarrel in a short time," he wrote to Shelburne.

The next day Oswald sent Shelburne a postscript regarding his conversation with Franklin. Oswald knew that Franklin's gout and kidney stones had been bothering him lately; a Franklin associate had commented to Oswald that Franklin was feeling his age more than ever. "This, the gentleman told me, led the Doctor to express himself very strongly as to his desire of quick dispatch, as he wanted much to go home and have the chance of a few years repose, having but a short time to live in the world, and had also much private business to do," Oswald wrote to Shelburne. "I should therefore hope it may be possible soon to bring their business near to a final close, and that they will not be any way stiff as to those articles he calls *advisable*, or will drop them altogether. Those he calls necessary will hardly be any obstacle."

AS THINGS HAPPENED, it wasn't Franklin's health that influenced the course of the negotiations so much as the health of Lord Rockingham. The British prime minister contracted a wicked strain of influenza that was sweeping across Europe and suddenly died. Shelburne became prime minister, and the added responsibilities diverted him from strict attention to the negotiations in Paris.

The arrival of John Adams in Paris didn't help matters. His chronic grumpiness hadn't improved on the trip from the Hague. "I have several times performed this journey of about three hundred and twenty-five miles in three days," he recorded. "But rains of unusual violence and duration had ruined the roads in such a manner that though the utmost diligence was employed, and no expence in horses or anything else was spared to hasten our progress, we could not arrive one moment sooner. We were dragged by the strength of six horses so often through the mire that our carriage, though a very strong one, was broken, and we obliged to wait until it could be repaired."

Adams disliked the French capital and its ways as much as ever. "The first thing essential to be done in Paris is always to send for a tailor, peruke-maker and shoe-maker, for this nation has established such a domination over the fashion that neither clothes, wigs nor shoes made in any other country will be tolerated in Paris or Versailles," he wrote. "This is one of the modes in which France taxes all Europe, and will tax America. It is a great branch of the policy of the court to preserve and increase this national influence over the ton, because it occasions an immense commerce between France and all the other parts of Europe. Paris furnishes the materials and the air, the manner and the grace, both to men and women everywhere else."

John Jay had arrived; Thomas Jefferson and Henry Laurens had not. So Adams would join Jay and Franklin as the American commissioners to negotiate the treaty. Adams characteristically distrusted anyone but himself. "Between two as subtle spirits as any in this world, the one malicious, the other I believe honest, I shall have a delicate, a nice, a critical part to act," he said. Franklin was the malicious one.

"Franklin's cunning will be to divide us. To this end he will provoke, he will insinuate, he will intrigue, he will manoeuvre. My curiosity will at least be employed in observing his invention and his artifice."

From a distance Adams had concluded that Franklin lacked the will or the energy to stand up to the British. He also believed, somewhat paradoxically, that Franklin was too lenient toward the French. In any event, the negotiations required the principled firmness on which he most prided himself. And he decided that Jay, however subtle, would be his ally against Franklin. Jay at least was honest and devoted to America. A close associate of Jay told Adams, "Mr. Jay declares roundly that he will never set his hand to a bad peace. Congress may appoint another minister, but he will make a good peace or none." Adams recorded, "To this resolution my heart and voice pronounced a devout amen."

Adams warmed to Jay on another point. Each was a reflexive Francophobe. "He says they are not a moral people," Adams wrote in his diary. "They know not what it is. He don't like any Frenchman. The Marquis de la Fayette is clever, but he is a Frenchman. Our allies don't play fair, he told me. They were endeavouring to deprive us of the fishery, the western lands, and the navigation of the Mississippi. They would even bargain with the English to deprive us of them. They want to play the western lands, Mississippi and whole Gulf of Mexico into the hands of Spain."

Jay could be as skeptical of Franklin as Adams was, but on this last point he had no worries. When Jay had been in Spain seeking money to fund the American war effort, and the Spanish had suggested that land in the Mississippi Valley would be suitable compensation, Franklin insisted that Jay hold firm. "Poor as we are, yet as I know we shall be rich, I would rather agree with them to buy at a great price the whole of their right on the Mississippi than sell a drop of its waters," he said. "A neighbour might as well ask me to sell my street door."

Franklin told Adams much the same thing, adding the fisheries for geographic balance. "The fisheries and Mississippi could not be given up," Franklin said to Adams, in Adams's retelling. "Nothing was clearer to him than that the fisheries were essential to the northern states, and the Mississippi to the southern, and indeed both to all."

Nonetheless, Franklin didn't spend much time haggling over fish, which in those days were understood to include whales. He hadn't identified with New England since fleeing Boston at seventeen, and cod and whales meant much less to Philadelphians than to the Gloucestermen and Nantucketers of Adams's constituency. Franklin let Adams handle the piscine part of the negotiation, which Adams did with lawyerly tenacity.

In another area, Franklin was the most stubborn of the three commissioners. "Dr. Franklin is very staunch against the Tories, more decided a great deal on this point than Mr. Jay or myself," Adams observed. To Shelburne's demand for compensation to Loyalists whose property had been seized by American states, and to an additional demand that British creditors be able to collect what Americans owed them, Franklin responded that the cases weren't at all comparable. The British were to blame for the war; they couldn't expect to come out whole. As for the Loyalists, they were traitors to their own country. If British creditors or the Loyalists wanted compensation, they should look to the British government.

This was Franklin's personal view, reflecting the anger he still felt toward Britain. But in answering Shelburne, he made another argument. He said matters of compensation and debt were beyond the control of the American national government. The Congress lacked the authority to compel the states to do anything—witness the financial straits the national government had been in since the start of the revolution. The most the Congress might do would be to recommend to the states that they compensate the Loyalists and open their courts to British creditors. But the British government must understand that such recommendations had no binding force.

THIS SUITED SHELBURNE, who needed the political cover Franklin's formula provided, and it was written into the agreement concluded on November 30, 1782, between the American commissioners and their British counterparts. The agreement said that "creditors on either side shall meet with no lawful impediment" to the recovery of their debts, and that the Congress "shall earnestly recommend to the legislatures of the respective states" that they provide restitution to the Loyalists for confiscated property. Shelburne and the British, no less than Franklin and the Americans, understood the flimsiness of these formulations, but the wording served the political purpose of making the treaty palatable to both sides.

Richard Oswald turned out to have been right about Franklin's necessary and advisable provisions. The necessary ones—American independence, the old boundary of Canada, and fishing rights—were included in the treaty without difficulty. The advisable ones were dispensed with. Franklin had never really expected the British to apologize for the war, or to pay reparations. Free trade would happen or not, regardless of treaty. As for Canada, that had been a bargaining chip from the start. Franklin wasn't even sure he *wanted* Canada. Having tried and failed to talk the Canadians into joining America's revolution willingly, he couldn't in republican conscience insist they be handed forcibly over after the war.

Better than Canada was the boundary settlement in the West. The British agreed—for the same reasons Franklin had made regarding Canada—to deliver Ohio and the eastern half of the Mississippi Valley to the United States. Aside from independence, this was the most important provision of the treaty, for it guaranteed the future growth of America, along lines Franklin had sketched out a generation earlier. At that time he had hoped the growth would be within the British empire; now it would be the growth of an independent United States.

The agreement of November 1782 was formalized as the "Preliminary Articles of Peace" in January 1783. Getting to a full treaty required separate agreements among the other belligerents. Not until September 1783 would all those pieces be in place; ratification of the treaty would take months longer.

But Franklin was more than ready for the fighting to end. "I long with you for the return of peace, on the general principles of humanity," he wrote to Jonathan Shipley amid the negotiations. Franklin didn't regret having supported the struggle that yielded American independence, but he wished it hadn't been necessary. "After much occasion to consider the folly and mischiefs of a state of warfare, and the little or no advantage obtained even by those nations who have conducted it with the most success, I have been apt to think that there has never been or ever will be any such thing as a good war or a bad peace."

NEWS TRAVELED SLOWLY across the North Atlantic in winter. Word of the Paris accord hadn't reached America when
Washington sent ominous news to Joseph Jones, a Virginia delegate
to the Congress. "In the course of a few days Congress will, I expect,
receive an address from the army on the subject of their grievances,"
Washington wrote from Newburgh, New York, where the Continental
Army was wintering. "This address, though couched in very respectful terms, is one of those things which though unpleasing, is just now
unavoidable, for I was very apprehensive once that matters would have
taken a more unfavourable turn, from the variety of discontents which
prevailed at this time."

The lull in the fighting since Yorktown, rather than easing the tension in the ranks of the troops, had made it worse. They no longer had
the excitement of battle to engage their patriotic sentiments and distract them from their dissatisfaction at short rations and late pay. And
the Congress and the states, without the specter of imminent defeat
hanging over their heads, were stingier and tardier than ever. "The
temper of the army is much soured, and has become more irritable
than at any period since the commencement of the war," Washington
wrote. He had hoped to take his first leave of absence in more than
seven years and spend the winter at Mount Vernon. But he decided he
couldn't risk it. "The dissatisfactions of the army had arisen to a great
and alarming height, and combinations among the officers to resign in
a body, at given periods, were beginning to take place, when by some
address and management their resolutions have been converted into
the form in which they will now appear before Congress."

Washington hoped the Congress would deal prudently with his
soldiers' complaints. "Policy, in my opinion, should dictate soothing
measures, as it is an uncontrovertible fact that no part of the com-

munity has undergone equal hardships and borne them with the same patience and fortitude that the army has done," he told Jones. Washington thought the disquiet among the officers was especially significant. "Hitherto the officers have stood between the lower order of the soldiery and the public, and in more instances than one have quelled, at the hazard of their lives, very dangerous mutinies. But if their discontents should be suffered to rise equally high, I know not what the consequences may be."

The limbo of uncertainty regarding the war made everything worse. "We are held in a very disagreeable state of suspence," Washington wrote to his brother John in January 1783. "The army as usual is without pay, and a great part of the soldiery without shirts; and though the patience of them is equally threadbare, it seems to be a matter of small concern to those at a distance"—the members of the Congress. "In truth, if one was to hazard an opinion for them on this subject, it would be that the army having contracted a habit of encountering distress and difficulties and of living without money, it would be injurious to it to introduce other customs."

Alexander Hamilton shared Washington's jaundiced view of the Congress, despite being a member himself. The end of active fighting had been too much for Hamilton's impatience; he resigned his commission to start his civilian career, becoming a lawyer and, before long, a New York delegate to the Congress. He kept in touch with Washington, and amid the restiveness of the officers and men at Washington's camp, he refloated some of his earlier ideas about reforming the government. He asked for Washington's help in putting them into practice. "Flattering myself that your knowledge of me will induce you to receive the observations I make as dictated by a regard to the public good, I take the liberty to suggest to you my ideas on some matters of delicacy and importance," Hamilton wrote to Washington.

"I view the present juncture as a very interesting one," he continued. "I need not observe how far the temper and situation of the army make it so. The state of our finances was perhaps never more critical. I am under injunctions which will not permit me to disclose some facts that would at once demonstrate this position, but I think it probable you will be possessed of them through another channel. It is however certain that there has scarcely been a period of the revolution which called more for wisdom and decision in Congress. Unfortunately for us we are a body not governed by reason or foresight but by circumstances. It is probable we shall not take the proper measures, and if we do not a few months may open an embarrassing scene. This will be the case whether we have peace or a continuance of the war."

Hamilton projected two scenarios. "If the war continues, it would seem that the army must in June subsist itself to *defend the country*. If peace should take place, it will subsist itself to *procure justice to itself.*" The latter case was the more troubling one. "It appears to be a prevailing opinion in the army that the disposition to recompense their services will cease with the necessity for them, and that if they once lay down their arms, they will part with the means of obtaining justice." Hamilton couldn't gainsay the prevailing opinion. "It is to be lamented that appearances afford too much ground for their distrust."

What should be done? Hamilton recommended using the army to force the hand of the legislature. "The claims of the army urged with moderation, but with firmness, may operate on those weak minds which are influenced by their apprehensions more than their judgments, so as to produce a concurrence in the measures which the exigencies of affairs demand," Hamilton said. "They may add weight to the applications of Congress to the several states."

Such a course entailed risk. "The difficulty will be to keep a complaining and suffering army within the bounds of moderation," Hamilton said. This was where Washington came in. "It will be advisable not to discountenance their endeavours to procure redress, but rather by the intervention of confidential and prudent persons, *to take the direction of them.*" Yet Washington must keep his hand hidden. "It is of moment to the public tranquility that Your Excellency should preserve the confidence of the army without losing that of the people. This will enable you in case of extremity to guide the torrent and bring order, perhaps even good, out of confusion. 'Tis a part that requires address, but 'tis one which your own situation as well as the welfare of the community points out."

A man less self-confident than Hamilton would have shied at recommending to the commander in chief a course that verged on mutiny. But Hamilton was nothing if not self-confident. He proceeded to instruct his former mentor on the mood of Washington's own army. "I will not conceal from Your Excellency a truth which it is necessary you should know. An idea is propagated in the army that delicacy carried to an extreme prevents your espousing its interests with sufficient warmth. The falsehood of this opinion no one can be better acquainted with than myself, but it is not the less mischievous for being false. Its tendency is to impair that influence which you may exert with advantage, should any commotions unhappily ensue, to moderate the pretensions of the army and make their conduct correspond with their duty." Washington must show his men that he had their interests at heart.

Hamilton closed on an unconvincingly modest note. "The intimations I have thrown out will suffice to give Your Excellency a proper conception of my sentiments. You will judge of their reasonableness or fallacy." As a postscript he added, "General Knox has the confidence of the army and is a man of sense. I think he may be safely made use of. Situated as I am, Your Excellency will feel the confidential nature of these observations."

Washington read Hamilton's letter with care and concern. He thanked his erstwhile protégé for airing his views so freely. And he concurred in the need for reform. But to employ the army to pressure the Congress was out of bounds. Washington would have no part of it. "I shall pursue the same steady line of conduct which has governed me hitherto," he told Hamilton. He would rely on the Congress and the states to do the right thing. "The just claims of the army ought, and it is to be hoped will, have their weight with every sensible legislature in the Union."

MANY OF WASHINGTON'S OFFICERS LACKED his patience and his confidence in America's elected officials. In early March a notice was circulated anonymously among the officers in camp for a meeting; accompanying the notice was a manifesto of grievances, also anonymous. "After a pursuit of seven long years, the object for which we set out is at length brought within our reach," the manifesto declared. "Yes, my friends, that suffering courage of yours was active once; it has conducted the United States of America through a doubtful and a bloody war. It has placed her in the chair of independency, and peace returns again to bless—whom? A country willing to redress your wrongs, cherish your worth and reward your services, a country courting your return to private life, with tears of gratitude and smiles of admiration, longing to divide with you that independency which your gallantry has given, and those riches which your wounds have preserved? Is this the case? Or is it rather a country that tramples upon your rights, disdains your cries and insults your distresses?" Too clearly, it was the latter. "If this, then, be your treatment, while the swords you wear are necessary for the defence of America, what have you to expect from peace, when your voice shall sink, and your strength dissipate by division? When those very swords, the instruments and companions of your glory, shall be taken from your sides, and no remaining mark of military distinction left but your wants, infirmities and scars? Can you then consent to be the only sufferers by this revolution, and retiring from the field, grow old in poverty, wretchedness and contempt? Can you consent to wade through the vile mire of dependency, and owe the miserable remnant of that life to charity, which has hitherto been spent in honor? If you can—go!—and carry with you the jest of Tories and scorn of Whigs—the ridicule, and what is worse, the pity of the world. Go, starve, and be forgotten!"

There was an alternative, the manifesto asserted. "If your spirit should revolt at this, if you have sense enough to discover, and spirit enough to oppose tyranny under whatever garb it may assume; whether it be the plain coat of republicanism, or the splendid robe of royalty; if you have yet learned to discriminate between a people and a cause, between men and principles—awake; attend to your situation and redress yourselves." It was now or never. "If the present moment be lost, every future effort is in vain, and your threats then will be as empty as your entreaties now."

A welter of feelings gripped Washington as he read the manifesto. The insubordination of the irregular meeting angered him; the sedition inherent in the thought of using the army against the Congress appalled him. Hamilton had suggested the same thing, but Hamilton had proposed that Washington lead the effort. Washington assumed that Hamilton accepted his refusal to do so. These anonymous conspirators were presuming to take matters into their own hands. It was mutiny again, but by officers rather than the rank and file.

At the same time, Washington was puzzled. "There is something very mysterious in this business," he wrote to Hamilton. Washington thought he had a good sense of the mood in the camp. He was aware of the dissatisfaction of the officers and men at being repeatedly spurned by the Congress, but he was fairly certain the unhappiness hadn't reached levels that would prompt his soldiers to entertain the suggestions of the anonymous writer. "It appears reports have been propagated in Philadelphia that dangerous combinations were forming in the army, and this at a time when there was not a syllable of the kind in agitation in camp," Washington told Hamilton. If there was plotting anywhere, it seemed to be in the Congress. "It is firmly believed by some the scheme was not only planned but also digested and matured in Philadelphia." Washington didn't entirely share this view, yet. "My opinion shall be suspended till I have better ground to found one on." But the circumstantial evidence was compelling. "The matter was managed with great art, for as soon as the minds of the officers were thought to be prepared for the transaction, the anonymous invitations and address to the officers were put in circulation through every state line in the army." Washington told Hamilton he had issued a general order forbidding the proposed meeting—"to arrest on the spot the foot that stood wavering on a tremendous precipice, to prevent the officers from being taken by surprise while the passions were all inflamed, and to rescue them from plunging themselves into a gulf of civil horror from which there might be no receding."

Washington had done his part, and would do more. Meanwhile, he said, Hamilton must do *his* part. The Congress must give the soldiers some measure of satisfaction. "The situation of these gentlemen I do verily believe is distressing beyond description. It is affirmed to me that a large part of them have no better prospects before them than a gaol"—for debt—"if they are turned loose without liquidation of accounts and an assurance of that justice to which they are so worthily entitled." Washington had a message he hoped Hamilton would relate to the obstructionists in the Congress. "It may, in my opinion, with propriety be suggested to them, if any disastrous consequences should follow, by reason of their delinquency, that they must be answerable to God and their country for the ineffable horror which may be occasioned thereby."

Washington had indeed forbidden the rogue meeting of officers, but in the same general orders he authorized another meeting, to be held a few days later. This maneuver bought time for reflection among the officers; it also gave the malcontents a chance to air their grievances without implicating the rest in mutiny by mere attendance at an unsanctioned affair.

Except that Washington didn't intend for the malcontents to have their chance, or their say. The officers duly gathered, expecting to hear from Horatio Gates, who expected to speak. A whiff of the Conway cabal occasionally drifted over the camp; Gates let officers continue to think of him as an alternative to Washington.

Yet just as Gates was starting, Washington entered the meeting hall and seized the stage. Neither Gates nor any of the restive officers could do anything but listen. "Gentlemen," he said, "by an anonymous summons, an attempt has been made to convene you together. How inconsistent with the rules of propriety! how unmilitary! and how subversive of all order and discipline!" As bad as the summons was the anonymous manifesto. "The address is drawn with great art and is designed to answer the most insidious purposes," Washington said. "It is calculated to impress the mind with an idea of premeditated injustice in the sovereign power of the United States, and rouse all those resentments which must unavoidably flow from such a belief."

Washington spoke more personally than he had ever done to his army. "I was among the first who embarked in the cause of our common country," he said. "I have never left your side one moment, but when called from you on public duty. . . . I have been the constant companion and witness of your distresses, and not among the last to feel and acknowledge your merits. . . . I have ever considered my own military reputation as inseparably connected with that of the army. . . . My heart has ever expanded with joy when I have heard its praises, and my indignation has arisen when the mouth of detraction has been opened against it." The anonymous writer presumed to speak more truly for the interests of the army than its general did; how dare he!

The writer cast the darkest aspersions on the motives of the Congress. Washington didn't hide the fact that the operations of that body had tested his patience. But he had never doubted the motives of its members. "That honourable body entertain exalted sentiments of the services of the army, and from a full conviction of its merits and sufferings will do it complete justice. . . . Why then should we distrust them and, in consequence of that distrust, adopt measures which may cast a shade over that glory which has been so justly acquired, and tarnish the reputation of an army which is celebrated through all Europe for its fortitude and patriotism? And for what is this done? To bring the object we seek for nearer? No! Most certainly, in my opinion, it will cast it at a greater distance." The army must turn its back on this counsel of ignoble shortsightedness. "Let me conjure you, in the name of our common country, as you value your own sacred honor, as you respect the rights of humanity, and as you regard the military and national character of America, to express your utmost horror and detestation of the man who wishes, under any specious pretenses, to overturn the liberties of our country, and who wickedly attempts to open the flood gates of civil discord and deluge our rising empire in blood."

The correct course would have the opposite effect. "By thus determining, and thus acting, you will pursue the plain and direct road to the attainment of your wishes. You will defeat the insidious designs of our enemies, who are compelled to resort from open force to secret artifice. You will give one more distinguished proof of unexampled patriotism and patient virtue, rising superior to the pressure of the most complicated sufferings. And you will, by the dignity of your conduct, afford occasion for posterity to say, when speaking of the glorious example you have exhibited to mankind, 'Had this day been wanting, the world had never seen the last stage of perfection to which human nature is capable of attaining.'"

SAMUEL SHAW HAD a clear view of the whole affair. "The meeting of the officers was in itself exceedingly respectable, the matters they were called to deliberate upon were of the most serious nature, and the unexpected attendance of the commander-in-chief heightened the solemnity of the scene," he wrote. "Every eye was fixed upon the illustrious man, and attention to their beloved general held the assembly mute. He opened the meeting by apologizing for his appearance there, which was by no means his intention when he published the order which directed them to assemble. But the diligence used in circulating the anonymous pieces rendered it necessary that he should give his sentiments to the army on the nature and tendency of them, and determined him to avail himself of the present opportunity; and, in order to do it with greater perspicuity, he had committed his thoughts to writing, which, with the indulgence of his brother officers, he would take the liberty of reading to them." And so he did.

But it was what came next that really impressed Shaw. "After he had concluded his address, he said that as a corroborating testimony of the good disposition in Congress towards the army, he would communicate to them a letter received from a worthy member of that body, and one who on all occasions had ever approved himself their fast friend. This was an exceedingly sensible letter; and, while it pointed out the difficulties and embarrassments of Congress, it held up very forcibly the idea that the army should, at all events, be generously dealt with. One circumstance in reading this letter must not be omitted. His Excellency, after reading the first paragraph, made a short pause, took out his spectacles, and begged the indulgence of his audience while he put them on, observing at the same time, that he had grown gray in their service, and now found himself growing blind. There was something so natural, so unaffected, in this appeal, as rendered it superior to the most studied oratory; it forced its way to the heart, and you might see sensibility moisten every eye."

After Washington's performance shamed even the distrustful into doing the right thing—the assembled officers unanimously rejected what they called the "infamous propositions" of the anonymous manifesto—Shaw reflected on the whole affair. "Happy for America that she has a *patriot army,* and equally so that a *Washington* is its leader," he said. "I rejoice in the opportunities I have had of seeing this great man in a variety of situations: calm and intrepid where the battle raged, patient and persevering under the pressure of misfortune, moderate and possessing himself in the full career of victory. Great as these qualifications deservedly render him, he never appeared to me more truly so than at the assembly we have been speaking of. On other occasions he has been supported by the exertions of an army and the countenance of his friends, but in this he stood single and alone. There was no saying where the passions of an army, which were not a little inflamed, might lead, but it was generally allowed that longer forbearance was dangerous, and moderation had ceased to be a virtue. Under these circumstances he appeared, not at the head of his troops, but as it were in opposition to them; and for a dreadful moment the interests of the army and its general seemed to be in competition! He spoke—every doubt was dispelled, and the tide of patriotism rolled again in its wonted course. Illustrious man! What he says of the army may with equal justice be applied to his own character: 'Had this day been wanting, the world had never seen the last stage of perfection to which human nature is capable of attaining.'"

THE RESTIVE OFFICERS WEREN'T the only ones shamed into doing the right thing by Washington's bravura performance. Accounts of the Newburgh showdown reached Philadelphia within days; within mere hours of that, a solid majority in the Congress approved a bond issue to pay the officers what they were owed.

Then, as though heaven had been holding its breath, the day after *that* a French ship arrived with word of the peace agreement. The Congress received the official word from Benjamin Franklin. At times during the war Franklin had thought he wouldn't live to see the struggle completed. Now that it was over, it didn't seem long at all. "I congratulate you and our country on the happy prospects afforded us by the finishing so speedily this glorious revolution," he wrote.

Washington announced the good news to the army. "The Commander in Chief orders the cessation of hostilities between the United States of America and the King of Great Britain, to be publicly proclaimed tomorrow," he declared on April 18. The tomorrow in question was the eighth anniversary of the battles of Lexington and Concord. "After which the chaplains with the several brigades will render thanks to the Almighty God for all his mercies, particularly for his overruling the wrath of man, to his own glory, and causing the rage of war to cease amongst the nations." Washington added his own thanks. "The Commander in Chief, far from endeavouring to stifle the feeling of joy in his own bosom, offers his most cordial congratulations on the occasion to all the officers of every denomination, to all the troops of the United States in general, and in particular to those gallant and persevering men who had resolved to defend the invaded rights of their country so long as the war should continue." History would remember them all. "Happy, thrice happy, shall they be pronounced hereafter who have contributed anything, who have performed the meanest office, in erecting this stupendous fabric of freedom and empire on the broad basis of independency."

Washington was certain the men shared his noble feelings on this glorious day. But he didn't forget that soldiers were soldiers. He concluded his order: "An extra ration of liquor to be issued to every man tomorrow to drink: Perpetual Peace, Independence and Happiness to the United States of America."

Another toast ended Washington's own military career. After the British gave up Charleston in December 1782, their last stronghold was New York. British troops remained in the city until the definitive peace treaty was signed in September 1783, after which the British government ordered their evacuation. Between the time the order took to cross the Atlantic and the preparations necessary to end a seven-year occupation, the British didn't depart New York until late November. Thereupon Washington led the Continental Army on a triumphant march down the length of Manhattan Island.

A week of savoring the triumph and restoring American government to the city culminated in word that Washington was finally going home. "At 12 o'clock the officers repaired to Fraunces Tavern, in Pearl Street, where Gen. Washington had appointed to meet them, and to take his final leave of them," Benjamin Tallmadge, one of Washington's staff, recalled. "We had been assembled but a few moments when His Excellency entered the room. His emotion, too strong to be concealed, seemed to be reciprocated by every officer present. After partaking of a slight refreshment, in almost breathless silence the General filled his glass with wine, and, turning to the officers, he said: 'With a heart full of love and gratitude, I now take leave of you. I most devoutly wish that your latter days may be as prosperous and happy as your former ones have been glorious and honourable.' After the officers had taken a glass of wine, Gen. Washington said: 'I cannot come to each of you, but shall feel obliged if each of you will come and take me by the hand.'"

Henry Knox was the first to grasp Washington's hand; the handshake became an embrace. One after another the rest of the officers stepped forward. "Such a scene of sorrow and weeping I had never before witnessed, and hope I may never be called upon to witness again," Tallmadge remarked. "It was indeed too affecting to be of long continuance, for tears of deep sensibility filled every eye, and the heart seemed so full that it was ready to burst from its wonted abode."

At length the weepy embraces were finished. Washington picked up his hat. "The time for separation had come, and waving his hand to his grieving children around him, he left the room," Tallmadge wrote. "And passing through a corps of light infantry who were paraded to receive him, he walked silently on to Whitehall, where a barge was in waiting. We all followed in mournful silence to the wharf, where a prodigious crowd had assembled to witness the departure of the man who, under God, had been the great agent in establishing the glory and independence of these United States. As soon as he was seated, the barge put off into the river, and when out in the stream, our great and beloved General waved his hat and bid us a silent adieu."

BENJAMIN FRANKLIN'S RETURN to private life struck a different note. His standing offer to resign remained, but he continued to serve at the pleasure of the Congress. And the Congress didn't see fit to accept his resignation. Or perhaps it just didn't get around to considering the matter. Franklin couldn't tell which was the case. But with the war over and the peace treaty signed, he felt little compulsion to keep at work. He reminded anyone who would listen that he was far past retirement age. In wishing John Jay and his wife bon voyage when Jay left for America to take up a new position as foreign secretary under the Articles of Confederation, Franklin said, "Mr. Jay was so kind as to offer his friendly services to me in America. He will oblige me much by endeavouring to forward my discharge from this employment. Repose is now my only ambition."

He needed the repose. His gout and kidney stones tormented him more than ever. "I cannot bear a carriage upon pavement," he wrote. He hoped his release would come soon, before he was unable to travel back to America, if travel at all.

Some days he wondered if he should just stay in France. "I am here among a people that love and respect me, a most amiable nation to live with," he wrote in the summer of 1784. "Perhaps I may conclude to die among them, for my friends in America are dying off one after another, and I have been so long abroad that I should now be almost a stranger in my own country."

There was a particular poignancy to this letter, for it was addressed to one who really was a stranger in his own country—and a stranger to his own father. William Franklin had survived arrest in New Jersey, imprisonment in Connecticut, internal exile in occupied New York, and finally actual exile to Britain, where he discovered that American Loyalists were treated as reminders of a colonial conflict best forgotten. He had recently written to Franklin, reviving a correspondence that had lapsed almost a decade earlier. "Dear and honoured Father," William wrote, "Ever since the termination of the unhappy contest between Great Britain and America, I have been anxious to write to you, and to endeavour to revive that affectionate intercourse and connexion which till the commencement of the late troubles had been the pride and happiness of my life." But he had hesitated, partly from fear of compromising the position Franklin held as a representative of the American government, and partly from uncertainty as to whether Franklin wanted to hear from his Loyalist son. William knew that Franklin had strongly disapproved of his views during the war; perhaps he still did. William didn't take any of those views back. "I am happy that I can with confidence appeal not only to you but to my God that I have uniformly acted from a strong sense of what I conceived my duty to my King, and regard to my country, required," he said. "If I have been mistaken, I cannot help it. It is an error of judgment that the maturest reflection I am capable of cannot rectify. And I verily believe were the same circumstances to occur again tomorrow, my conduct would be exactly similar to what it was heretofore, notwithstanding the cruel sufferings, scandalous neglects, and ill-treatment which we poor unfortunate Loyalists have in general experienced." Yet that was in the past. "On a subject so disagreeable I have no desire to say more, and I hope everything which has happened relative to it may be mutually forgotten," William wrote. "I flatter myself that you are actuated by the same disposition, and that my advances towards a renewal of our former affectionate intercourse will be as acceptable to you as they are agreeable to myself."

Franklin responded at once. "Dear son," he said, "I received your letter of the 22d past, and am glad to find that you desire to revive the affectionate intercourse that formerly existed between us. It will be very agreeable to me."

But it would be on his own terms. "Nothing has ever hurt me so much and affected me with such keen sensations as to find myself deserted in my old age by my only son; and not only deserted, but to find him taking up arms against me, in a cause wherein my good fame, fortune and life were all at stake," Franklin told William. "You conceived, you say, that your duty to your king and regard for your country required this. I ought not to blame you for differing in sentiment with me in public affairs. We are men, all subject to errors. Our opinions are not in our power; they are formed and governed much by circumstances that are often as inexplicable as they are irresistible. Your situation was such that few would have censured your remaining neuter, though *there are natural duties which precede political ones, and cannot be extinguished by them.*"

Franklin felt himself getting angry. "This is a disagreeable subject," he wrote. "I drop it. And we will endeavour as you propose mutually to forget what has happened relating to it, as well as we can."

Which turned out to be not very well, in Franklin's case. William Temple Franklin had been communicating with his father, hoping to reconstruct the family the revolution had broken apart. Allowing himself some license, he let William think Franklin was more willing to forgive and forget than he actually was. And when the Congress at length accepted Franklin's resignation, and Franklin decided that Philadelphia, after all, was where he should go to die, Temple arranged a meeting between his father and his grandfather.

Franklin and Temple crossed the English Channel to Southampton. They stayed at a popular tavern and greeted such of Franklin's old friends as were healthy enough to make the journey from London. The reunion of Franklin and William took place amid the bustle of the tavern and the coming and going of Franklin's friends. Temple tried to get the two to let go of the past, if only so that he no longer had to feel that he was betraying one by embracing the other. William was amenable, although not on the condition his father imposed: William wouldn't apologize for choosing his king over his father. Franklin, perhaps still feeling the contempt so conspicuously displayed by the king's men in the Cockpit a decade before, refused to bend. He and William awkwardly conducted some family business, and then they separated, as far apart as ever.

THE OUTCOME OF THE WAR made heroes of the Patriots. George Washington was applauded all the way home to Mount Vernon, where he was permitted to resume his life as a farmer—but only until postwar troubles prompted his countrymen to summon him back into service. He presided over the convention that wrote a new charter to replace the Articles of Confederation; after the Constitution was ratified, he presided over the national government it created. Eight years as America's chief executive left him but two before death claimed him, in 1799. During his final days, almost half a century after he had measured himself against British soldiers in the Ohio campaign against the French, and come out ahead, he took pleasure in being hailed as the greatest man in the United States, indeed the Father of His Country.

Benjamin Franklin joined Washington at the Constitutional Convention. Franklin was the oldest delegate and the most admired figure in the host city, Philadelphia; his presence conferred much-needed legitimacy on what had begun as an extraconstitutional coup against the Congress of the Articles. His gout and kidney stones still plagued him. His heart was slowly failing. He had to be carried to the convention hall each day in a sedan chair. He intervened in the discussions only occasionally, to urge compromise and humility on delegates too often quite full of themselves. The anger that had fueled his rebellion had cooled after the rebellion succeeded; the good humor that had characterized his earlier days emerged once more. It helped secure a unanimous vote of the state delegations on the convention's finished product, which he was pleased to see take effect not long before he breathed his last, in 1790.

John Adams was appointed American minister to Britain after the war, on that account missing the Constitutional Convention. But he supported the project from afar, and in the first election for president, he finished second to Washington, which made him vice president under the procedure the Constitution originally specified. As opinionated as ever, Adams became a leader of the Federalist party, and the party's candidate for president upon Washington's retirement. Adams defeated Thomas Jefferson, the leader of the other party, the Republicans. Yet lacking Washington's stature, he couldn't win a second time, losing to Jefferson in a rematch. Adams retired to Massachusetts, where he lived another quarter-century, until July 4, 1826. The remarkable coincidence of his dying on the fiftieth anniversary of the Declaration of Independence might have finally given him the recognition he had always craved, but just as he had been overshadowed in life by Washington and Franklin, he was eclipsed in death by Jefferson, the author of the Declaration, who astonishingly died on the very same jubilee day.

THE OUTCOME OF THE WAR produced a strikingly different result for the Loyalists. But even had their side prevailed, they would have achieved no such honor as the Patriots did in *their* victory. The Loyalists would have created no new country; they would have remained servants and subjects of the British crown. Doubtless King George would have rewarded them, but whether salaries, posts or even peerages would have compensated for the animus many of their fellow Americans felt for them was impossible to know.

Of course their side did *not* win. And neither the king nor Parliament was inclined to be generous toward Americans of any political stripe, preferring to ignore the whole unhappy affair of the failed war. The most the British government offered to the typical Loyalist was transport to England, Canada or the West Indies. At war's end some fifty thousand, possibly as many as one hundred thousand, sailed away, the great majority never to return.

Of the Loyalist leaders, Thomas Hutchinson had been the first to go. His audience with King George briefly earned him status other Loyalists could only envy, but it didn't translate into permanent preference of any sort. Hutchinson took refuge in the past, resuming work on a history of the Massachusetts Bay Colony he had been writing for many years. When he got to the part where he himself played a large role, he rebutted the bad press he had received at the time from the likes of Sam Adams. His 1780 death delayed publication of the third and final volume, which appeared only a half-century later.

Joseph Galloway never reunited with his wife, who had no desire for a reunion. Poverty weighed on Grace Growden Galloway, who increasingly favored her Growden ancestry over her Galloway connections; under poverty's burden she fell ill and died, in 1782. Joseph Galloway's burden included a conviction for treason Pennsylvania handed down in his absence. The conviction, which confirmed the seizure of his property, erased any lingering incentive to return to America. In the London papers and before Parliament, Galloway blamed William Howe for losing the war; after the Paris treaty rendered the matter moot, he abandoned politics for the study of religion. He died in 1803.

William Franklin fared decently at the hands of the British government, and badly at those of his father. The government gave him a pension; his father next to nothing. Benjamin Franklin's anger still smoldered against his son, and his will explained why the younger man was bequeathed but a pittance: "The part he acted against me in the late war, which is of public notoriety, will account for my leaving him no more of an estate he endeavoured to deprive me of." William Franklin died in 1813.

Benedict Arnold served as a brigadier general in the British army after his defection from Patriot ranks. He tangled with Continental Army forces led by Lafayette, who had orders from Washington to hang him if captured. Arnold displayed initiative on King George's behalf comparable to what he had shown for Washington; a raid on New London, Connecticut, left the Patriot-held port in ruins. Arnold and wife Peggy sailed to England shortly after the surrender at Yorktown. He urged the British government to continue the war; when this effort failed, and then the Paris treaty formally closed the conflict, his salary was reduced to peacetime rates, and he found himself again short of money. He moved to Canada to launch a merchant venture; when this, too, failed, he returned to England. In British minds his name was linked to that of John André, and Arnold suffered by the comparison. He dabbled in privateering following the outbreak of the French Revolution, was captured in the West Indies, and escaped the noose only by bribing his guards. His strength, long compromised by the leg wounds suffered in defense of the United States, diminished with passing years. He died in 1801.

The Loyalist slaves received better from the British government than many had feared when they heard the terms of the Paris treaty. The pact's seventh article specified that British troops would depart America "without causing any destruction or carrying away any Negroes or other property of the American inhabitants." Boston King witnessed the reaction in New York. "Peace was restored between America and Great Britain, which diffused universal joy among all parties, except us, who had escaped from slavery and taken refuge in the English army," he wrote. "A report prevailed at New York that all the slaves, in number 2000, were to be delivered up to their masters, although some of them had been three or four years among the English. This dreadful rumour filled us all with inexpressible anguish and terror, especially when we saw our old masters coming from Virginia, North Carolina, and other parts, and seizing upon their slaves in the streets of New York, or even dragging them out of their beds. Many of the slaves had very cruel masters, so that the thoughts of returning home with them embittered life to us. For some days we lost our appetite for food, and sleep departed from our eyes."

Fortunately for King and the others, the British army in New York honored its promises better than the British diplomats in Paris honored theirs. "Each of us received a certificate from the commanding officer at New York which dispelled all our fears, and filled us with joy and gratitude," King recounted. The certificate formally asserted the freedom of the former slaves.

Yet the certificate meant nothing beyond the bounds of British control, which were shrinking fast. More decisive for King's future was the transport the British provided him and the other Loyalists. "Soon after, ships were fitted out and furnished with every necessary for conveying us to Nova Scotia," King wrote.

King lived in Nova Scotia for several years, during which he experienced a religious conversion to the Methodist faith. Life was hard for the black Loyalists in Canada; mostly farmers, they suffered from the thin soil of the land they received from the British government, and many found the Canadian winters excruciating. A sizable group left for the British colony of Sierra Leone, and King went along as a preacher. During the next decade he traveled back and forth between West Africa and Britain. While in Britain he wrote his memoir; in Sierra Leone he died in 1802.

The Patriot slave Jeffrey Brace, the one who wrote of himself, "Poor African slave to liberate freemen, my tyrants," was surprised to discover in the wake of the war that he had liberated himself as well. "After we were disbanded, I returned to my old master at Woodbury, with whom I lived one year," Brace recalled. "My services in the American war having emancipated me from further slavery, and from being bartered or sold, my master consented that I might go where I pleased and seek my fortune." In the recounting, Brace was vague as to whether he was emancipated by Connecticut law, which freed some slaves who fought on the Patriot side, or by Benjamin Stiles, his master. Possibly Stiles muddled the issue on purpose, to get an extra year of labor from Brace. Regardless, Brace relocated to Vermont, married, and raised a family. In old age, having gone blind, he dictated his life story, which became a staple of abolitionist literature. He died in 1827.

Of all the Loyalists, Joseph Brant perhaps fared the best. He joined the Loyalist exodus from the United States, in his case under the duress of the clause of the Paris treaty that ceded to the new republic all the British lands east of the Mississippi River, including the homeland of the Iroquois. Brant led his Loyalist Iroquois to Canada, where they settled on land deeded to them by the British government to replace what they had lost. Brant visited England and was accorded honors by the British government, along with a pension for his services to the Crown. (His sister Molly Brant received a pension as well.) In time the animus in America against Brant diminished; George Washington as president invited him to Philadelphia to confer with the new government on Indian policy. Brant became a celebrity, the model of the "civilized savage." He dined in the best homes in Philadelphia and New York. He grew wealthy, tended by a coterie of servants and slaves. He died in 1807—a few years before a second war between the United States and Britain compelled Indians on the American frontier to choose sides once again.

Sources

PROLOGUE

1 "minds and hearts": Adams to Hezekiah Niles, Feb. 13, 1818, Founders Online, founders.archives.gov. Below, where no other archive or printed reference is given, Founders Online is the source.

2 "a vindictive asperity": Banastre Tarleton, *A History of the Campaigns of 1780 and 1781 in the Southern Provinces of North America* (1787), 31.

2 "But before this . . . with his bayonet": William Dobein James, *A Sketch of the Life of Brig. Gen. Francis Marion* (1821), Appendix, 1–7.

3 "Their numbers enabled them": Diary of Anthony Allaire, Oct. 7, 1780, in Lyman C. Draper, *King's Mountain and Its Heroes* (1881), 510.

3 "They were ordered": Isaac Shelby pamphlet, "Battle of King's Mountain," April 1823, in Draper, *King's Mountain*, 566.

PART I · FIRST DOUBTS

Chapter 1

13 "to build forts . . . the most part of their arms": "Expedition to the Ohio, 1754: Narrative."

16 "Three days ago": Washington to John Augustine Washington, May 31, 1754.

17 "Our sentinel gave notice . . . called to parley": "Account of the Capitulation of Fort Necessity," July 19, 1754.

17 "I told him that": "The Journal of M. de Villiers," note to "Account of the Capitulation of Fort Necessity."

18 "l'assasinat du Sr de Jumonville": Articles of Capitulation, July 3, 1754.

18 "I heard bullets whistle": Washington to John Augustine Washington, May 31, 1754.

Chapter 2

19 "Friday last": *Pennsylvania Gazette*, May 9, 1754, enclosed in Benjamin Franklin to Richard Partridge, May 9, 1754.

21 "It would be a very strange thing": Benjamin Franklin to James Parker, Mar. 20, 1751.

21 "The confidence of the French": *Pennsylvania Gazette*, May 9, 1754. Although this essay is unsigned, strong evidence points to Franklin as author.

22 "We had a great deal of disputation": Benjamin Franklin to Cadwallader Colden, July 21, 1754.

Chapter 3

23 "My temper . . . What is, is best": Bernard Bailyn, *The Ordeal of Thomas Hutchinson* (1974), 17.

23 "All the time": *The Diary and Letters of His Excellency Thomas Hutchinson*, edited by Peter Orlando Hutchinson (1883), 1:46.

24 "divided, disunited state": *Journal of the Proceedings of the Congress held at Albany in 1754*, in *Collections of the Massachusetts Historical Society* (1836), 67–69.

24 "It is supposed": Benjamin Franklin to Shirley, Dec. 4, 1754.

24 "Such an union . . . expect some preference": Benjamin Franklin to Shirley, Dec. 22, 1754.

26 "Observations concerning the Increase . . . What numbers of ships and seamen!": "Observations concerning the Increase of Mankind, Peopling of Countries, etc." 1751 (published 1754).

Chapter 4

28 "He once had a duel": Horace Walpole to Horace Mann, Aug. 28, 1755, in *The Letters of Horace Walpole*, edited by Peter Cunningham (1866), 2:461.

29 "Braddock is a very Iroquois . . . acquainted with General Braddock": Horace Walpole to Horace Mann, Aug. 25, 1755, *Letters*, 2:459.

29 "I cannot sufficiently express . . . His Majesty's dominions in America": *The History of an Expedition Against Fort Du Quesne, in 1755, under Major General Edward Braddock*, edited by Winthrop Sargent (1856), 153.

30 "General Braddock": *An Apology for the Life of George Ann Bellamy*, excerpted in *The Gentleman's Magazine*, vol. 55 (1785), 207.

32 "Billy is so fond": Benjamin Franklin to John Franklin, Apr. 2, 1747.

32 "My son": Benjamin Franklin to Cadwallader Colden, June 5, 1747.

32 "As peace cuts off": Benjamin Franklin to William Strahan, Oct. 19, 1748.

32 "A tall proper youth . . . I live long enough": Benjamin Franklin to Abiah Franklin, Apr. 12, 1750.

33 "We found the general . . . and said no more": *The Autobiography of Benjamin Franklin* (1888 ed.), 174–82.

Chapter 5

36 "I wish earnestly": Washington to Robert Orme, Mar. 15, 1755.

36 "which though imperfect": Washington to Robert Orme, Apr. 2, 1755.

36 "I can very truly say": Washington to Carter Burwell, Apr. 20, 1755.

37 "I have met": Washington to John Augustine Washington, May 6, 1755.

37 "I am very happy": Washington to Mary Ball Washington, May 6, 1755.

37 "We proceeded by slow marches . . . for them to spare many": Washington to Augustine Washington, May 14, 1755.

37 "We are to halt here": Washington to John Carlyle, May 14, 1755.

38 "As to any danger . . . in the military line": Washington to John Augustine Washington, May 14, 1755, not sent.

38 "I urged it . . . are now removed": Washington to John Augustine Washington, July 2, 1755.

40 "We continued our march": Washington to John Augustine Washington, July 18, 1755.

41 "I had four bullets": Washington to John Augustine Washington, July 18, 1755.

42 "The shocking scenes": "Remarks, 1787–1788."

42 "Who would have thought it?": Franklin, *Autobiography*, 183.

42 "to guard against a savage triumph": "Remarks, 1787–1788."

43 "This whole transaction": Franklin, *Autobiography*, 183–84.

PART II · WHEN THE WINDS BLOW

Chapter 6

47 "I have succeeded": Dumas in Paul A. W. Wallace, "Conrad Weiser and the Delawares," *Pennsylvania History* (1937), 149.

47 "It is by means": Francis Parkman, *France and England in North America*, part 7 (1910), 1:329–30.

48 "The inhabitants of the Great Cove": Adam Hoops to Robert Morris, Nov. 3, 1755, *Pennsylvania Archives*, edited by Samuel Hazard, vol. 2 (1852), 462–63.

48 "We are now . . . extended to them": John Bartram to Peter Collinson, Feb. 21, 1756, *Memorials of John Bartram and Humphry Marshall*, edited by William Darlington (1849), 205–6.

49 "Where a government": "Form of Association," Nov. 24, 1747.

50 "This Association . . . little less than treason": Thomas Penn to Richard Peters, Mar. 30, 1748, in headnote to *Plain Truth*, Nov. 17, 1747.

50 "He is a dangerous man": Thomas Penn to Richard Peters, June 9, 1748, ibid.

52 "It appeared that their number . . . his real sentiments": Franklin, *Autobiography*, 192–98.

Chapter 7

53 "I never saw a man": William Strahan to Deborah Franklin, Dec. 13, 1757.

53 "You Americans . . . to my lodgings": Franklin, *Autobiography*, 180.

54 "Mr. Franklin": Robert Morris to Ferdinand Paris, July 4, 1757, in note to Benjamin Franklin to Paris, Aug. 12, 1757.

55 "the privileges long enjoyed": William Franklin [Benjamin Franklin] to

The Citizen, Sept. 16, 1757, in *An Historical Review of the Constitution and Government of Pennsylvania* (1759), 439.

55 "On the assistance of these people": Washington to John Stanwix, Apr. 10, 1758.

55 "The Catawbas . . . to kill him for it": Washington to Francis Halkett, May 11, 1758.

56 "These scalping parties": Washington to Henry Bouquet, July 16, 1758.

57 "If Colonel Bouquet": Washington to Francis Halkett Aug. 2, 1758.

57 "That appearance of glory": Washington to John Robinson, Sept. 1, 1758.

57 "The enemy . . . happily succeeded": Washington to Francis Fauquier, Nov. 28, 1758.

59 "of a sprightly genius": "Joseph Brant," *Canadian Encyclopedia*.

59 "Because an uninterrupted trade": Benjamin Franklin in *London Chronicle*, Dec. 27, 1759.

60 "If the Indians . . . when the winds blow": *The Interest of Great Britain Considered*, Apr. 17, 1750.

62 "I shall probably make": Benjamin Franklin to William Strahan, Aug. 23, 1762.

62 "I have long been . . . as I am a Briton": Benjamin Franklin to Lord Kames, Jan. 3, 1760.

PART III · SO WIDELY DIFFERENT

Chapter 8

67 "Mr. Grenville gave us . . . the mother country": Jared Ingersoll to Thomas Fitch, Feb. 11, 1765, in *Prologue to Revolution: Sources and Documents on the Stamp Act Crisis, 1764–1766*, edited by Edmund S. Morgan (1959), 33.

69 "It will operate": "Scheme for Supplying the Colonies with a Paper Currency," c. Feb. 11–12, 1765.

69 "I think it will affect": Benjamin Franklin to David Hall, Feb. 14, 1765.

70 "You are now . . . Thank God": John Hughes to Benjamin Franklin, Sept. 8–17, 1765.

70 "I sent to ask": Deborah Franklin to Benjamin Franklin, Sept. 22, 1765.

71 "I honour much": Benjamin Franklin to Deborah Franklin, Nov. 9, 1765.

Chapter 9

72 "This occasioned murmuring . . . the brick work": Thomas Hutchinson, *The History of the Province of Massachusetts Bay, from 1749 to 1774* (1828), 120–24.

75 "It is uncertain . . . such purposes as these": Thomas Hutchinson to Benjamin Franklin, Nov. 18, 1765.

Chapter 10

77 "It is difficult . . . that can be devised": Joseph Galloway to Benjamin Franklin, Nov. 16, 1765.

79 "Men of the most exalted genius": Adams diary entry for Feb. 19, 1756.

79 "I sometimes . . . 3 farthing bastard": Adams diary entry for Mar. 15, 1756.

80 "Reputation ought . . . creep or fly?": Adams diary entry for Mar. 14, 1759.

80 "In all the calamities . . . never can be slaves": Adams statement against Stamp Act, Sept. 24, 1765.

81 "The year 1765 . . . will become inevitable": Adams diary entry for Dec. 18, 1765.

Chapter 11

83 "Resolved . . . make the most of it": William Wirt, *Sketches of the Life and Character of Patrick Henry* (1847), 49–55. The resolution as quoted here was the version that was circulated in contemporary newspapers. The version voted on by the burgesses was subsequently expunged, and so its precise wording is uncertain.

83 "They were opposed": Thomas Jefferson notes on Patrick Henry, n.d. but before Apr. 12, 1812.

84 "Peter Green": Washington diary entry for May 30, 1765.

84 "The Stamp Act imposed . . . repeal of it": Washington to Francis Dandridge, Sept. 20, 1765.

85 "I can never look . . . to accomplish": Washington to William Crawford, Sept. 17, 1767.

Chapter 12

87 "What is your name . . . to change their opinions": Examination before the Committee of the Whole of the House of Commons, Feb. 13, 1766.

Chapter 13

94 "The Marquis of Rockingham . . . the greatest pleasure": William Strahan to David Hall, May 10, 1766, *Pennsylvania Magazine of History and Biography* (1886), 10:220–21.

95 "If we examine . . . myself in person": "Benevolus," *London Chronicle*, Apr. 9–11, 1767.

97 "Had this happy method . . . out of their senses": Benjamin Franklin in *London Chronicle*, Jan. 5–7, 1768.

100 "what bounds the Farmer": Benjamin Franklin to William Franklin, Mar. 13, 1768.

PART IV · CAN A VIRTUOUS MAN HESITATE?

Chapter 14

103 "My old chariot": Washington to Robert Cary, June 6, 1768.

103 "In my opinion . . . absolutely necessary": Washington to George Mason, Apr. 5, 1769.

105 "A new Association": Washington to George William Fairfax, June 27, 1770.

106   "That there should be": Washington to Jonathan Boucher, July 30, 1770.
106   "The public affairs . . . at all events": Benjamin Franklin to Joseph Gal-
       loway, Mar. 21, 1770.

Chapter 15

108   "Having been a landwaiter . . . for that night": Thomas Hutchinson, *The
       History of the Colony of Massachusetts Bay*, 3:269–73.
111   "The evening of the fifth . . . upon those principles": "Autobiography of
       John Adams," part 1, sheet 12, Massachusetts Historical Society, masshist
       .org.
112   "When the multitude . . . cannot be eradicated": Adams argument for the
       defense, Dec. 3–4, 1770.
114   "The part I took": Adams diary, Mar. 5, 1773.

Chapter 16

115   "I went this morning . . . no farther trouble": Benjamin Franklin account
       of interview with Lord Hillsborough, Jan. 16, 1771.
118   "After a long audience . . . our present grievances": Benjamin Franklin to
       Thomas Cushing, Dec. 2, 1772.
120   "If no measures": Thomas Hutchinson to Thomas Whately, Jan. 20, 1769,
       in *The Representations of Governor Hutchinson and Others Contained in Cer-
       tain Letters Transmitted to England* (1773), 15–16.
120   "My resentment . . . the whole English empire": Benjamin Franklin to
       Thomas Cushing, Dec. 2, 1772.
121   "You mention the surprise": Benjamin Franklin to Samuel Cooper, July 7,
       1773.
122   "It was not in the power": Thomas Hutchinson, *The History of the Colony of
       Massachusetts Bay*, 3:401.

Chapter 17

123   "Rules by which a Great Empire": *Public Advertiser*, Sept. 11, 1773.
124   "Finding that two gentlemen": Benjamin Franklin to *London Chronicle*,
       Dec. 25, 1773.
125   "When the intelligence . . . must be the consequence": Thomas Hutchin-
       son, *The History of the Colony of Massachusetts Bay*, 3:422–40.

Chapter 18

129   "Dr. Franklin therefore . . . accusation against him": Alexander Wedder-
       burn speech to Privy Council, Jan. 29, 1774.

Chapter 19

133   "Will this country sit still": Lord North in House of Commons, Apr. 22,
       1774, in *The Parliamentary History of England from the Earliest Period to the
       Year 1803* (1813), 17:1280.
134   "Have we not tried this": Washington to Bryan Fairfax, July 4, 1774.
135   "I might add": Washington to Charles Thruston, Mar. 12, 1773.

135 "TWENTY THOUSAND Acres": Advertisement, July 15, 1773.

135 "To make matters as easy": Washington to Henry Riddell, Feb. 22, 1774.

136 "Though we are its subjects": Fairfax County Resolves, July 18, 1774.

136 "An innate spirit . . . can prevent it": Washington to Bryan Fairfax, Aug. 24, 1774.

137 "He never spoke": Adams to William Wirt, Jan. 23, 1818.

138 "life, liberty and property": Declaration and Resolves of the First Continental Congress, Oct. 14, 1774, Avalon Project, avalon.yale.edu.

139 "I expressed a full conviction . . . between them": Adams to William Wirt, Jan. 23, 1818.

140 "Permit me . . . the remembrance of": Washington to Robert Mackenzie, Oct. 9, 1774.

Chapter 20

142 "This line is just . . . Your affectionate Father": Benjamin Franklin to William Franklin, Feb. 2, 1774.

143 "Some tell me": Benjamin Franklin to William Franklin, Feb. 18, 1774.

143 "You will hear": Benjamin Franklin to Jane Mecom, Feb. 17, 1774.

143 "It is yet unknown": Benjamin Franklin to Massachusetts House Committee of Correspondence, Feb. 2, 1774.

144 "I suppose we never": Benjamin Franklin to Thomas Cushing, Mar. 22, 1774.

144 "I rejoice to find": Benjamin Franklin to Thomas Cushing, Sept. 15, 1774.

Chapter 21

146 "I see no prospect . . . the parent state": Hutchinson to Dartmouth, Feb. [no date given], 1774, *Diary and Letters of Thomas Hutchinson*, 1:112–17.

147 "How do you do . . . insensible of this": Diary entry for July 1, 1774, *Diary and Letters of Thomas Hutchinson*, 1:157–75.

150 "It is surprising": Hutchinson to unidentified correspondent, July 11, 1774, *Diary and Letters of Thomas Hutchinson*, 1:159n.

Chapter 22

151 "a cool, sullen silence . . . besides me would have done": Benjamin Franklin to William Franklin, Mar. 22, 1775.

158 "The blockade of Boston": Benjamin Franklin to Lord Dartmouth, Mar. 16, 1775 (not sent).

159 "I had no desire": Benjamin Franklin to William Franklin, Mar. 22, 1775.

Chapter 23

160 "With us here": Washington to John Connolly, Feb. 25, 1775.

160 "A great number": Washington to George Mercer, Apr. 5, 1775.

161 "General Gage acknowledges . . . in his choice?": Washington to George William Fairfax, May 31, 1775.

162 "Accordingly . . . so well after this": "Autobiography of John Adams," sheets 20–21 of manuscript in Adams Family Papers, Massachusetts Historical Society, masshist.org.

163 "Though I am truly sensible": Washington address to Continental Congress, June 16, 1775.

163 "You may believe me": Washington to Martha Washington, June 18, 1775.

163 "I am now embarked": Washington to Burwell Bassett, June 19, 1775.

PART V · REBELLION TO TYRANTS

Chapter 24

167 "I arrived here": Benjamin Franklin to David Hartley, May 8, 1775.

167 "The governor had called": Benjamin Franklin to Joseph Priestley, May 16, 1775.

168 "You see I am warm . . . satisfaction is made": Benjamin Franklin to Jonathan Shipley, July 7, 1775.

169 "You are a member": Benjamin Franklin to William Strahan, July 5, 1775 (unsent).

169 "The glass having gone": Hutchinson diary, Jan. 6, 1779, *Diary and Letters of Thomas Hutchinson*, 2:237–38.

170 "The Congress met": Benjamin Franklin to Joseph Priestley, July 7, 1775.

171 "The Congress is not yet . . . ripe for it": Adams to James Warren, July 6, 1775.

172 "In confidence": Adams to James Warren, July 24, 1775.

173 "The United Colonies of North America": Franklin's proposed articles of confederation, July 21, 1775.

Chapter 25

175 "I found . . . of the continent": Washington to John Augustine Washington, July 27, 1775.

177 "I understand . . . ever entitled": Washington to Thomas Gage, Aug. 11, 1775.

178 "George Washington, Esq. . . . . martyrs under misfortune": Thomas Gage to Washington, Aug. 13, 1775, *The Gentleman's Magazine and Historical Chronicle* (1775), 447.

179 "I have taken time": Washington to Thomas Gage, Aug. 20, 1775.

Chapter 26

180 "the oppressed inhabitants": Letter to the Inhabitants of Canada, May 29, 1775, *Journals of the Continental Congress* (1823), 1:75.

180 "It is to penetrate": Washington to Philip Schuyler, Aug. 20, 1775.

182 "I am now": Arnold to B. Douglas, June 9, 1770, *Historical Magazine* (1857), 1:119.

182 "You are entrusted": Washington to Arnold, Sept. 14, 1775.

183 "In case of a union": Instructions to Colonel Benedict Arnold, Sept. 15, 1775.

183 "Friends and brethren": Washington to the Inhabitants of Canada, Sept. 14, 1775.

Chapter 27

184 "Under the present circumstances . . . constantly and regularly sent": Minutes of conference at Cambridge, Oct. 18–24, 1775.

Chapter 28

188 "There are as many . . . best of princes!": Benjamin Franklin to Richard Bache, Oct. 19–24, 1775.

189 "Tell our good friend": Benjamin Franklin letter to *London Chronicle*, October 1775, printed in issue of Dec. 5–7, 1775.

189 "Your nation must stop": Benjamin Franklin to David Hartley, Sept. 12, 1775.

189 "I wish as ardently": Benjamin Franklin to David Hartley, Oct. 13, 1775.

190 "May it not be": William Strahan to Benjamin Franklin, Sept. 6, 1775.

190 "If you have shewn them": Benjamin Franklin to William Strahan, Oct. 3, 1775.

191 "O, reader": *Pennsylvania Evening Post*, Dec. 14, 1775. The headnote to this entry in the Franklin Papers makes the persuasive case for Franklin's authorship.

Chapter 29

192 "We have had": Arnold to Washington, Oct. 13, 1775.

192 "Excessive heavy rains . . . most hospitable manner": Arnold to Washington, Oct. 27–28, 1775.

193 "Our commander": Isaac N. Arnold, *The Life and Times of Benedict Arnold: His Patriotism and His Treason* (1880), 70.

193 "It is not in the power": Washington to Arnold, Dec. 5, 1775.

194 "I make no doubt": Arnold to Washington, Jan. 14, 1776.

194 "This unhappy affair . . . in the spring": Washington to Arnold, Jan. 27, 1776.

195 "Brothers . . . their own officers": Arnold speech in *The Journal of Isaac Senter* (1846), 23–24.

Chapter 30

197 "We are now without . . . we labour under": Washington to Joseph Reed, Jan. 14, 1776.

198 "The late freezing weather": Washington to Jonathan Trumbull, Feb. 19, 1776.

199 "When the enemy": Washington to John Hancock, Mar. 7–9, 1776.

199 "Our bombardment . . . Bunker Hill affair": Washington to John Hancock, Mar. 7–9, 1776.

200 "The town": Washington to John Hancock, Mar. 19, 1776.

200 "All officers and soldiers": Washington proclamation, Mar. 21, 1776.

201 "One or two have done": Washington to John Augustine Washington, Mar. 31, 1776.

201 "Much blood . . . I shall follow myself": Washington to John Augustine Washington, Mar. 31, 1776.

Chapter 31

203 "You are with all convenient dispatch": John Hancock to Benjamin Franklin et al., Mar. 20, 1776.

204 "I grow daily more feeble": Benjamin Franklin to Charles Carroll and Samuel Chase, May 27, 1776.

204 "It is impossible": Benjamin Franklin et al. to John Hancock, May 1, 1776.

204 "We have tried in vain": Benjamin Franklin et al. to John Hancock, May 8, 1776.

205 "I have forwarded to General Schuyler": John Hancock to Benjamin Franklin et al., May 24, 1776.

205 "Two men-of-war": Benjamin Franklin et al. to John Hancock, May 10, 1776.

205 "My dear brother . . to expect infirmities": Jane Mecom to Catherine Greene, June 1, 1776.

205 "concern and surprise": Washington to Benjamin Franklin, May 20, 1776.

206 "I see more certainly . . . I am just recovering": Benjamin Franklin to Washington, June 21, 1776.

Chapter 32

207 "I am very glad": Washington to John Augustine Washington, May 31, 1776.

207 "Resolved: That these United Colonies": Resolution of Independence by Richard Henry Lee, June 7, 1776.

208 "Mr. Jefferson . . . as I can": John Adams to Timothy Pickering, Aug. 6, 1882.

209 "I have made it a rule": Thomas Jefferson's anecdotes of Benjamin Franklin, c. Dec. 4, 1818.

209 "Will Doctor Franklin": Thomas Jefferson to Benjamin Franklin, June 21, 1776.

209 "reduce them to arbitrary power . . . self-evident": Carl Becker, *The Declaration of Independence* (1933), 160–71; Julian P. Boyd, *The Declaration of Independence* (1945), 22–38.

210 "We must be unanimous . . . all hang separately": *Boston Weekly Magazine*, Dec. 15, 1838.

PART VI · A SCENE OF HORROR AND DISTRESS

Chapter 33

213 "The stoppage of communication": David Hartley to Benjamin Franklin, June 8, 1776.

214 "You will learn": Lord Howe to Benjamin Franklin, June 20–July 12, 1776.

214 "The official dispatches . . . honourable private station": Benjamin Franklin to Lord Howe, July 20, 1776.

216 "I am sorry": Lord Howe to Benjamin Franklin, Aug. 16, 1776.

216 "The temper of the colonies": Benjamin Franklin to Lord Howe, Aug. 20, 1776.

217 "This morning two deserters": Washington to John Hancock, Aug. 7, 1776.

217 "An attack is now": Washington to Jesse Root, Aug. 7, 1776.

217 "Brave men": Washington to Samuel Miles, Aug. 8, 1776.

218 "The General exhorts": Washington general orders, Aug. 9, 1776.

218 "The enemy's whole reinforcement": Washington general orders, Aug. 13, 1776.

219 "Very unexpectedly . . . of this continent": Washington to Lund Washington, Aug. 19, 1776.

220 "The distinction": Washington to Israel Putnam, Aug. 25, 1776.

221 "I have no doubt": Washington to John Hancock, Aug. 23, 1776.

221 "Almost the whole": Washington to John Hancock, Aug. 26, 1776.

221 "This may possibly be": Washington to William Heath, Aug. 26, 1776.

222 "The extreme fatigue": Washington to John Hancock, Aug. 31, 1776.

Chapter 34

223 "that the first ball . . . of our independence": John Adams quoted by Benjamin Rush in *A Memorial Containing Travels Through Life or Sundry Incidents in the Life of Dr. Benjamin Rush*, edited by Louis Alexander Biddle (1905), 103–4.

223 "On the road . . . and mutton": Adams diary for Sept. 9, 1776.

225 "They were now met . . . into any negotiation": Henry Strachey notes of conference in Paul Leicester Ford, "Lord Howe's Commission to Pacify the Colonies," *Atlantic Monthly*, June 1896, 760–62.

226 "Dr. Franklin, with an easy air": Adams diary, Sept. 17, 1776.

Chapter 35

227 "I suppose": Adams diary, Sept. 17, 1776.

228 "I cannot but think": William Franklin to Benjamin Franklin, July 3, 1774.

228 "As to 'doing justice before they ask it'": Benjamin Franklin to William Franklin, Sept. 7, 1774.

228 "I heartily wish . . . I'll drop it": William Franklin to Benjamin Franklin, Dec. 24, 1774.

229 "Methinks 'tis time": Benjamin Franklin to William Franklin, Aug. 1, 1774.

230 "It has long appeared . . . breaking of the ice": William Franklin to Lord Germain, Mar. 28, 1776, *Documents Relating to the Colonial History of the State of New Jersey*, edited by Frederick W. Ricord and Wm. Nelson, vol. 10 (1886), 702–11.

232 "Having by proclamation . . . I owe His Majesty": William Franklin to New Jersey legislators, June 17, 1776, *Documents Relating to the Colonial History of the State of New Jersey*, 10:719–28.

235 "My troubles": Elizabeth Franklin to Benjamin Franklin, Aug. 6, 1776.

236 "Dear Billy": Benjamin Franklin to William Temple Franklin, Sept. 19, 1776.

237 "Honoured sir . . . no time to be lost": William Temple Franklin to Benjamin Franklin, Sept. 21, 1776.

237 "You are mistaken . . . Your affectionate Grandfather": Benjamin Franklin to William Temple Franklin, Sept. 22, 1776.

238 "I hope you will return": Benjamin Franklin to William Temple Franklin, Sept. 28, 1776.

239 "Governor Livingston": Washington to Jonathan Trumbull, Mar. 23, 1777.

239 "Mr. Franklin's conduct": Washington to Jonathan Trumbull, Apr. 21, 1777.

239 "I suffer so much": William Franklin in Chaim M. Rosenberg, *The Loyalist Conscience: Principled Opposition to the American Revolution* (2018), 59.

240 "All I request": William Franklin to Washington, July 22, 1777.

240 "I heartily sympathise": Washington to William Franklin, July 25, 1777.

Chapter 36

242 "most disagreeable": Dunmore proclamation, Nov. 7, 1775, *Encyclopedia Virginia*.

242 "base and insidious arts": Declaration of the General Convention, Dec. 14, 1775, in *Proceedings of the Convention of Delegates* (1816), 66.

243 "Our Dunmore has at length": Lund Washington to George Washington, Dec. 3, 1775.

244 "If the Virginians are wise": Washington to Joseph Reed, Dec. 15, 1775.

244 "As the General": Washington general orders, Dec. 30, 1775.

Chapter 37

245 "This is a most unfortunate affair . . . have occasioned": Washington to John Augustine Washington, Nov, 19, 1776.

247 "I wish to Heaven . . . pretty well up": Washington to Lund Washington, Dec. 10 and 17, 1776.

247 "A little after 12 o'clock . . . I ever beheld": Diary entry for Sept. 20, 1776, *Diary of Frederick Mackenzie: Giving a Daily Narrative of His Military Service as an Officer of the Regiment of Royal Welch Fusiliers during the Years 1775–1781* (1930), 1:58–61.

PART VII · MALIGNANT FACTION

Chapter 38

253 "We beg leave": Benjamin Franklin et al. to Vergennes, Dec. 23, 1776.

253 "All their humble petitions . . . clothed and armed": Benjamin Franklin to Vergennes, Jan. 5, 1777.

255 "North America now offers": Benjamin Franklin et al. to Vergennes, Jan. 5, 1777.

Chapter 39

257 "The hearts of the French": Benjamin Franklin et al. to Committee of Secret Correspondence, Jan. 17, 1777.

258 "This haven is safe": Meschinet de Richemond to Benjamin Franklin, Jan. 14, 1777.

258 "In the present peril": Benjamin Franklin et al., resolution, Feb. 5, 1777.

258 "The United States shall not": Benjamin Franklin et al., resolution, Feb. 2, 1777.

259 "I cannot speak": Benjamin Franklin to Washington, Apr. 2, 1777.

259 "Count Pulaski": Benjamin Franklin to Washington, May 29, 1777.

259 "The gentleman": Benjamin Franklin to Washington, Sept. 4, 1777.

259 "a young nobleman": Benjamin Franklin et al. to Washington, August or September 1777.

260 "Every new arrival": Washington to Benjamin Franklin, Aug. 17, 1777.

260 "The bearer of this": Benjamin Franklin model letter, Apr. 2, 1777.

261 "I am much obliged": Benjamin Franklin to Juliana Ritchie, Jan. 19, 1777.

262 "I went to Paris": Edward Bancroft to the Marquis of Carmarthen, Sept. 17, 1784, in Samuel Flagg Bemis, "British Secret Service and the French-American Alliance," *American Historical Review*, April 1924, 494.

Chapter 40

263 "My first visit . . . to be satisfied": Minutes of conversation with Benjamin Franklin, by Philip Gibbes, Feb. 5, 1777.

Chapter 41

267 "Christmas-day at night": Washington to Joseph Reed, Dec. 23, 1776.

267 "The quantity of ice . . . immediately checked them": Washington to John Hancock, Dec. 27, 1776.

268 "Our situation . . . might have stores": Washington to John Hancock, Jan. 5, 1777.

269 "The enemy are in great consternation": Washington to William Heath, Jan. 5, 1777.

269 "The severity of the season": Washington to John Hancock, Jan. 7, 1777.

Chapter 42

271 "The Commissioners received" . . . 7,730,000 livres: Benjamin Franklin et al. to Vergennes and Aranda, Sept. 25, 1777.

272 "We are scarce allowed": Benjamin Franklin et al. to Committee for Foreign Affairs, Nov. 30, 1777.

272 "I have this moment . . . infinite to America": Washington to Israel Putnam, Aug. 1, 1777.

273 "The conduct of the enemy": Washington to Jonathan Trumbull, Aug. 4, 1777.

273 "Since General Howe's remove . . . last mentioned power": Washington to John Augustine Washington, Aug. 5–9, 1777.

274 "I am now of opinion": Washington to Horatio Gates, Aug. 20, 1777.

275 "Had the Chesapeake Bay": Washington to John Hancock, Aug. 21, 1777.

275 "I have issued orders": Washington to John Hancock, Aug. 22, 1777.

275 "I am sorry to inform . . . losses now sustained": Washington to John Hancock, Sept. 11, 1777.

276 "The morning was extremely foggy . . . by being in actions": Washington to John Hancock, Oct. 5, 1777.

277 "I have obtained . . . on a retreat": Washington to John Hancock, Oct. 7, 1777.

Chapter 43

278 "I have but to give": Proclamation by John Burgoyne, June 29, 1777, in *The Gentleman's Magazine*, August 1777, 360.

278 "One word": "Molly Brant (Konwatsi'tsiaiénni)," *Canadian Encyclopedia*.

279 "Your resolution": Barry St. Leger to Henry Bird, Aug. 2, 1777, in William L. Stone, *Life of Joseph Brant—Thayendanegea* (1838), 1:222.

280 "the vengeance of the state": Proclamation by Barry St. Leger, undated (August 1777), in William W. Campbell, *Annals of Tryon County* (1831), 78.

280 "I beheld": Stone, *Life of Joseph Brant*, 1:243.

281 "The British sent for": *Life of Mary Jemison*, edited by James E. Seaver (1856 ed.), 116–17.

281 "I was surprized . . . thanks of your country": Washington to Arnold, Apr. 2, 1777,

282 "I am stationed . . . aspersed and calumniated": Arnold to Washington, July 27, 1777.

285 "Enclosed . . . to the public": Washington to Arnold, Jan. 20, 1778.

Chapter 44

286 "Is Philadelphia taken? . . . prisoners of war!": *Boston News-Letter and City Record*, Aug. 12, 1826.

286 "You mistake the matter": Note to Announcement by the American Commissioners, Dec. 4, 1777.

287 "The completing such a treaty": Benjamin Franklin et al. to Vergennes, Dec. 8, 1777.

287 The deputy tendered congratulations: Richard Henry Lee, *Life of Arthur Lee* (1829), 1:357.

287 "Though I have no reason . . . war upon us": Minutes of conversation, Jan. 5, 1778.

290 "gone forever": Richard Henry Lee, *Life of Arthur Lee* (1829), 1:374.

290 "There shall be a firm . . . ports of either party": Treaty of Amity and Commerce, Feb. 6, 1778.

291 "If war should break out . . . intimate union": Franco-American treaty of alliance, Feb. 6, 1778.

Chapter 45

294 "When I arrived . . . bigot and fanatic": Adams diary, Feb. 11, 1779.

295 "But Mr. Franklin . . . title to the legislator of America": Adams diary, June 23, 1779.

296 "That he was a great genius": Adams diary, Apr. 21, 1778.

296 "We were invited . . . revenge and rancour": Adams diary, Apr. 10, 1778.

297 "Dined with Madam Helvetius . . . Cavete Americani!": John Adams diary, Apr. 15, 1778.

297 "She entered the room . . . a mere recluse": Abigail Adams to Lucy Cranch, Sept. 5, 1784, in *Letters of Mrs. Adams*, edited by Charles Francis Adams (1841), 2:55–56.

299 "The life of Dr. Franklin . . . after it was done": Adams diary, May 27, 1778.

Chapter 46

301 "General Howe has withdrawn": Washington to Horatio Gates, Dec. 2, 1777.

301 "Viewing the subject . . . reflection or consideration": Washington to John Hancock, Dec. 22, 1777.

302 "Three or four days . . . relieve or prevent": Washington to John Hancock, Dec. 23, 1777.

303 "The present situation": Washington to Peter Colt, Feb. 7, 1778.

304 "For some days past": Washington to George Clinton, Feb. 16, 1778.

304 "Friends . . . violent death": Washington circular letter, Feb. 18, 1778.

305 "By death and desertion": Washington to John Cadwalader, Mar. 20, 1778.

306 "You and I": Alexander Hamilton to George Clinton, Feb. 13, 1778.

306 "He appears to be": Washington to John Hancock, May 9, 1777.

306 "He is entitled": Benjamin Rush to John Adams, Oct. 13, 1777.

307 "Heaven has been . . . myself mistaken": Washington to Horatio Gates, Jan. 4, 1778.

308 "I find with great satisfaction": Thomas Conway to Washington, Jan. 27, 1778.

308 "He is one of the vermin": Alexander Hamilton to George Clinton, Feb. 13, 1778.

308 "I was not unapprized": Washington to Henry Laurens, Jan. 31, 1778.

308 "My caution to avoid": Washington to Patrick Henry, Mar. 28, 1778.

309 "A period is fast approaching": Washington to John Banister, Apr. 21, 1778.

310 "A most important crisis": Washington to Henry Laurens Apr. 30, 1778.

PART VIII · LAWRENCE GROWDEN'S DAUGHTER

Chapter 47

313 "When my brother and I . . ." better for him: *The Narrative of Lieut. Gen. Sir William Howe in a Committee of the House of Commons* (1780), 41–42.

314 "Washington appeared": Sarah Logan Fisher diary entry for Aug. 23, 1777, in "'A Diary of Trifling Occurrences': Philadelphia 1776–1778," edited by Nicholas B. Wainwright, *Pennsylvania of History and Biography* (1958), 443. This source will be cited as Sarah Logan Fisher Diary.

314 "An express came in . . . on our parts": Diary entries for Aug. 26–Sept. 26, 1777, Sarah Logan Fisher Diary, 444–51.

317 "I appointed him . . . to act upon it": *The Narrative of Lieut. Gen. Sir William Howe in a Committee of the House of Commons* (1780), 43–44.

318 "Scarcely any meat": Entry for Oct. 23, 1777, Sarah Logan Fisher Diary, 454.

318 "Low and distressed": Entry for Nov. 1, 1777, Sarah Logan Fisher Diary, 455.

318 "This day may be remembered": Entry for May 18, 1777, *Extracts from the Journal of Elizabeth Drinker*, edited by Henry D. Biddle (1889), 103.

319 "I assured him": *Narrative of Lieut. Gen. Sir William Howe*, 33n.

319 "This evening parted": Entry for June 17, 1778, "Diary of Grace Growden Galloway," edited by Raymond C. Werner, *Pennsylvania Magazine of History and Biography* (1931), 36.

Chapter 48

320 "You are immediately": Washington to Arnold, June 19, 1778.

320 "Let me know": Washington to Arnold, June 30, 1778.

320 "My wounds": Arnold to Washington, July 18, 1778.

321 "I confess myself": Washington to Arnold, Aug. 3, 1778.

321 "Major Franks": Entry for June 20, 1778, "Diary of Grace Galloway," 36.

321 "He told me he could do": Entry for July 6, 1778, ibid., 38.

321 "He told me to do nothing": Entries for July 6 and 9, 1778, ibid., 38.

322 "I was quite mad," "Everything wears," and "Oh, God!": Entries for July 10, 11 and 21, 1778, ibid., 39–41.

322 "I told them": Entry for July 21, 1778, ibid., 40–41.

323 "My heart was ready to burst": Entry for Aug. 1, 1778, ibid., 44.

323 "Went to General Arnold": Entry for Aug. 10, 1778, ibid., 48.

323 "A little after ten . . . glad it is over": Entry for Aug. 20, 1778, ibid., 51–53.

325 "I dreamed . . . speedy and a prosperous voyage": Entry for Nov. 2, 1778, ibid., 55–56.

326 "As I was walking": Entry for Nov. 13, 1778, ibid., 57.

326 "The liberty of doing": Entry for Nov. 25, 1778, ibid., 59–60.

326 "He told me . . . indifferent to him": Entry for Dec. 16, 1778, ibid., 63–64.

327 "I asked her": Entries for Apr. 4 and 18, 1779, ibid., 71–72, 75.

327 "Got my spirits": Entry for Apr. 20, 1779, ibid., 75–76.

PART IX · TREASON OF THE DEEPEST DYE

Chapter 49

333 "Lord North consented . . . the present negotiation": "Observations by Mr. Hartley," in *The Revolutionary Diplomatic Correspondence of the United States*, edited by Francis Wharton (1889), 3:130–31.

333 "A little time . . . relatively lesser evils": David Hartley to Benjamin Franklin, Apr. 22, 1779.

334 "But this is merely . . . the spirit of it": Benjamin Franklin to David Hartley, May 4, 1779.

Chapter 50

338 "Came on 442 Indians": Entry for Nov. 11, 1778, "Journal of William McKendry," *Proceedings of the Massachusetts Historical Society* (1886), 449–50.

338 "Your rebels came": Joseph Brant to John Cantine, Dec. 13, 1778, *Public Papers of George Clinton*, vol. 4 (1900), 364.

338 "The expedition . . . will inspire them": Washington to John Sullivan, May 31, 1779.

339 "We marched . . . others inconsiderable": John Sullivan to Washington, Aug. 30, 1779.

Chapter 51

343 "The villainous attacks": Arnold to Washington, Mar. 19, 1779.

343 "Having made every sacrifice": Arnold to Washington, May 5, 1779.

344 "You will rest assured": Washington to Arnold, Aug. 3, 1778.

344 "Let me congratulate you": Washington to Arnold, Mar. 28, 1780.

344 "You are to proceed": Washington to Arnold, Aug. 3, 1780.

345 "In the very first instance": John André to Joseph Stansbury, May 10, 1779, in Carl Van Doren, *Secret History of the American Revolution* (1941), 439–40.

345 "a post in which . . . to plan matters": Arnold to John André, July 12 and 15, 1780 (two letters), in Van Doren, *Secret History*, 463–65.

346 "The heart which is conscious": Arnold to Washington, Sept. 25, 1780.

347 "In the midst of my letter . . . cannot make her hate": Alexander Hamilton to Elizabeth Schuyler, Sept. 25, 1780.

349 "Major André came . . . spilt in consequence": Arnold to Washington, Oct. 1, 1780.

350 "I agreed to meet . . . an impostor": John André to Washington, Sept. 24, 1780.

351 "Sympathy towards a soldier": John André to Washington, Oct. 1, 1780.

PART X · UP GOES HUDDY

Chapter 52

355 "Do you wish to know . . . existence as a nation": *Journals of Shaw*, 82–83.

356 "Be prepared . . . to Pennsylvania": *Journals of Shaw*, 84–85.

357 "Opposition . . . in short, everything": Washington to Anthony Wayne, Jan. 3, 1781.

358 "The event . . . for the issue": Washington to John Hancock, Jan. 5, 1781.

360 "The rest of our army": Washington to Rochambeau, Jan. 20, 1781.

360 "It was expected . . . immediate relief": Washington to Meshech Weare et al., Jan. 22, 1781.

Chapter 53

363 "The efforts . . . vigorous offensive": Washington to John Laurens, Jan. 15, 1781.

364 "It was agreed . . . of Charles Town": Washington to Henry Knox, Feb. 16, 1781.

365 "Every day convinces me": Washington to Benjamin Lincoln, Apr. 4, 1781.

367 "to commence an operation": Washington diary, May 22, 1781.

367 "All the French troops": Washington to John Hancock, May 27, 1781.

367 "The progress . . . of the former": Washington to Thomas Jefferson, June 8, 1781.

369 "It will be . . . much more probable": Rochambeau to Washington, June 12, 1871, with enclosure from de Grasse of Mar. 29, 1781.

369 "You cannot . . . his appearance in?": Washington to Rochambeau, June 13, 1781.

370 "What is to be . . . our primary object": Rochambeau to Washington, with Washington response, July 19, 1781.

Chapter 54

375 "The serenity of his countenance . . . our great ally": James Thacher, *A Military Journal During the American Revolutionary War* (1823), 182–83, 322–33.

377 "I take particular satisfaction": Washington to de Grasse, Sept. 15, 1781.

377 "But having already taken . . . some cannon and powder": Memorandum in Washington to de Grasse, Sept. 17, 1781.

378 "The enterprise against York": Washington to de Grasse, Sept. 28, 1781.

378 "I marched . . . with great vigor": Washington to John Hancock, Oct. 1, 1781.

379 "We were informed . . . as possible": Washington to John Hancock, Oct. 12, 1781.

380 "From the bank . . . 'to step back.'": Thacher, *Military Journal*, 339–42.

381 "The engineers . . . mortally wounded": Washington to John Hancock, Oct. 16, 1781.

382 "The whole of our works": Thacher, *Military Journal*, 343.

382 "Sir": Cornwallis to Washington, Oct. 17, 1781.

382 "At about twelve o'clock . . . of American independence": Thacher, *Military Journal*, 346–49.

Chapter 55

385 "An unwillingness to quit": Sheila L. Skemp, *William Franklin: Son of a Patriot, Servant of a King* (1990), 227.

385 "This article": Articles of Capitulation, Oct. 18, 1781, Avalon Project, avalon.law.yale.edu.

386 "The unhappy fate": Thomas Hutchinson (son) to Thomas Hutchinson, Dec. 8, 1781, *Diary and Letters of Thomas Hutchinson*, 2:373–74.

386 "Were it not": William Franklin to William Strahan, May 12, 1782, "Letters from William Franklin to William Strahan," edited by Charles Henry Hart, *Pennsylvania Magazine of History and Biography* (1911), 462.

387 "We the Refugees": Sheila Skemp, *William Franklin*, 256–57. This book is the principal source for the account here of the circumstances surrounding the Huddy execution.

387 "the most wanton": Washington to Henry Clinton, Apr. 21, 1782.

388 "barbarous outrage": Henry Clinton to Washington, Apr. 25, 1781.

Chapter 56

390 "I was but . . . almost equally certain": Thomas Andros, *The Old Jersey Captive, or A Narrative of the Captivity of Thomas Andros* (1833), 5–12.

393 "They were English . . . no pen can describe": Thomas Dring, *Recollections of the Jersey Prison-Ship*, edited by Albert G. Greene (1829), 88–89, 117–24.

Chapter 57

396 "beloved . . . mercy and goodness": "Memoirs of the Life of Boston King," *Methodist Magazine*, March 1798, republished at Black Loyalists: Our History, Our People, blackloyalist.com.

401 "This was a glorious era . . . fighting for liberty": *The Blind African Slave*,

or Memoirs of Boyrereau Brinch, Nicknamed Jeffrey Brace, edited by Kari J. Winter (2004 ed.), 156–66.

PART XI · NEVER A GOOD WAR

Chapter 58

409 "All the world agree . . . continuance of the war": Benjamin Franklin to Washington, Apr. 2, 1782.

410 "I have heretofore congratulated": Benjamin Franklin to Washington, Apr. 8, 1782.

410 "I am pleased to see": Benjamin Franklin to David Hartley, Apr. 5, 1782.

411 "The project of dividing us": Benjamin Franklin to David Hartley, Apr. 13, 1782.

411 "I have conversed": Benjamin Franklin to Lord Shelburne, Apr. 18, 1782.

411 "He tells me": Benjamin Franklin to Vergennes, Apr. 15, 1782.

412 "These papers will inform you": Benjamin Franklin to Adams, Apr. 20, 1782.

412 "To make a peace durable . . . of their estates": Benjamin Franklin notes for conversation with Richard Oswald, c. Apr. 19, 1782.

413 "His Lordship": Benjamin Franklin journal of peace negotiations, May 9 to July 1, 1782.

414 "I then entered . . . his manner pleasing": Benjamin Franklin journal of peace negotiations, May 9 to July 1, 1782.

417 "They want to treat . . . have taken place": Benjamin Franklin journal of peace negotiations, May 9 to July 1, 1782.

419 "Some he said . . . a short time": Richard Oswald to Shelburne, July 10, 1782, in United States Senate, 61st Congress, 3rd session, Document 870 (1912), 7:79–81.

420 "This, the gentleman told me": Richard Oswald to Shelburne, July 11, 1782, ibid., 81–82.

421 "I have several times . . . a devout amen": Adams to the *Boston Patriot*, Apr. 6, 1811.

422 "He says": Adams diary, Nov. 5, 1782.

422 "Poor as we are": Benjamin Franklin to John Jay, Oct. 2, 1780.

422 "The fisheries and Mississippi": Adams diary, Nov. 20, 1782.

423 "Dr. Franklin is very staunch": Adams diary, Nov. 26, 1782.

423 "creditors on either side": Treaty of Paris, Sept. 30, 1783, Avalon Project, avalon.law.yale.edu.

424 "I long with you": Benjamin Franklin to Jonathan Shipley, June 10, 1782.

Chapter 59

425 "In the course . . . consequences may be": Washington to Joseph Jones, Dec. 14, 1782.

426 "We are held": Washington to John Augustine Washington, Jan. 16, 1783.

426 "Flattering myself . . . these observations": Alexander Hamilton to Washington, Feb. 13, 1783.

428 "I shall pursue": Washington to Alexander Hamilton, Mar. 4, 1783.

428 "After a pursuit . . . your entreaties now": Anonymous manifesto, in *Journals of the Continental Congress*, Apr. 29, 1783, 296–97.

429 "There is something . . . occasioned thereby": Washington to Alexander Hamilton, Mar. 12, 1783.

431 "Gentlemen . . . capable of attaining": Washington address, Mar. 15, 1783.

432 "The meeting of the officers . . . moisten every eye": *The Journals of Major Samuel Shaw*, 103–4.

433 "infamous propositions": *Journals of the Continental Congress*, Apr. 29, 1783, 311.

433 "Happy for America . . . capable of attaining": *Journals of Shaw*, 104–5.

Chapter 60

435 "I congratulate you": Benjamin Franklin to Robert Livingstone, Jan. 21, 1783.

435 "The Commander in Chief . . . United States of America": General Orders, Apr. 18, 1783.

436 "At 12 o'clock . . . a silent adieu": *Memoir of Col. Benjamin Tallmadge* (1858), 63–64.

437 "Mr. Jay": Benjamin Franklin to John and Mrs. Jay, May 13, 1784.

437 "I cannot bear": Benjamin Franklin to Thomas Mifflin, June 16, 1784.

437 "I am here among a people": Benjamin Franklin to William Franklin, Aug. 16, 1784.

438 "Dear and honoured Father": William Franklin to Benjamin Franklin, July 22, 1784.

438 "Dear son . . . as well as we can": Benjamin Franklin to William Franklin, Aug. 16, 1784.

Chapter 61

442 "The part he acted against me": Benjamin Franklin will, July 17, 1788, Jared Sparks, *The Life of Benjamin Franklin* (1844), 599.

443 "without causing any destruction": Article Seven, Treaty of Paris, Sept. 3, 1783.

443 "Peace was restored . . . to Nova Scotia": "Memoirs of the Life of Boston King," *Methodist Magazine*, March 1798, republished at Black Loyalists: Our History, Our People, blackloyalist.com.

444 "After we were disbanded": *The Blind African Slave, or Memoirs of Boyrereau Brinch, Nicknamed Jeffrey Brace*, edited by Kari J. Winter (2004 ed.), 165–66.

Acknowledgments

Anyone who writes about the founding era of American history is now more deeply in debt than ever to the National Archives, for the creation of Founders Online, a portal to scores of thousands of documents from the Revolutionary and early national periods. Without this marvelous source base, the present book would have been years longer in the research.

As always, I owe much to my students and colleagues at the University of Texas at Austin, for their questions and comments. And to Kris Puopolo, Dan Meyer and Bill Thomas at Doubleday, for their consummate professionalism. And finally, to my readers, for the interest that makes my work possible.

Index

ABOUT THE AUTHOR

H. W. Brands holds the Jack S. Blanton Sr. Chair in History at the University of Texas at Austin. For three decades he has been writing histories and biographies. Two of his books, *The First American* and *Traitor to His Class,* were finalists for the Pulitzer Prize.

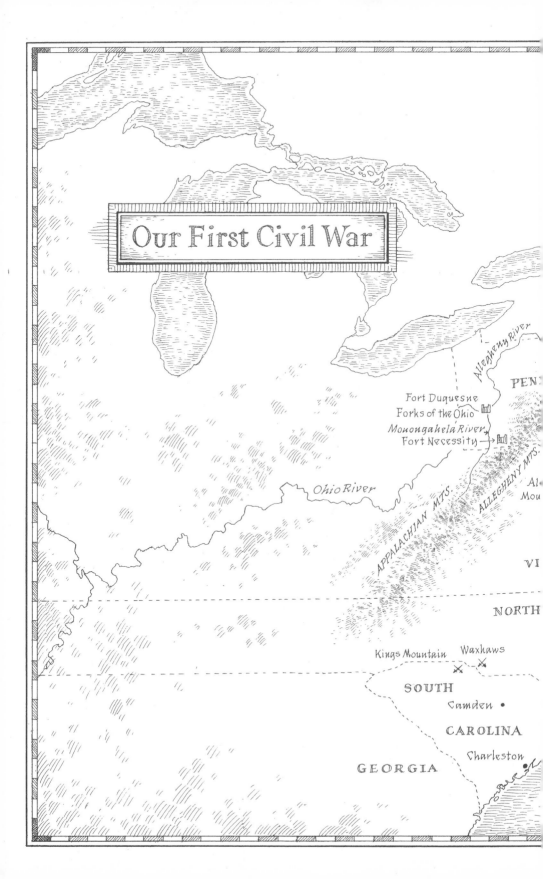

Our First Civil War

Allegheny River

PEN

Fort Duquesne
Forks of the Ohio
Monongahela River
Fort Necessity

APPALACHIAN MTS.

ALLEGHENY MTS.

Al
Mou

Ohio River

VI

NORTH

Kings Mountain   Waxhaws

SOUTH

Camden •

CAROLINA

Charleston

GEORGIA